THE CULT

BATMAN

DC COMICS
NEW YORK, NY

WRITER

JIM
STARLIN

THE CU

COLOR ARTIST

BILL
WRAY

ILLUSTRATOR

BERNIE WRIGHTSON

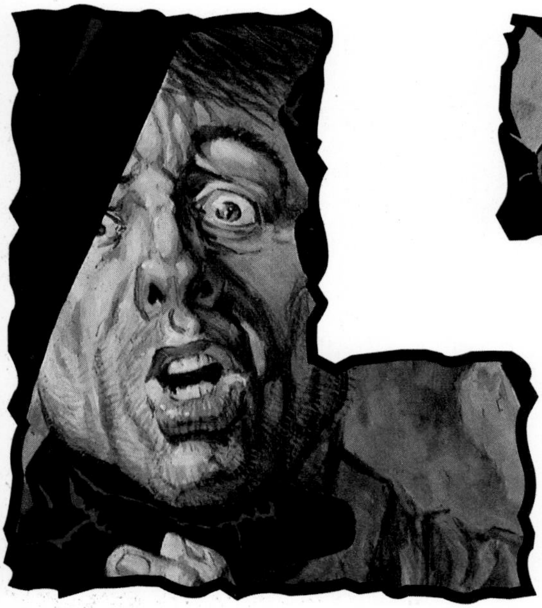

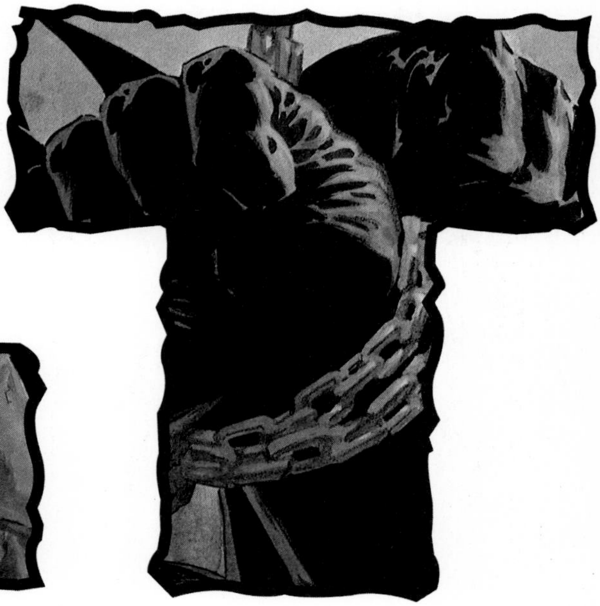

LETTERER

JOHN COSTANZA

Jenette Kahn
President & Editor-in-Chief

Dick Giordano
V.P.–Editorial Director

Denny O'Neil
Editor, Original Series

Dan Thorsland
Editor, Collected Edition

Jim Chadwick
Director–Design Services

Joe Orlando
V.P.–Creative Director

Paul Levitz
Executive V.P. & Publisher

Bruce Bristow
V.P.–Sales & Marketing

Patrick Caldon
V.P.–Controller

Terri Cunningham
Director–Editorial
Administration

Chantal d'Aulnis
V.P.–Business Affairs

Matthew Ragone
Circulation Director

Bob Rozakis
Production Director

BATMAN: THE CULT
Published by DC Comics Inc.
Copyright ©1991. All rights reserved.
Originally published in magazine form by
DC Comics Inc. as BATMAN: THE CULT #1-4.
Copyright ©1988 DC Comics Inc.
All rights reserved.

Cover illustration by Bernie Wrightson

Book design by Bruning, Motter + Associates

DC Comics Inc., 666 Fifth Ave., NY, NY 10103

A Warner Bros. Inc. Company
Printed in Canada. First Printing.

BURN THIS BOOK

by
Jim
Starlin

W

HEN I WAS A KID,

Batman and Superman were the only super-heroes around. That was way back in the prehistoric late fifties.

Sure, there were a few other super-powered characters kicking about, like Aquaman, Green Arrow, and the Martian Manhunter, but they could only be found in five-page back-up stories in DETECTIVE, ADVENTURE and a few other comics. The only guys who had their own books were Supes and the Bat Guy. Oh yeah, DC did have this one gal named Wonder Woman, but her book was strictly for girls. I wouldn't have been caught dead reading it. So my induction into the exploits of flashy do-gooders in long underwear came at the hands of two old vets, the sole survivors of the heroes that abounded in the forties.

To tell you the truth, back in my younger days I liked Super-man better than Batman — a pretty strange admission from a guy who grew up to do what he thinks is some of his best writing on the gent with the pointy ears. It wasn't that the Superman stories of the fifties were any less simpleminded and silly than Batman's were; it was just that Supes was better suited to the bland fare he was forced to deal out. I mean, I was only a kid, but even I knew Batman's portrayal of criminal life wasn't up to snuff. I stuck with him, though; what choice did I have? When you need a super-hero fix, a lame hero is better than no hero at all.

What I didn't know at the time was that a few years earlier the comic book industry had been gutted by a series of Senate House Committee hearings. Groups of pious, right-thinking people had pressured our elected government officials into a witch hunt on comic book creators. The focus of this exercise in First Amendment bashing was, of course, EC Comics, the grand masters of the horror genre. But the entire industry suffered because of these hearings. Companies went out of business, respected writers and artists were forced to find employment in other fields, some of them forever after denying they ever had anything to do with the funny book business.

What was left of the industry survived by forming the Comics Code, a self-regulating organization whose job it was (and still is) to keep the American kid's reading matter pure and wholesome.

At DC, violence was cut down to the absolute minimum. Sex, which had never been mentioned in any DC books that I know of, was raised to an even more forbidden plateau. Watch what shape you draw those rocket ships!

But then a strange thing began to happen as I grew older. Somewhere in the mid-sixties Batman started to mature. His stories began to get more interesting. Over the years the artistically strait-jacketing restrictions began to loosen up. This welcome growth can only be credited to the talented writers and artists who slowly and subtly raised the standards of Batman's books during those reemerging years. I tell you, it was like a breath of fresh air.

The seventies came around and I found myself entering the comics biz. There was a brand-new glut of super-heroes blooming and a flock of fledgling writers and artists migrating to New York to tell their tales. But out of all this craziness, Batman always remained one of the best. Sure, he had his less than glorious moments along the way, but you just knew that he'd eventually return to his rightful place at the top of the heap. And he always did.

The eighties brought on a more adult version of comics. The readership was getting older and demanded stories with more meat on them. Writers leapt at the chance to expand the depths of the imaginary characters they'd grown up with and whose destinies they now directed. Some pretty nice stuff came out of this new freedom: Moore's Swamp Thing, Miller's Daredevil and Batman, Byrne's Superman and many others.

But something else once again reared its ugly head during this decade. The self-righteous began to unfurl the crimson banners of censorship. The Attorney General of the United States instituted a pressure campaign to clean up the magazine market. Born-again TV evangelists did entire shows on the evils of comics. Tipper Gore led a movement against the record industry. And now in the nineties, the good Rev. Wyldman and Jesse Helms seek to disembowel the National Endowment for the Arts. It all begins to sound terribly familiar, don't it?

I couldn't help but inject some of these tensions into THE CULT. Here we have Deacon Blackfire masquerading as a religious leader, hiding behind moral self-righteousness while he furthers his

own private agenda. I'll admit his goals and methods are a hell of a lot more extreme than the groups that lobby in our state capital, but they both have one thing in common: they brought Batman to his knees.

After the Comics Code was forced upon Batman, the Dark Knight was stripped of his fearsome anger and forced to be something he wasn't: a happy, smiling father-figure chasing aliens around a Day-Glo Gotham City. It was years before determined writers brought back the Batman we all know and love. In THE CULT that subjugation was fictional and Jason Todd rescued Bats in considerably less time, but when certain parties voiced concern over the violence in the story I couldn't help but feel a twinge of déjà vu.

Now, don't get me wrong. I don't live under the illusion that what we do in comics is grand literature. We're not producing ULYSSES or A TALE OF TWO CITIES. What we're putting out is mass market entertainment. Occasionally something thought-provoking comes down the tubes, but that's not this industry's main goal. Entertainment is.

But entertainment or fine art, it makes no difference. Free speech of any kind is protected by the First Amendment and we have to remember that that protection is something we have to fight for. And don't believe for a second that there isn't a bogeyman just outside the door.

There are folks who don't want you to read stories like the one you have in your hands. Too much death. Too much violence. Too much horror. They form committees against tales of this sort. They pass laws forbidding their sale. They burn books like this.

The idea is to go back to a simpler time when all the real and terrible problems that face us these days didn't exist – or were at least swept under the carpet where they belonged. The censors think that by banning certain books this goal can be reached. Kill the messenger and the message will be the one you want to hear. Makes sense to me.

So there you have it. It's a simple choice, really: you can either accept the sway of public opinion and read whatever is acceptable at the time or you can stand up and tell them to keep their filthy hands off your First Amendment rights.

But whatever your choice, remember this: Today it may only be a rap group or a horror story or a comic book that gets suppressed. Tomorrow, though, it might be a novel by James Joyce or D. H. Lawrence they're referring to when they cry, "Burn this book!"

Jim Starlin
November 1990

CHAPTER 1

ORDEAL

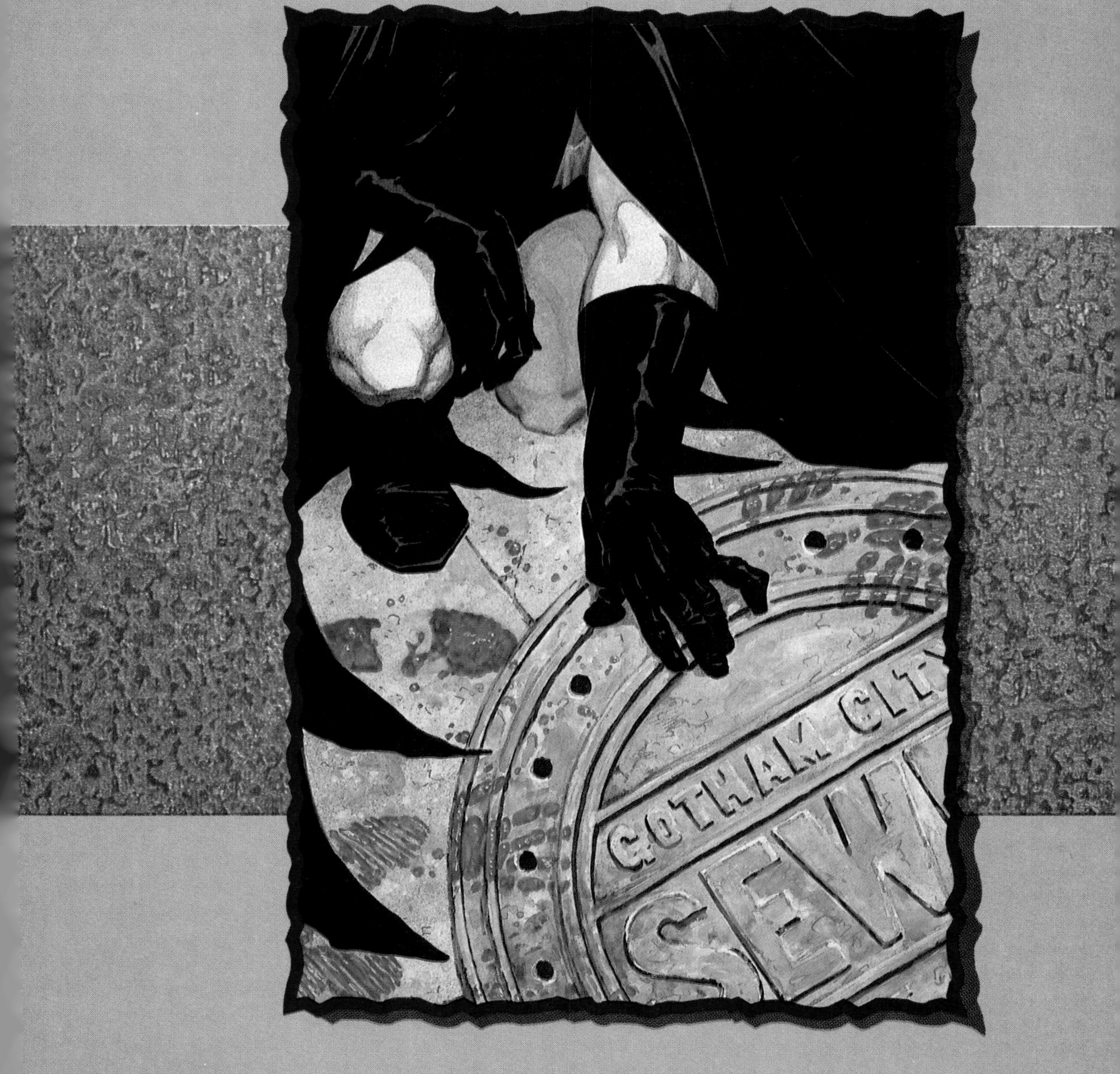

GOTHAM

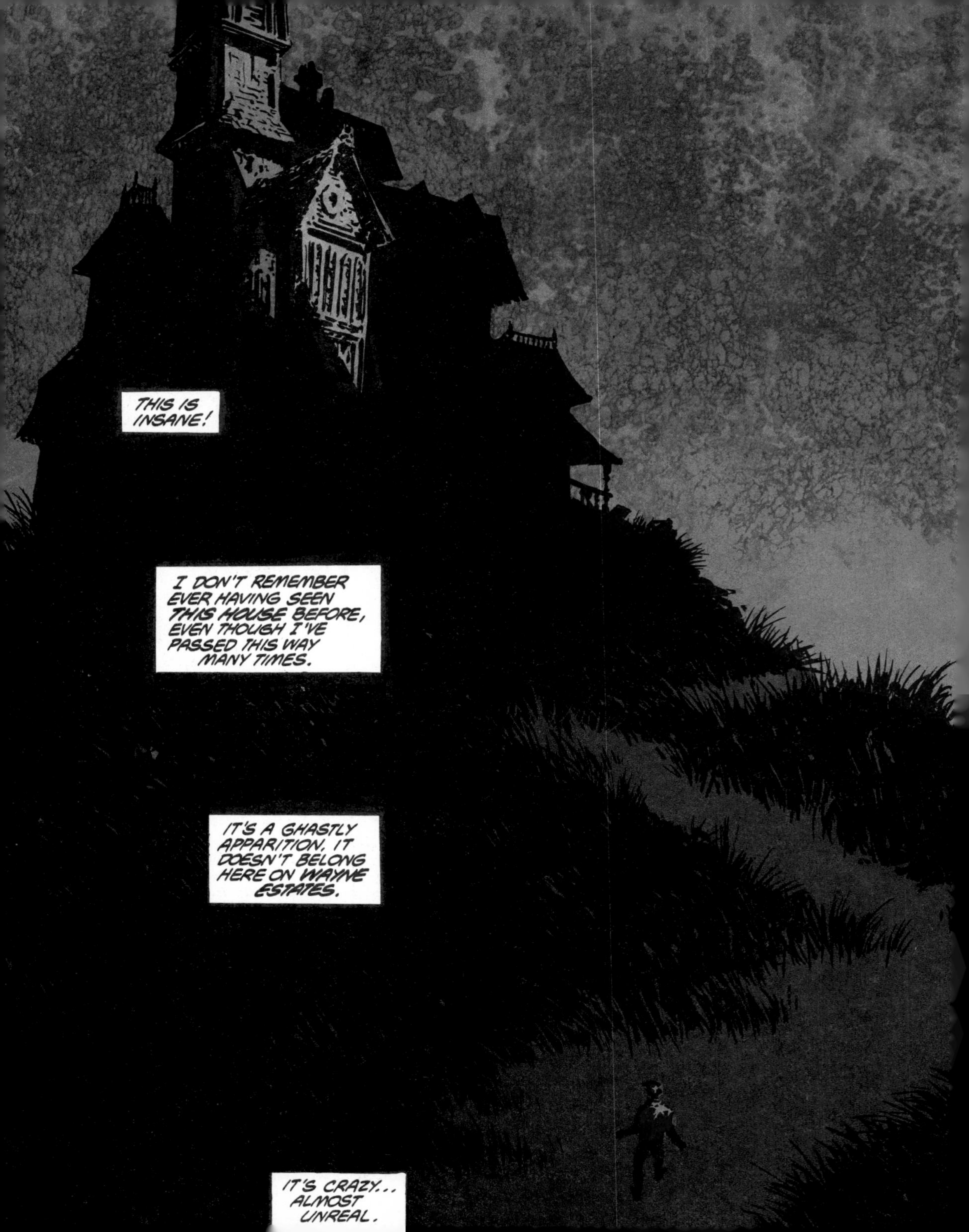
THIS IS INSANE!
I DON'T REMEMBER EVER HAVING SEEN THIS HOUSE BEFORE, EVEN THOUGH I'VE PASSED THIS WAY MANY TIMES.
IT'S A GHASTLY APPARITION. IT DOESN'T BELONG HERE ON WAYNE ESTATES.
IT'S CRAZY... ALMOST UNREAL.

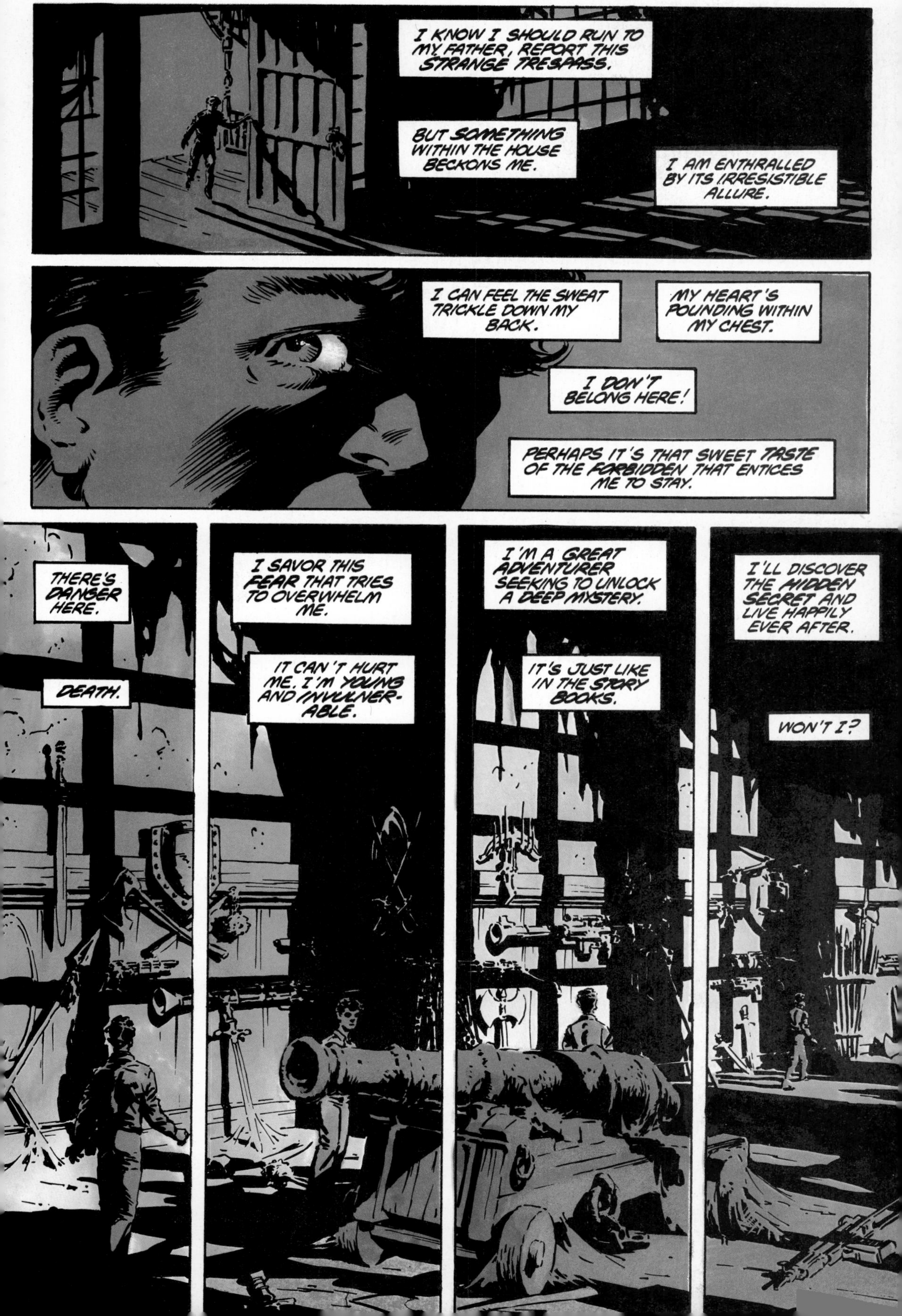
I KNOW I SHOULD RUN TO MY FATHER, REPORT THIS STRANGE TRESPASS.
BUT SOMETHING WITHIN THE HOUSE BECKONS ME.
I AM ENTHRALLED BY ITS IRRESISTIBLE ALLURE.
I CAN FEEL THE SWEAT TRICKLE DOWN MY BACK.
MY HEART'S POUNDING WITHIN MY CHEST.
I DON'T BELONG HERE!
PERHAPS IT'S THAT SWEET TASTE OF THE FORBIDDEN THAT ENTICES ME TO STAY.
THERE'S DANGER HERE.
DEATH.
I SAVOR THIS FEAR THAT TRIES TO OVERWHELM ME.
IT CAN'T HURT ME. I'M YOUNG AND INVULNER-ABLE.
I'M A GREAT ADVENTURER SEEKING TO UNLOCK A DEEP MYSTERY.
IT'S JUST LIKE IN THE STORY BOOKS.
I'LL DISCOVER THE HIDDEN SECRET AND LIVE HAPPILY EVER AFTER.
WON'T I?

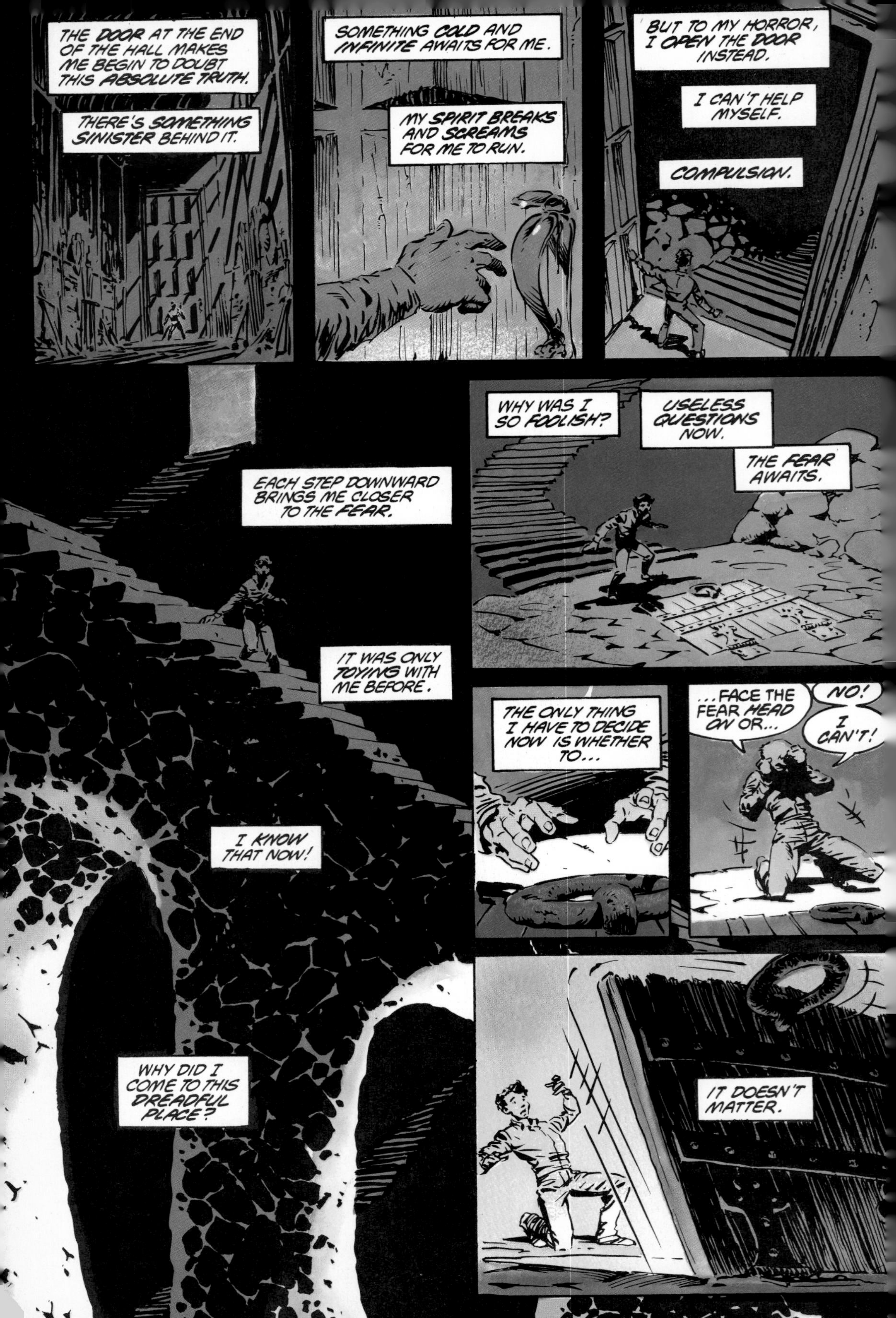
THE DOOR AT THE END OF THE HALL MAKES ME BEGIN TO DOUBT THIS ABSOLUTE TRUTH.
THERE'S SOMETHING SINISTER BEHIND IT.
SOMETHING COLD AND INFINITE AWAITS FOR ME.
MY SPIRIT BREAKS AND SCREAMS FOR ME TO RUN.
BUT TO MY HORROR, I OPEN THE DOOR INSTEAD.
I CAN'T HELP MYSELF.
COMPULSION.
EACH STEP DOWNWARD BRINGS ME CLOSER TO THE FEAR.
IT WAS ONLY TOYING WITH ME BEFORE.
I KNOW THAT NOW!
WHY DID I COME TO THIS DREADFUL PLACE?
WHY WAS I SO FOOLISH?
USELESS QUESTIONS NOW.
THE FEAR AWAITS.
THE ONLY THING I HAVE TO DECIDE NOW IS WHETHER TO...
...FACE THE FEAR HEAD ON OR...
NO!
I CAN'T!
IT DOESN'T MATTER.

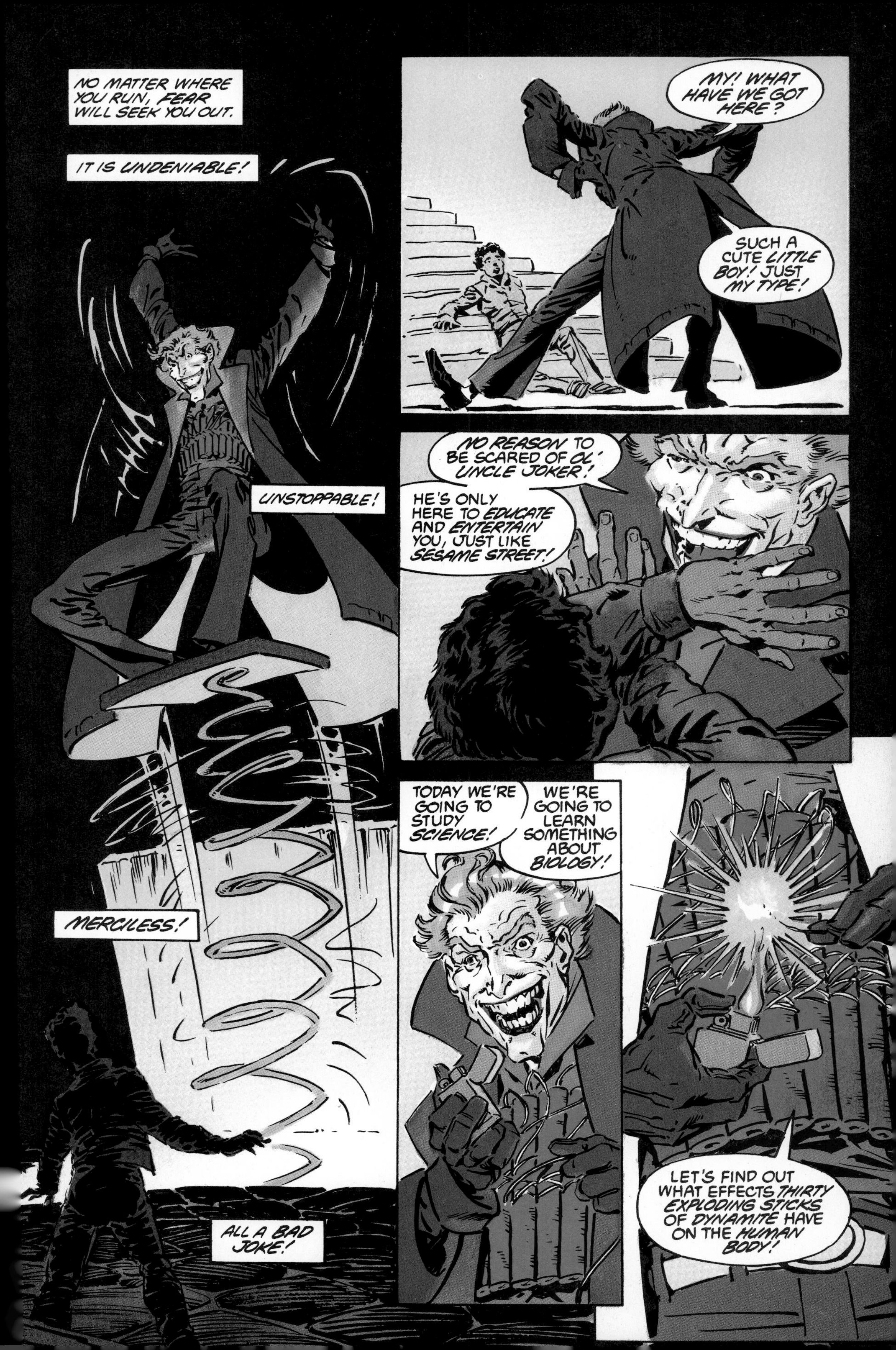
NO MATTER WHERE YOU RUN, FEAR WILL SEEK YOU OUT.
IT IS UNDENIABLE!
UNSTOPPABLE!
MERCILESS!
ALL A BAD JOKE!
MY! WHAT HAVE WE GOT HERE?
SUCH A CUTE LITTLE BOY! JUST MY TYPE!
NO REASON TO BE SCARED OF OL' UNCLE JOKER!
HE'S ONLY HERE TO EDUCATE AND ENTERTAIN YOU, JUST LIKE SESAME STREET!
TODAY WE'RE GOING TO STUDY SCIENCE!
WE'RE GOING TO LEARN SOMETHING ABOUT BIOLOGY!
LET'S FIND OUT WHAT EFFECTS THIRTY EXPLODING STICKS OF DYNAMITE HAVE ON THE HUMAN BODY!

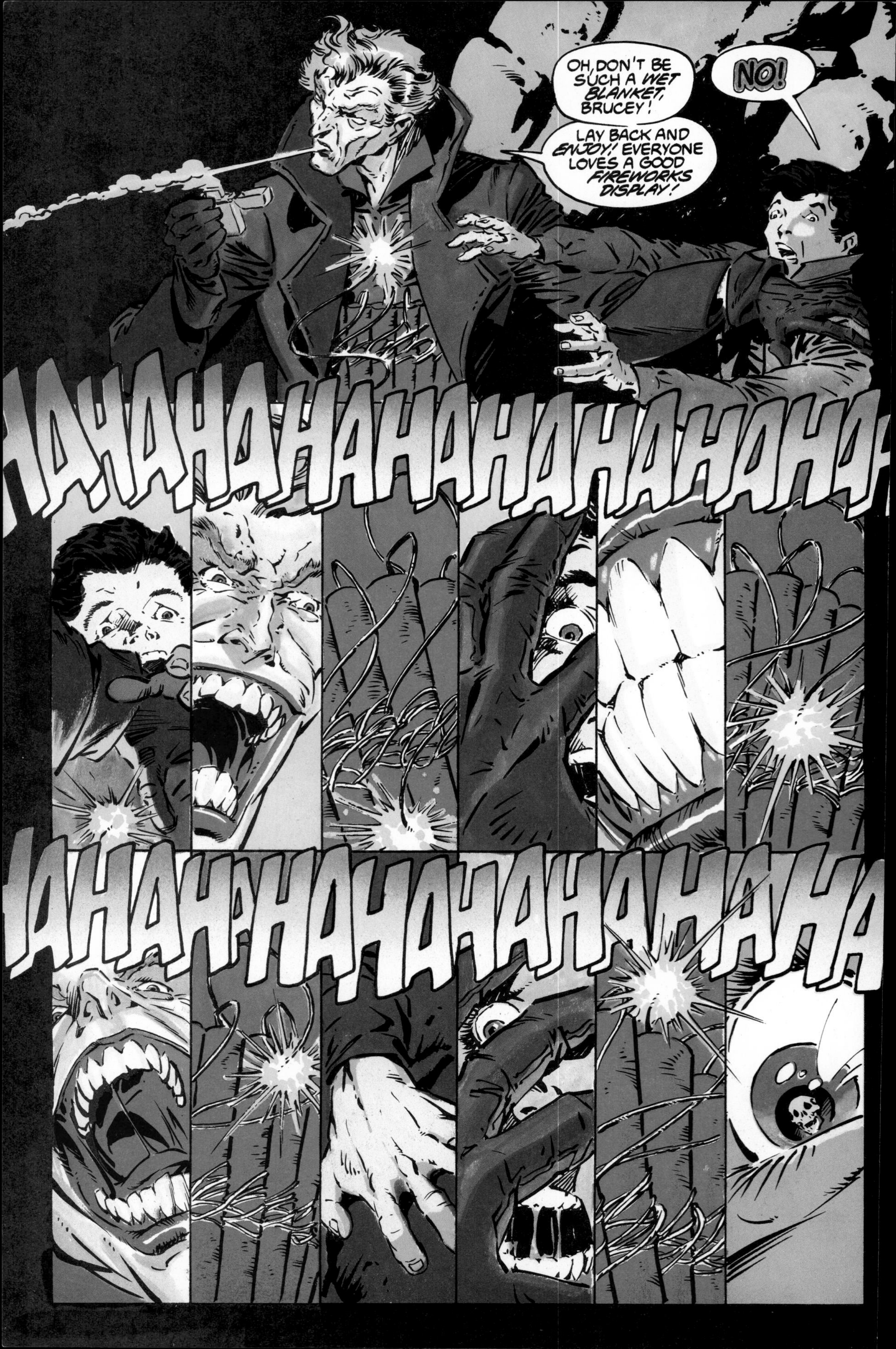
OH, DON'T BE SUCH A WET BLANKET, BRUCEY!
LAY BACK AND ENJOY! EVERYONE LOVES A GOOD FIREWORKS DISPLAY!
NO!
HAHAHAHAHAHAHAHAHAHAHAHA
HAHAHAHAHAHAHAHAHAHAHAHAHA

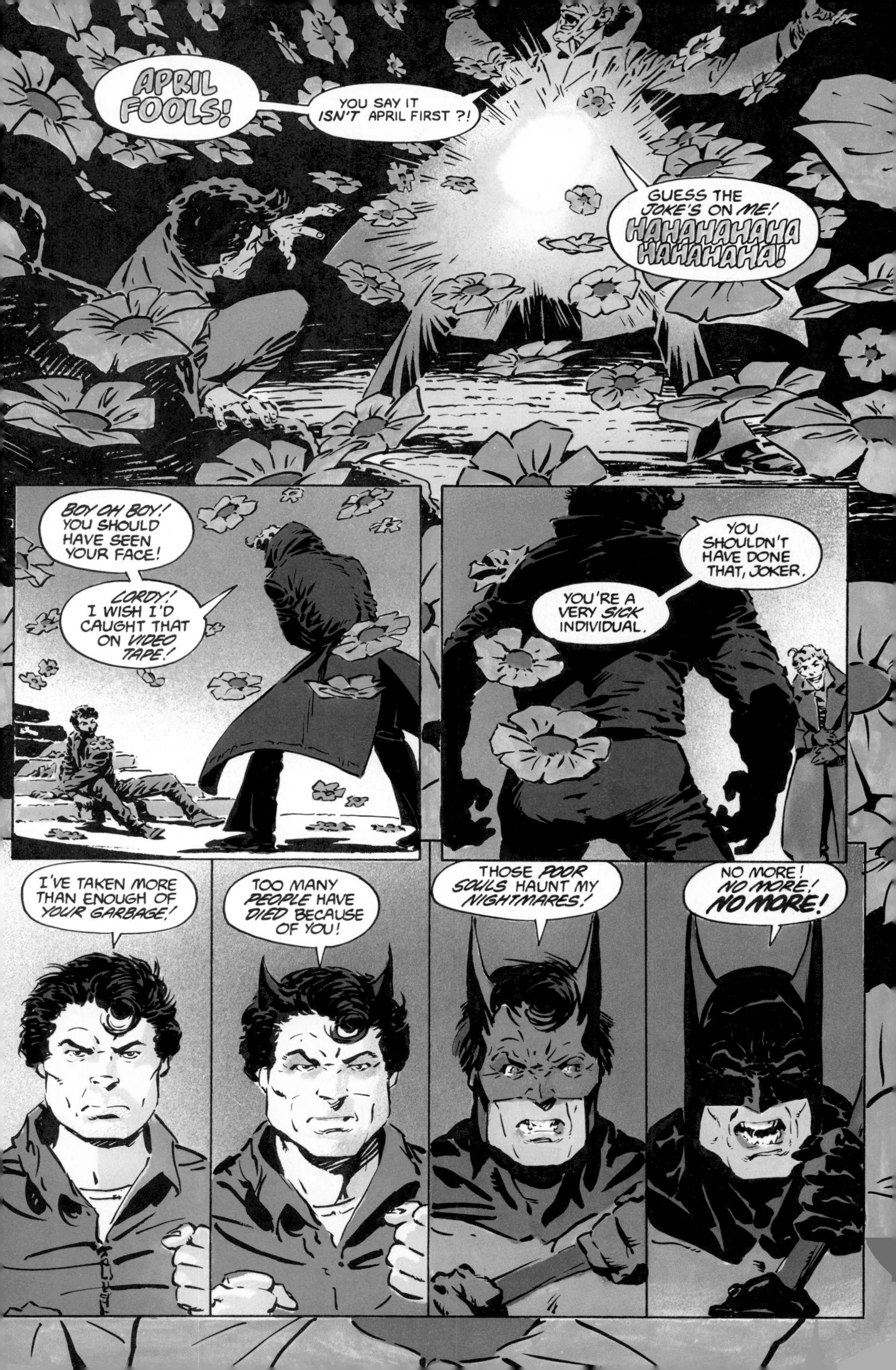
APRIL FOOLS!
YOU SAY IT ISN'T APRIL FIRST ?!
GUESS THE JOKE'S ON ME! HAHAHAHAHA HAHAHAHA!
BOY OH BOY! YOU SHOULD HAVE SEEN YOUR FACE!
CORDY! I WISH I'D CAUGHT THAT ON VIDEO TAPE!
YOU SHOULDN'T HAVE DONE THAT, JOKER.
YOU'RE A VERY SICK INDIVIDUAL.
I'VE TAKEN MORE THAN ENOUGH OF YOUR GARBAGE!
TOO MANY PEOPLE HAVE DIED BECAUSE OF YOU!
THOSE POOR SOULS HAUNT MY NIGHTMARES!
NO MORE! NO MORE! NO MORE!

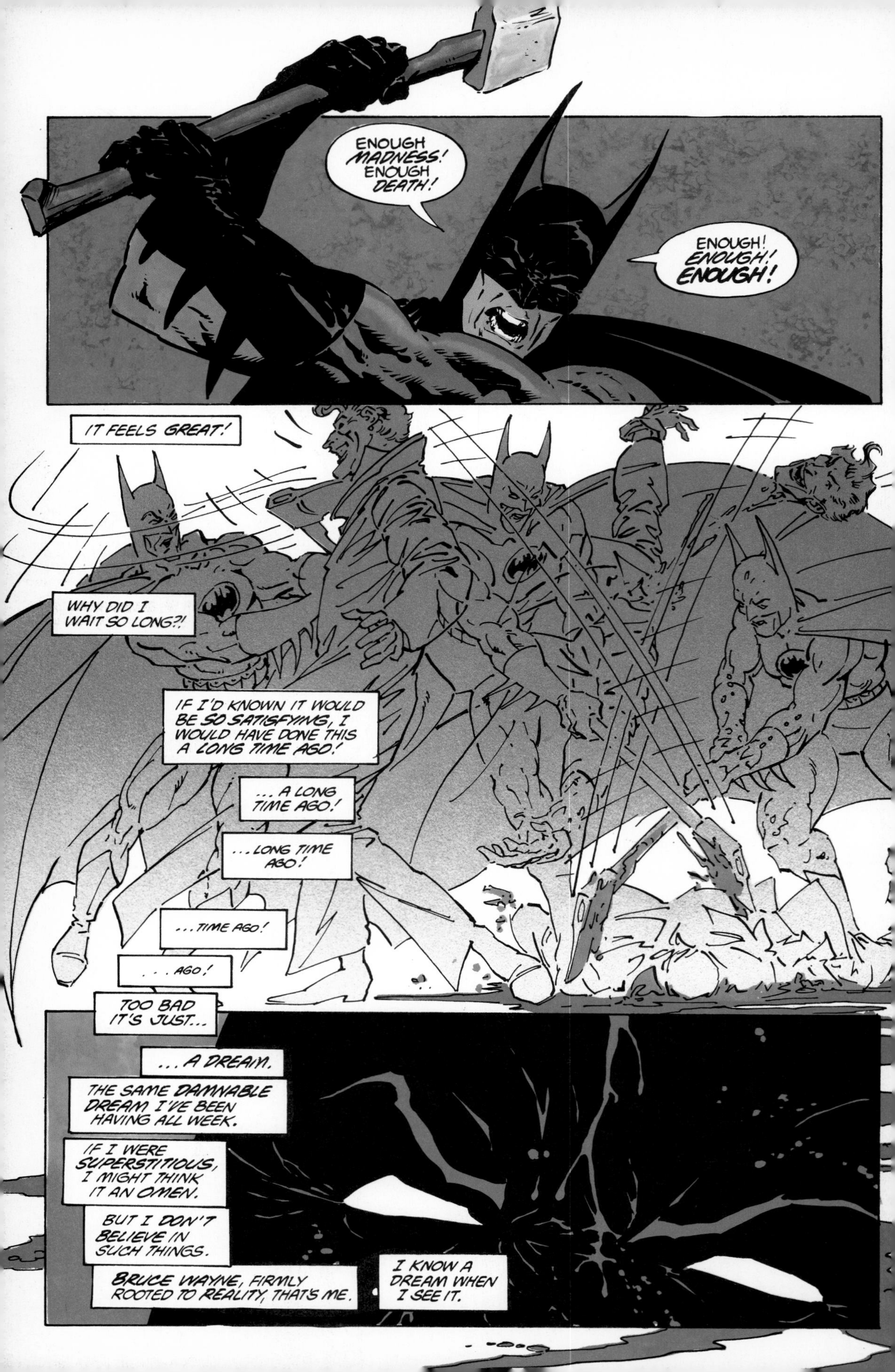
ENOUGH MADNESS! ENOUGH DEATH!
ENOUGH! ENOUGH! ENOUGH!
IT FEELS GREAT!
WHY DID I WAIT SO LONG?!
IF I'D KNOWN IT WOULD BE SO SATISFYING, I WOULD HAVE DONE THIS A LONG TIME AGO!
... A LONG TIME AGO!
... LONG TIME AGO!
... TIME AGO!
. . . AGO!
TOO BAD IT'S JUST...
... A DREAM.
THE SAME DAMNABLE DREAM I'VE BEEN HAVING ALL WEEK.
IF I WERE SUPERSTITIOUS, I MIGHT THINK IT AN OMEN.
BUT I DON'T BELIEVE IN SUCH THINGS.
BRUCE WAYNE, FIRMLY ROOTED TO REALITY, THAT'S ME.
I KNOW A DREAM WHEN I SEE IT.

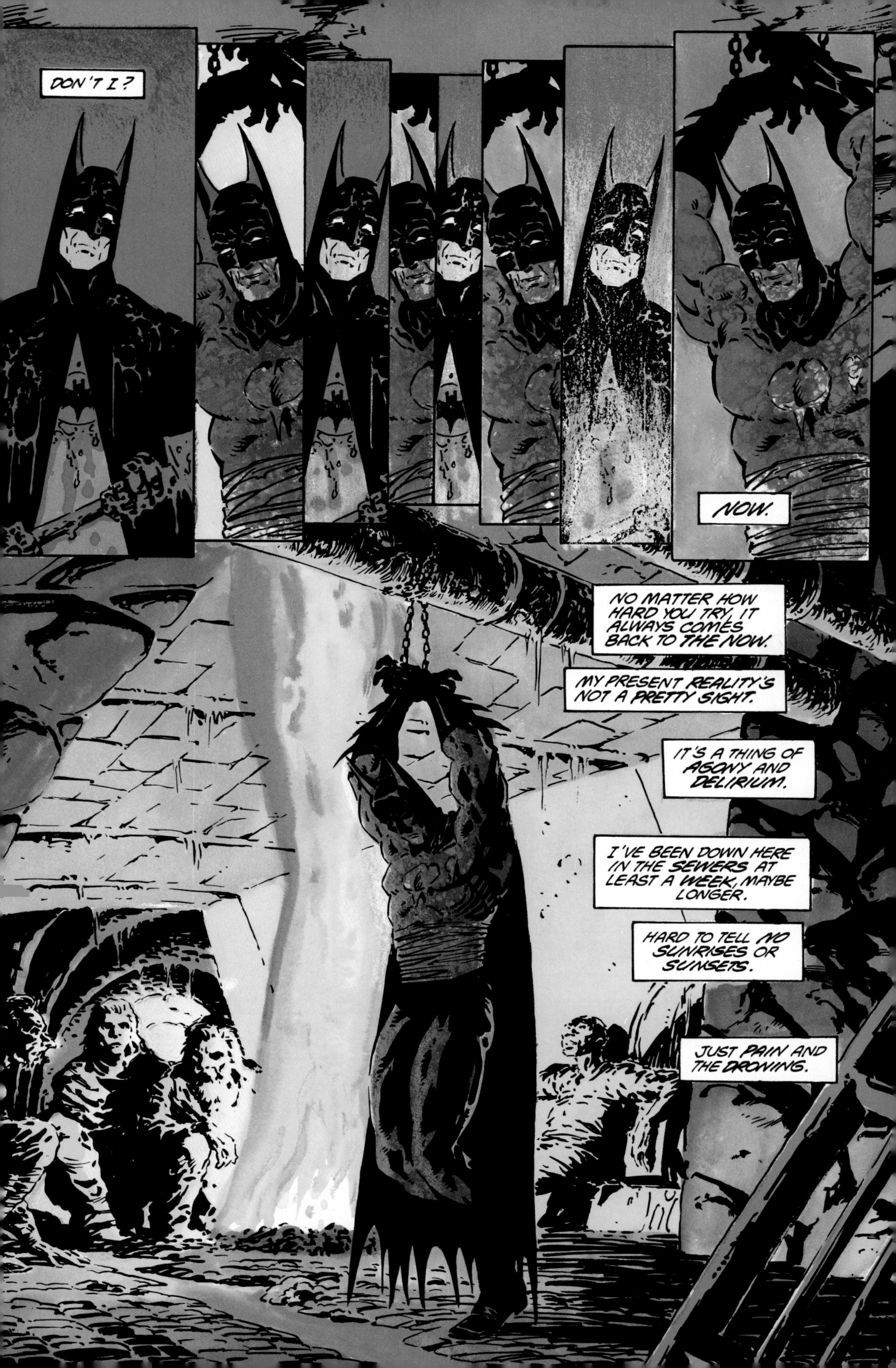
DON'T I?
NOW.
NO MATTER HOW HARD YOU TRY, IT ALWAYS COMES BACK TO THE NOW.
MY PRESENT REALITY'S NOT A PRETTY SIGHT.
IT'S A THING OF AGONY AND DELIRIUM.
I'VE BEEN DOWN HERE IN THE SEWERS AT LEAST A WEEK, MAYBE LONGER.
HARD TO TELL NO SUNRISES OR SUNSETS.
JUST PAIN AND THE DRONING.

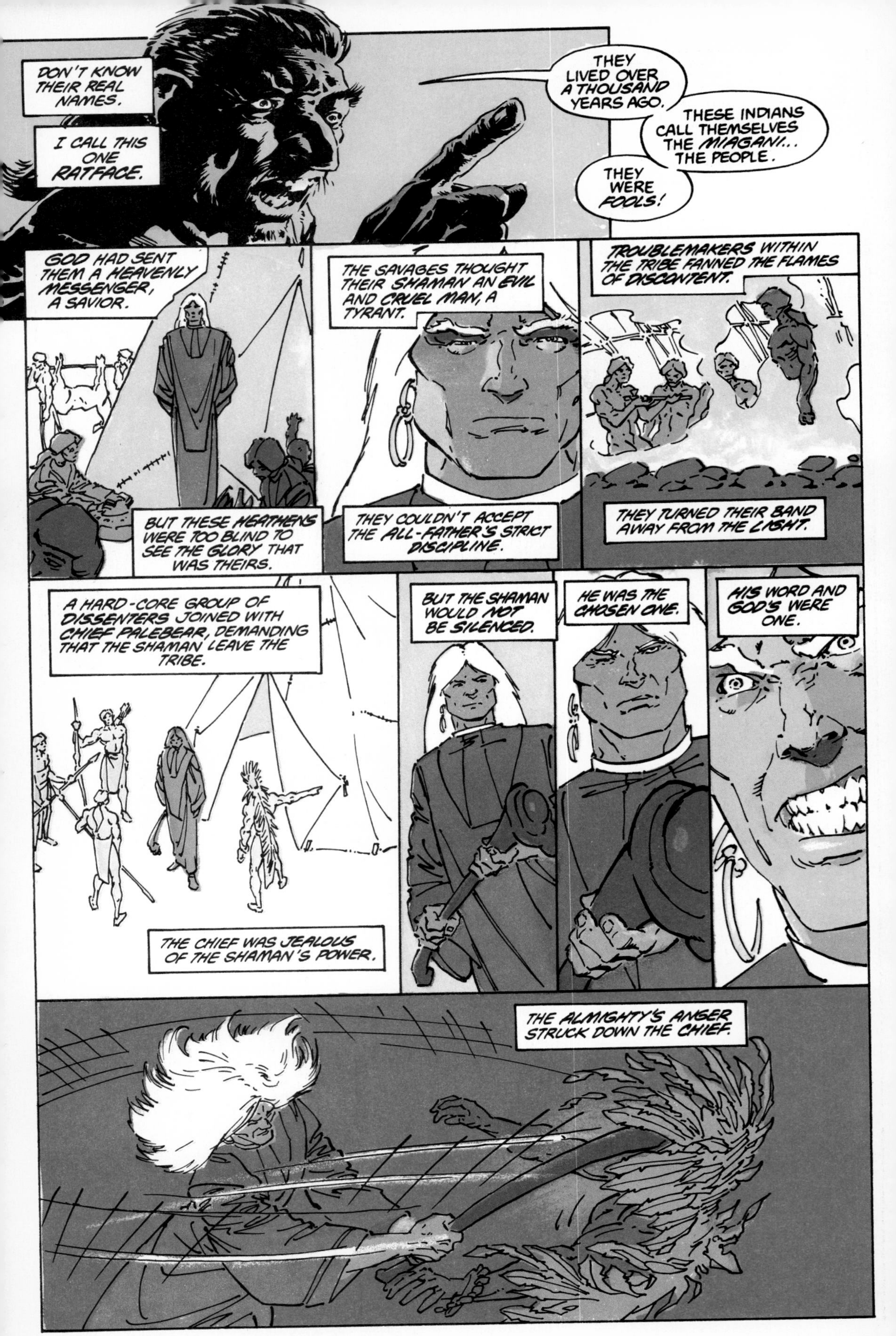
DON'T KNOW THEIR REAL NAMES.
I CALL THIS ONE RATFACE.
THEY LIVED OVER A THOUSAND YEARS AGO.
THESE INDIANS CALL THEMSELVES THE MIAGANI... THE PEOPLE.
THEY WERE FOOLS!
GOD HAD SENT THEM A HEAVENLY MESSENGER, A SAVIOR.
BUT THESE HEATHENS WERE TOO BLIND TO SEE THE GLORY THAT WAS THEIRS.
THE SAVAGES THOUGHT THEIR SHAMAN AN EVIL AND CRUEL MAN, A TYRANT.
THEY COULDN'T ACCEPT THE ALL-FATHER'S STRICT DISCIPLINE.
TROUBLEMAKERS WITHIN THE TRIBE FANNED THE FLAMES OF DISCONTENT.
THEY TURNED THEIR BAND AWAY FROM THE LIGHT.
A HARD-CORE GROUP OF DISSENTERS JOINED WITH CHIEF PALEBEAR, DEMANDING THAT THE SHAMAN LEAVE THE TRIBE.
THE CHIEF WAS JEALOUS OF THE SHAMAN'S POWER.
BUT THE SHAMAN WOULD NOT BE SILENCED.
HE WAS THE CHOSEN ONE.
HIS WORD AND GOD'S WERE ONE.
THE ALMIGHTY'S ANGER STRUCK DOWN THE CHIEF.

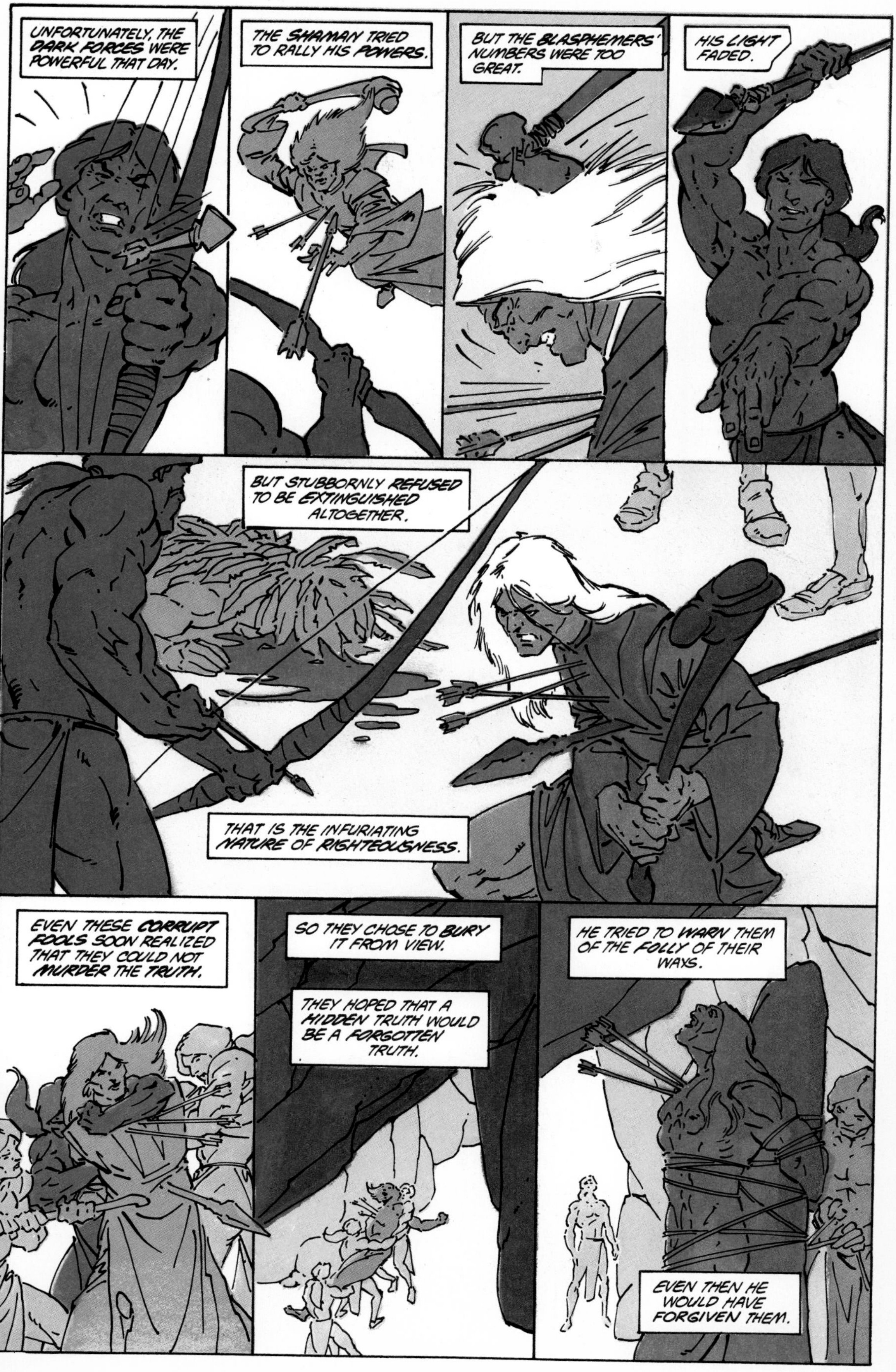
UNFORTUNATELY, THE DARK FORCES WERE POWERFUL THAT DAY.
THE SHAMAN TRIED TO RALLY HIS POWERS.
BUT THE BLASPHEMERS' NUMBERS WERE TOO GREAT.
HIS LIGHT FADED.
BUT STUBBORNLY REFUSED TO BE EXTINGUISHED ALTOGETHER.
THAT IS THE INFURIATING NATURE OF RIGHTEOUSNESS.
EVEN THESE CORRUPT FOOLS SOON REALIZED THAT THEY COULD NOT MURDER THE TRUTH.
SO THEY CHOSE TO BURY IT FROM VIEW.
THEY HOPED THAT A HIDDEN TRUTH WOULD BE A FORGOTTEN TRUTH.
HE TRIED TO WARN THEM OF THE FOLLY OF THEIR WAYS.
EVEN THEN HE WOULD HAVE FORGIVEN THEM.

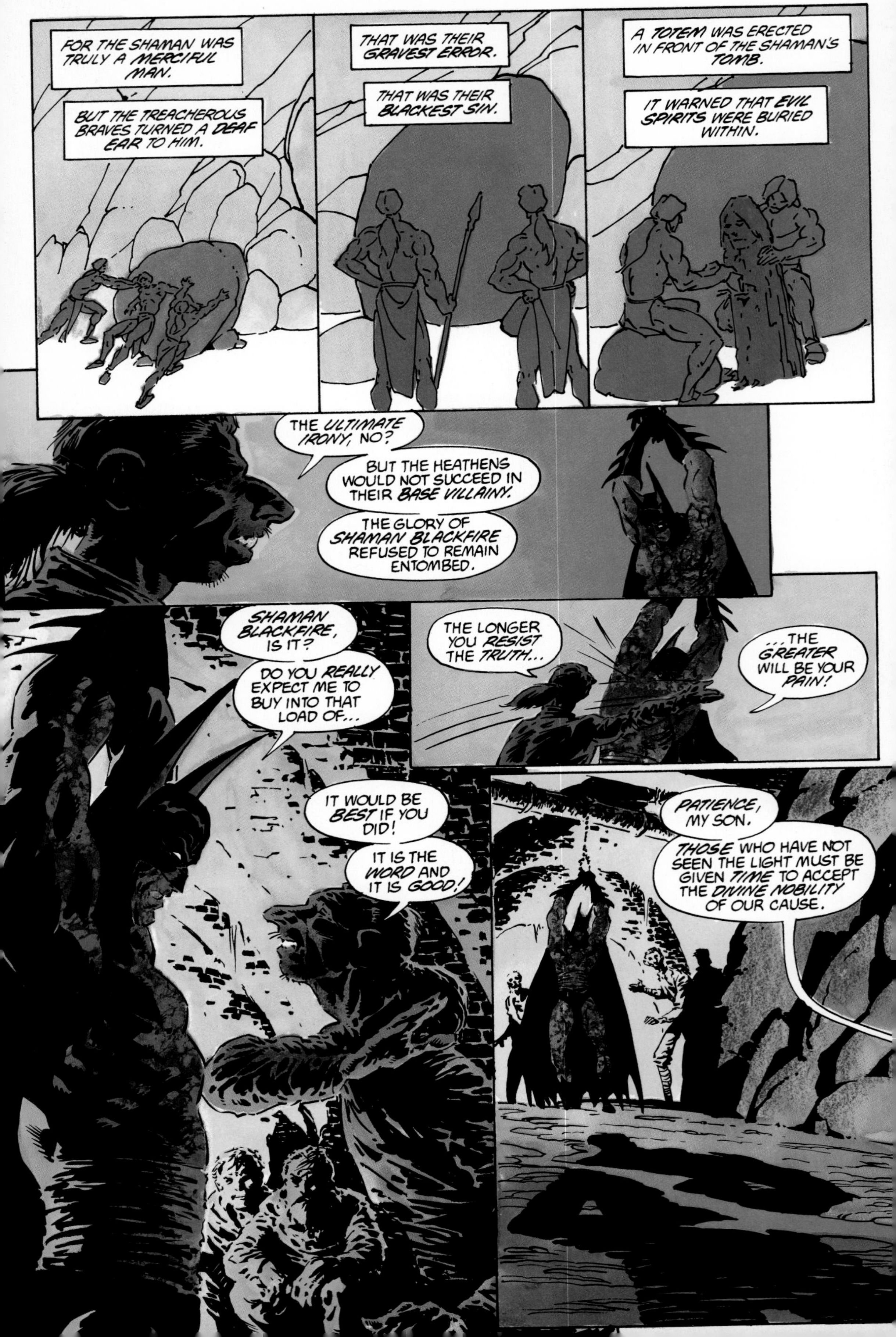
FOR THE SHAMAN WAS TRULY A MERCIFUL MAN.
BUT THE TREACHEROUS BRAVES TURNED A DEAF EAR TO HIM.
THAT WAS THEIR GRAVEST ERROR.
THAT WAS THEIR BLACKEST SIN.
A TOTEM WAS ERECTED IN FRONT OF THE SHAMAN'S TOMB.
IT WARNED THAT EVIL SPIRITS WERE BURIED WITHIN.
THE ULTIMATE IRONY, NO?
BUT THE HEATHENS WOULD NOT SUCCEED IN THEIR BASE VILLAINY.
THE GLORY OF SHAMAN BLACKFIRE REFUSED TO REMAIN ENTOMBED.
SHAMAN BLACKFIRE, IS IT?
DO YOU REALLY EXPECT ME TO BUY INTO THAT LOAD OF...
THE LONGER YOU RESIST THE TRUTH...
...THE GREATER WILL BE YOUR PAIN!
IT WOULD BE BEST IF YOU DID!
IT IS THE WORD AND IT IS GOOD!
PATIENCE, MY SON.
THOSE WHO HAVE NOT SEEN THE LIGHT MUST BE GIVEN TIME TO ACCEPT THE DIVINE NOBILITY OF OUR CAUSE.

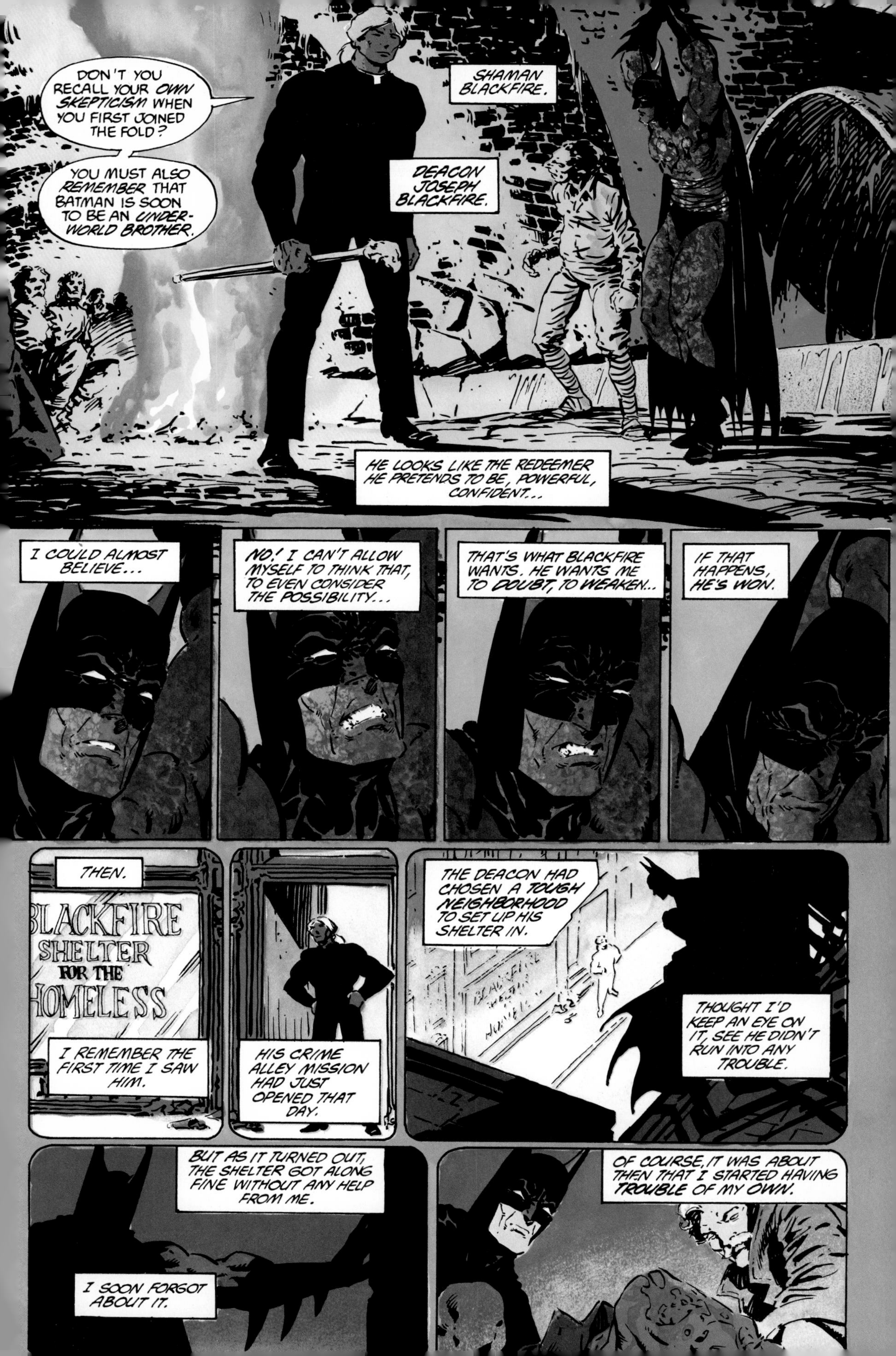

DON'T YOU RECALL YOUR OWN SKEPTICISM WHEN YOU FIRST JOINED THE FOLD?
YOU MUST ALSO REMEMBER THAT BATMAN IS SOON TO BE AN UNDER-WORLD BROTHER.
SHAMAN BLACKFIRE.
DEACON JOSEPH BLACKFIRE.
HE LOOKS LIKE THE REDEEMER HE PRETENDS TO BE, POWERFUL, CONFIDENT...
I COULD ALMOST BELIEVE...
NO! I CAN'T ALLOW MYSELF TO THINK THAT, TO EVEN CONSIDER THE POSSIBILITY...
THAT'S WHAT BLACKFIRE WANTS. HE WANTS ME TO DOUBT, TO WEAKEN...
IF THAT HAPPENS, HE'S WON.
THEN.
BLACKFIRE SHELTER FOR THE HOMELESS
I REMEMBER THE FIRST TIME I SAW HIM.
HIS CRIME ALLEY MISSION HAD JUST OPENED THAT DAY.
THE DEACON HAD CHOSEN A TOUGH NEIGHBORHOOD TO SET UP HIS SHELTER IN.
THOUGHT I'D KEEP AN EYE ON IT, SEE HE DIDN'T RUN INTO ANY TROUBLE.
BUT AS IT TURNED OUT, THE SHELTER GOT ALONG FINE WITHOUT ANY HELP FROM ME.
I SOON FORGOT ABOUT IT.
OF COURSE, IT WAS ABOUT THEN THAT I STARTED HAVING TROUBLE OF MY OWN.

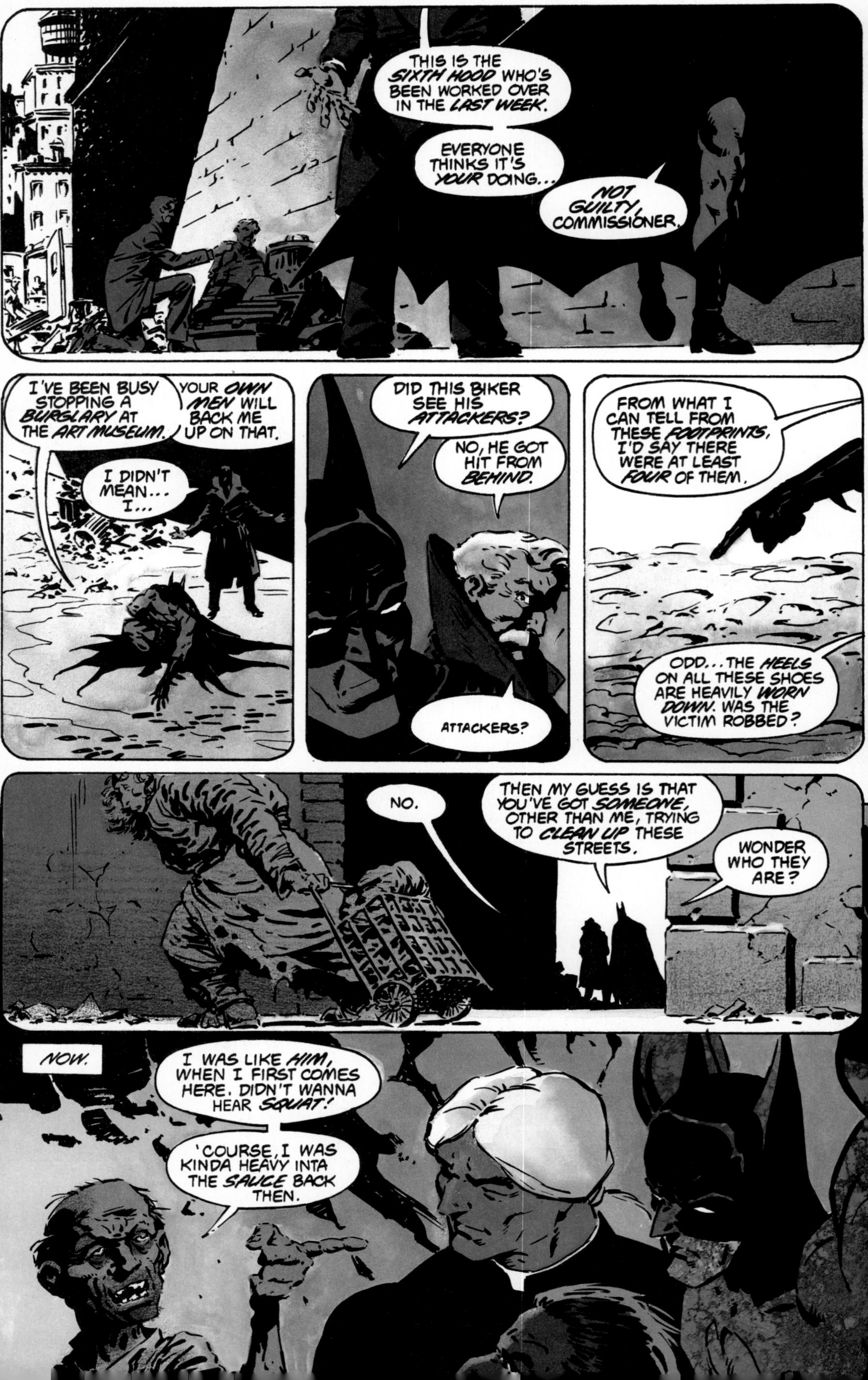
THIS IS THE SIXTH HOOD WHO'S BEEN WORKED OVER IN THE LAST WEEK.
EVERYONE THINKS IT'S YOUR DOING...
NOT GUILTY, COMMISSIONER.
I'VE BEEN BUSY STOPPING A BURGLARY AT THE ART MUSEUM.
YOUR OWN MEN WILL BACK ME UP ON THAT.
I DIDN'T MEAN... I...
DID THIS BIKER SEE HIS ATTACKERS?
NO, HE GOT HIT FROM BEHIND.
ATTACKERS?
FROM WHAT I CAN TELL FROM THESE FOOTPRINTS, I'D SAY THERE WERE AT LEAST FOUR OF THEM.
ODD... THE HEELS ON ALL THESE SHOES ARE HEAVILY WORN DOWN. WAS THE VICTIM ROBBED?
NO.
THEN MY GUESS IS THAT YOU'VE GOT SOMEONE, OTHER THAN ME, TRYING TO CLEAN UP THESE STREETS.
WONDER WHO THEY ARE?
NOW.
I WAS LIKE HIM, WHEN I FIRST COMES HERE. DIDN'T WANNA HEAR SQUAT!
'COURSE, I WAS KINDA HEAVY INTA THE SAUCE BACK THEN.

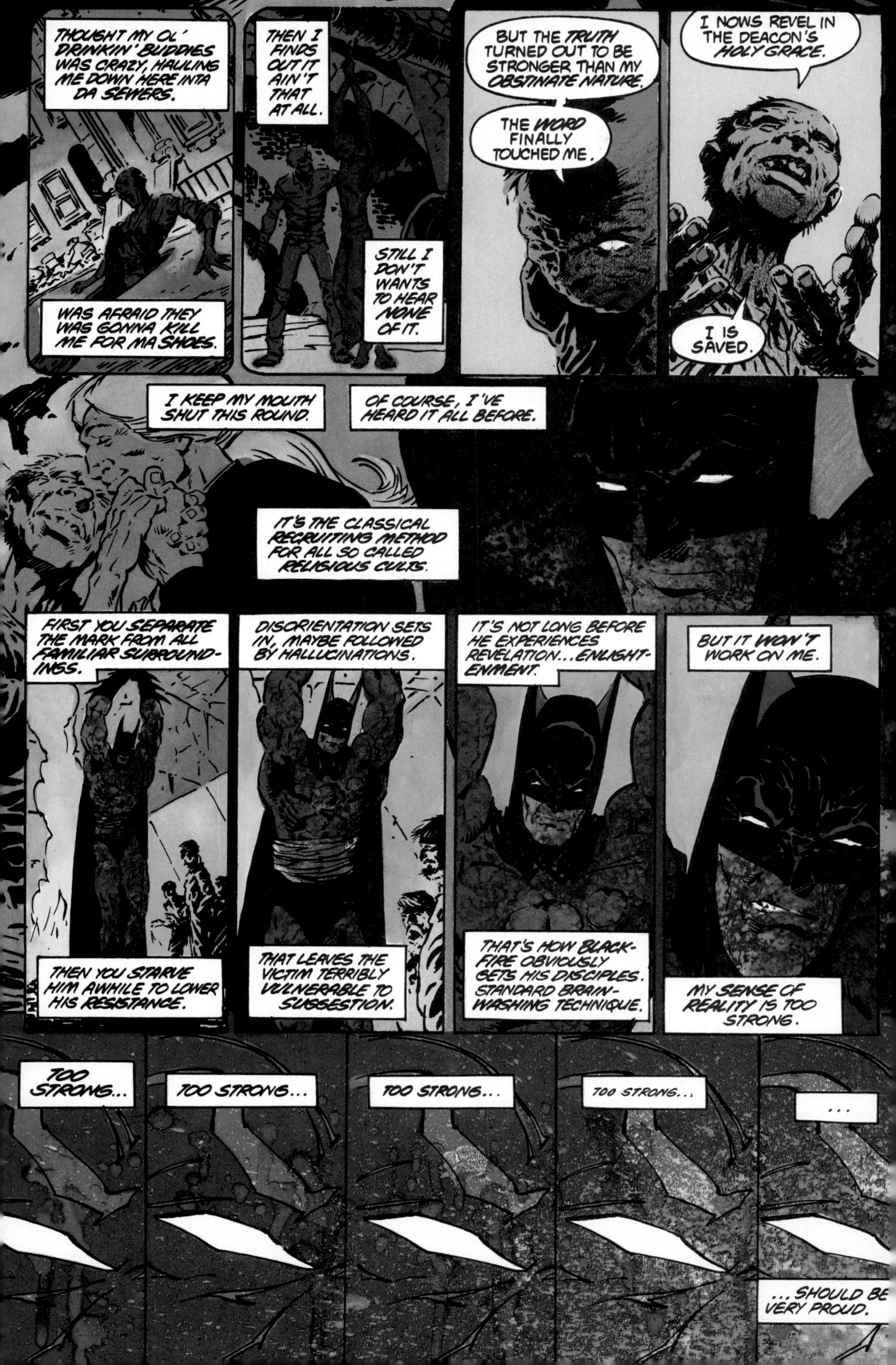
THOUGHT MY OL' DRINKIN' BUDDIES WAS CRAZY, HAULING ME DOWN HERE INTA DA SEWERS.
WAS AFRAID THEY WAS GONNA KILL ME FOR MA SHOES.
THEN I FINDS OUT IT AIN'T THAT AT ALL.
STILL I DON'T WANTS TO HEAR NONE OF IT.
BUT THE TRUTH TURNED OUT TO BE STRONGER THAN MY OBSTINATE NATURE.
THE WORD FINALLY TOUCHED ME.
I NOWS REVEL IN THE DEACON'S HOLY GRACE.
I IS SAVED.
I KEEP MY MOUTH SHUT THIS ROUND.
OF COURSE, I'VE HEARD IT ALL BEFORE.
IT'S THE CLASSICAL RECRUITING METHOD FOR ALL SO CALLED RELIGIOUS CULTS.
FIRST YOU SEPARATE THE MARK FROM ALL FAMILIAR SURROUND-INGS.
THEN YOU STARVE HIM AWHILE TO LOWER HIS RESISTANCE.
DISORIENTATION SETS IN, MAYBE FOLLOWED BY HALLUCINATIONS.
THAT LEAVES THE VICTIM TERRIBLY VULNERABLE TO SUGGESTION.
IT'S NOT LONG BEFORE HE EXPERIENCES REVELATION... ENLIGHT-ENMENT.
THAT'S HOW BLACK-FIRE OBVIOUSLY GETS HIS DISCIPLES. STANDARD BRAIN-WASHING TECHNIQUE.
BUT IT WON'T WORK ON ME.
MY SENSE OF REALITY IS TOO STRONG.
TOO STRONG...
TOO STRONG...
TOO STRONG...
TOO STRONG...
...
...SHOULD BE VERY PROUD.

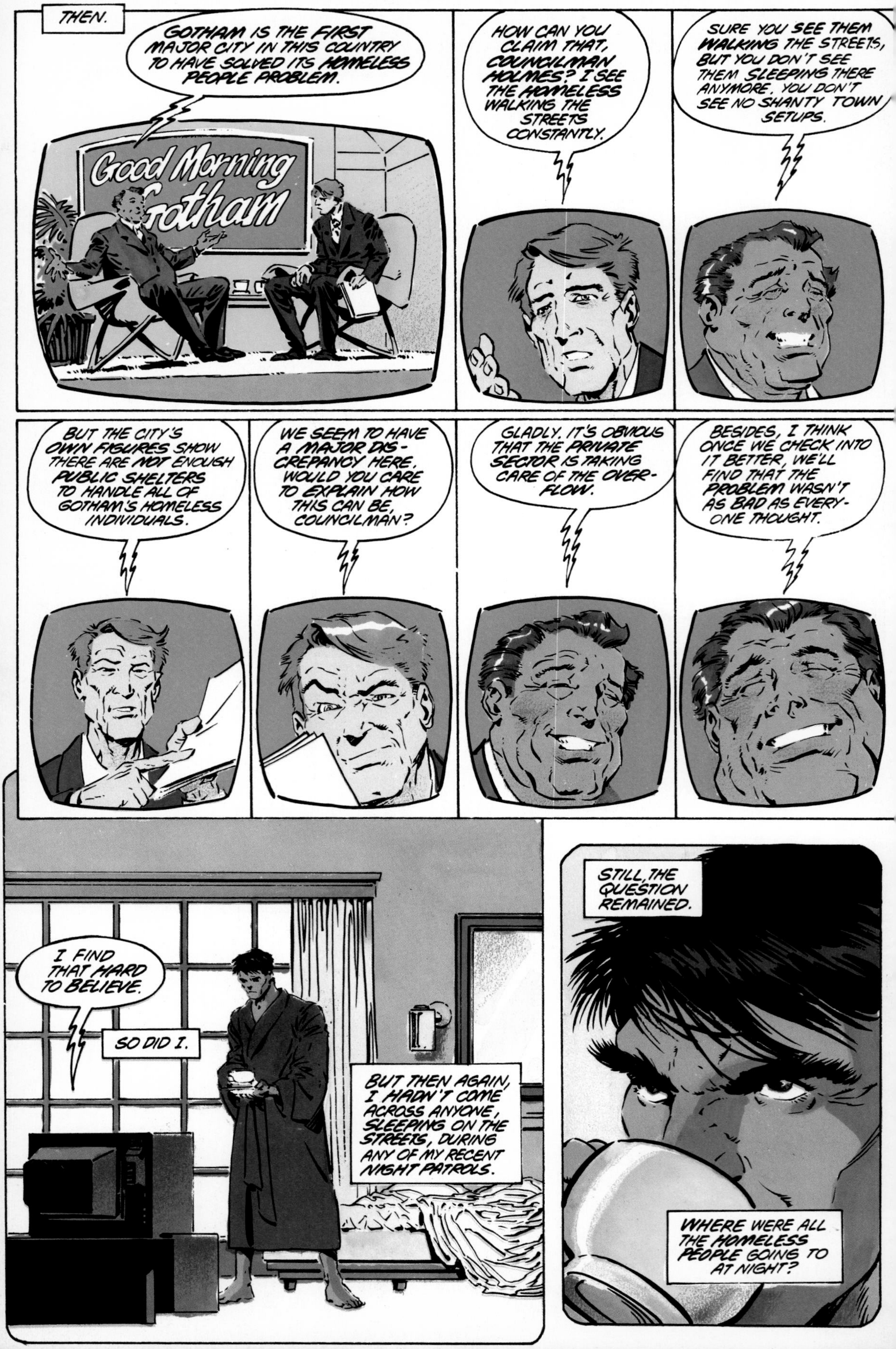
THEN.
GOTHAM IS THE FIRST MAJOR CITY IN THIS COUNTRY TO HAVE SOLVED ITS HOMELESS PEOPLE PROBLEM.
Good Morning Gotham
HOW CAN YOU CLAIM THAT, COUNCILMAN HOLMES? I SEE THE HOMELESS WALKING THE STREETS CONSTANTLY.
SURE YOU SEE THEM WALKING THE STREETS, BUT YOU DON'T SEE THEM SLEEPING THERE ANYMORE. YOU DON'T SEE NO SHANTY TOWN SETUPS.
BUT THE CITY'S OWN FIGURES SHOW THERE ARE NOT ENOUGH PUBLIC SHELTERS TO HANDLE ALL OF GOTHAM'S HOMELESS INDIVIDUALS.
WE SEEM TO HAVE A MAJOR DIS-CREPANCY HERE. WOULD YOU CARE TO EXPLAIN HOW THIS CAN BE, COUNCILMAN?
GLADLY. IT'S OBVIOUS THAT THE PRIVATE SECTOR IS TAKING CARE OF THE OVER-FLOW.
BESIDES, I THINK ONCE WE CHECK INTO IT BETTER, WE'LL FIND THAT THE PROBLEM WASN'T AS BAD AS EVERY-ONE THOUGHT.
I FIND THAT HARD TO BELIEVE.
SO DID I.
BUT THEN AGAIN, I HADN'T COME ACROSS ANYONE, SLEEPING ON THE STREETS, DURING ANY OF MY RECENT NIGHT PATROLS.
STILL, THE QUESTION REMAINED.
WHERE WERE ALL THE HOMELESS PEOPLE GOING TO AT NIGHT?

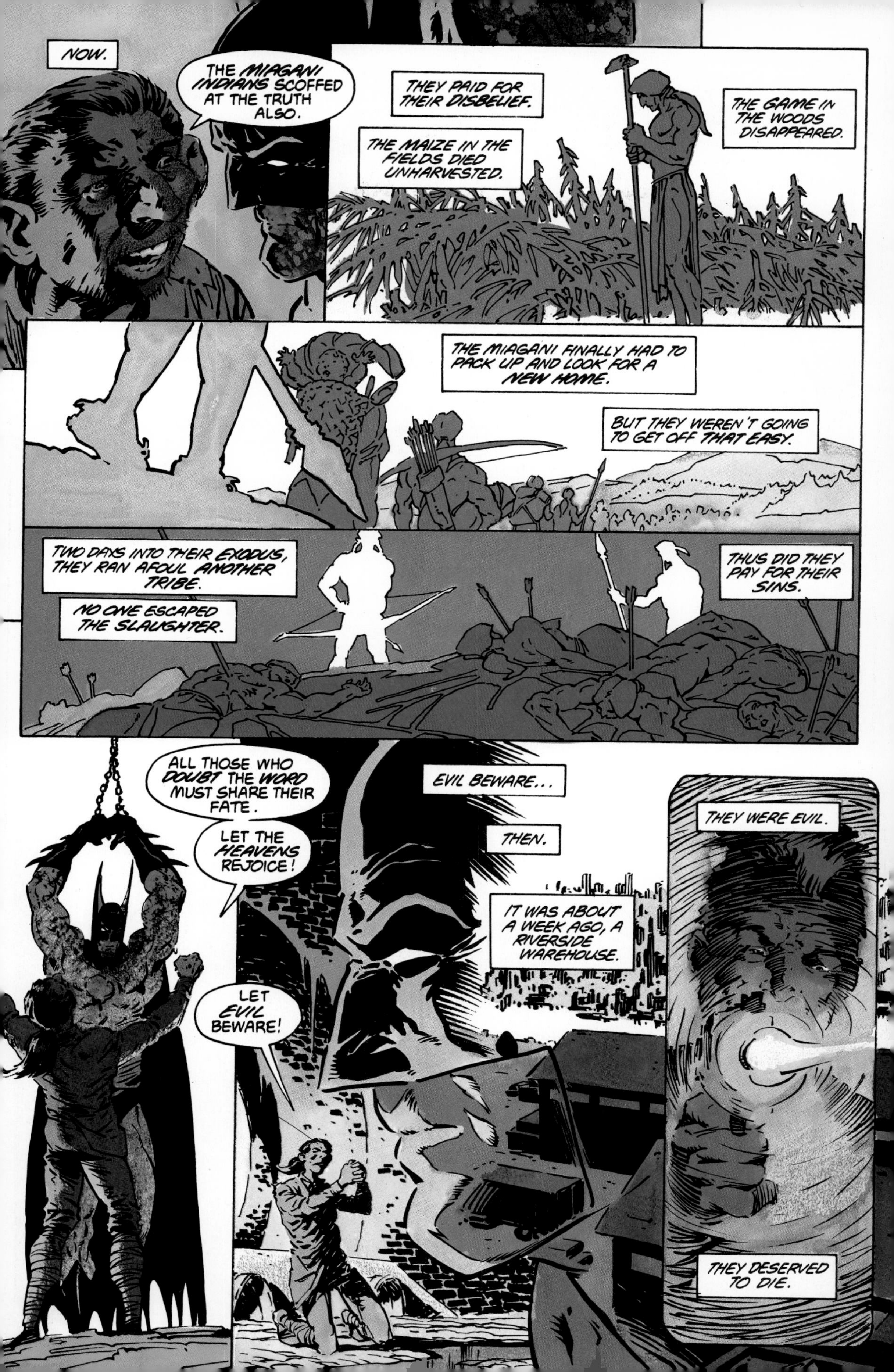
NOW.
THE MIAGANI INDIANS SCOFFED AT THE TRUTH ALSO.
THEY PAID FOR THEIR DISBELIEF.
THE MAIZE IN THE FIELDS DIED UNHARVESTED.
THE GAME IN THE WOODS DISAPPEARED.
THE MIAGANI FINALLY HAD TO PACK UP AND LOOK FOR A NEW HOME.
BUT THEY WEREN'T GOING TO GET OFF THAT EASY.
TWO DAYS INTO THEIR EXODUS, THEY RAN AFOUL ANOTHER TRIBE.
NO ONE ESCAPED THE SLAUGHTER.
THUS DID THEY PAY FOR THEIR SINS.
ALL THOSE WHO DOUBT THE WORD MUST SHARE THEIR FATE.
LET THE HEAVENS REJOICE!
LET EVIL BEWARE!
EVIL BEWARE...
THEN.
IT WAS ABOUT A WEEK AGO, A RIVERSIDE WAREHOUSE.
THEY WERE EVIL.
THEY DESERVED TO DIE.

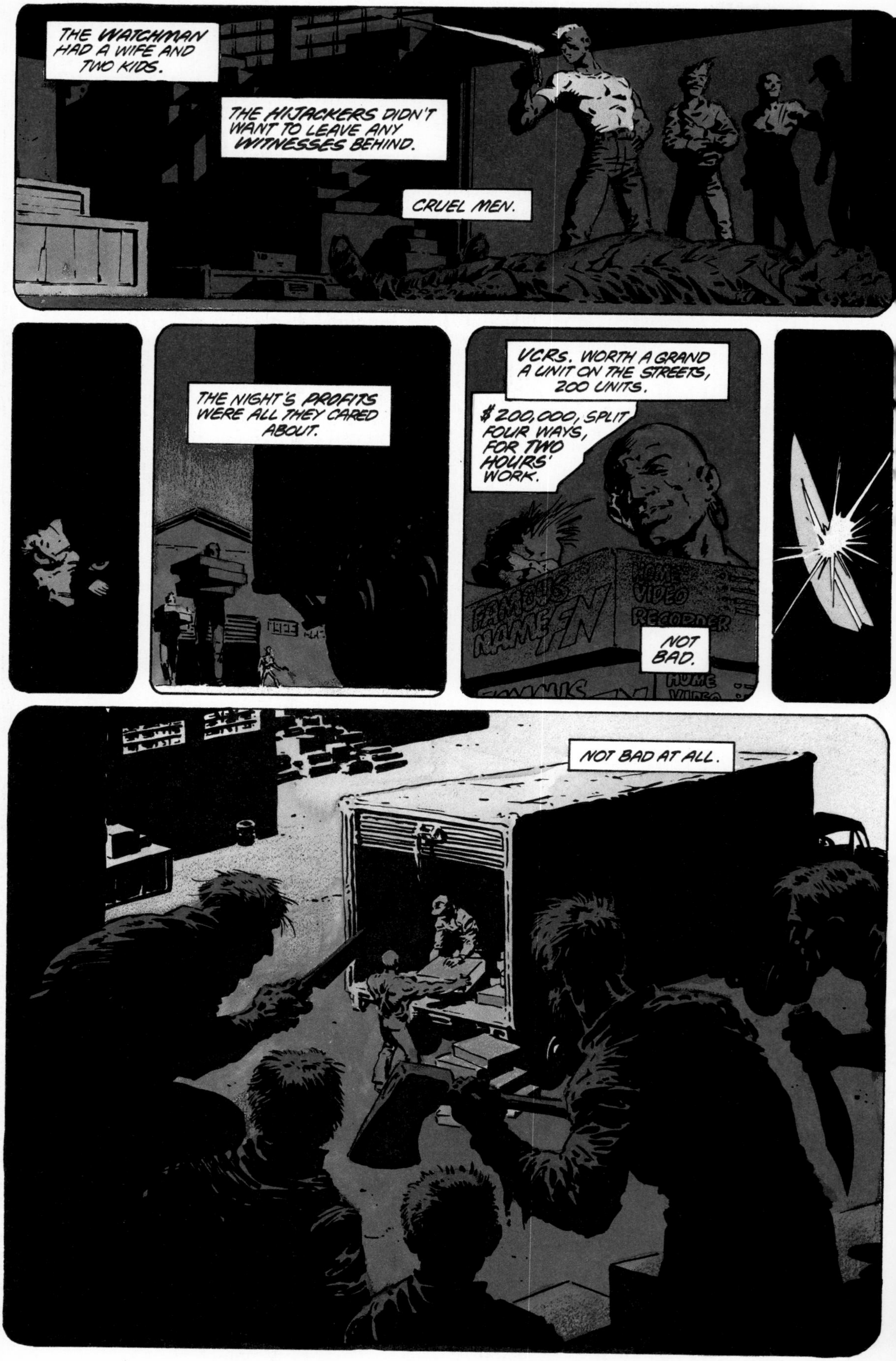
THE WATCHMAN HAD A WIFE AND TWO KIDS.
THE HIJACKERS DIDN'T WANT TO LEAVE ANY WITNESSES BEHIND.
CRUEL MEN.
THE NIGHT'S PROFITS WERE ALL THEY CARED ABOUT.
VCRs. WORTH A GRAND A UNIT ON THE STREETS, 200 UNITS.
$200,000, SPLIT FOUR WAYS, FOR TWO HOURS' WORK.
HOME VIDEO RECORDER
NOT BAD.
NOT BAD AT ALL.

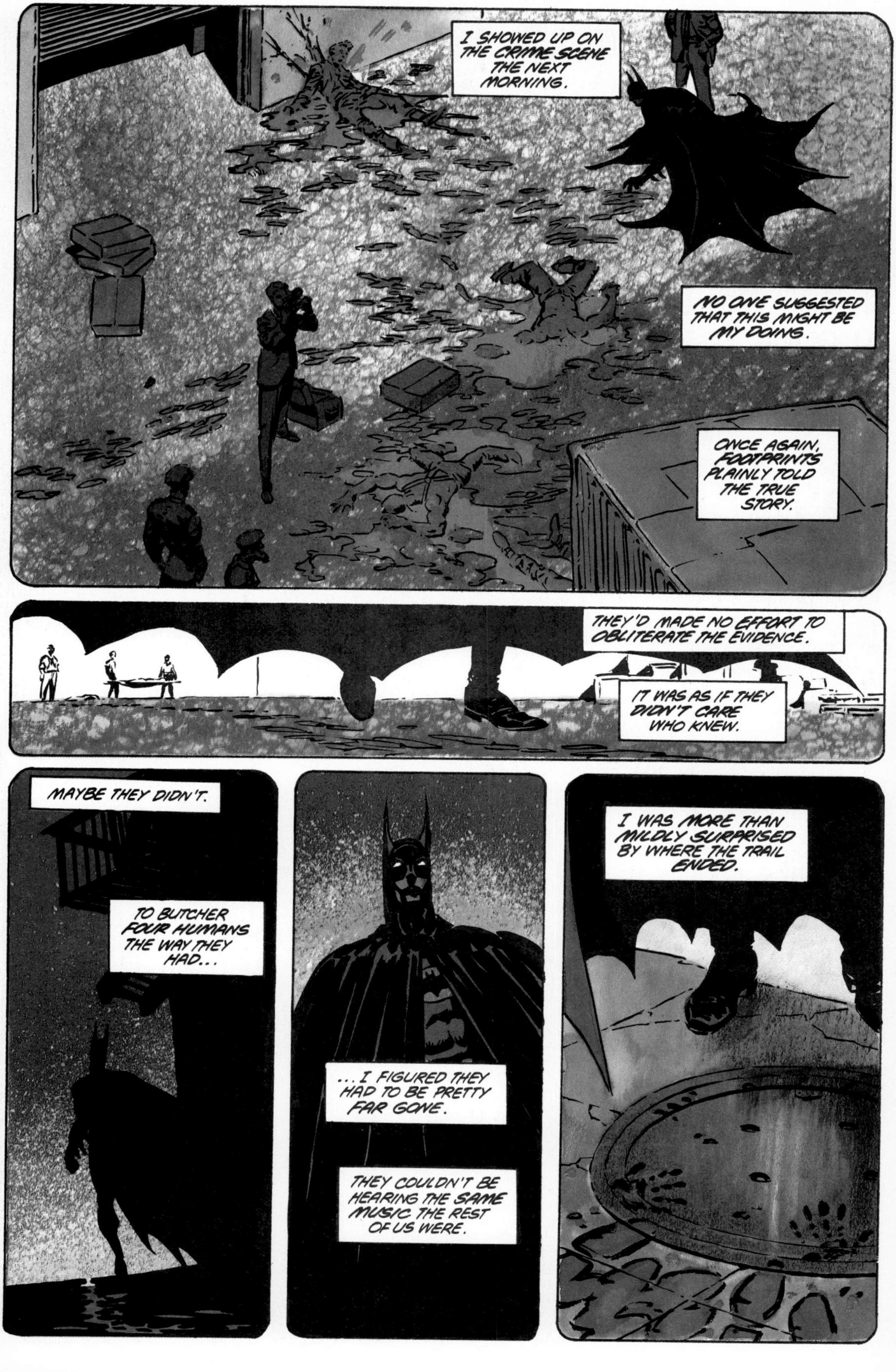
I SHOWED UP ON THE CRIME SCENE THE NEXT MORNING.
NO ONE SUGGESTED THAT THIS MIGHT BE MY DOING.
ONCE AGAIN, FOOTPRINTS PLAINLY TOLD THE TRUE STORY.
THEY'D MADE NO EFFORT TO OBLITERATE THE EVIDENCE.
IT WAS AS IF THEY DIDN'T CARE WHO KNEW.
MAYBE THEY DIDN'T.
TO BUTCHER FOUR HUMANS THE WAY THEY HAD...
...I FIGURED THEY HAD TO BE PRETTY FAR GONE.
THEY COULDN'T BE HEARING THE SAME MUSIC THE REST OF US WERE.
I WAS MORE THAN MILDLY SURPRISED BY WHERE THE TRAIL ENDED.

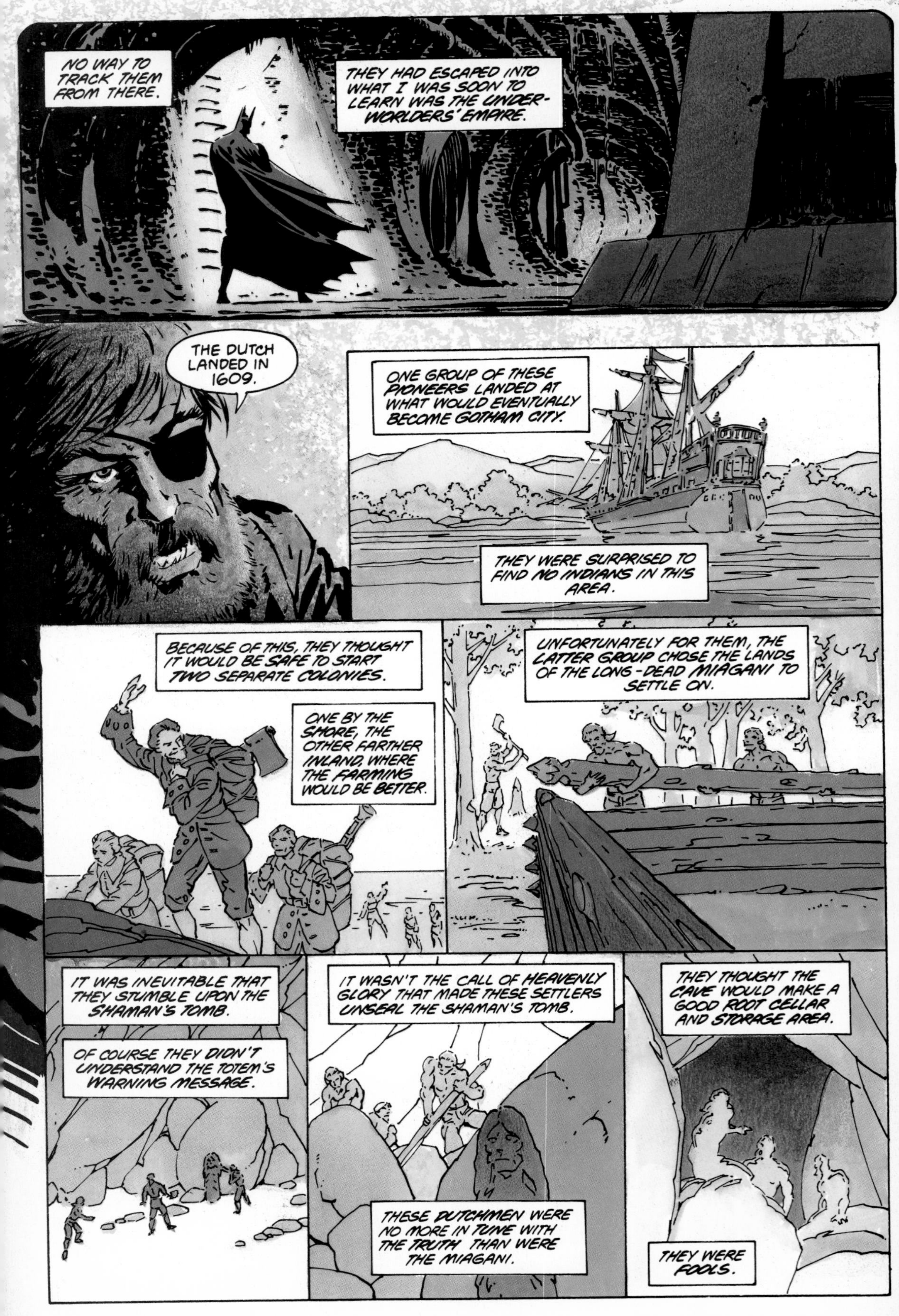
NO WAY TO TRACK THEM FROM THERE.
THEY HAD ESCAPED INTO WHAT I WAS SOON TO LEARN WAS THE UNDER-WORLDERS' EMPIRE.
THE DUTCH LANDED IN 1609.
ONE GROUP OF THESE PIONEERS LANDED AT WHAT WOULD EVENTUALLY BECOME GOTHAM CITY.
THEY WERE SURPRISED TO FIND NO INDIANS IN THIS AREA.
BECAUSE OF THIS, THEY THOUGHT IT WOULD BE SAFE TO START TWO SEPARATE COLONIES.
ONE BY THE SHORE, THE OTHER FARTHER INLAND, WHERE THE FARMING WOULD BE BETTER.
UNFORTUNATELY FOR THEM, THE LATTER GROUP CHOSE THE LANDS OF THE LONG-DEAD MIAGANI TO SETTLE ON.
IT WAS INEVITABLE THAT THEY STUMBLE UPON THE SHAMAN'S TOMB.
OF COURSE THEY DIDN'T UNDERSTAND THE TOTEM'S WARNING MESSAGE.
IT WASN'T THE CALL OF HEAVENLY GLORY THAT MADE THESE SETTLERS UNSEAL THE SHAMAN'S TOMB.
THESE DUTCHMEN WERE NO MORE IN TUNE WITH THE TRUTH THAN WERE THE MIAGANI.
THEY THOUGHT THE CAVE WOULD MAKE A GOOD ROOT CELLAR AND STORAGE AREA.
THEY WERE FOOLS.

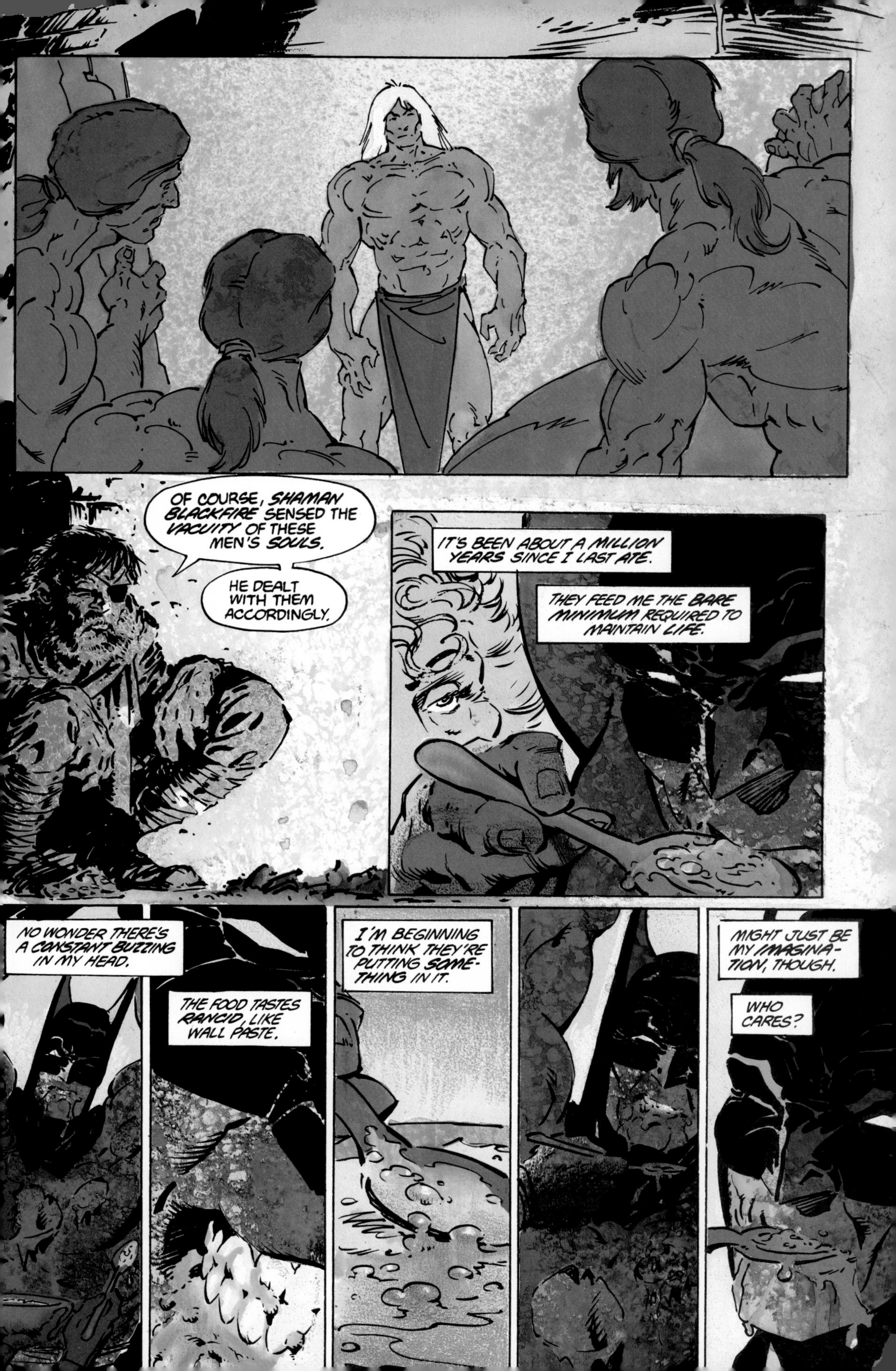
OF COURSE, SHAMAN BLACKFIRE SENSED THE VACUITY OF THESE MEN'S SOULS.
HE DEALT WITH THEM ACCORDINGLY.
IT'S BEEN ABOUT A MILLION YEARS SINCE I LAST ATE.
THEY FEED ME THE BARE MINIMUM REQUIRED TO MAINTAIN LIFE.
NO WONDER THERE'S A CONSTANT BUZZING IN MY HEAD.
THE FOOD TASTES RANCID, LIKE WALL PASTE.
I'M BEGINNING TO THINK THEY'RE PUTTING SOME-THING IN IT.
MIGHT JUST BE MY IMAGINA-TION, THOUGH.
WHO CARES?

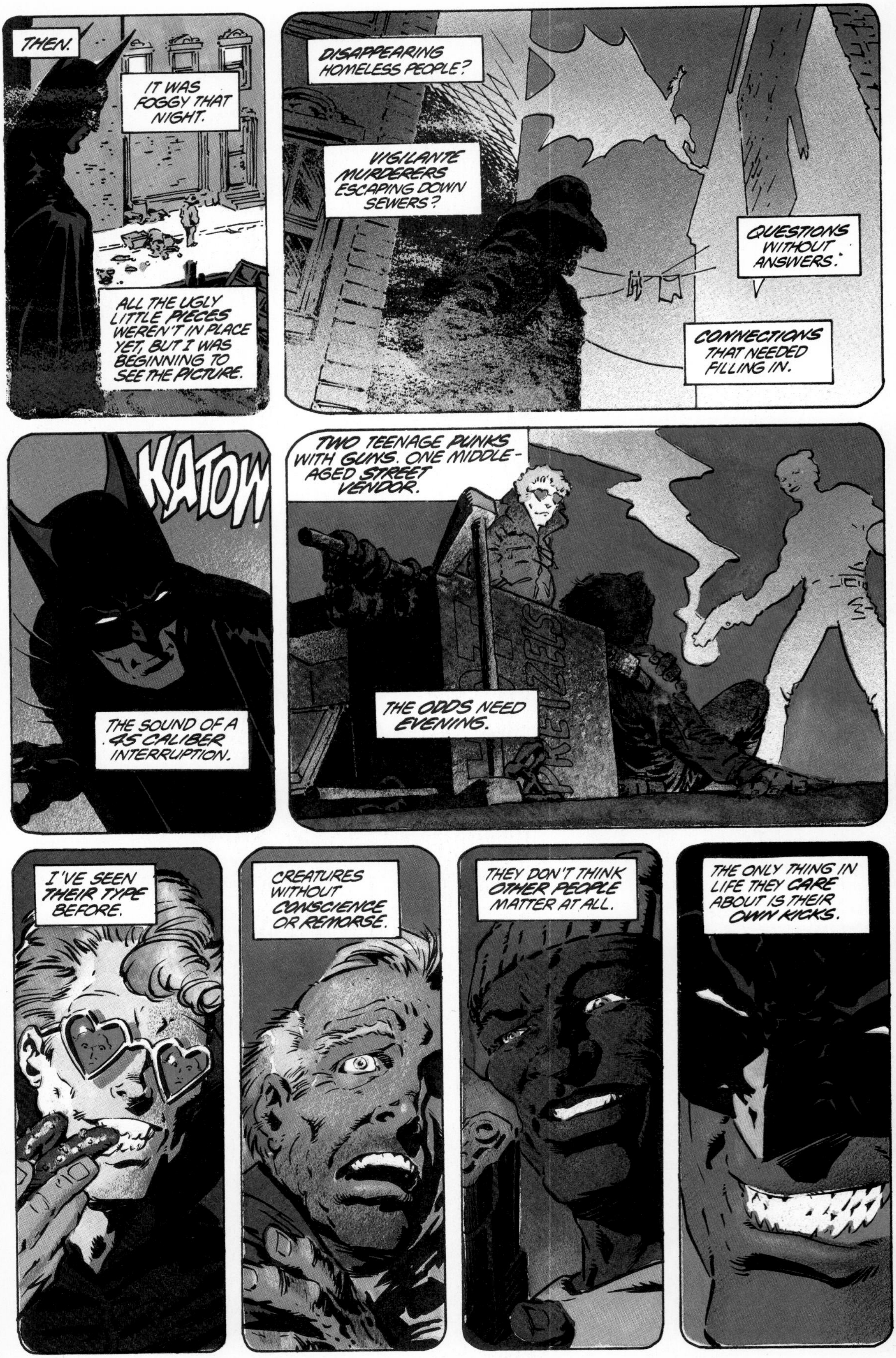
THEN.
IT WAS FOGGY THAT NIGHT.
ALL THE UGLY LITTLE PIECES WEREN'T IN PLACE YET, BUT I WAS BEGINNING TO SEE THE PICTURE.
DISAPPEARING HOMELESS PEOPLE?
VIGILANTE MURDERERS ESCAPING DOWN SEWERS?
QUESTIONS WITHOUT ANSWERS.
CONNECTIONS THAT NEEDED FILLING IN.
KATOW
THE SOUND OF A 45 CALIBER INTERRUPTION.
TWO TEENAGE PUNKS WITH GUNS. ONE MIDDLE-AGED STREET VENDOR.
PRETZELS
THE ODDS NEED EVENING.
I'VE SEEN THEIR TYPE BEFORE.
CREATURES WITHOUT CONSCIENCE OR REMORSE.
THEY DON'T THINK OTHER PEOPLE MATTER AT ALL.
THE ONLY THING IN LIFE THEY CARE ABOUT IS THEIR OWN KICKS.

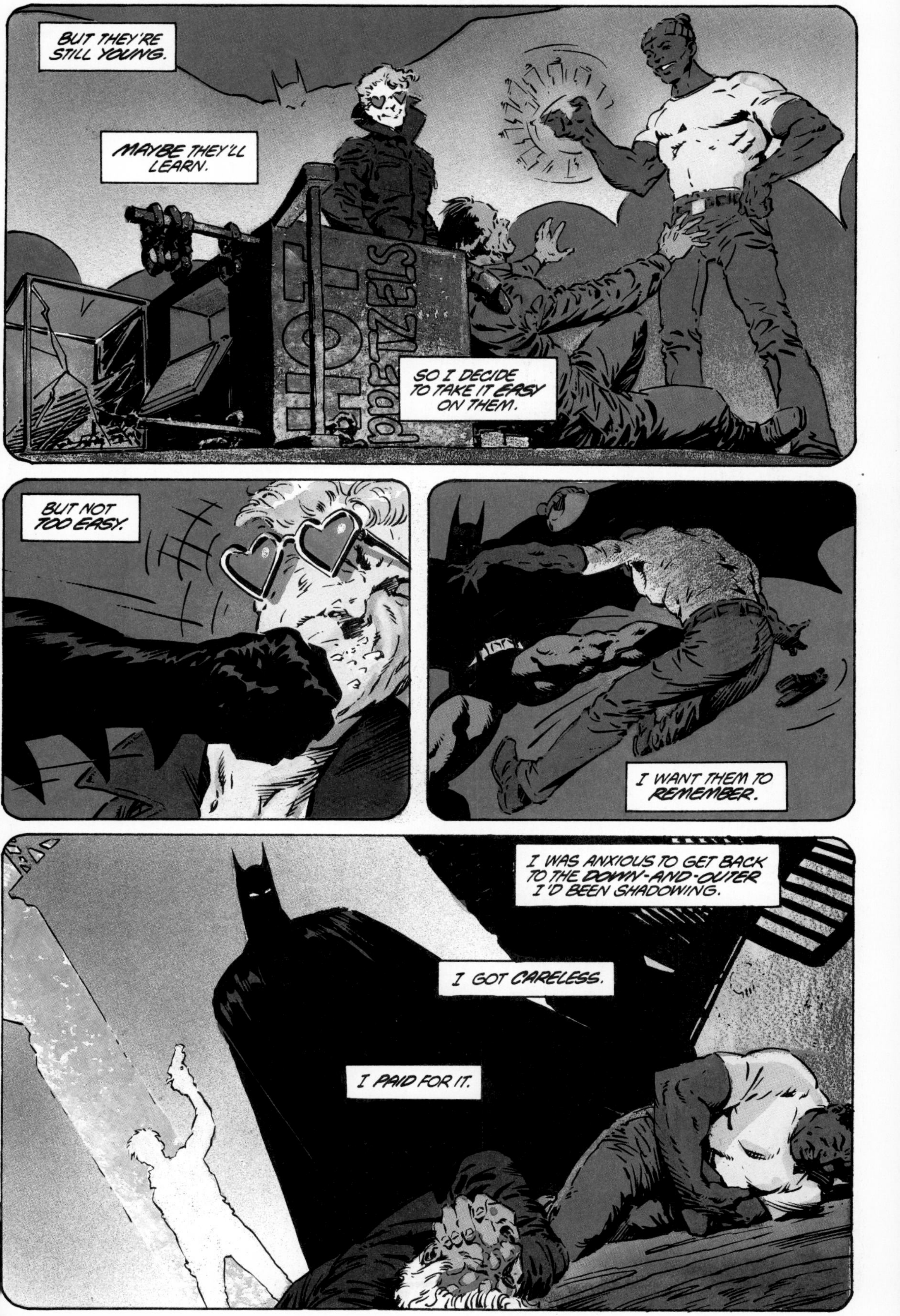
BUT THEY'RE STILL YOUNG.
MAYBE THEY'LL LEARN.
SO I DECIDE TO TAKE IT EASY ON THEM.
BUT NOT TOO EASY.
I WANT THEM TO REMEMBER.
I WAS ANXIOUS TO GET BACK TO THE DOWN-AND-OUTER I'D BEEN SHADOWING.
I GOT CARELESS.
I PAID FOR IT.

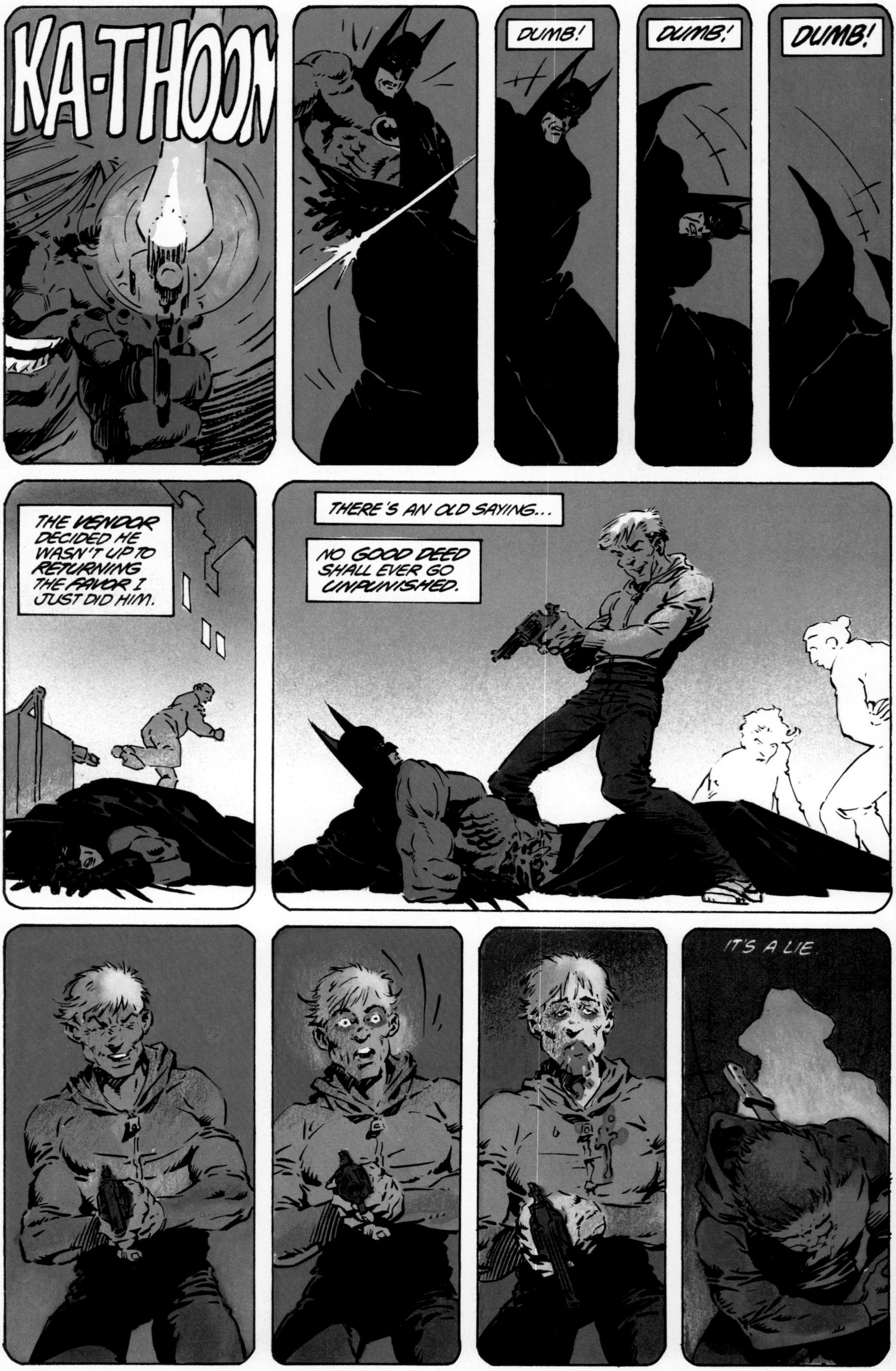
KA-THOOM
DUMB!
DUMB!
DUMB!
THE VENDOR DECIDED HE WASN'T UP TO RETURNING THE FAVOR I JUST DID HIM.
THERE'S AN OLD SAYING...
NO GOOD DEED SHALL EVER GO UNPUNISHED.
IT'S A LIE.

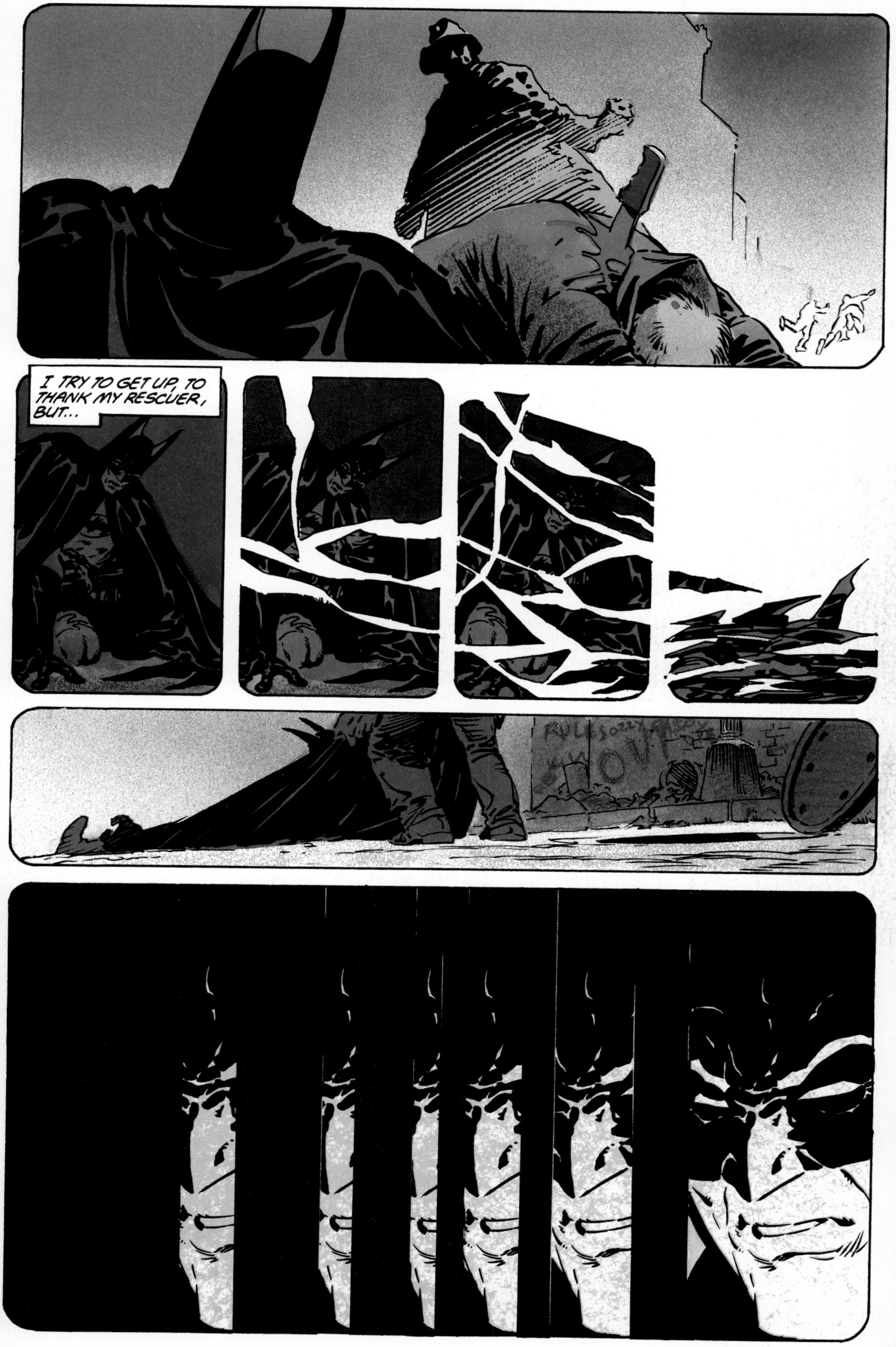
I TRY TO GET UP, TO THANK MY RESCUER, BUT...

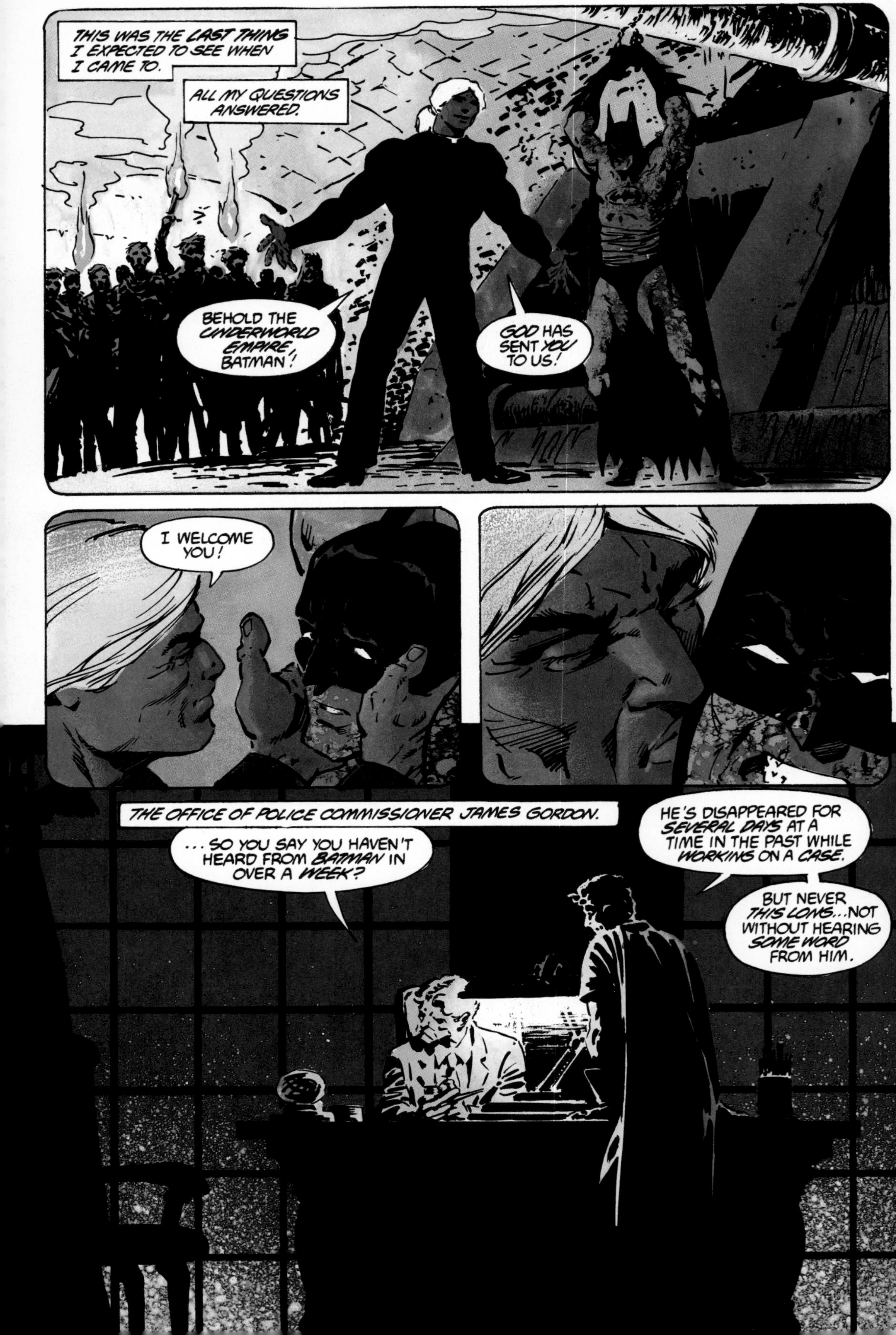
THIS WAS THE LAST THING I EXPECTED TO SEE WHEN I CAME TO.
ALL MY QUESTIONS ANSWERED.
BEHOLD THE UNDERWORLD EMPIRE, BATMAN!
GOD HAS SENT YOU TO US!
I WELCOME YOU!
THE OFFICE OF POLICE COMMISSIONER JAMES GORDON.
...SO YOU SAY YOU HAVEN'T HEARD FROM BATMAN IN OVER A WEEK?
HE'S DISAPPEARED FOR SEVERAL DAYS AT A TIME IN THE PAST WHILE WORKING ON A CASE.
BUT NEVER THIS LONG...NOT WITHOUT HEARING SOME WORD FROM HIM.

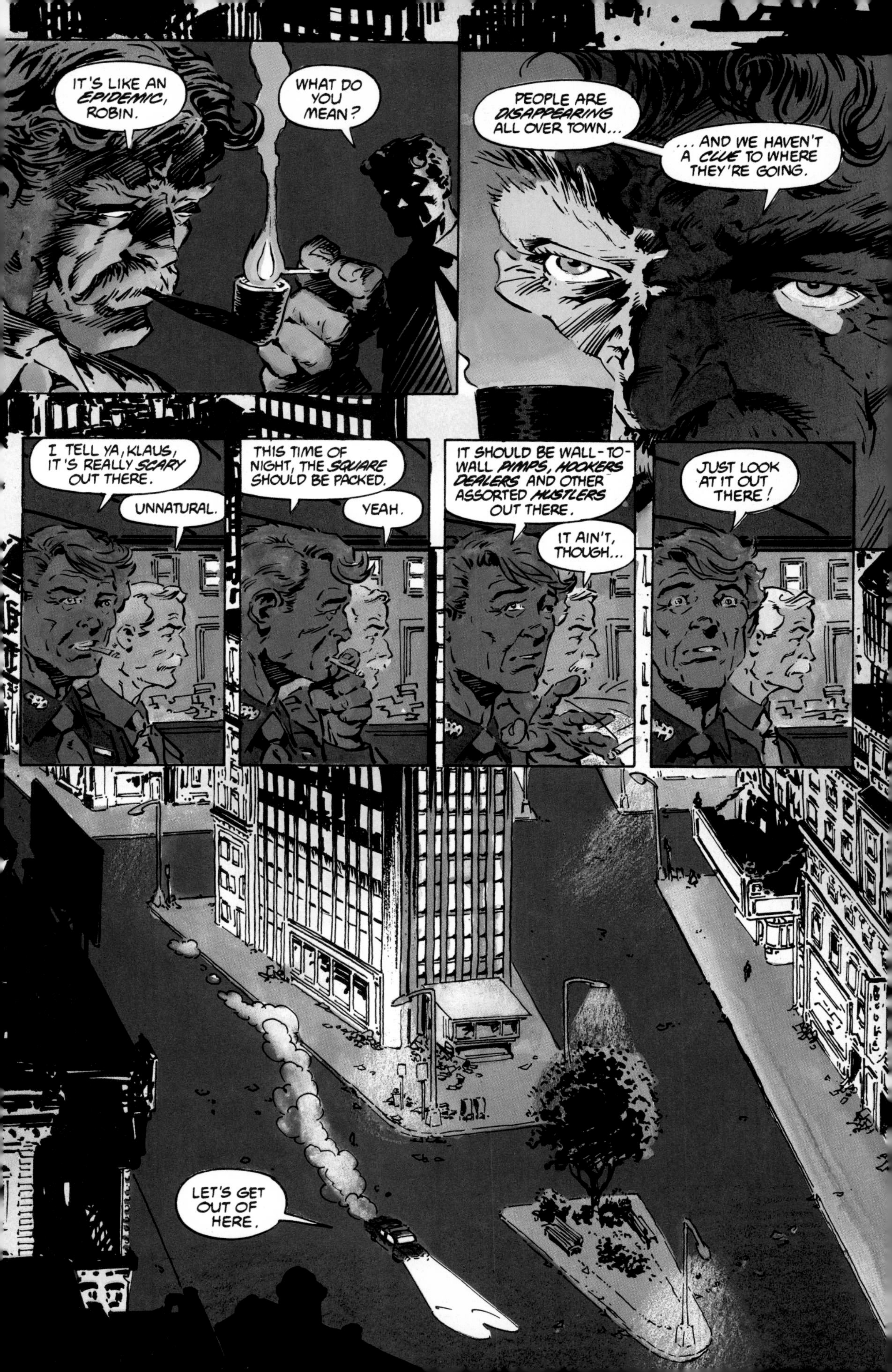

IT'S LIKE AN *EPIDEMIC*, ROBIN.
WHAT DO YOU MEAN?
PEOPLE ARE *DISAPPEARING* ALL OVER TOWN...
...AND WE HAVEN'T A *CLUE* TO WHERE THEY'RE GOING.
I TELL YA, KLAUS, IT'S REALLY *SCARY* OUT THERE.
UNNATURAL.
THIS TIME OF NIGHT, THE *SQUARE* SHOULD BE PACKED.
YEAH.
IT SHOULD BE WALL-TO-WALL *PIMPS, HOOKERS DEALERS* AND OTHER ASSORTED *HUSTLERS* OUT THERE.
IT AIN'T, THOUGH...
JUST LOOK AT IT OUT THERE!
LET'S GET OUT OF HERE.

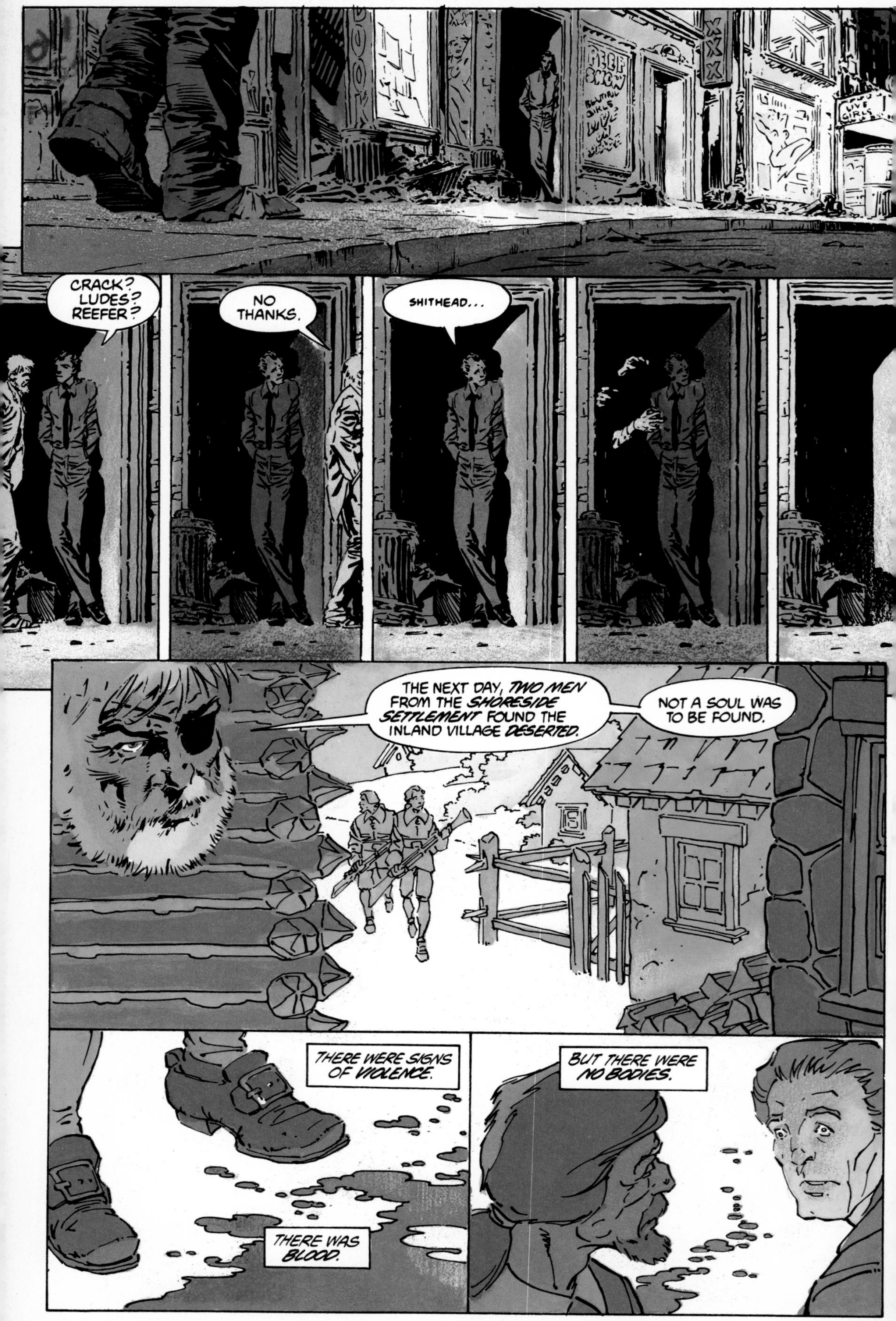
PEEP SHOW
CRACK? LUDES? REEFER?
NO THANKS.
SHITHEAD...
THE NEXT DAY, TWO MEN FROM THE SHORESIDE SETTLEMENT FOUND THE INLAND VILLAGE DESERTED.
NOT A SOUL WAS TO BE FOUND.
THERE WERE SIGNS OF VIOLENCE.
THERE WAS BLOOD.
BUT THERE WERE NO BODIES.

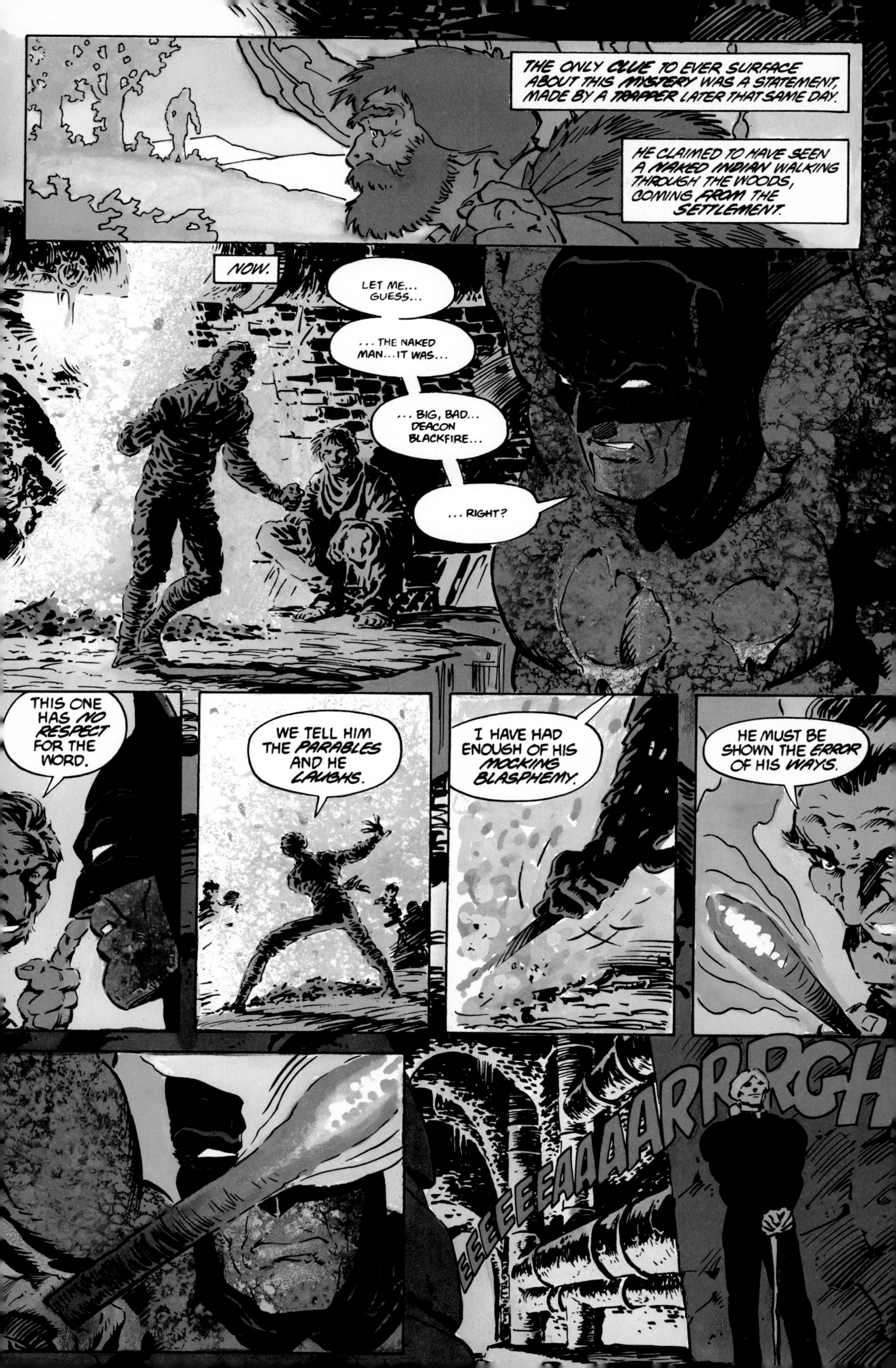
THE ONLY CLUE TO EVER SURFACE ABOUT THIS MYSTERY WAS A STATEMENT, MADE BY A TRAPPER LATER THAT SAME DAY.
HE CLAIMED TO HAVE SEEN A NAKED INDIAN WALKING THROUGH THE WOODS, COMING FROM THE SETTLEMENT.
NOW.
LET ME... GUESS...
...THE NAKED MAN...IT WAS...
...BIG, BAD... DEACON BLACKFIRE...
...RIGHT?
THIS ONE HAS NO RESPECT FOR THE WORD.
WE TELL HIM THE PARABLES AND HE LAUGHS.
I HAVE HAD ENOUGH OF HIS MOCKING BLASPHEMY.
HE MUST BE SHOWN THE ERROR OF HIS WAYS.
EEEEEEAAAAARRRRGH

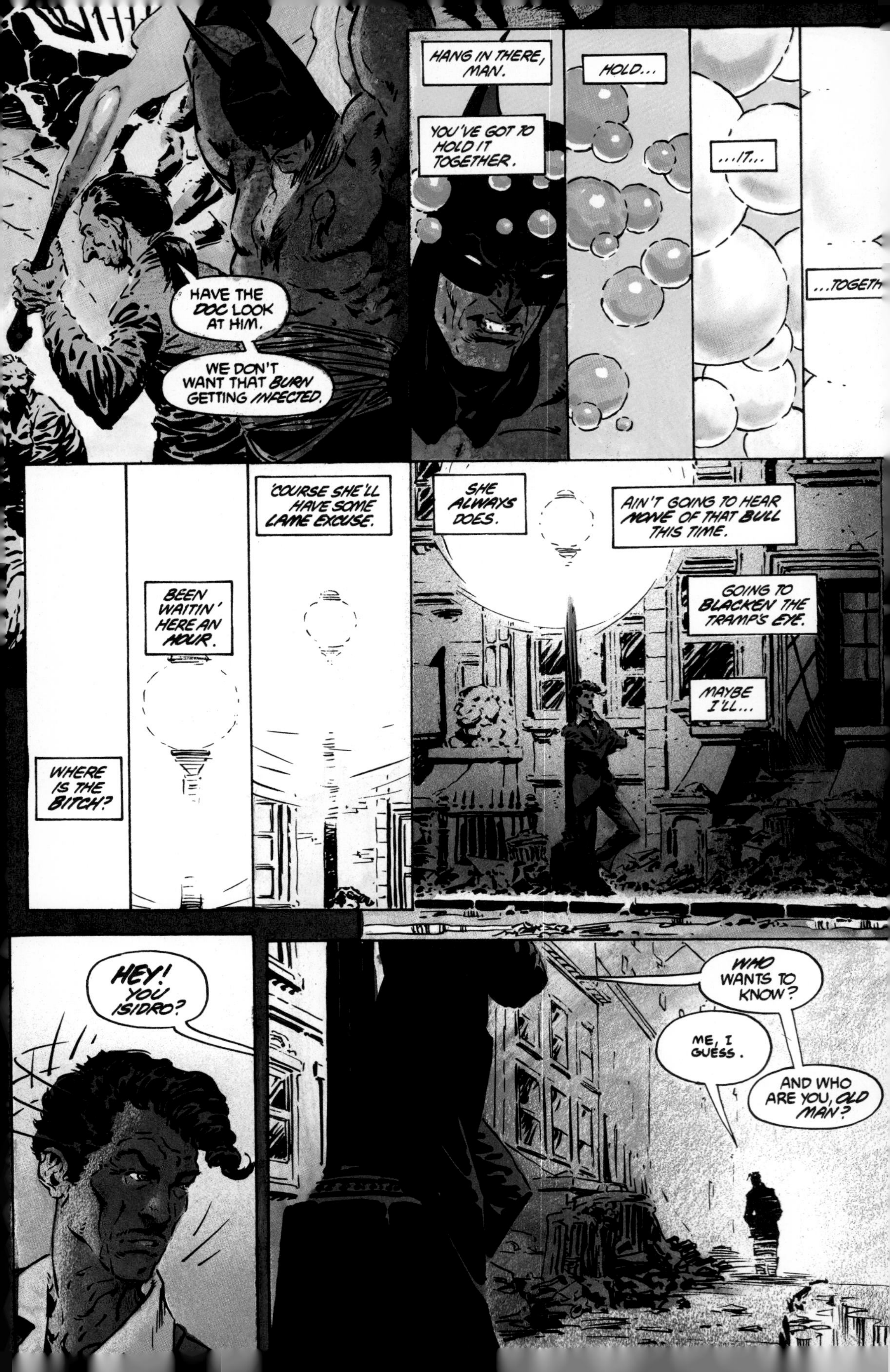
HAVE THE DOC LOOK AT HIM.
WE DON'T WANT THAT BURN GETTING INFECTED.
HANG IN THERE, MAN.
YOU'VE GOT TO HOLD IT TOGETHER.
HOLD...
...IT...
...TOGETH
WHERE IS THE BITCH?
BEEN WAITIN' HERE AN HOUR.
'COURSE SHE'LL HAVE SOME LAME EXCUSE.
SHE ALWAYS DOES.
AIN'T GOING TO HEAR NONE OF THAT BULL THIS TIME.
GOING TO BLACKEN THE TRAMP'S EYE.
MAYBE I'LL...
HEY! YOU ISIDRO?
WHO WANTS TO KNOW?
ME, I GUESS.
AND WHO ARE YOU, OLD MAN?

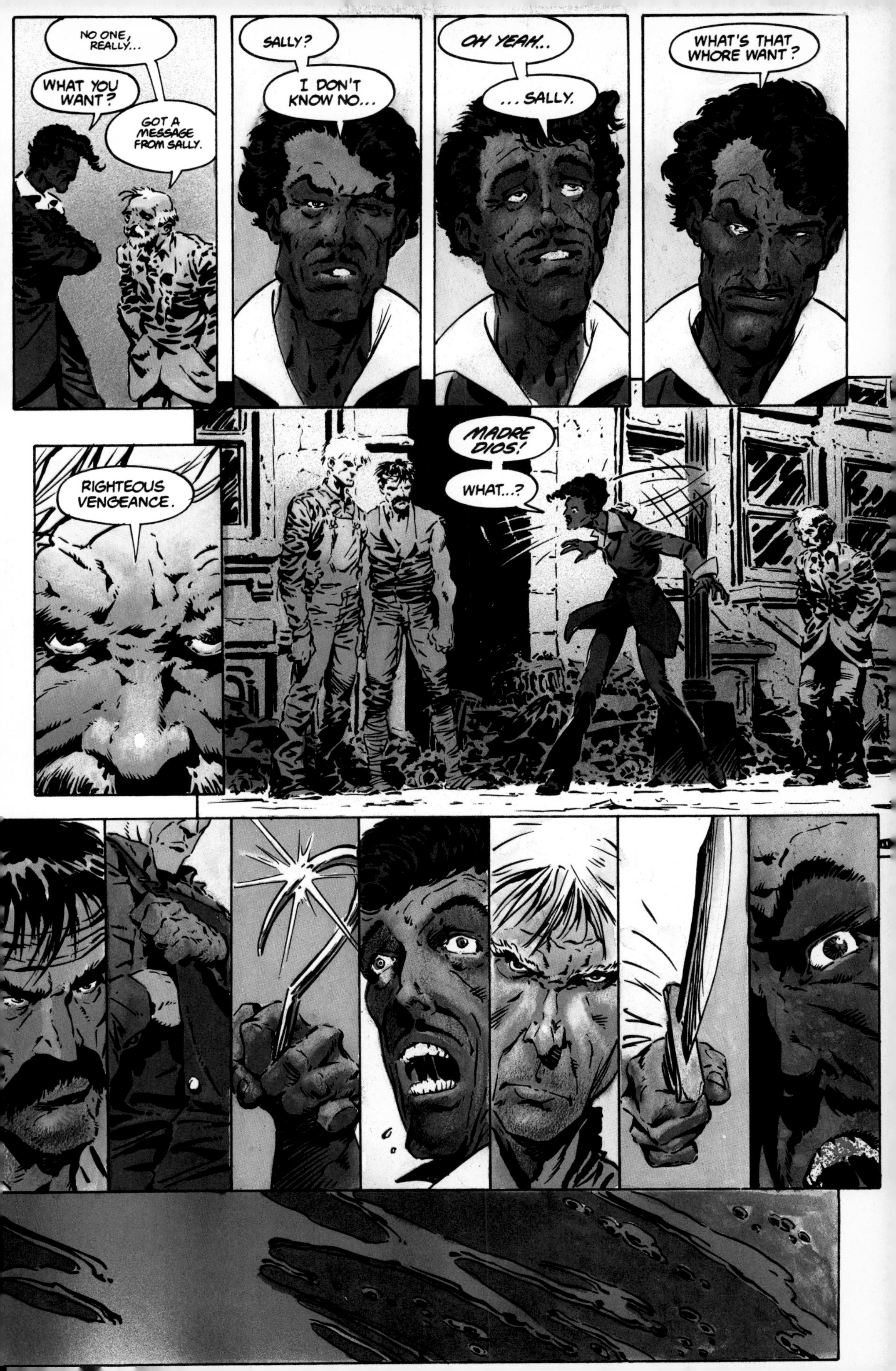
NO ONE, REALLY...
WHAT YOU WANT?
GOT A MESSAGE FROM SALLY.
SALLY?
I DON'T KNOW NO...
OH YEAH...
... SALLY.
WHAT'S THAT WHORE WANT?
RIGHTEOUS VENGEANCE.
MADRE DIOS!
WHAT...?

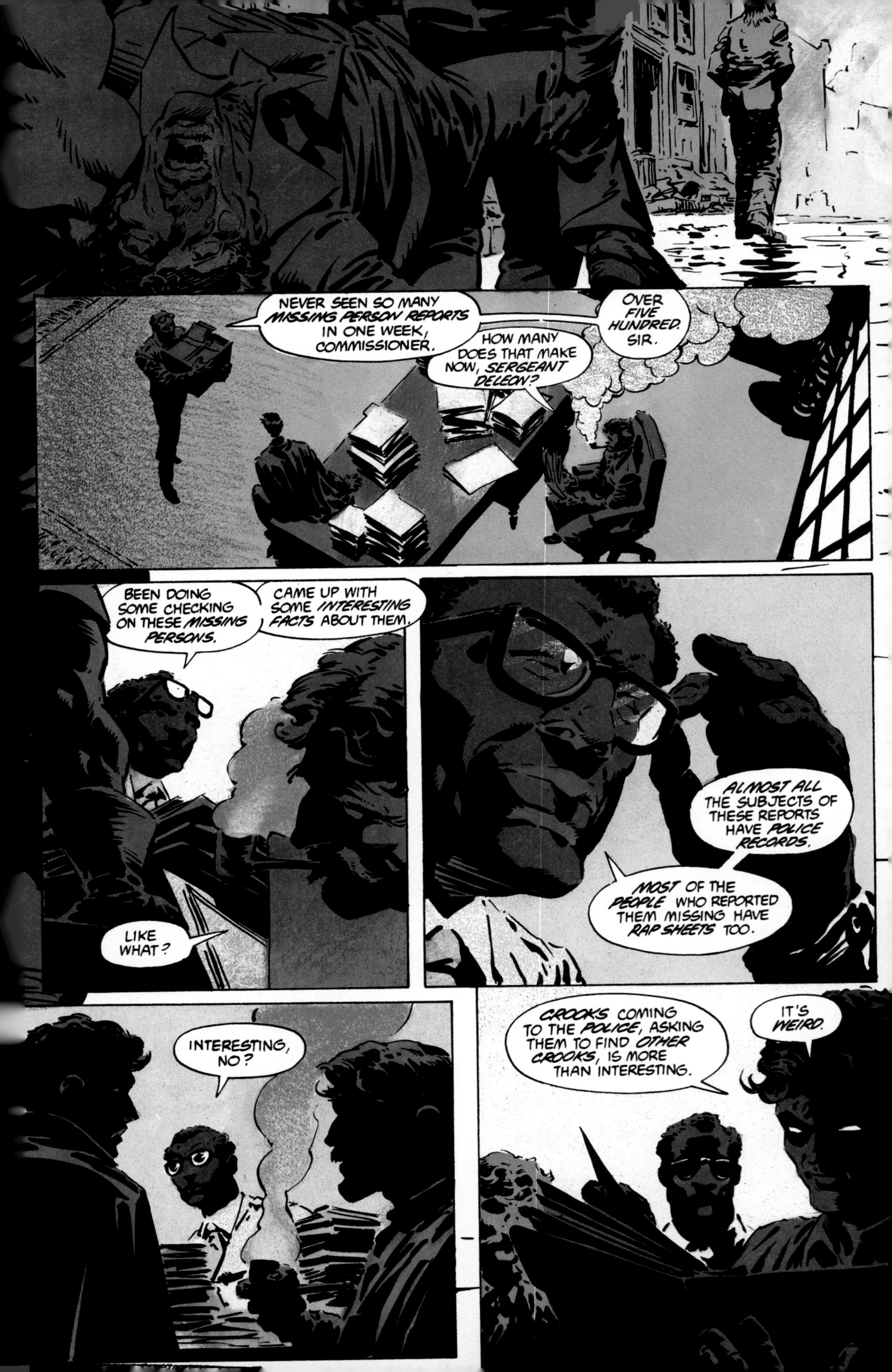
NEVER SEEN SO MANY MISSING PERSON REPORTS IN ONE WEEK, COMMISSIONER.
HOW MANY DOES THAT MAKE NOW, SERGEANT DELEON?
OVER FIVE HUNDRED. SIR.
BEEN DOING SOME CHECKING ON THESE MISSING PERSONS.
CAME UP WITH SOME INTERESTING FACTS ABOUT THEM.
LIKE WHAT?
ALMOST ALL THE SUBJECTS OF THESE REPORTS HAVE POLICE RECORDS.
MOST OF THE PEOPLE WHO REPORTED THEM MISSING HAVE RAP SHEETS TOO.
INTERESTING, NO?
CROOKS COMING TO THE POLICE, ASKING THEM TO FIND OTHER CROOKS, IS MORE THAN INTERESTING.
IT'S WEIRD.

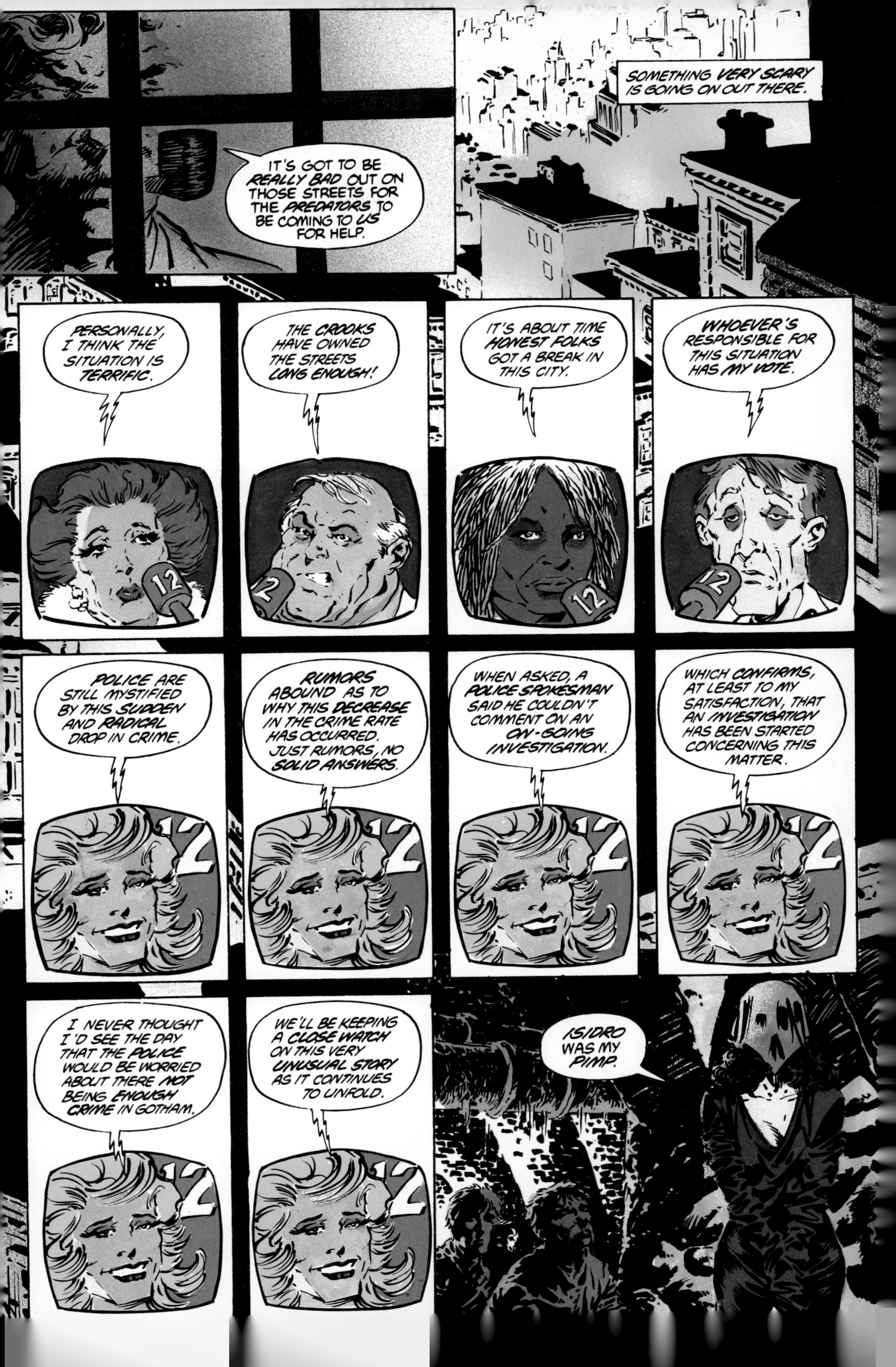
SOMETHING VERY SCARY IS GOING ON OUT THERE.
IT'S GOT TO BE REALLY BAD OUT ON THOSE STREETS FOR THE PREDATORS TO BE COMING TO US FOR HELP.
PERSONALLY, I THINK THE SITUATION IS TERRIFIC.
THE CROOKS HAVE OWNED THE STREETS LONG ENOUGH!
IT'S ABOUT TIME HONEST FOLKS GOT A BREAK IN THIS CITY.
WHOEVER'S RESPONSIBLE FOR THIS SITUATION HAS MY VOTE.
POLICE ARE STILL MYSTIFIED BY THIS SUDDEN AND RADICAL DROP IN CRIME.
RUMORS ABOUND AS TO WHY THIS DECREASE IN THE CRIME RATE HAS OCCURRED. JUST RUMORS, NO SOLID ANSWERS.
WHEN ASKED, A POLICE SPOKESMAN SAID HE COULDN'T COMMENT ON AN ON-GOING INVESTIGATION.
WHICH CONFIRMS, AT LEAST TO MY SATISFACTION, THAT AN INVESTIGATION HAS BEEN STARTED CONCERNING THIS MATTER.
I NEVER THOUGHT I'D SEE THE DAY THAT THE POLICE WOULD BE WORRIED ABOUT THERE NOT BEING ENOUGH CRIME IN GOTHAM.
WE'LL BE KEEPING A CLOSE WATCH ON THIS VERY UNUSUAL STORY AS IT CONTINUES TO UNFOLD.
ISIDRO WAS MY PIMP.

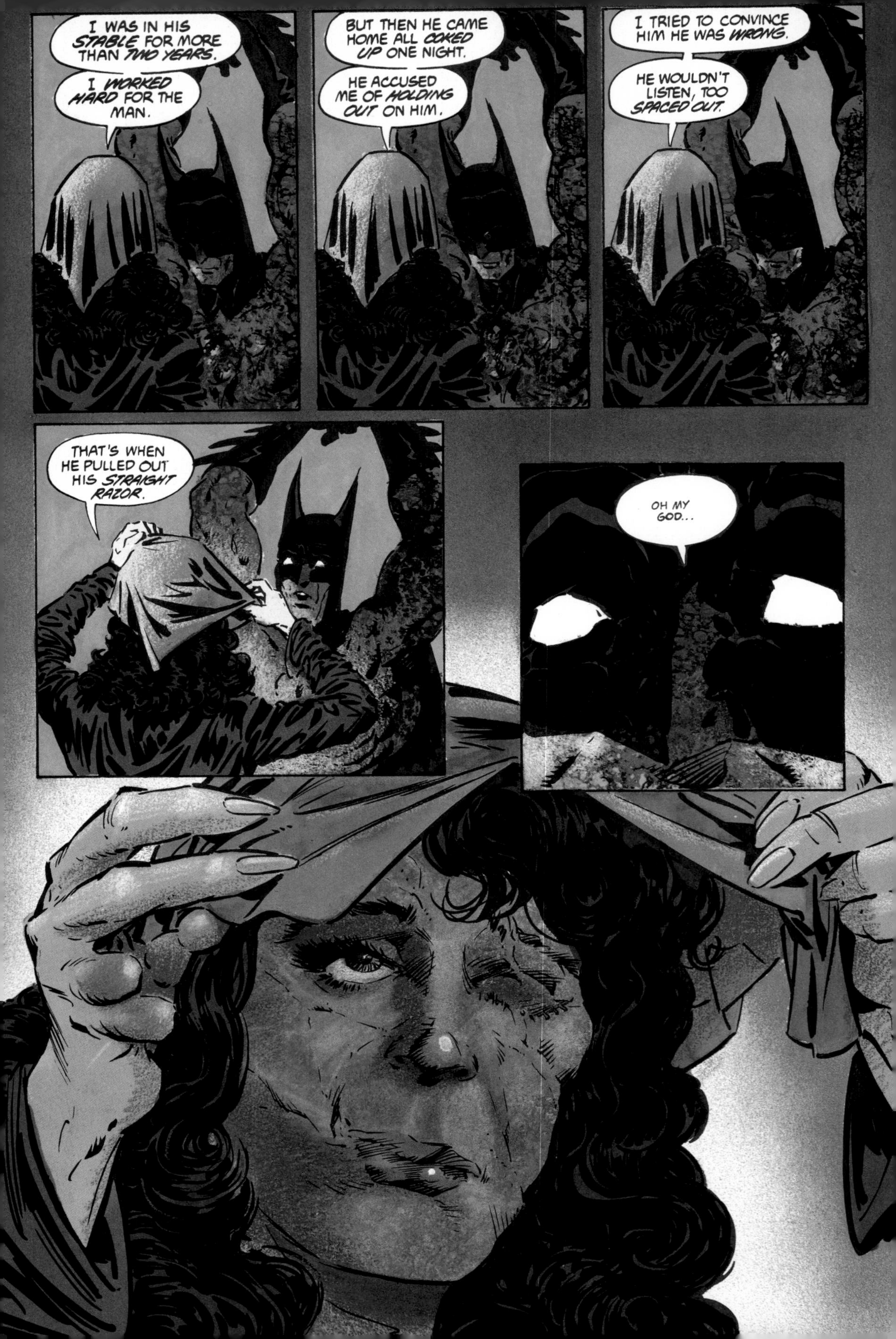
I WAS IN HIS STABLE FOR MORE THAN TWO YEARS.
I WORKED HARD FOR THE MAN.
BUT THEN HE CAME HOME ALL COKED UP ONE NIGHT.
HE ACCUSED ME OF HOLDING OUT ON HIM.
I TRIED TO CONVINCE HIM HE WAS WRONG.
HE WOULDN'T LISTEN, TOO SPACED OUT.
THAT'S WHEN HE PULLED OUT HIS STRAIGHT RAZOR.
OH MY GOD...

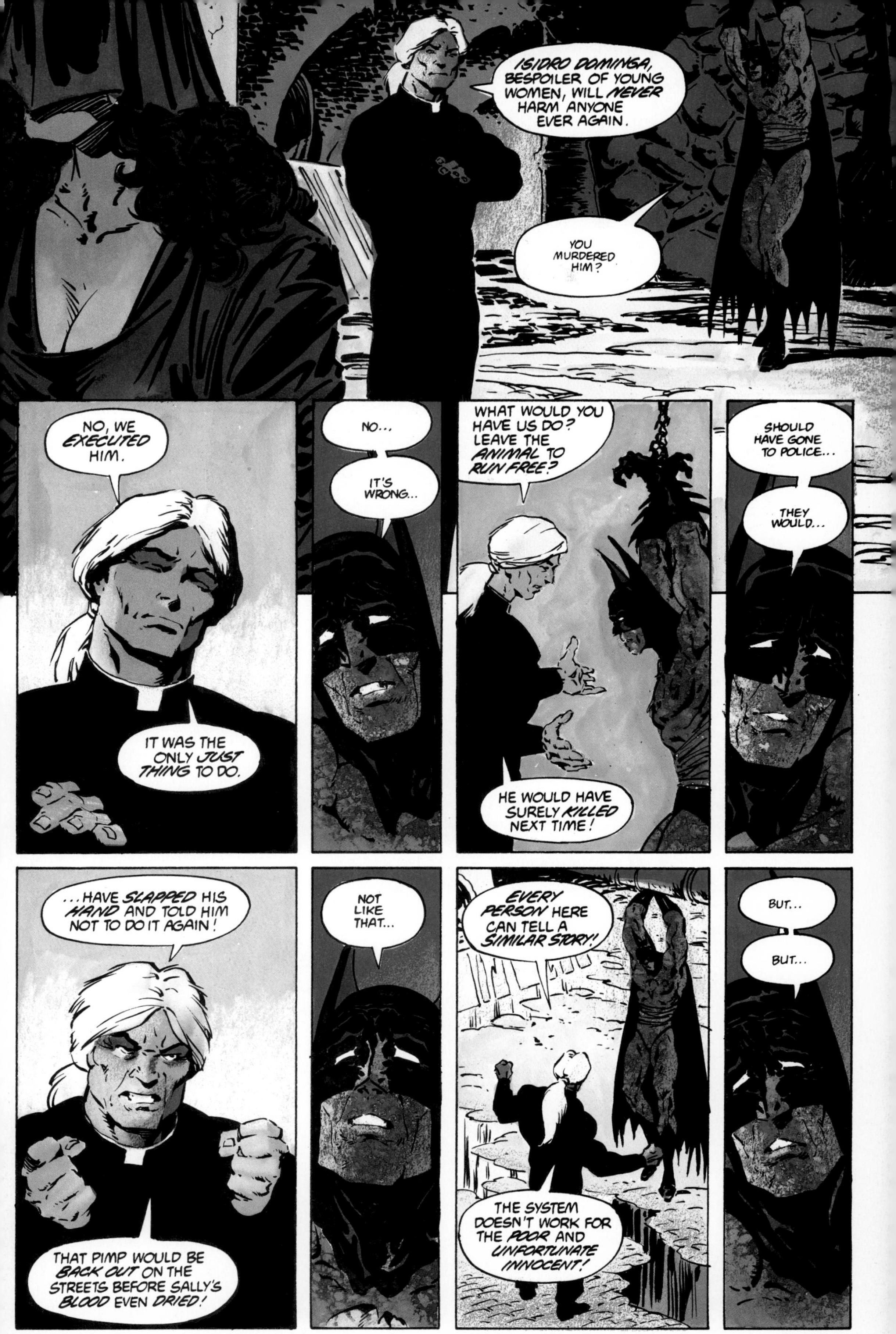
ISIDRO DOMINGA, BESPOILER OF YOUNG WOMEN, WILL NEVER HARM ANYONE EVER AGAIN.
YOU MURDERED HIM?
NO, WE EXECUTED HIM.
IT WAS THE ONLY JUST THING TO DO.
NO...
IT'S WRONG...
WHAT WOULD YOU HAVE US DO? LEAVE THE ANIMAL TO RUN FREE?
HE WOULD HAVE SURELY KILLED NEXT TIME!
SHOULD HAVE GONE TO POLICE...
THEY WOULD...
...HAVE SLAPPED HIS HAND AND TOLD HIM NOT TO DO IT AGAIN!
THAT PIMP WOULD BE BACK OUT ON THE STREETS BEFORE SALLY'S BLOOD EVEN DRIED!
NOT LIKE THAT...
EVERY PERSON HERE CAN TELL A SIMILAR STORY!
THE SYSTEM DOESN'T WORK FOR THE POOR AND UNFORTUNATE INNOCENT!
BUT...
BUT...

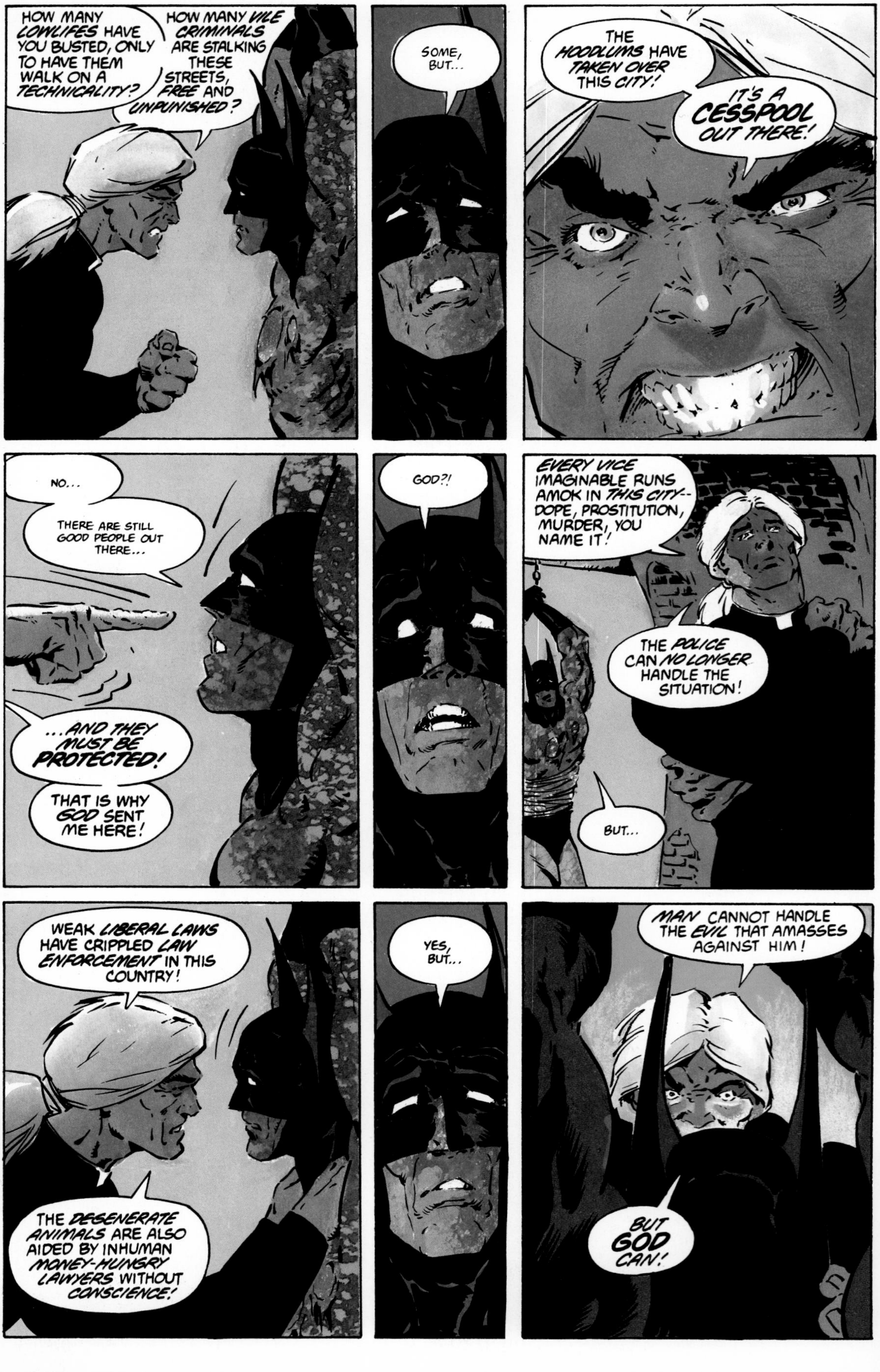
HOW MANY LOWLIFES HAVE YOU BUSTED, ONLY TO HAVE THEM WALK ON A TECHNICALITY?
HOW MANY VILE CRIMINALS ARE STALKING THESE STREETS, FREE AND UNPUNISHED?
SOME, BUT...
THE HOODLUMS HAVE TAKEN OVER THIS CITY!
IT'S A CESSPOOL OUT THERE!
NO...
THERE ARE STILL GOOD PEOPLE OUT THERE...
...AND THEY MUST BE PROTECTED!
THAT IS WHY GOD SENT ME HERE!
GOD?!
EVERY VICE IMAGINABLE RUNS AMOK IN THIS CITY--DOPE, PROSTITUTION, MURDER, YOU NAME IT!
THE POLICE CAN NO LONGER HANDLE THE SITUATION!
BUT...
WEAK LIBERAL LAWS HAVE CRIPPLED LAW ENFORCEMENT IN THIS COUNTRY!
THE DEGENERATE ANIMALS ARE ALSO AIDED BY INHUMAN MONEY-HUNGRY LAWYERS WITHOUT CONSCIENCE!
YES, BUT...
MAN CANNOT HANDLE THE EVIL THAT AMASSES AGAINST HIM!
BUT GOD CAN!

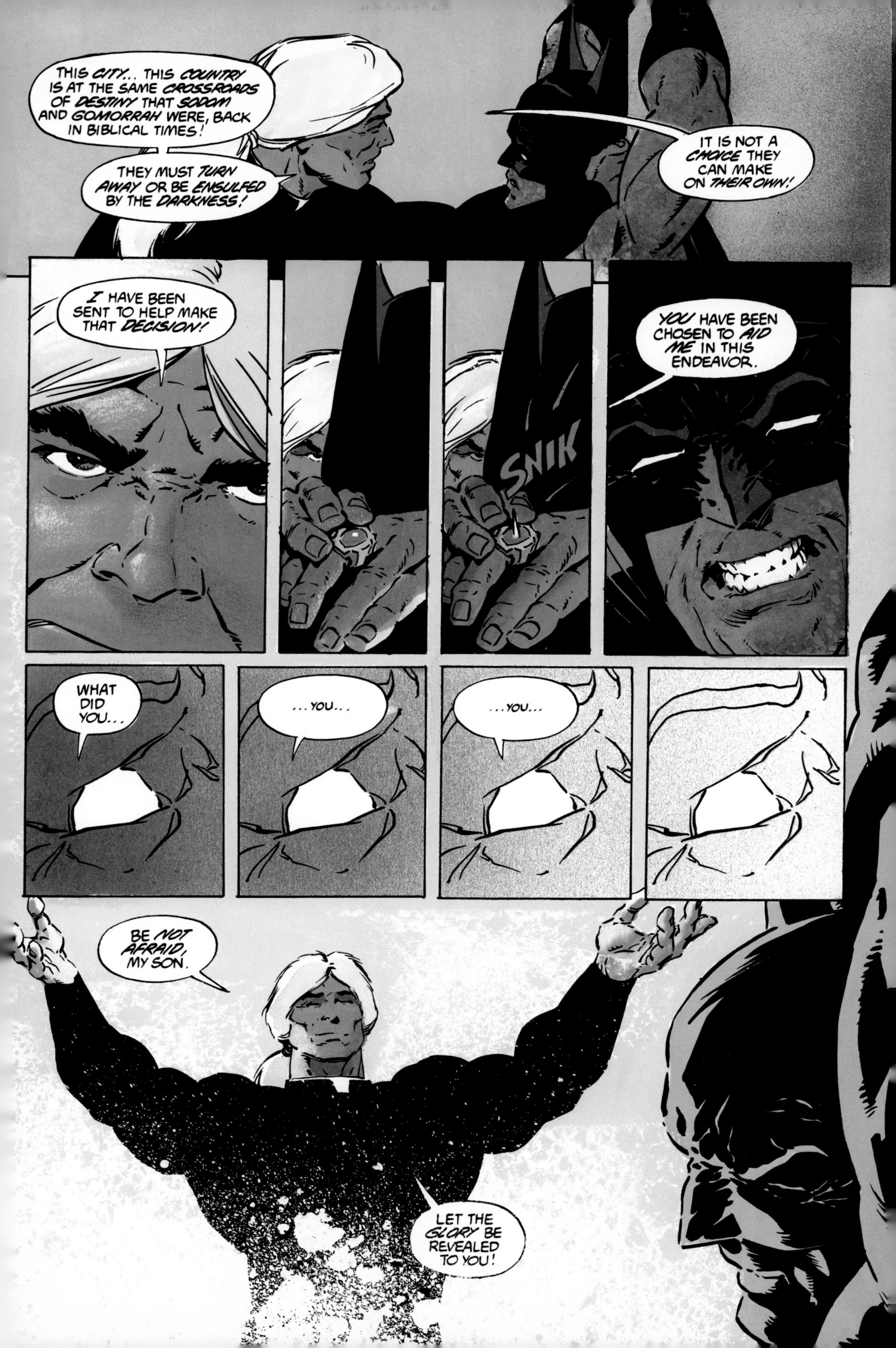
THIS CITY... THIS COUNTRY IS AT THE SAME CROSSROADS OF DESTINY THAT SODOM AND GOMORRAH WERE, BACK IN BIBLICAL TIMES!
THEY MUST TURN AWAY OR BE ENGULFED BY THE DARKNESS!
IT IS NOT A CHOICE THEY CAN MAKE ON THEIR OWN!
I HAVE BEEN SENT TO HELP MAKE THAT DECISION!
SNIK
YOU HAVE BEEN CHOSEN TO AID ME IN THIS ENDEAVOR.
WHAT DID YOU...
...YOU...
...YOU...
BE NOT AFRAID, MY SON.
LET THE GLORY BE REVEALED TO YOU!

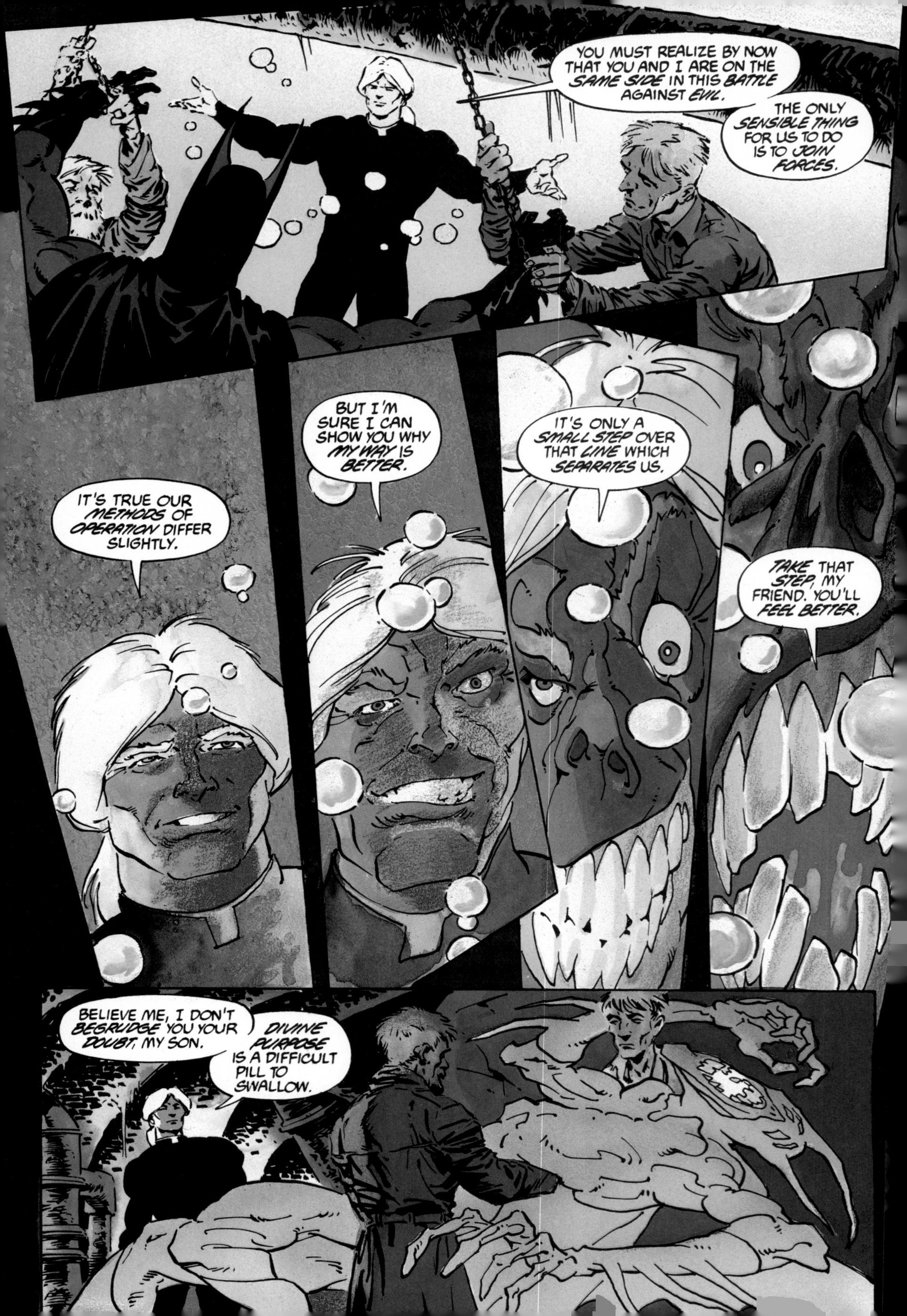
YOU MUST REALIZE BY NOW THAT YOU AND I ARE ON THE SAME SIDE IN THIS BATTLE AGAINST EVIL.
THE ONLY SENSIBLE THING FOR US TO DO IS TO JOIN FORCES.
IT'S TRUE OUR METHODS OF OPERATION DIFFER SLIGHTLY.
BUT I'M SURE I CAN SHOW YOU WHY MY WAY IS BETTER.
IT'S ONLY A SMALL STEP OVER THAT LINE WHICH SEPARATES US.
TAKE THAT STEP, MY FRIEND. YOU'LL FEEL BETTER.
BELIEVE ME, I DON'T BEGRUDGE YOU YOUR DOUBT, MY SON.
DIVINE PURPOSE IS A DIFFICULT PILL TO SWALLOW.

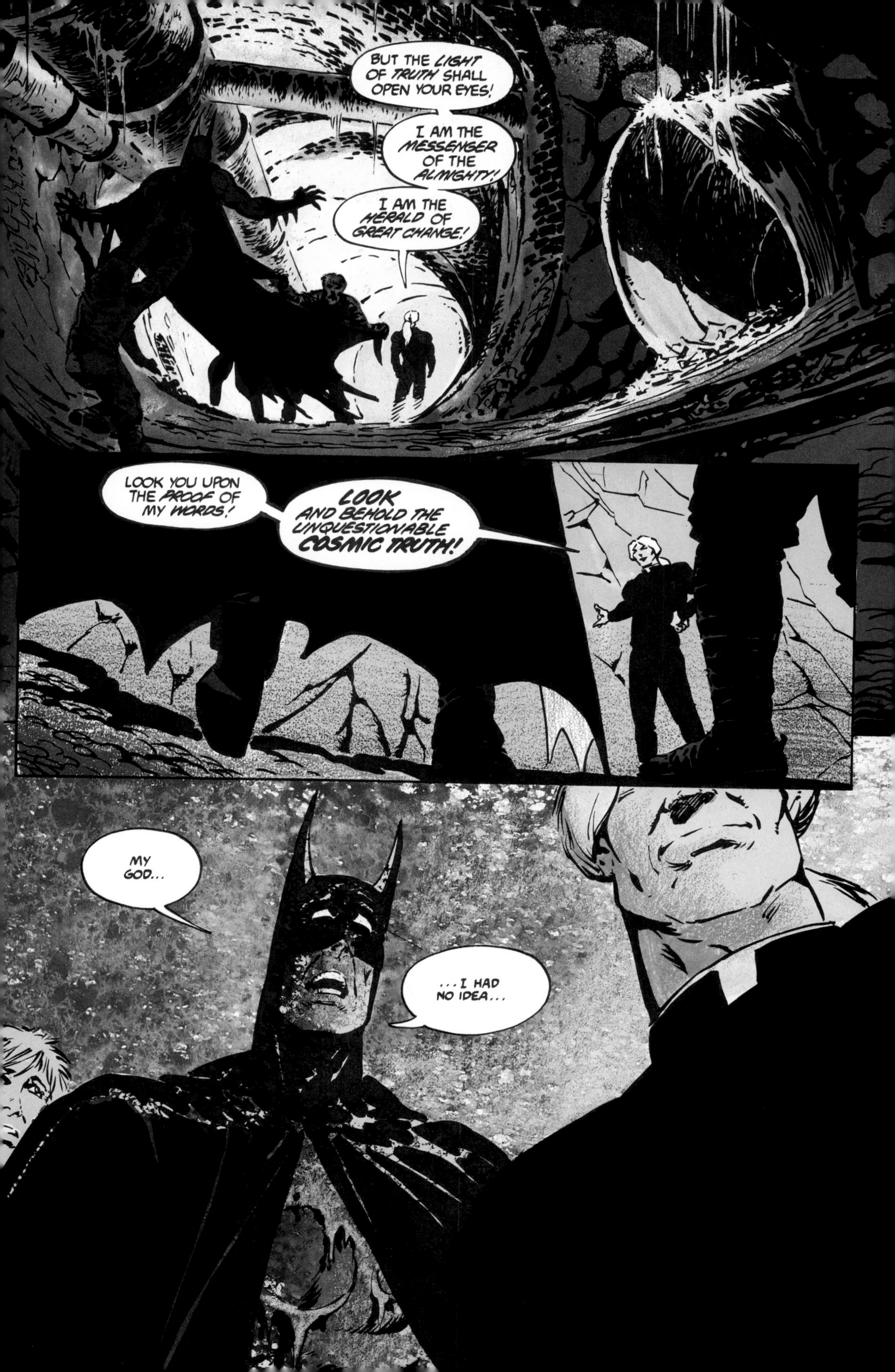
BUT THE LIGHT OF TRUTH SHALL OPEN YOUR EYES!
I AM THE MESSENGER OF THE ALMIGHTY!
I AM THE HERALD OF GREAT CHANGE!
LOOK YOU UPON THE PROOF OF MY WORDS!
LOOK AND BEHOLD THE UNQUESTIONABLE COSMIC TRUTH!
MY GOD...
...I HAD NO IDEA...

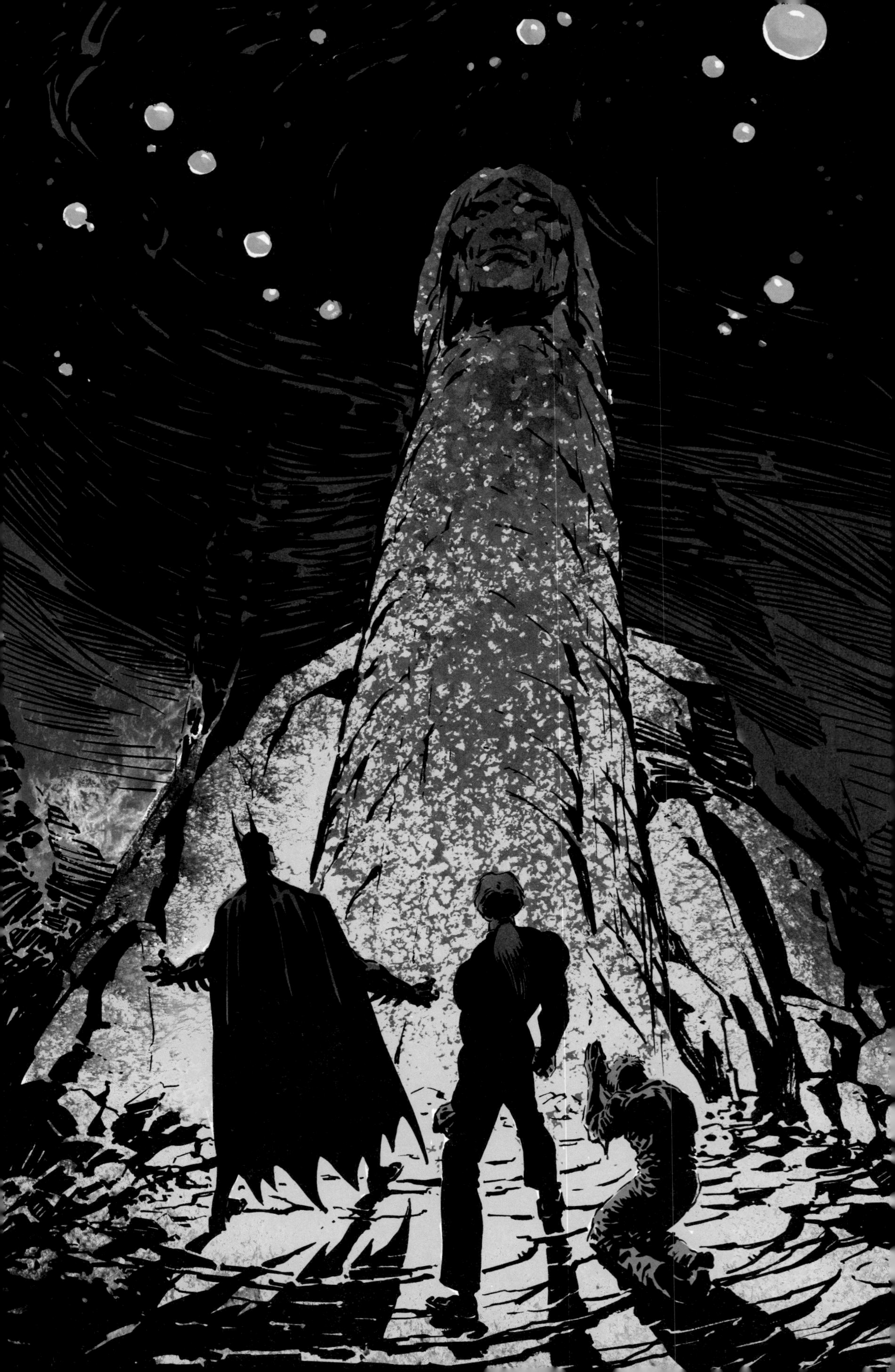

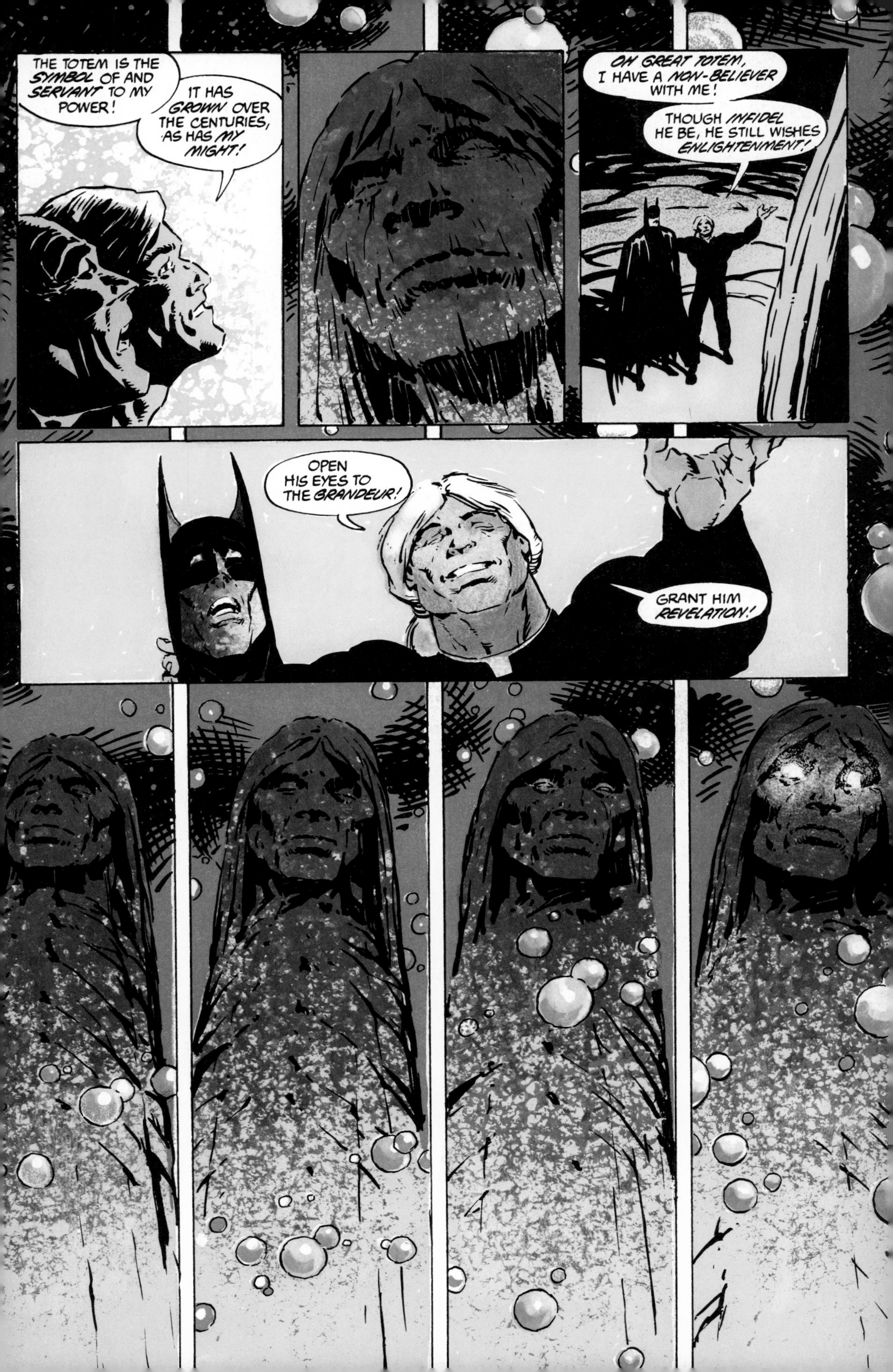
THE TOTEM IS THE SYMBOL OF AND SERVANT TO MY POWER!
IT HAS GROWN OVER THE CENTURIES, AS HAS MY MIGHT!
OH GREAT TOTEM, I HAVE A NON-BELIEVER WITH ME!
THOUGH INFIDEL HE BE, HE STILL WISHES ENLIGHTENMENT!
OPEN HIS EYES TO THE GRANDEUR!
GRANT HIM REVELATION!

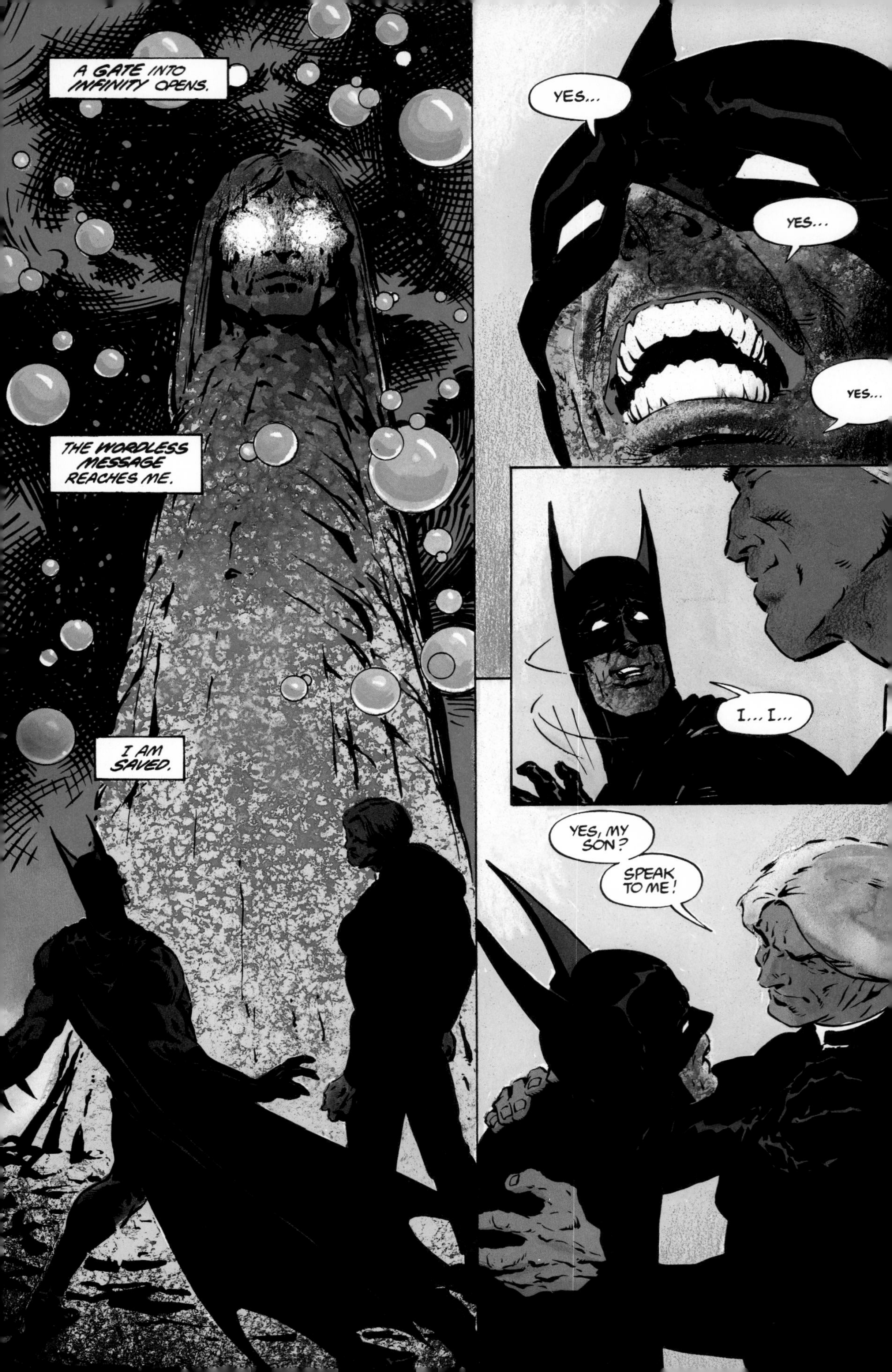
A GATE INTO INFINITY OPENS.
THE WORDLESS MESSAGE REACHES ME.
I AM SAVED.
YES...
YES...
YES...
I... I...
YES, MY SON?
SPEAK TO ME!

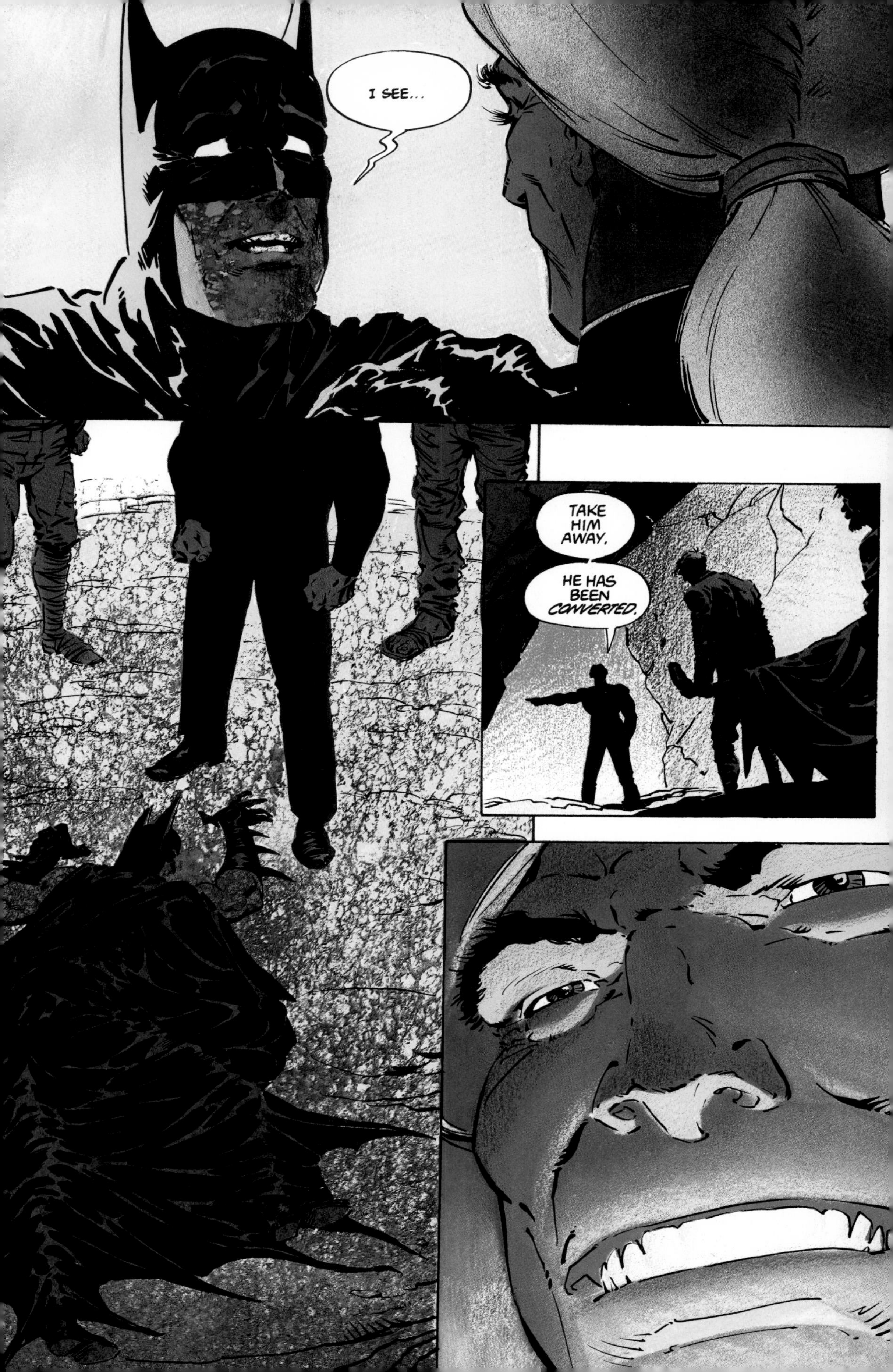
I SEE...
TAKE HIM AWAY.
HE HAS BEEN *CONVERTED*.

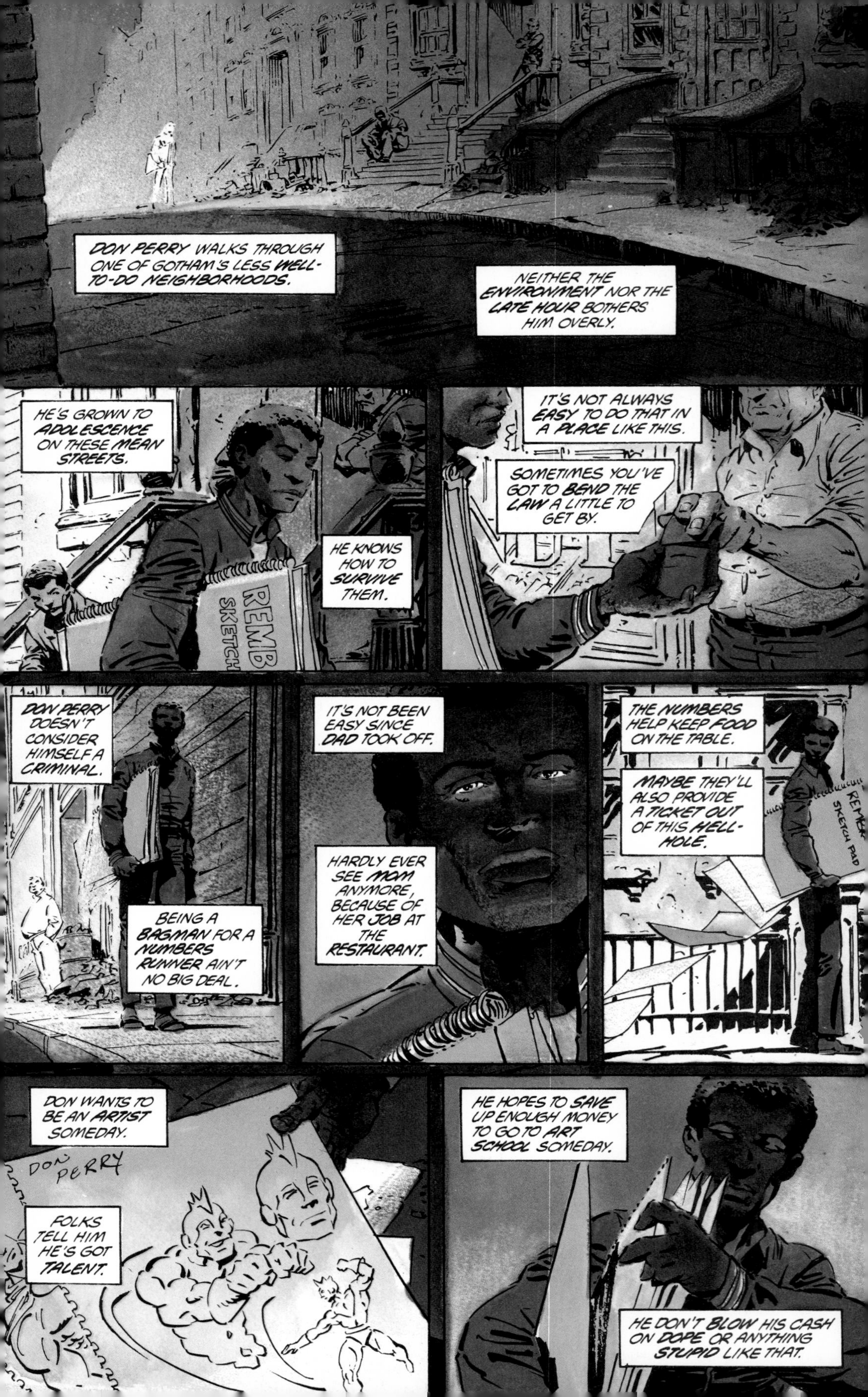
DON PERRY WALKS THROUGH ONE OF GOTHAM'S LESS WELL-TO-DO NEIGHBORHOODS.
NEITHER THE ENVIRONMENT NOR THE LATE HOUR BOTHERS HIM OVERLY.
HE'S GROWN TO ADOLESCENCE ON THESE MEAN STREETS.
HE KNOWS HOW TO SURVIVE THEM.
REMB SKETCH
IT'S NOT ALWAYS EASY TO DO THAT IN A PLACE LIKE THIS.
SOMETIMES YOU'VE GOT TO BEND THE LAW A LITTLE TO GET BY.
DON PERRY DOESN'T CONSIDER HIMSELF A CRIMINAL.
BEING A BAGMAN FOR A NUMBERS RUNNER AIN'T NO BIG DEAL.
IT'S NOT BEEN EASY SINCE DAD TOOK OFF.
HARDLY EVER SEE MOM ANYMORE, BECAUSE OF HER JOB AT THE RESTAURANT.
THE NUMBERS HELP KEEP FOOD ON THE TABLE.
MAYBE THEY'LL ALSO PROVIDE A TICKET OUT OF THIS HELL-HOLE.
REMBR SKETCH PAD
DON WANTS TO BE AN ARTIST SOMEDAY.
DON PERRY
FOLKS TELL HIM HE'S GOT TALENT.
HE HOPES TO SAVE UP ENOUGH MONEY TO GO TO ART SCHOOL SOMEDAY.
HE DON'T BLOW HIS CASH ON DOPE OR ANYTHING STUPID LIKE THAT.

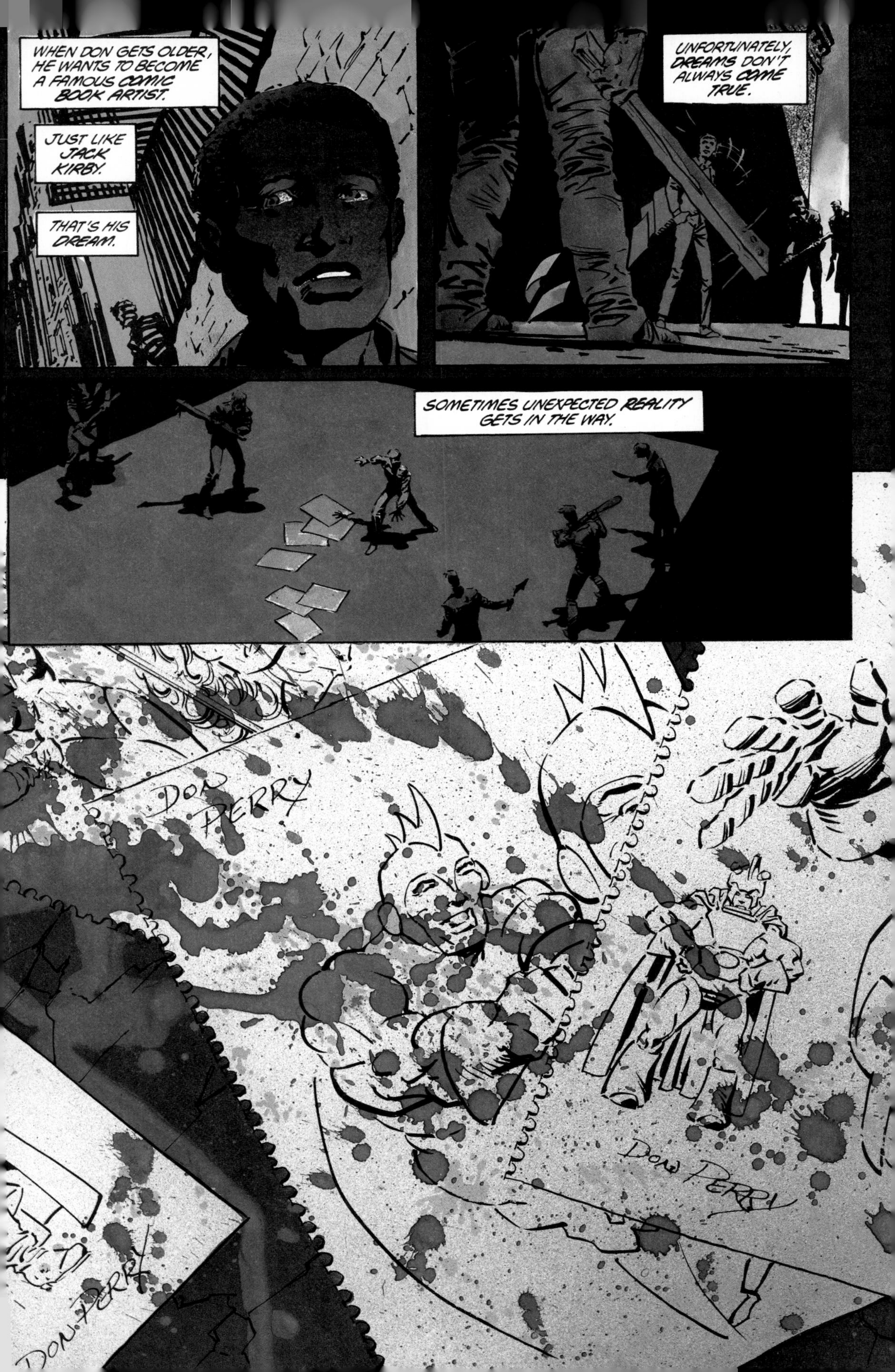
WHEN DON GETS OLDER, HE WANTS TO BECOME A FAMOUS COMIC BOOK ARTIST.
JUST LIKE JACK KIRBY.
THAT'S HIS DREAM.
UNFORTUNATELY, DREAMS DON'T ALWAYS COME TRUE.
SOMETIMES UNEXPECTED REALITY GETS IN THE WAY.
DON PERRY
DON PERRY
DON PERRY

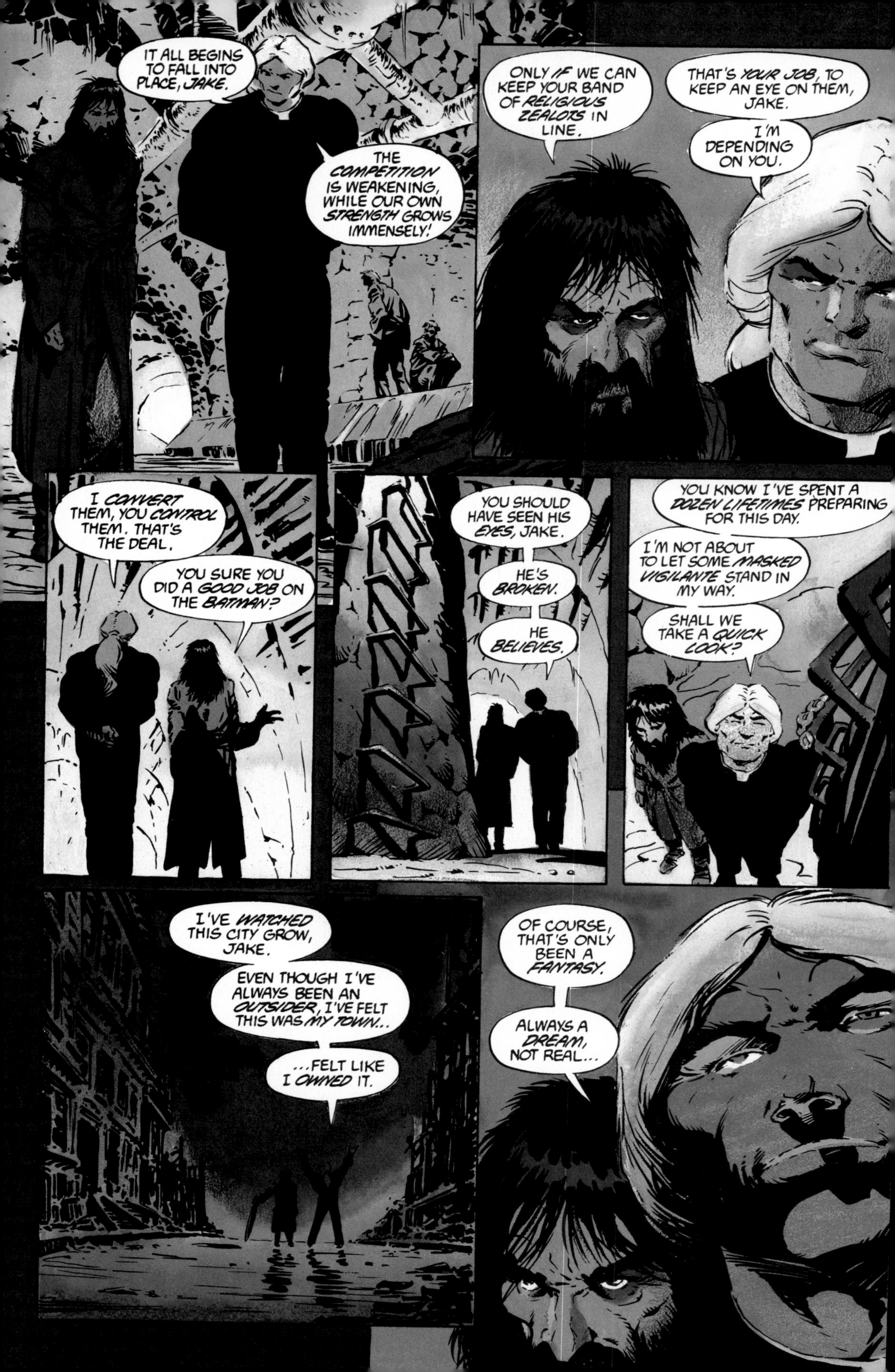
IT ALL BEGINS TO FALL INTO PLACE, JAKE.
THE COMPETITION IS WEAKENING, WHILE OUR OWN STRENGTH GROWS IMMENSELY!
ONLY IF WE CAN KEEP YOUR BAND OF RELIGIOUS ZEALOTS IN LINE.
THAT'S YOUR JOB, TO KEEP AN EYE ON THEM, JAKE.
I'M DEPENDING ON YOU.
I CONVERT THEM, YOU CONTROL THEM. THAT'S THE DEAL.
YOU SURE YOU DID A GOOD JOB ON THE BATMAN?
YOU SHOULD HAVE SEEN HIS EYES, JAKE.
HE'S BROKEN.
HE BELIEVES.
YOU KNOW I'VE SPENT A DOZEN LIFETIMES PREPARING FOR THIS DAY.
I'M NOT ABOUT TO LET SOME MASKED VIGILANTE STAND IN MY WAY.
SHALL WE TAKE A QUICK LOOK?
I'VE WATCHED THIS CITY GROW, JAKE.
EVEN THOUGH I'VE ALWAYS BEEN AN OUTSIDER, I'VE FELT THIS WAS MY TOWN...
...FELT LIKE I OWNED IT.
OF COURSE, THAT'S ONLY BEEN A FANTASY.
ALWAYS A DREAM, NOT REAL...

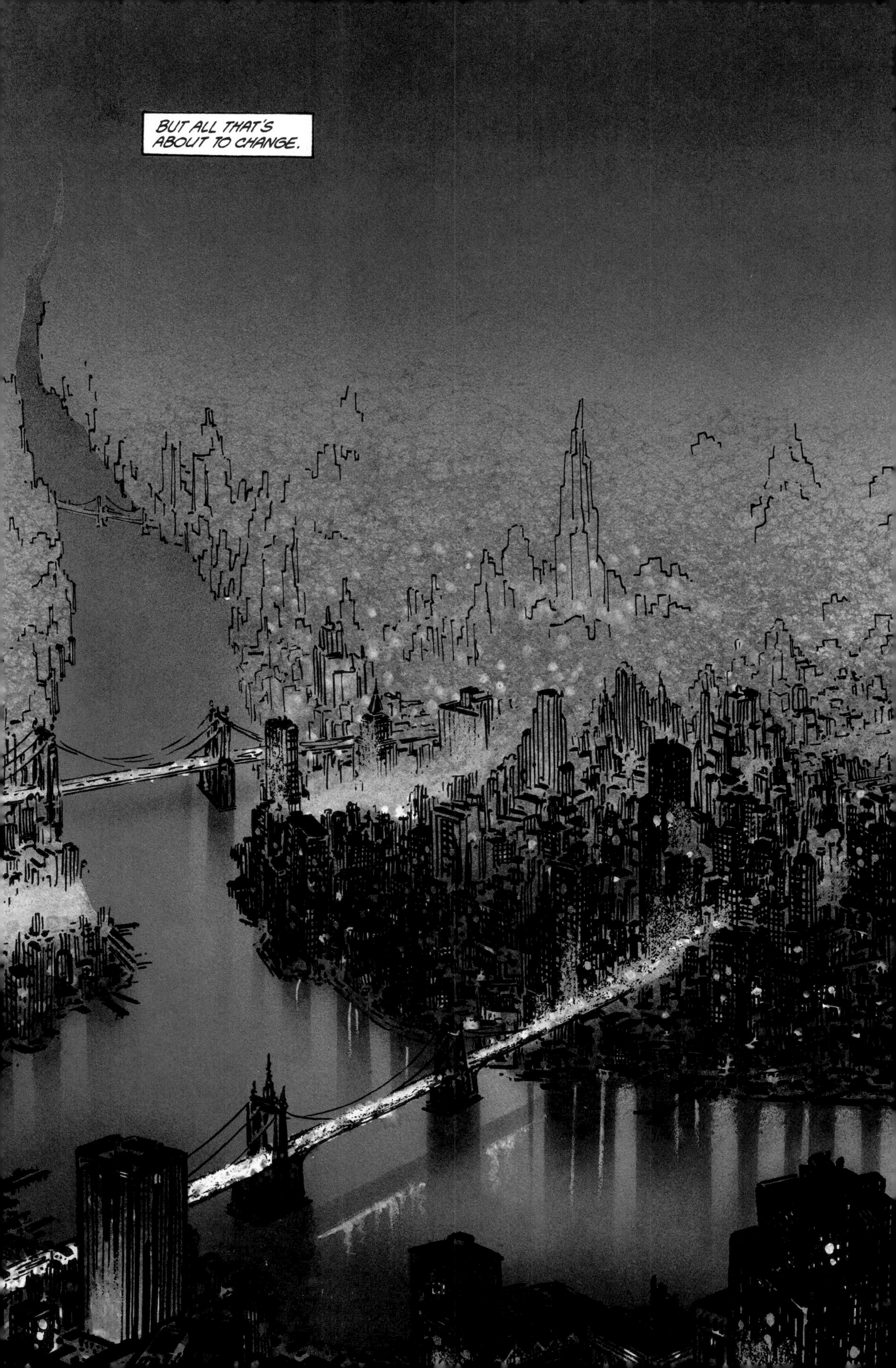
BUT ALL THAT'S ABOUT TO CHANGE.

CHAPTER 2

CAPTURE

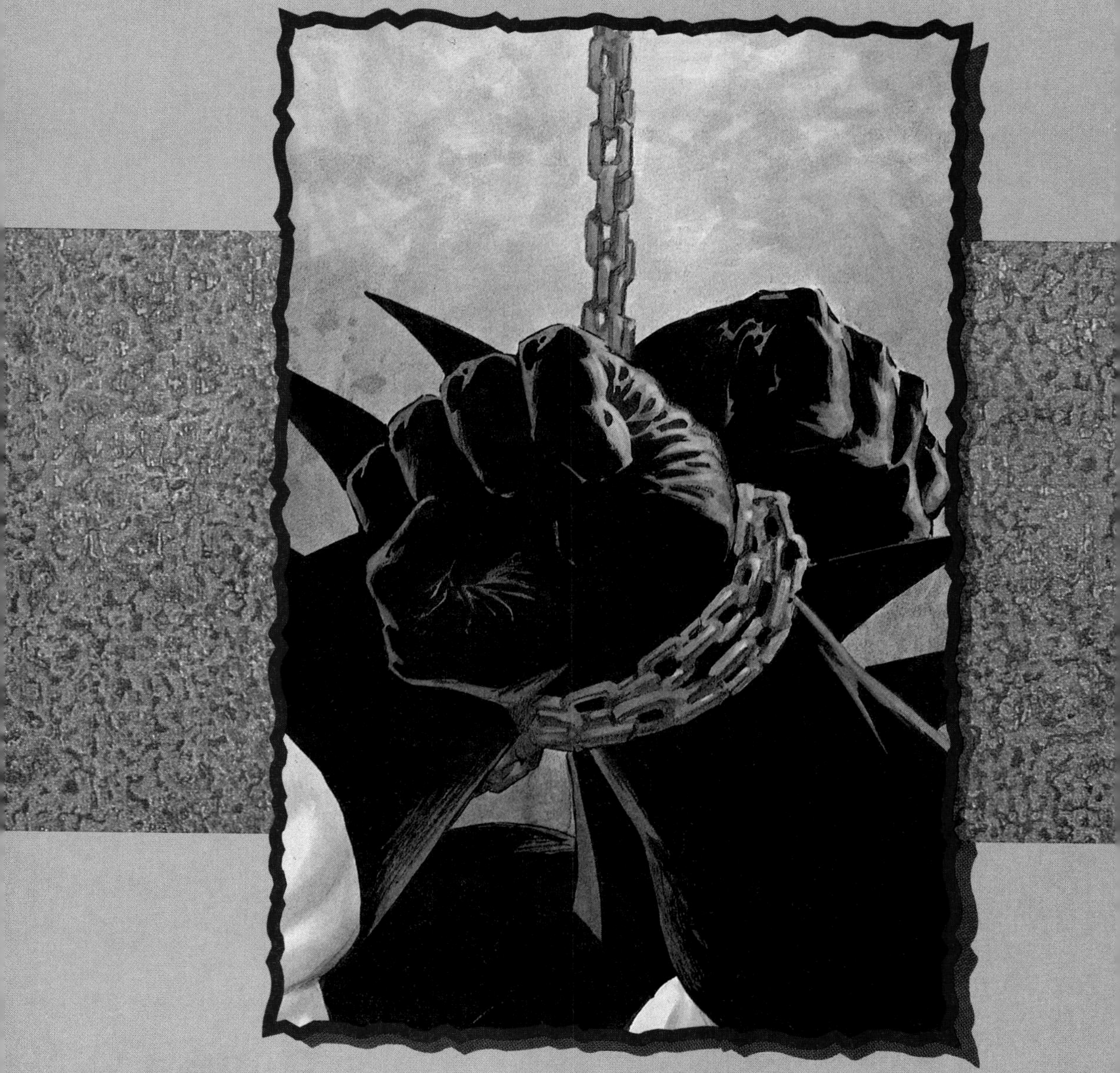

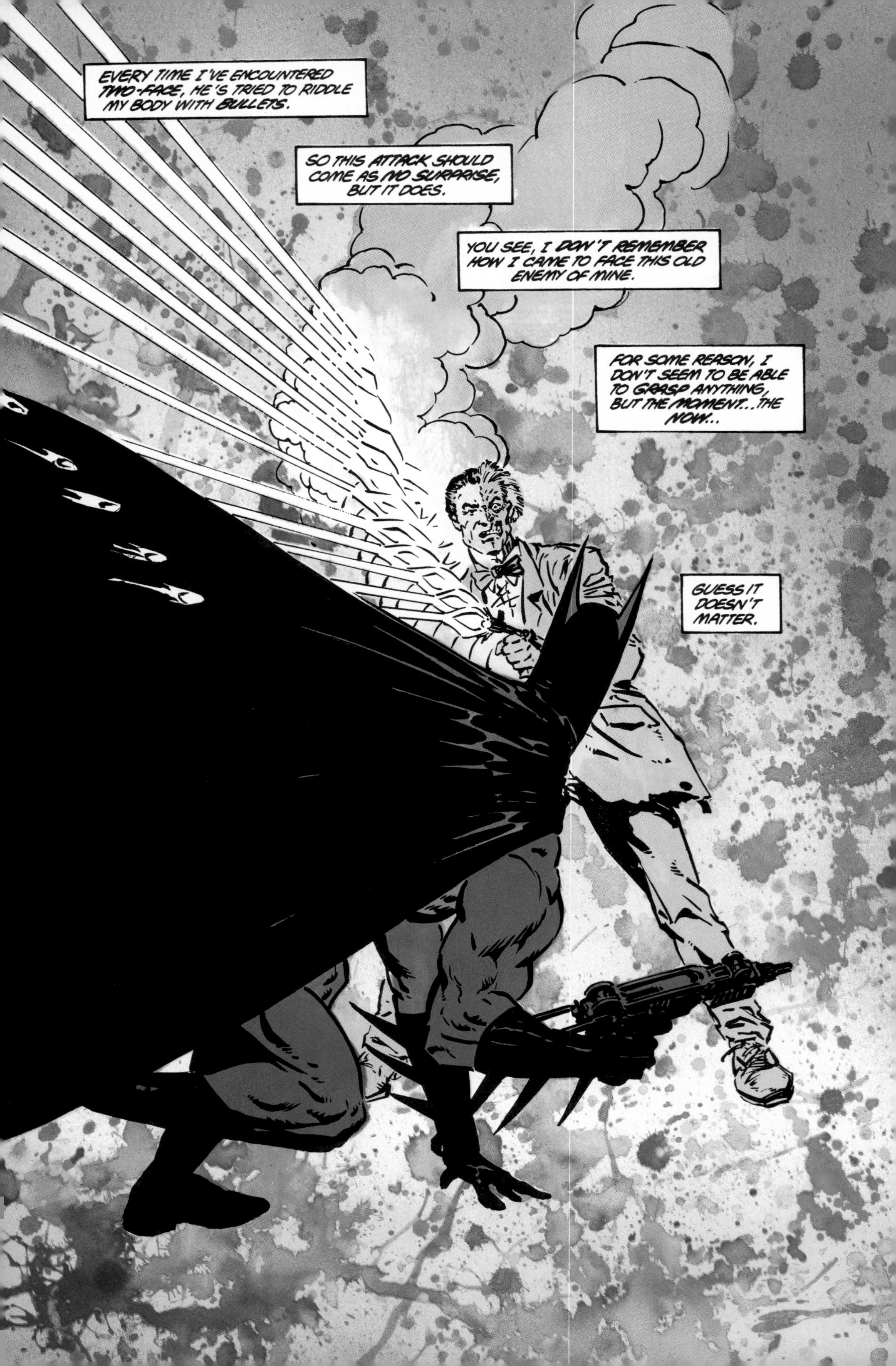
EVERY TIME I'VE ENCOUNTERED TWO-FACE, HE'S TRIED TO RIDDLE MY BODY WITH BULLETS.
SO THIS ATTACK SHOULD COME AS NO SURPRISE, BUT IT DOES.
YOU SEE, I DON'T REMEMBER HOW I CAME TO FACE THIS OLD ENEMY OF MINE.
FOR SOME REASON, I DON'T SEEM TO BE ABLE TO GRASP ANYTHING, BUT THE MOMENT...THE NOW...
GUESS IT DOESN'T MATTER.

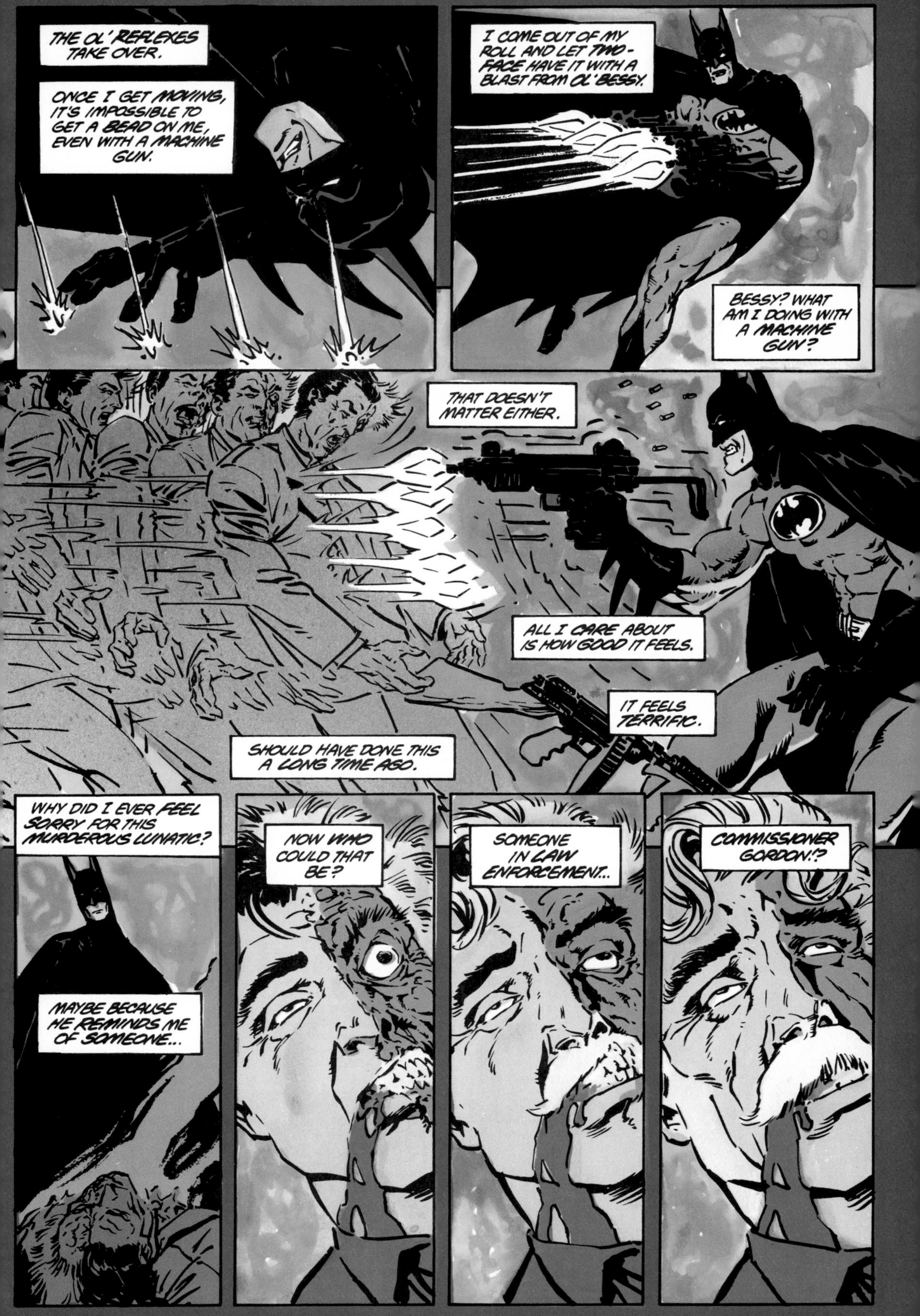
THE OL' REFLEXES TAKE OVER.
ONCE I GET MOVING, IT'S IMPOSSIBLE TO GET A BEAD ON ME, EVEN WITH A MACHINE GUN.
I COME OUT OF MY ROLL AND LET TWO-FACE HAVE IT WITH A BLAST FROM OL' BESSY.
BESSY? WHAT AM I DOING WITH A MACHINE GUN?
THAT DOESN'T MATTER EITHER.
ALL I CARE ABOUT IS HOW GOOD IT FEELS.
IT FEELS TERRIFIC.
SHOULD HAVE DONE THIS A LONG TIME AGO.
WHY DID I EVER FEEL SORRY FOR THIS MURDEROUS LUNATIC?
MAYBE BECAUSE HE REMINDS ME OF SOMEONE...
NOW WHO COULD THAT BE?
SOMEONE IN LAW ENFORCEMENT...
COMMISSIONER GORDON!?

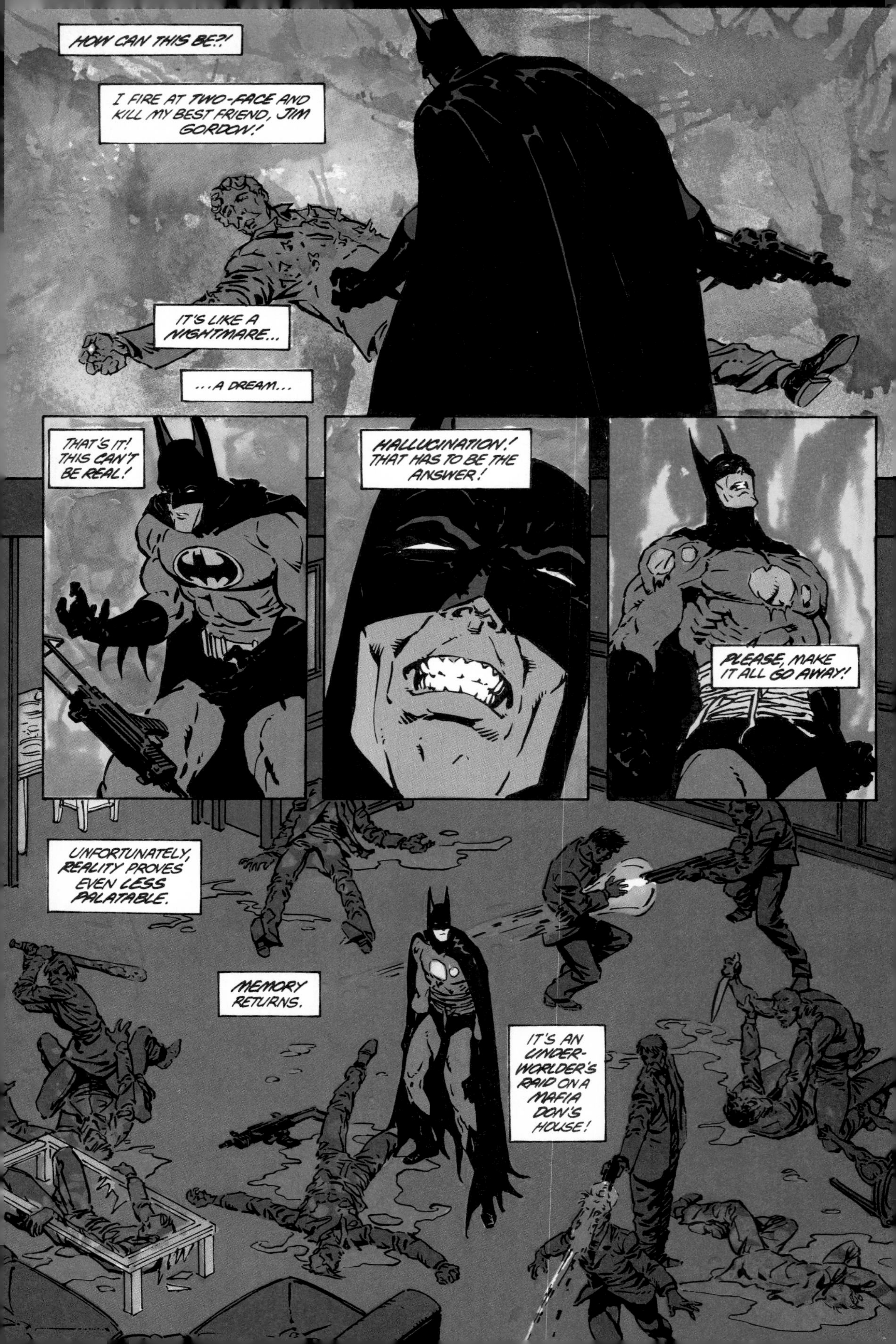
HOW CAN THIS BE?!
I FIRE AT TWO-FACE AND KILL MY BEST FRIEND, JIM GORDON!
IT'S LIKE A NIGHTMARE...
...A DREAM...
THAT'S IT! THIS CAN'T BE REAL!
HALLUCINATION! THAT HAS TO BE THE ANSWER!
PLEASE, MAKE IT ALL GO AWAY!
UNFORTUNATELY, REALITY PROVES EVEN LESS PALATABLE.
MEMORY RETURNS.
IT'S AN UNDER-WORLDER'S RAID ON A MAFIA DON'S HOUSE!

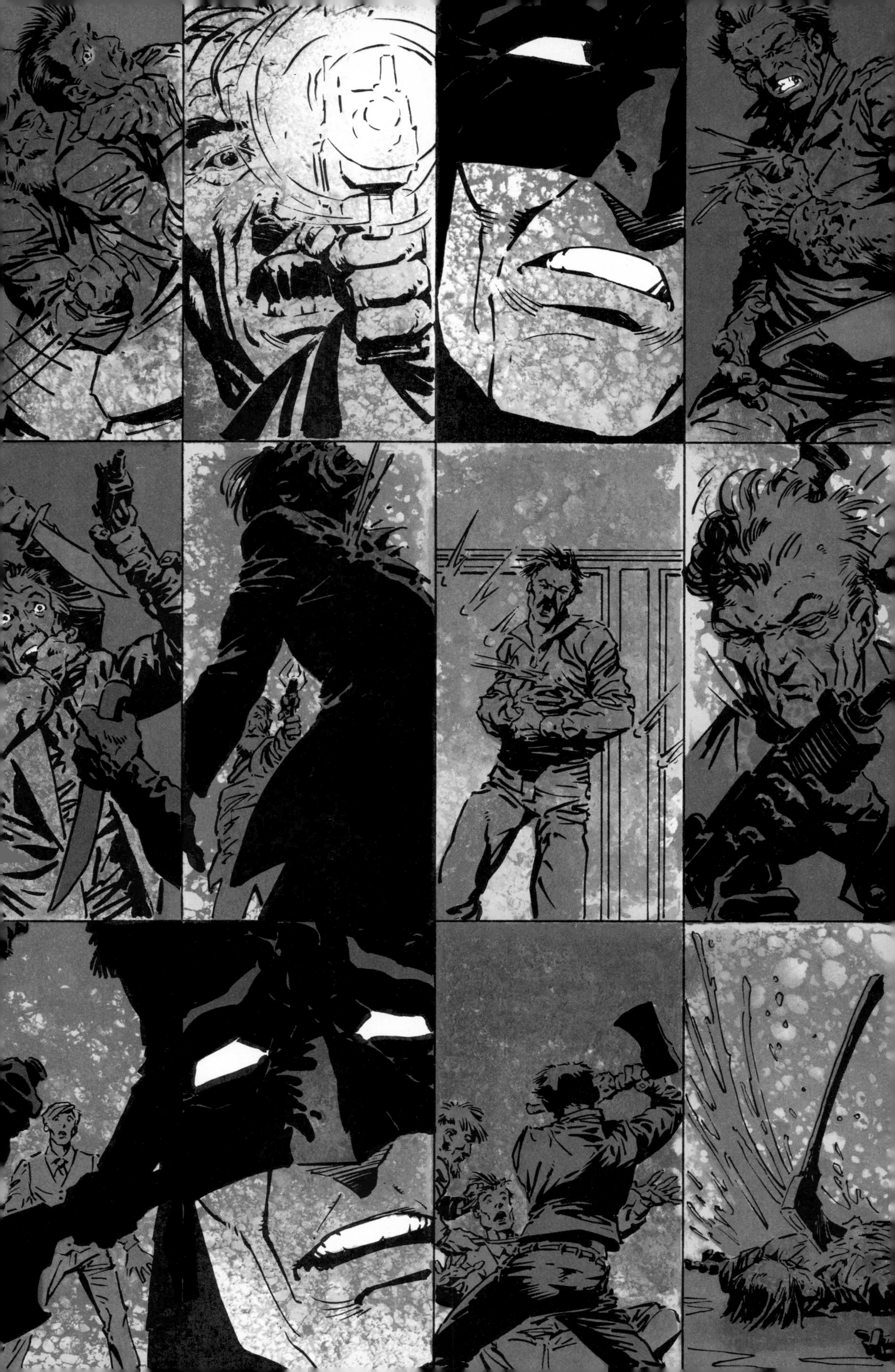

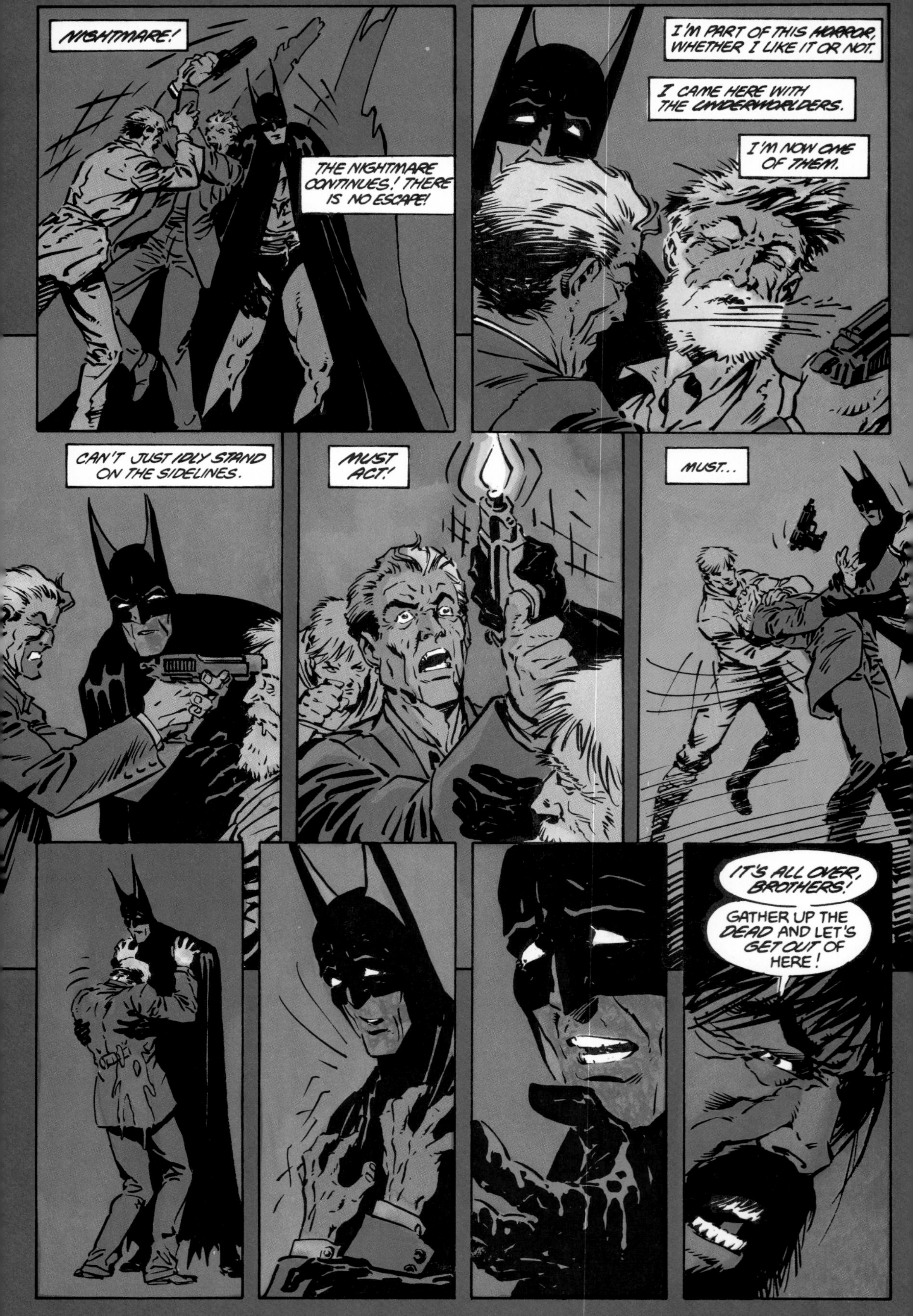
NIGHTMARE!
THE NIGHTMARE CONTINUES! THERE IS NO ESCAPE!
I'M PART OF THIS HORROR, WHETHER I LIKE IT OR NOT.
I CAME HERE WITH THE UNDERWORLDERS.
I'M NOW ONE OF THEM.
CAN'T JUST IDLY STAND ON THE SIDELINES.
MUST ACT!
MUST...
IT'S ALL OVER, BROTHERS!
GATHER UP THE DEAD AND LET'S GET OUT OF HERE!

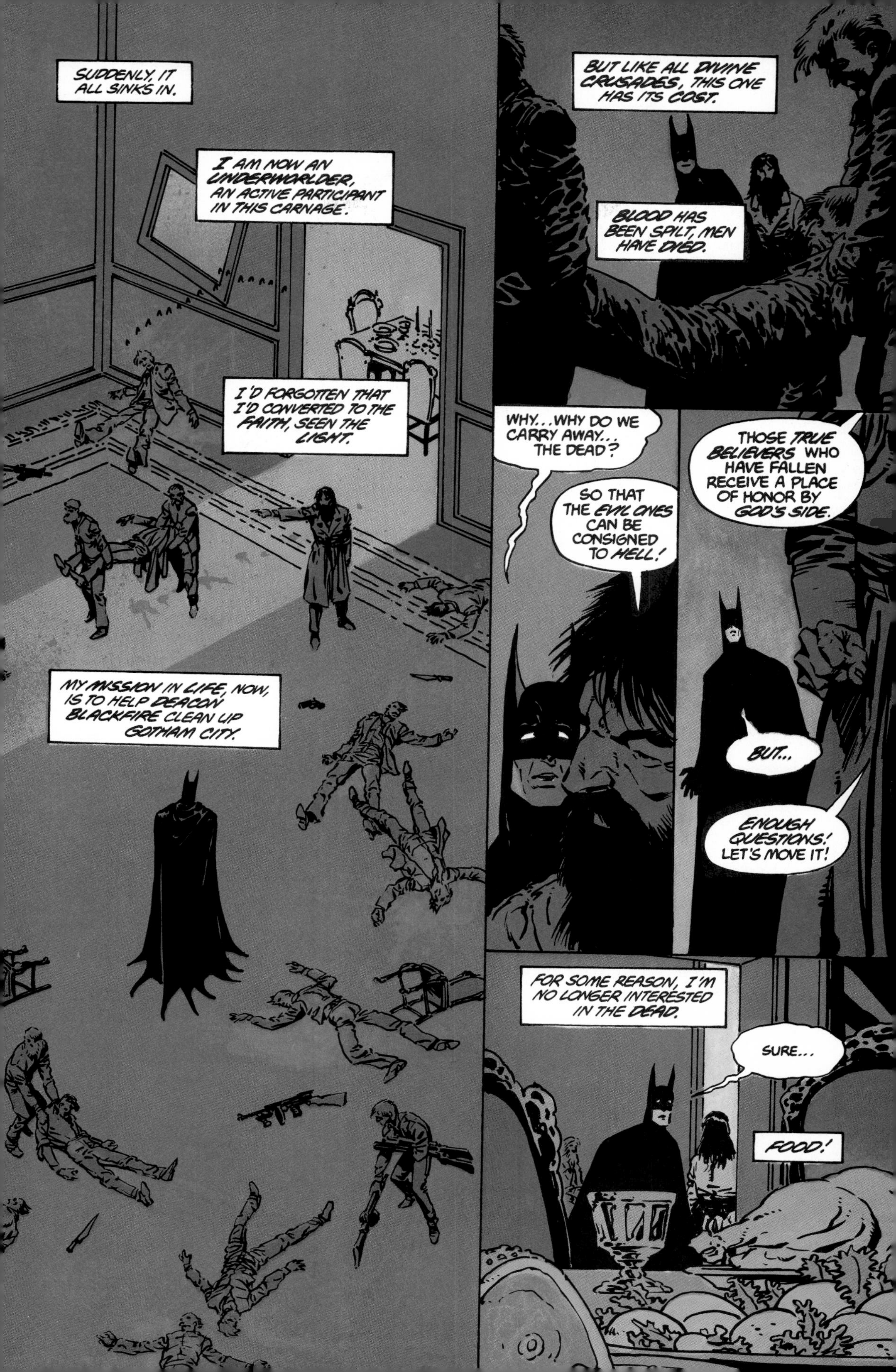
SUDDENLY, IT ALL SINKS IN.
I AM NOW AN UNDERWORLDER, AN ACTIVE PARTICIPANT IN THIS CARNAGE.
I'D FORGOTTEN THAT I'D CONVERTED TO THE FAITH, SEEN THE LIGHT.
MY MISSION IN LIFE, NOW, IS TO HELP DEACON BLACKFIRE CLEAN UP GOTHAM CITY.
BUT LIKE ALL DIVINE CRUSADES, THIS ONE HAS ITS COST.
BLOOD HAS BEEN SPILT, MEN HAVE DIED.
WHY...WHY DO WE CARRY AWAY... THE DEAD?
SO THAT THE EVIL ONES CAN BE CONSIGNED TO HELL!
THOSE TRUE BELIEVERS WHO HAVE FALLEN RECEIVE A PLACE OF HONOR BY GOD'S SIDE.
BUT...
ENOUGH QUESTIONS! LET'S MOVE IT!
FOR SOME REASON, I'M NO LONGER INTERESTED IN THE DEAD.
SURE...
FOOD!

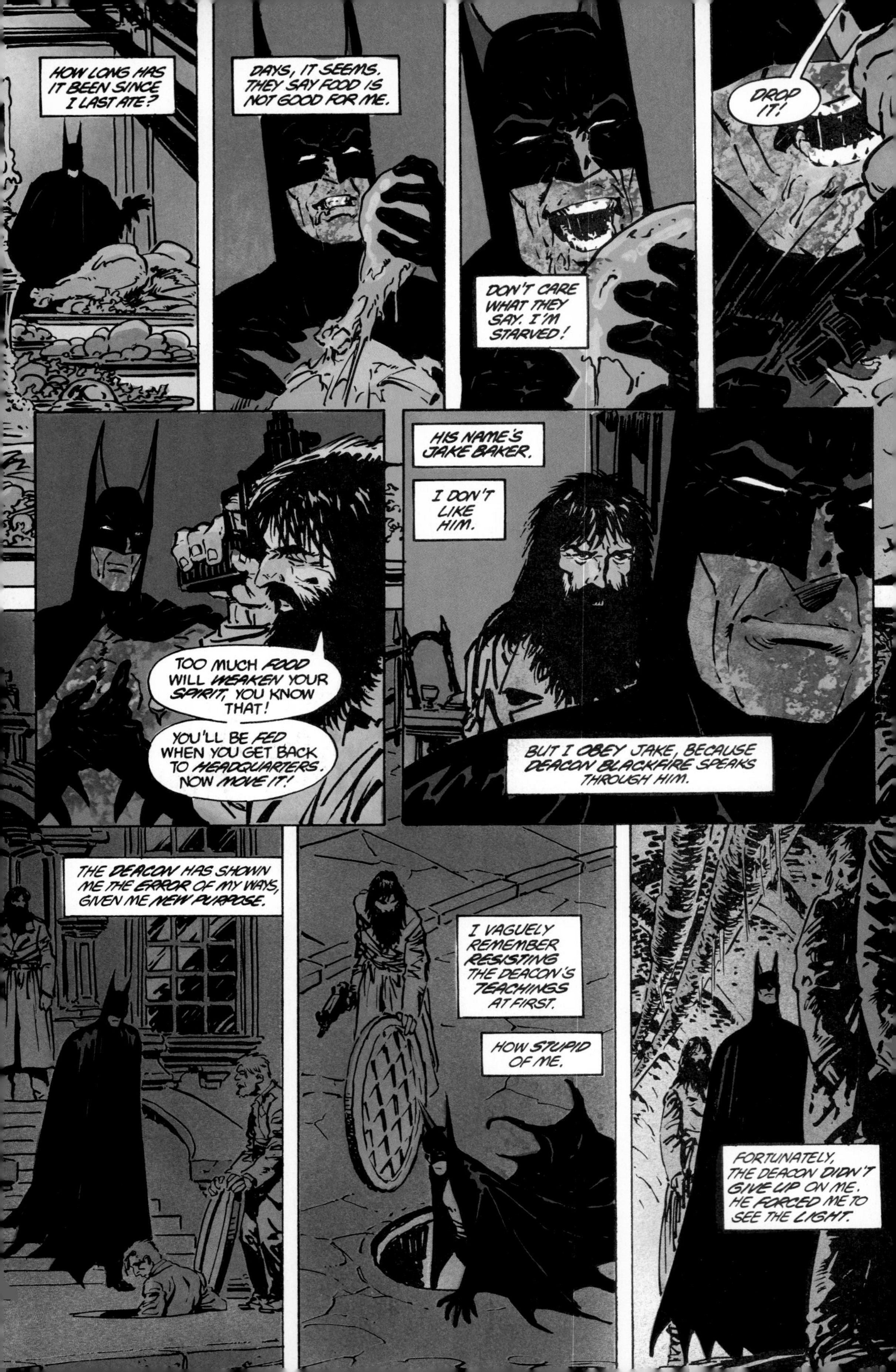

HOW LONG HAS IT BEEN SINCE I LAST ATE?
DAYS, IT SEEMS. THEY SAY FOOD IS NOT GOOD FOR ME.
DON'T CARE WHAT THEY SAY. I'M STARVED!
DROP IT!
TOO MUCH FOOD WILL WEAKEN YOUR SPIRIT, YOU KNOW THAT!
YOU'LL BE FED WHEN YOU GET BACK TO HEADQUARTERS. NOW MOVE IT!
HIS NAME'S JAKE BAKER.
I DON'T LIKE HIM.
BUT I OBEY JAKE, BECAUSE DEACON BLACKFIRE SPEAKS THROUGH HIM.
THE DEACON HAS SHOWN ME THE ERROR OF MY WAYS, GIVEN ME NEW PURPOSE.
I VAGUELY REMEMBER RESISTING THE DEACON'S TEACHINGS AT FIRST.
HOW STUPID OF ME.
FORTUNATELY, THE DEACON DIDN'T GIVE UP ON ME. HE FORCED ME TO SEE THE LIGHT.

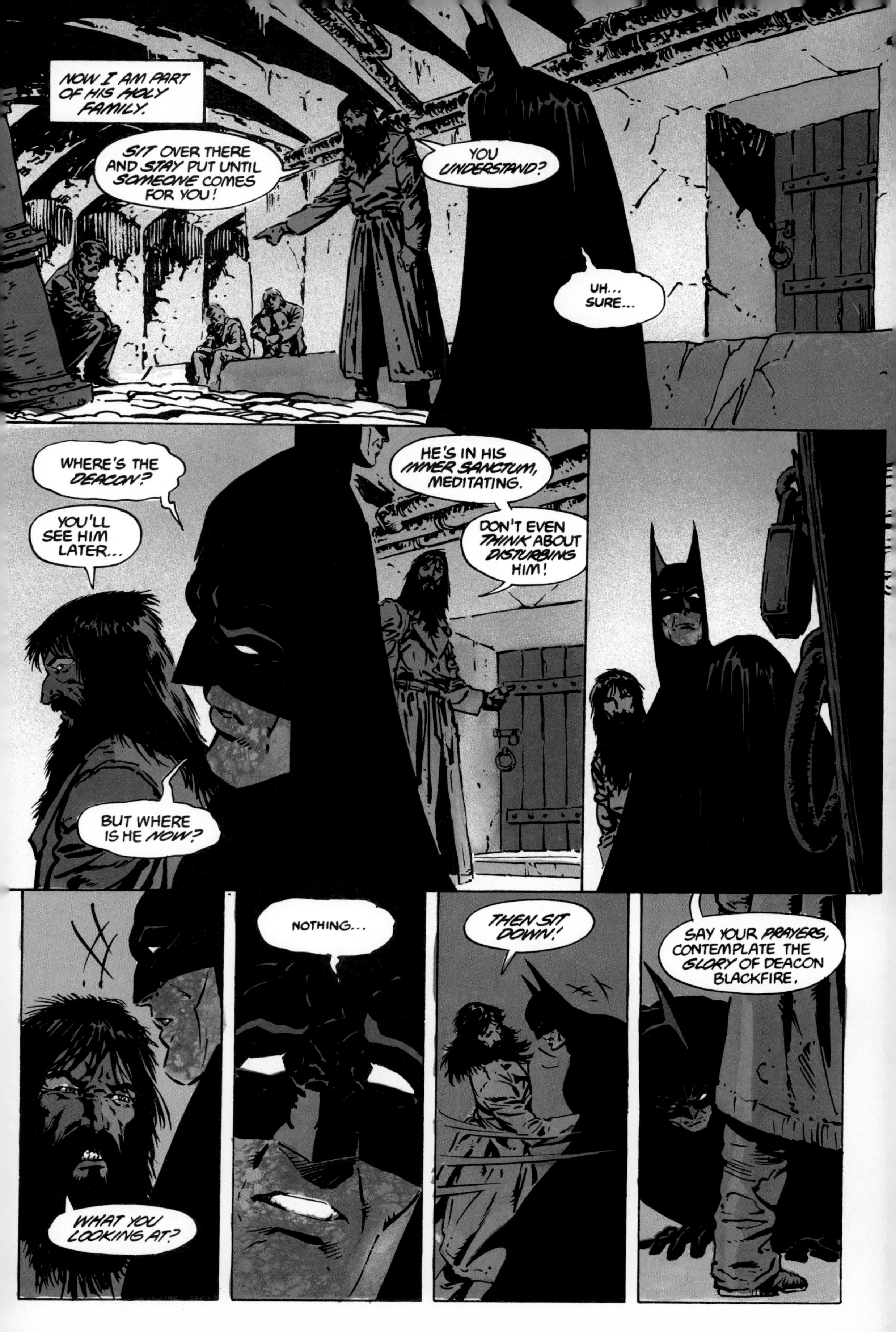
NOW I AM PART OF HIS HOLY FAMILY.
SIT OVER THERE AND STAY PUT UNTIL SOMEONE COMES FOR YOU!
YOU UNDERSTAND?
UH... SURE...
WHERE'S THE DEACON?
YOU'LL SEE HIM LATER...
HE'S IN HIS INNER SANCTUM, MEDITATING.
DON'T EVEN THINK ABOUT DISTURBING HIM!
BUT WHERE IS HE NOW?
WHAT YOU LOOKING AT?
NOTHING...
THEN SIT DOWN!
SAY YOUR PRAYERS, CONTEMPLATE THE GLORY OF DEACON BLACKFIRE.

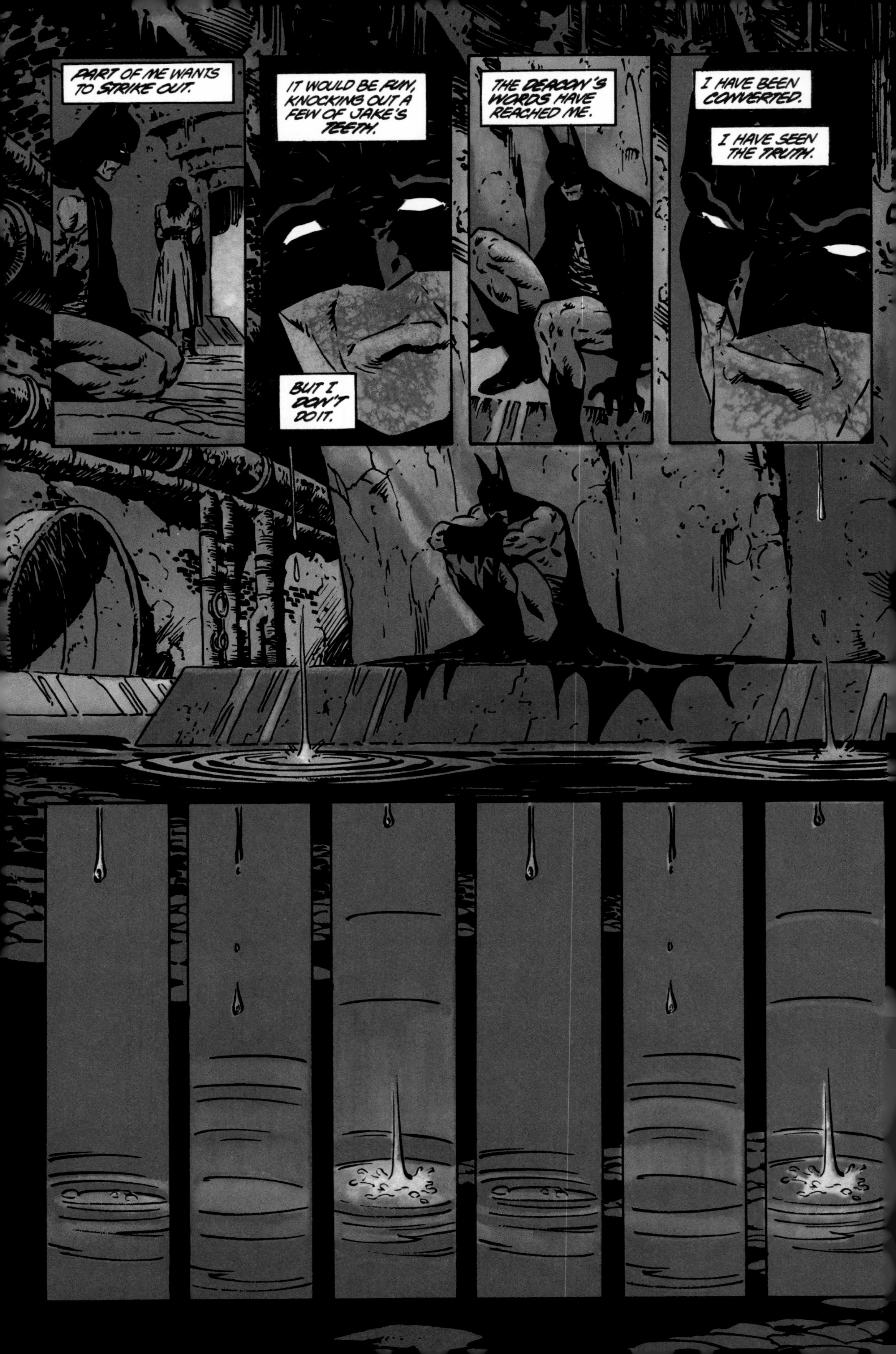
PART OF ME WANTS TO STRIKE OUT.
IT WOULD BE FUN, KNOCKING OUT A FEW OF JAKE'S TEETH.
BUT I DON'T DO IT.
THE DEACON'S WORDS HAVE REACHED ME.
I HAVE BEEN CONVERTED.
I HAVE SEEN THE TRUTH.

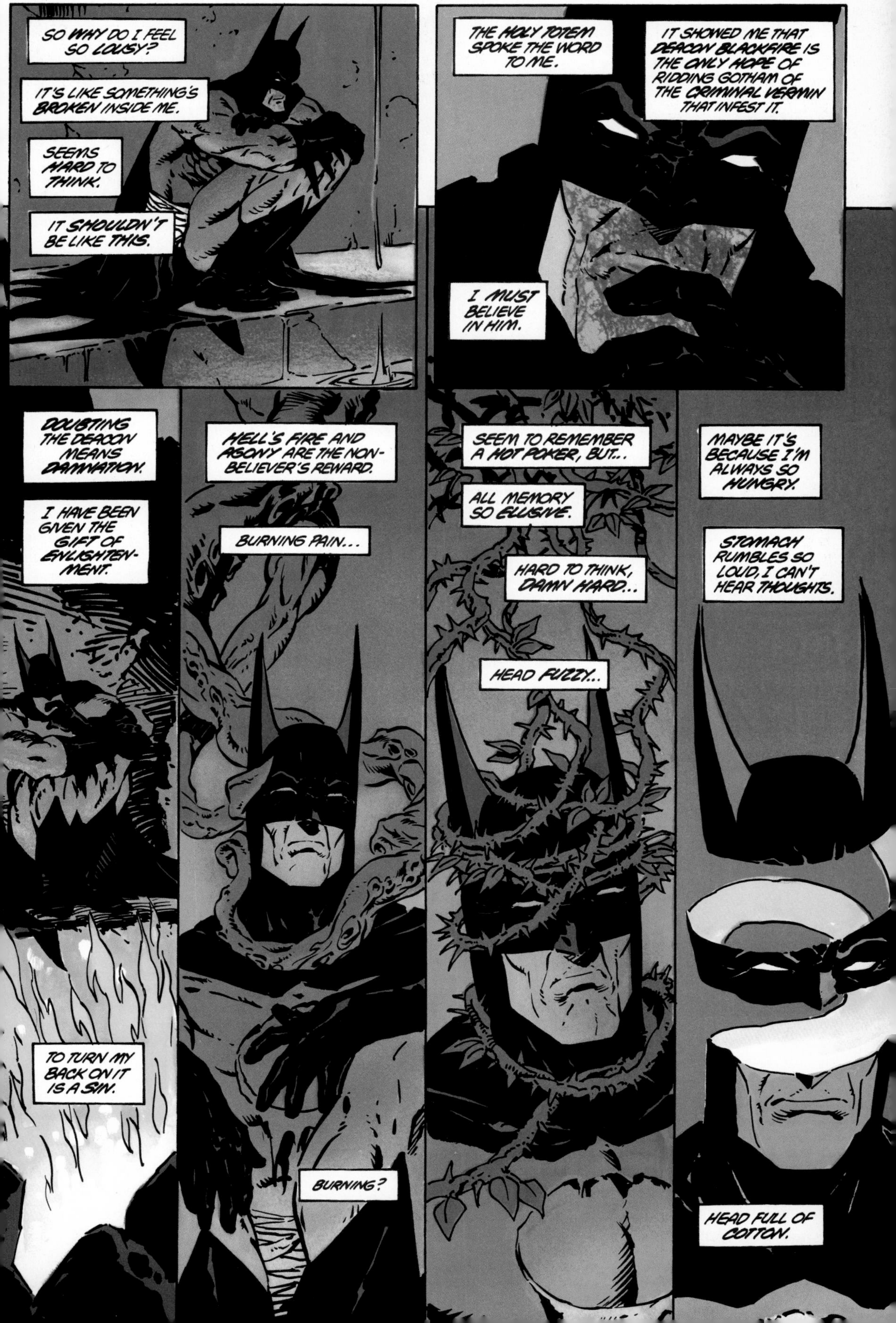
SO WHY DO I FEEL SO LOUSY?
IT'S LIKE SOMETHING'S BROKEN INSIDE ME.
SEEMS HARD TO THINK.
IT SHOULDN'T BE LIKE THIS.
THE HOLY TOTEM SPOKE THE WORD TO ME.
IT SHOWED ME THAT DEACON BLACKFIRE IS THE ONLY HOPE OF RIDDING GOTHAM OF THE CRIMINAL VERMIN THAT INFEST IT.
I MUST BELIEVE IN HIM.
DOUBTING THE DEACON MEANS DAMNATION.
I HAVE BEEN GIVEN THE GIFT OF ENLIGHTENMENT.
TO TURN MY BACK ON IT IS A SIN.
HELL'S FIRE AND AGONY ARE THE NON-BELIEVER'S REWARD.
BURNING PAIN...
BURNING?
SEEM TO REMEMBER A HOT POKER, BUT...
ALL MEMORY SO ELUSIVE.
HARD TO THINK, DAMN HARD...
HEAD FUZZY...
MAYBE IT'S BECAUSE I'M ALWAYS SO HUNGRY.
STOMACH RUMBLES SO LOUD, I CAN'T HEAR THOUGHTS.
HEAD FULL OF COTTON.

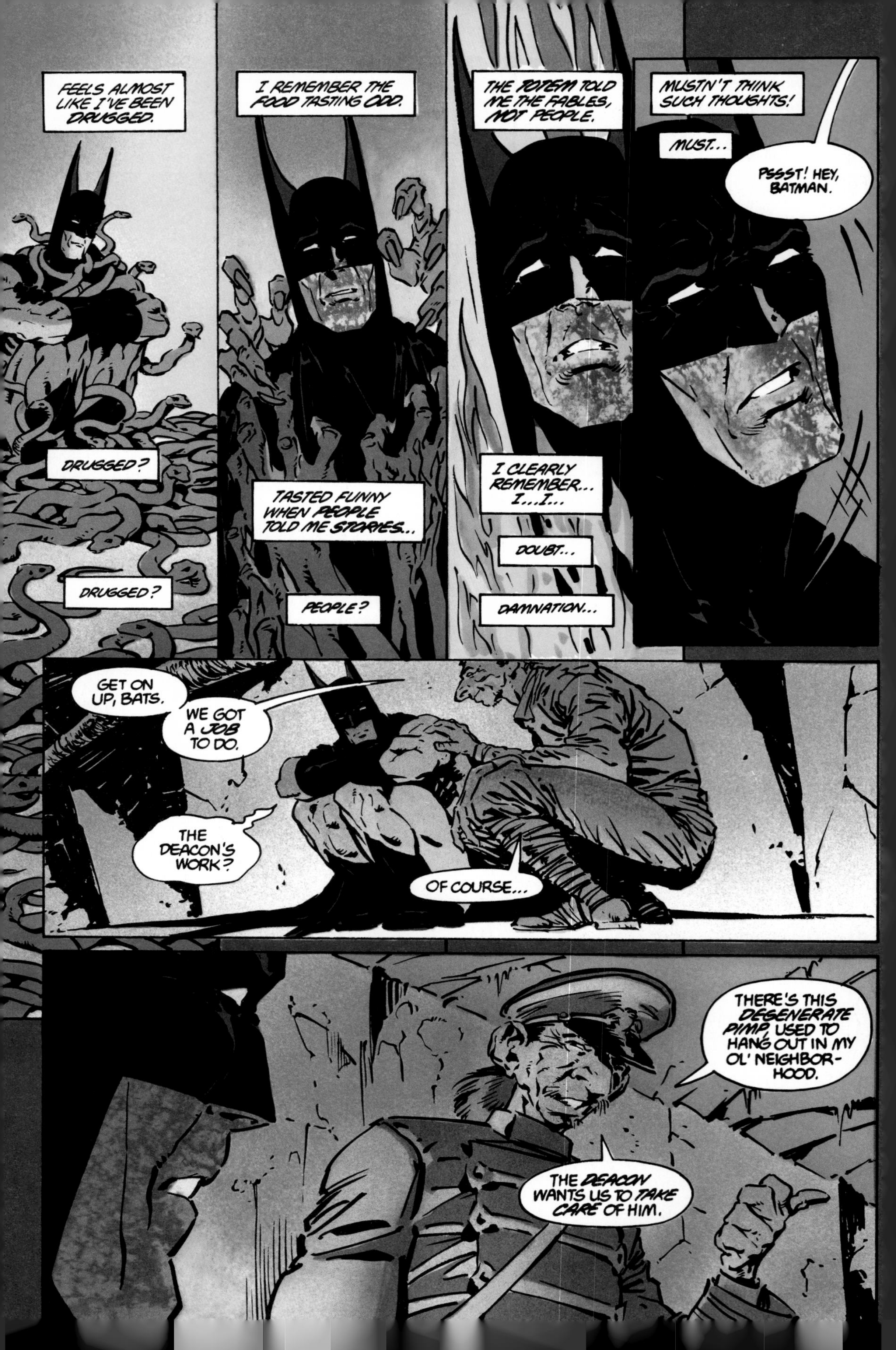
FEELS ALMOST LIKE I'VE BEEN DRUGGED.
DRUGGED?
DRUGGED?
I REMEMBER THE FOOD TASTING ODD.
TASTED FUNNY WHEN PEOPLE TOLD ME STORIES...
PEOPLE?
THE TOTEM TOLD ME THE FABLES, NOT PEOPLE.
I CLEARLY REMEMBER... I...I...
DOUBT...
DAMNATION...
MUSTN'T THINK SUCH THOUGHTS!
MUST...
PSSST! HEY, BATMAN.
GET ON UP, BATS.
WE GOT A JOB TO DO.
THE DEACON'S WORK?
OF COURSE...
THERE'S THIS DEGENERATE PIMP, USED TO HANG OUT IN MY OL' NEIGHBOR-HOOD.
THE DEACON WANTS US TO TAKE CARE OF HIM.

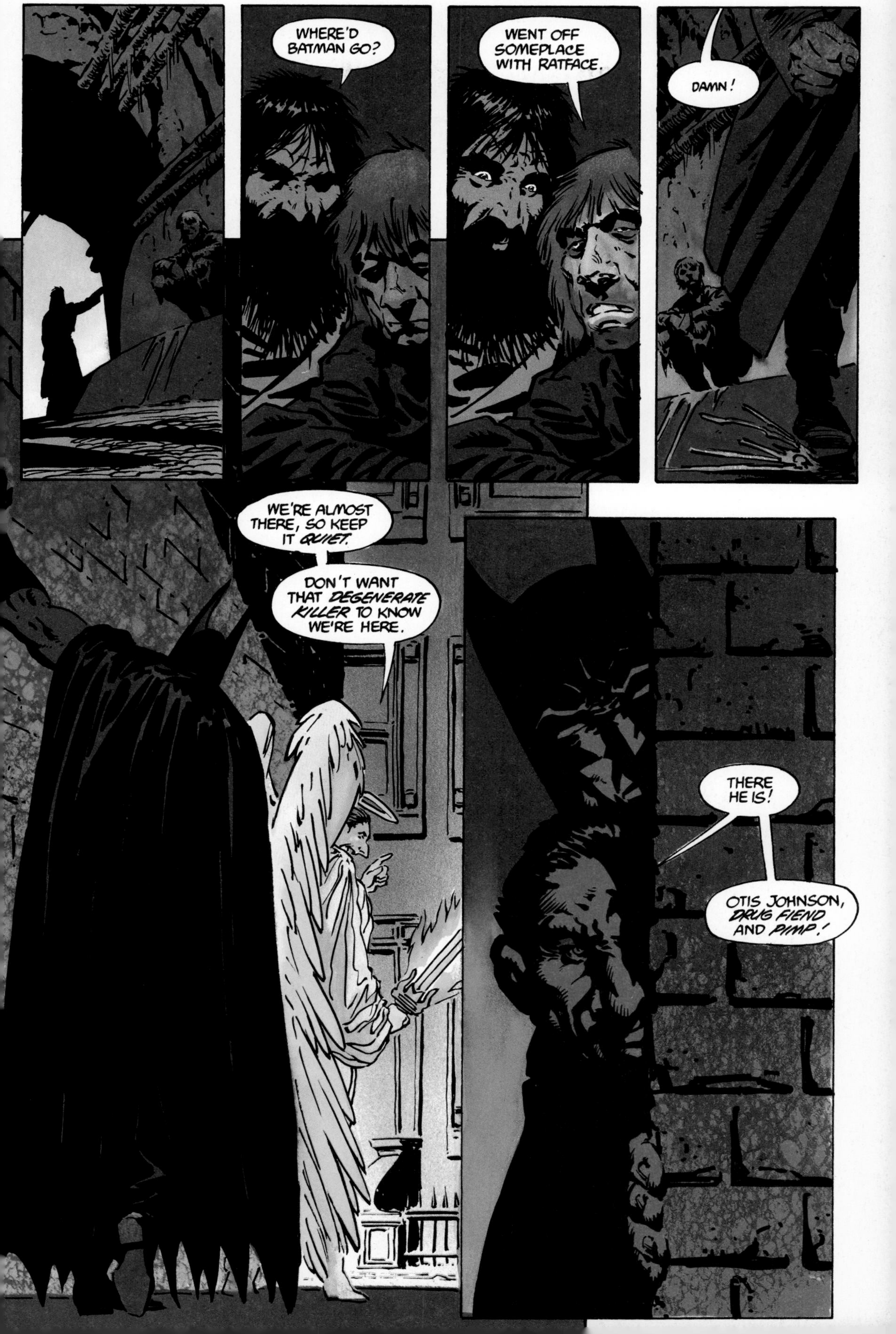
WHERE'D BATMAN GO?
WENT OFF SOMEPLACE WITH RATFACE.
DAMN!
WE'RE ALMOST THERE, SO KEEP IT QUIET.
DON'T WANT THAT DEGENERATE KILLER TO KNOW WE'RE HERE.
THERE HE IS!
OTIS JOHNSON, DRUG FIEND AND PIMP!

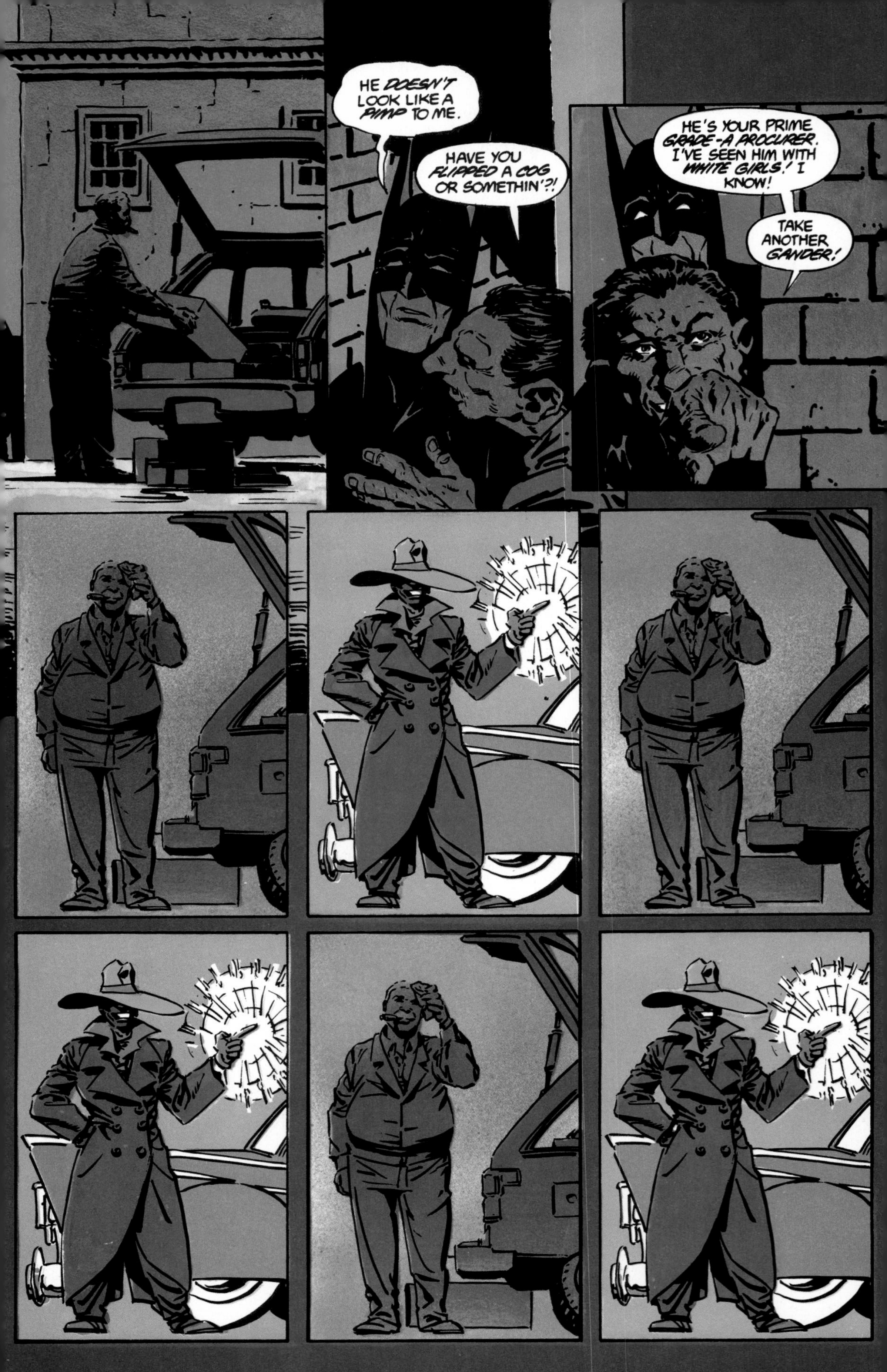
HE DOESN'T LOOK LIKE A PIMP TO ME.
HAVE YOU FLIPPED A COG OR SOMETHIN'?!
HE'S YOUR PRIME GRADE-A PROCURER. I'VE SEEN HIM WITH WHITE GIRLS! I KNOW!
TAKE ANOTHER GANDER!

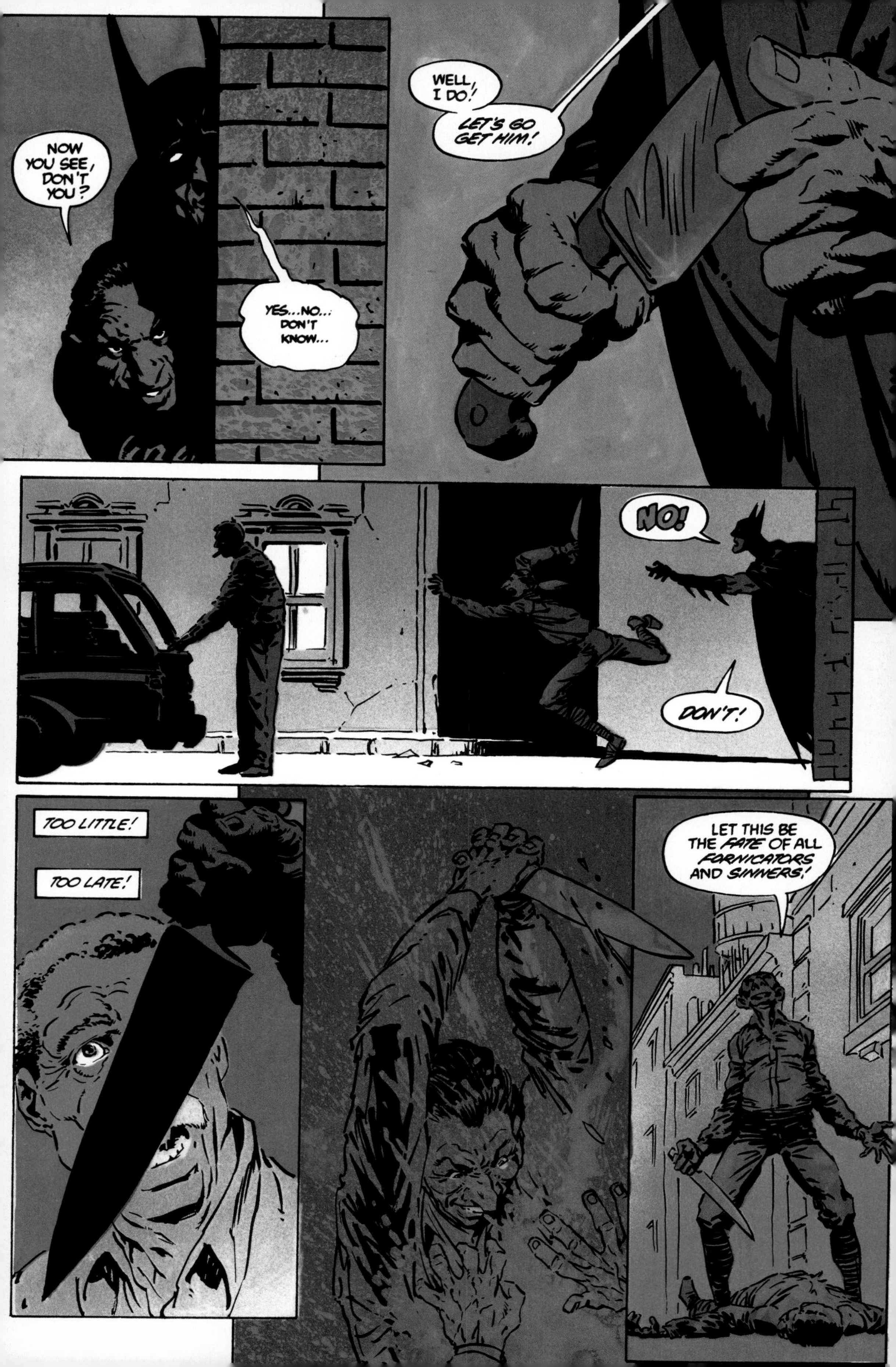
NOW YOU SEE, DON'T YOU?
YES...NO... DON'T KNOW...
WELL, I DO!
LET'S GO GET HIM!
NO!
DON'T!
TOO LITTLE!
TOO LATE!
LET THIS BE THE FATE OF ALL FORNICATORS AND SINNERS!

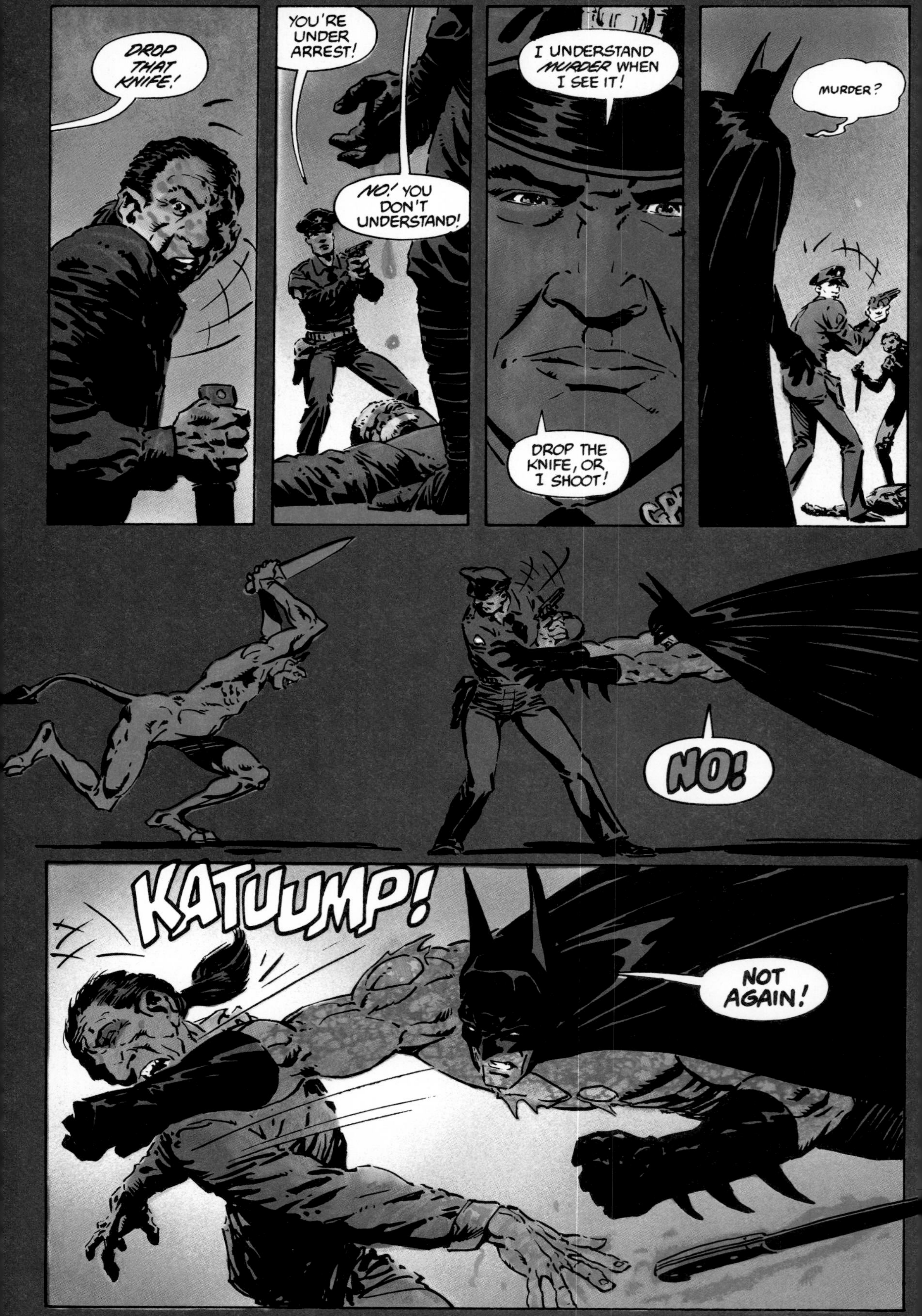
DROP THAT KNIFE!
YOU'RE UNDER ARREST!
NO! YOU DON'T UNDERSTAND!
I UNDERSTAND MURDER WHEN I SEE IT!
DROP THE KNIFE, OR I SHOOT!
MURDER?
NO!
KATUUMP!
NOT AGAIN!

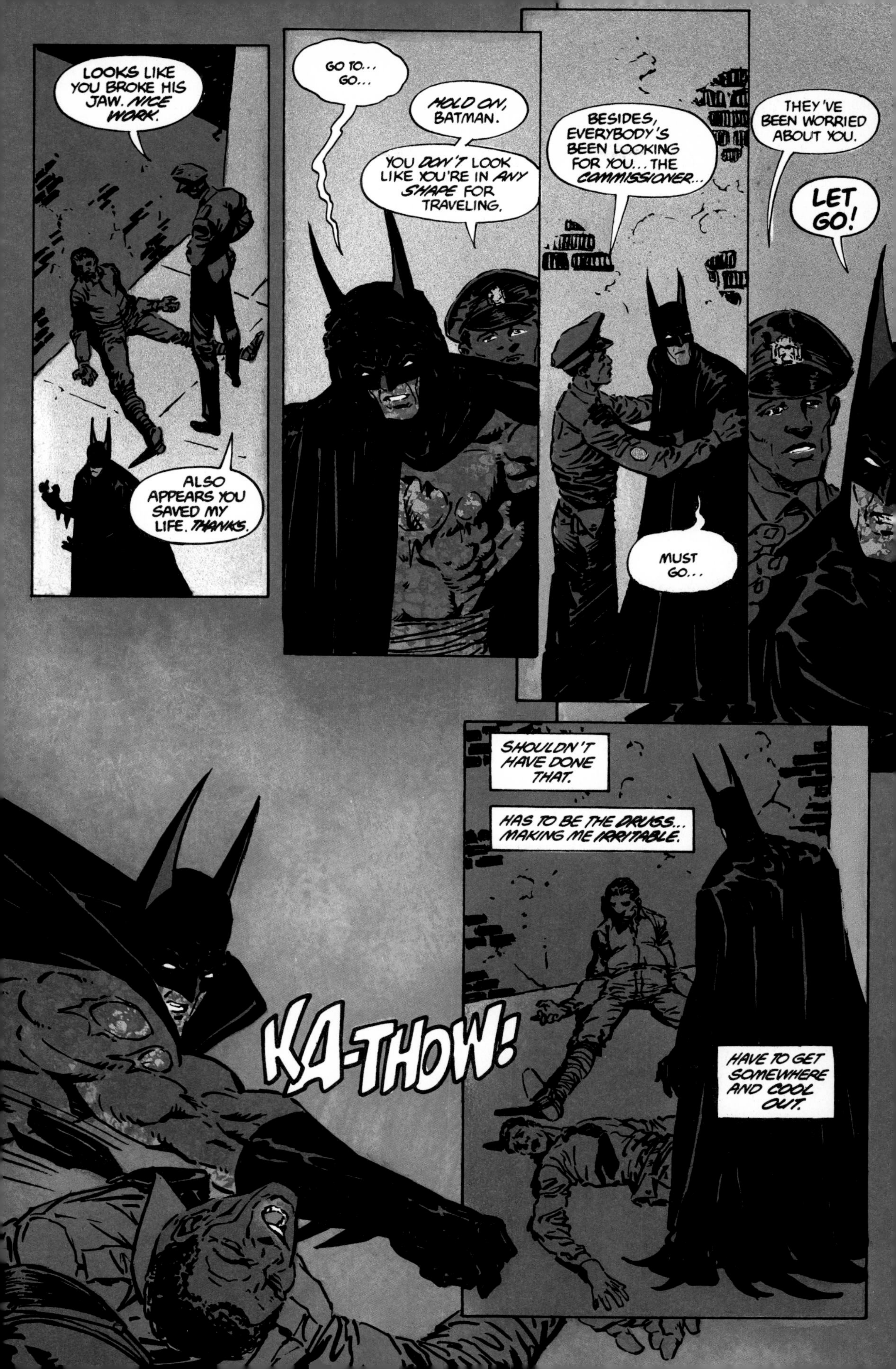
LOOKS LIKE YOU BROKE HIS JAW. NICE WORK.
ALSO APPEARS YOU SAVED MY LIFE. THANKS.
GO TO... GO...
HOLD ON, BATMAN.
YOU DON'T LOOK LIKE YOU'RE IN ANY SHAPE FOR TRAVELING.
BESIDES, EVERYBODY'S BEEN LOOKING FOR YOU... THE COMMISSIONER...
MUST GO...
THEY'VE BEEN WORRIED ABOUT YOU.
LET GO!
KA-THOW!
SHOULDN'T HAVE DONE THAT.
HAS TO BE THE DRUGS... MAKING ME IRRITABLE.
HAVE TO GET SOMEWHERE AND COOL OUT.

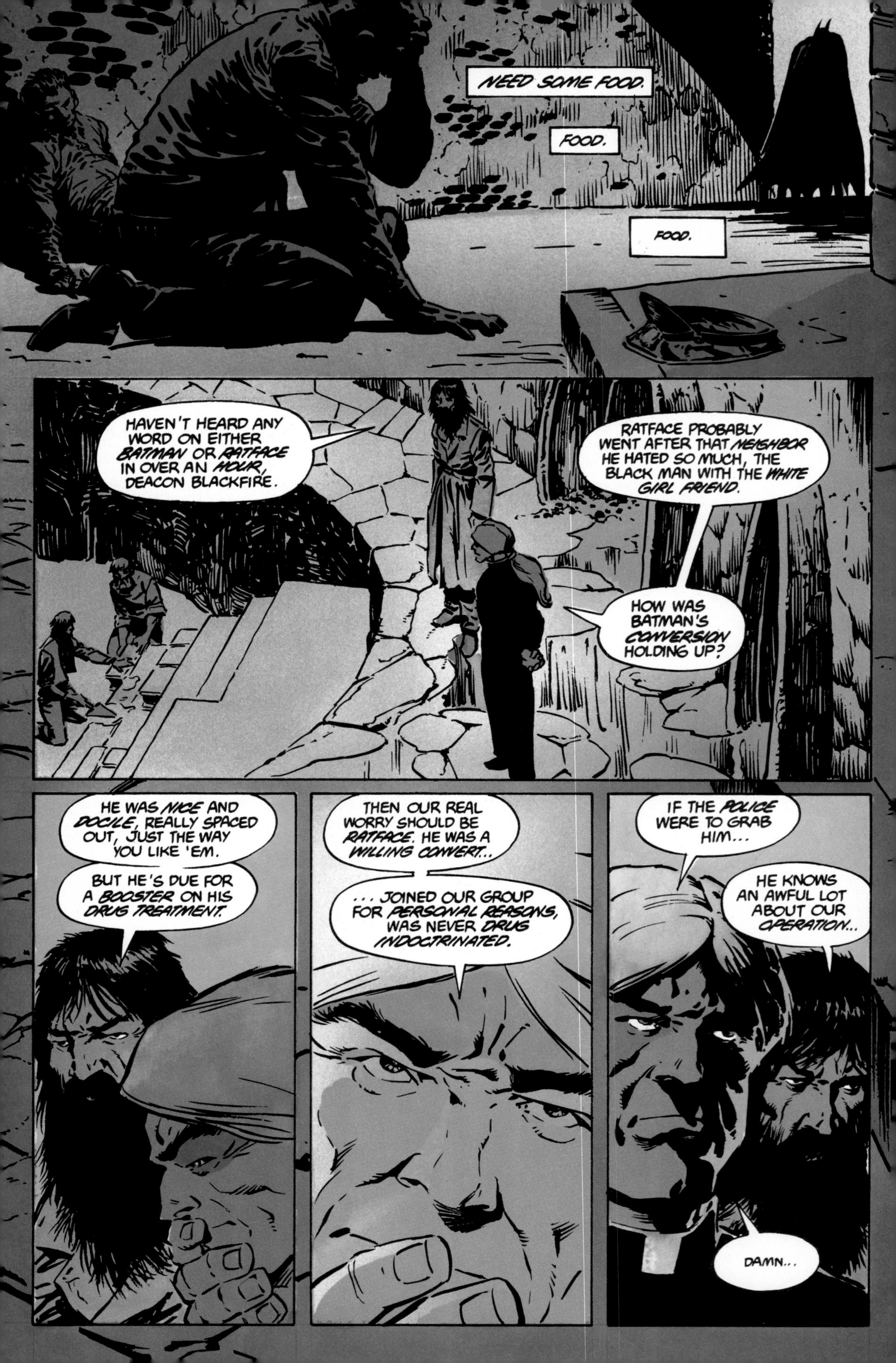
NEED SOME FOOD.
FOOD.
FOOD.
HAVEN'T HEARD ANY WORD ON EITHER BATMAN OR RATFACE IN OVER AN HOUR, DEACON BLACKFIRE.
RATFACE PROBABLY WENT AFTER THAT NEIGHBOR HE HATED SO MUCH, THE BLACK MAN WITH THE WHITE GIRL FRIEND.
HOW WAS BATMAN'S CONVERSION HOLDING UP?
HE WAS NICE AND DOCILE, REALLY SPACED OUT, JUST THE WAY YOU LIKE 'EM.
BUT HE'S DUE FOR A BOOSTER ON HIS DRUG TREATMENT.
THEN OUR REAL WORRY SHOULD BE RATFACE. HE WAS A WILLING CONVERT...
...JOINED OUR GROUP FOR PERSONAL REASONS, WAS NEVER DRUG INDOCTRINATED.
IF THE POLICE WERE TO GRAB HIM...
HE KNOWS AN AWFUL LOT ABOUT OUR OPERATION...
DAMN...

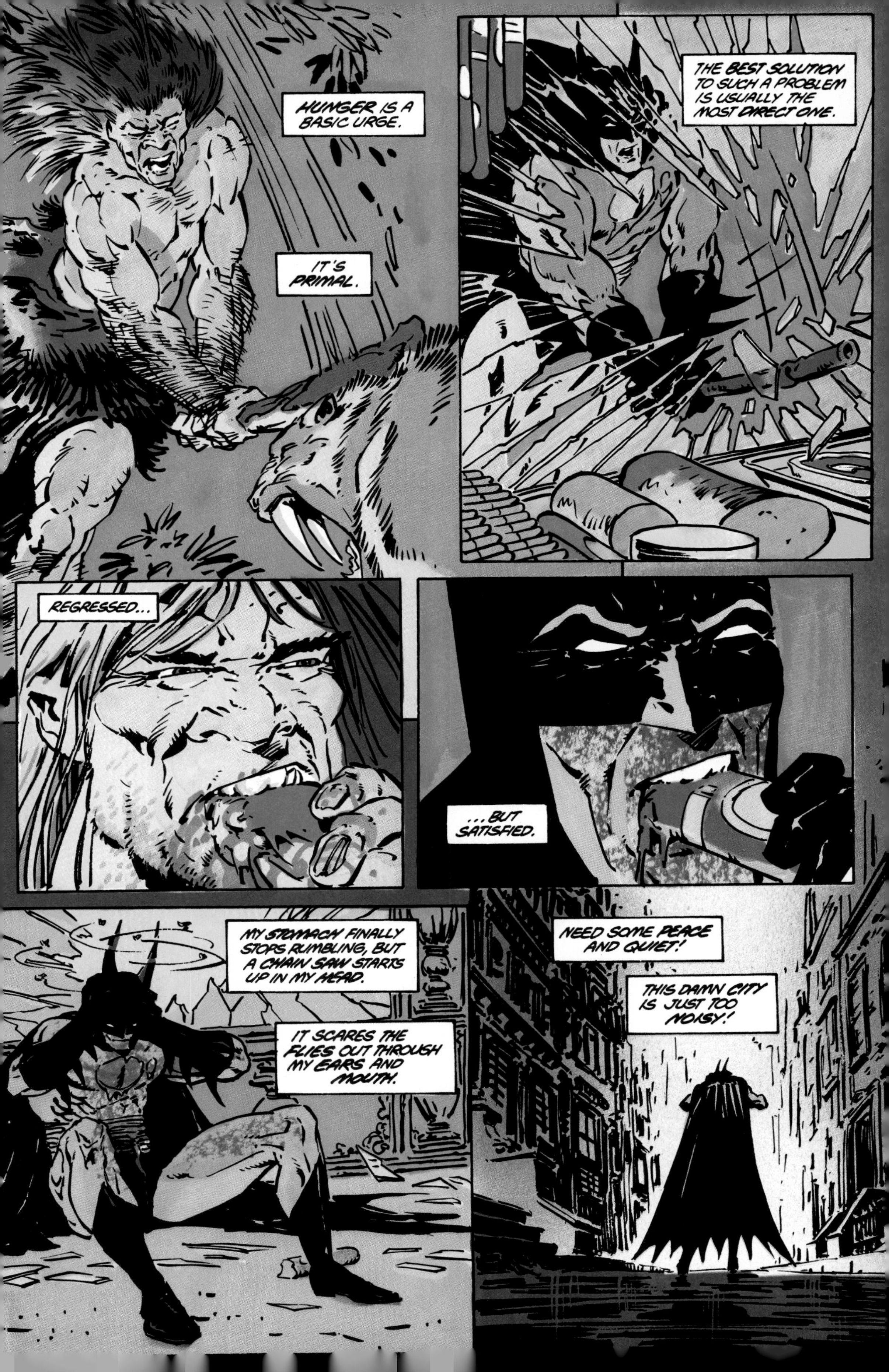
HUNGER IS A BASIC URGE.
IT'S PRIMAL.
THE BEST SOLUTION TO SUCH A PROBLEM IS USUALLY THE MOST DIRECT ONE.
REGRESSED...
...BUT SATISFIED.
MY STOMACH FINALLY STOPS RUMBLING, BUT A CHAIN SAW STARTS UP IN MY HEAD.
IT SCARES THE FLIES OUT THROUGH MY EARS AND MOUTH.
NEED SOME PEACE AND QUIET!
THIS DAMN CITY IS JUST TOO NOISY!

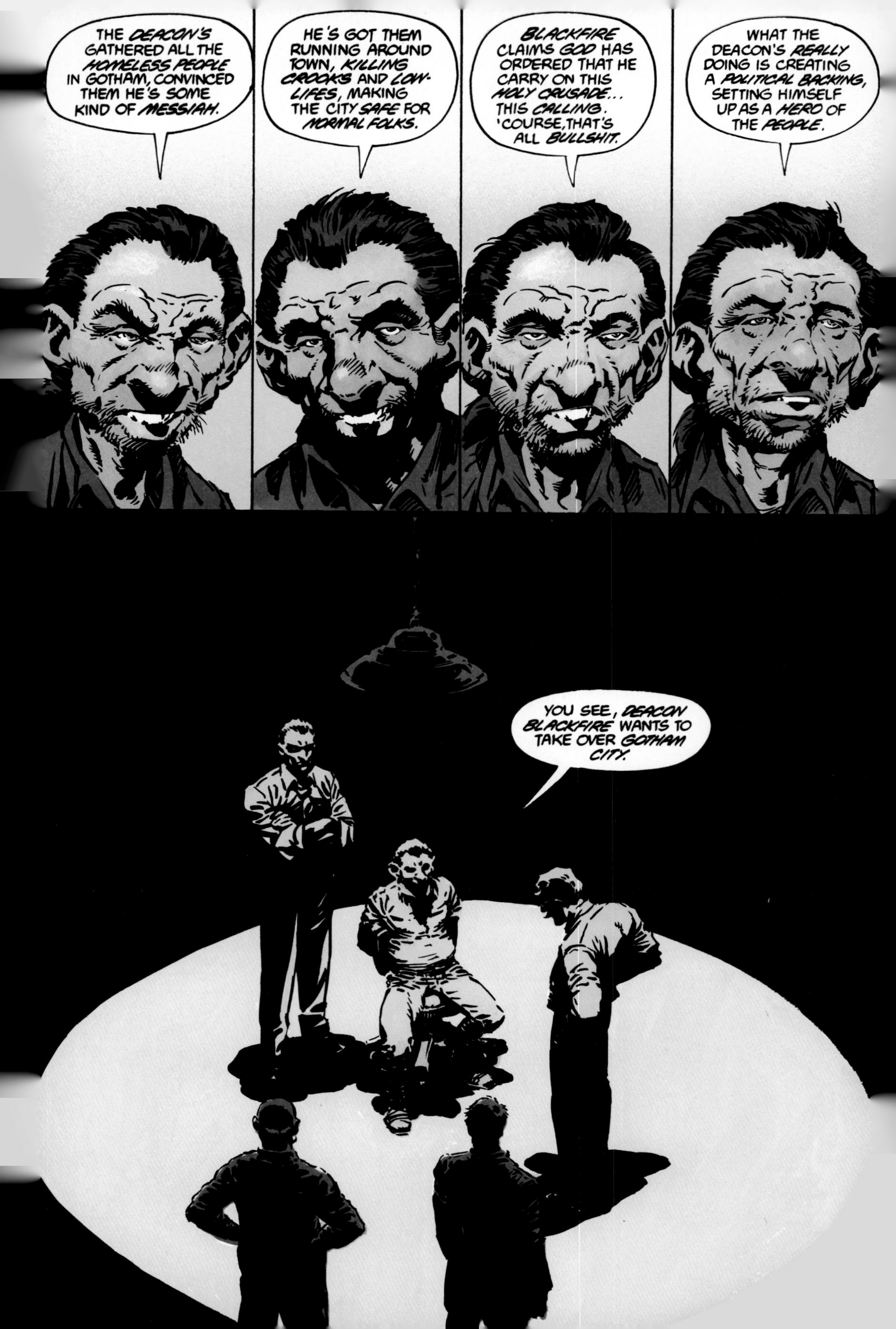
THE DEACON'S GATHERED ALL THE HOMELESS PEOPLE IN GOTHAM, CONVINCED THEM HE'S SOME KIND OF MESSIAH.
HE'S GOT THEM RUNNING AROUND TOWN, KILLING CROOKS AND LOW-LIFES, MAKING THE CITY SAFE FOR NORMAL FOLKS.
BLACKFIRE CLAIMS GOD HAS ORDERED THAT HE CARRY ON THIS HOLY CRUSADE... THIS CALLING. 'COURSE, THAT'S ALL BULLSHIT.
WHAT THE DEACON'S REALLY DOING IS CREATING A POLITICAL BACKING, SETTING HIMSELF UP AS A HERO OF THE PEOPLE.
YOU SEE, DEACON BLACKFIRE WANTS TO TAKE OVER GOTHAM CITY.

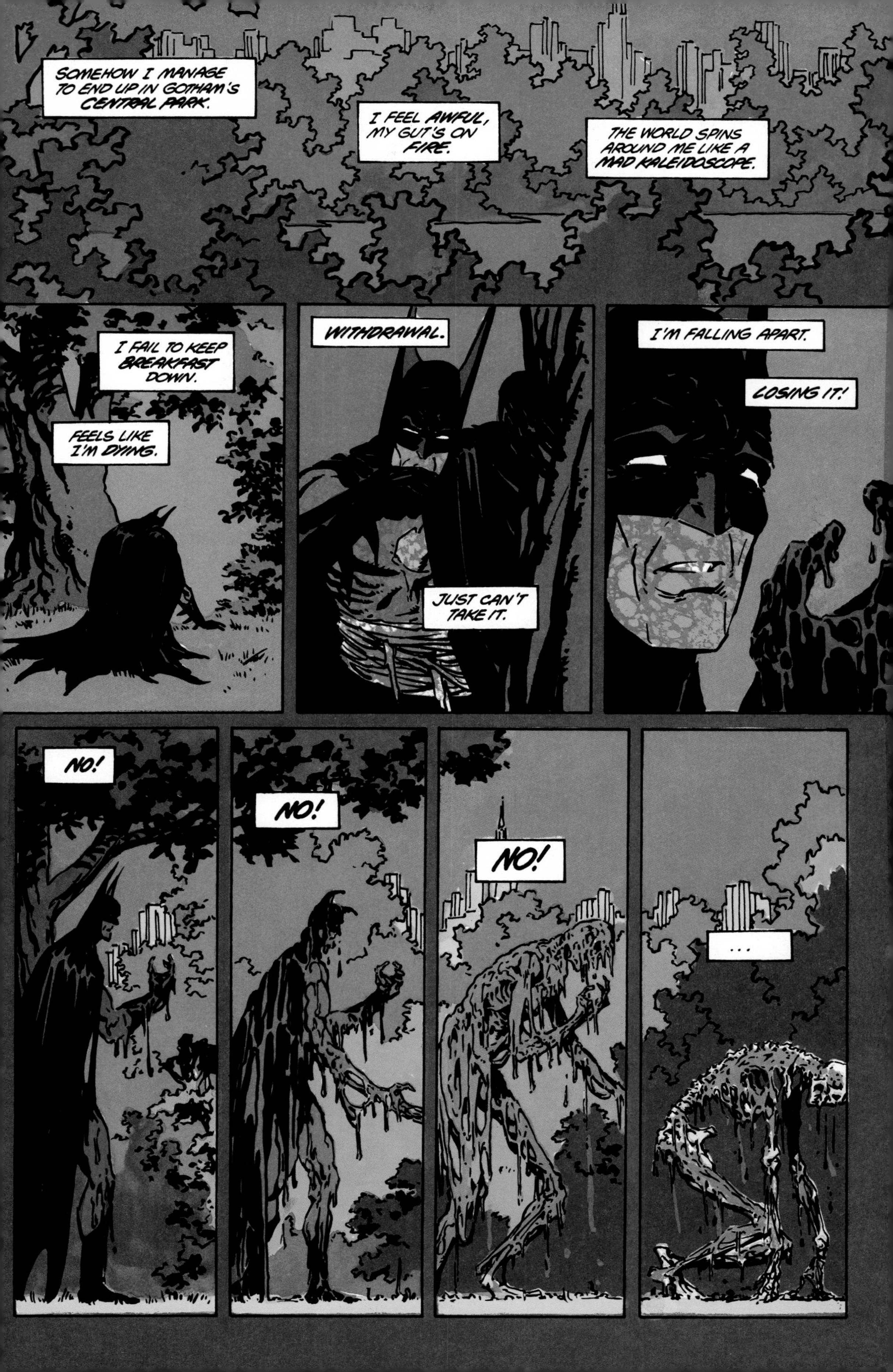
SOMEHOW I MANAGE TO END UP IN GOTHAM'S CENTRAL PARK.
I FEEL AWFUL, MY GUT'S ON FIRE.
THE WORLD SPINS AROUND ME LIKE A MAD KALEIDOSCOPE.
I FAIL TO KEEP BREAKFAST DOWN.
FEELS LIKE I'M DYING.
WITHDRAWAL.
JUST CAN'T TAKE IT.
I'M FALLING APART.
LOSING IT!
NO!
NO!
NO!
...

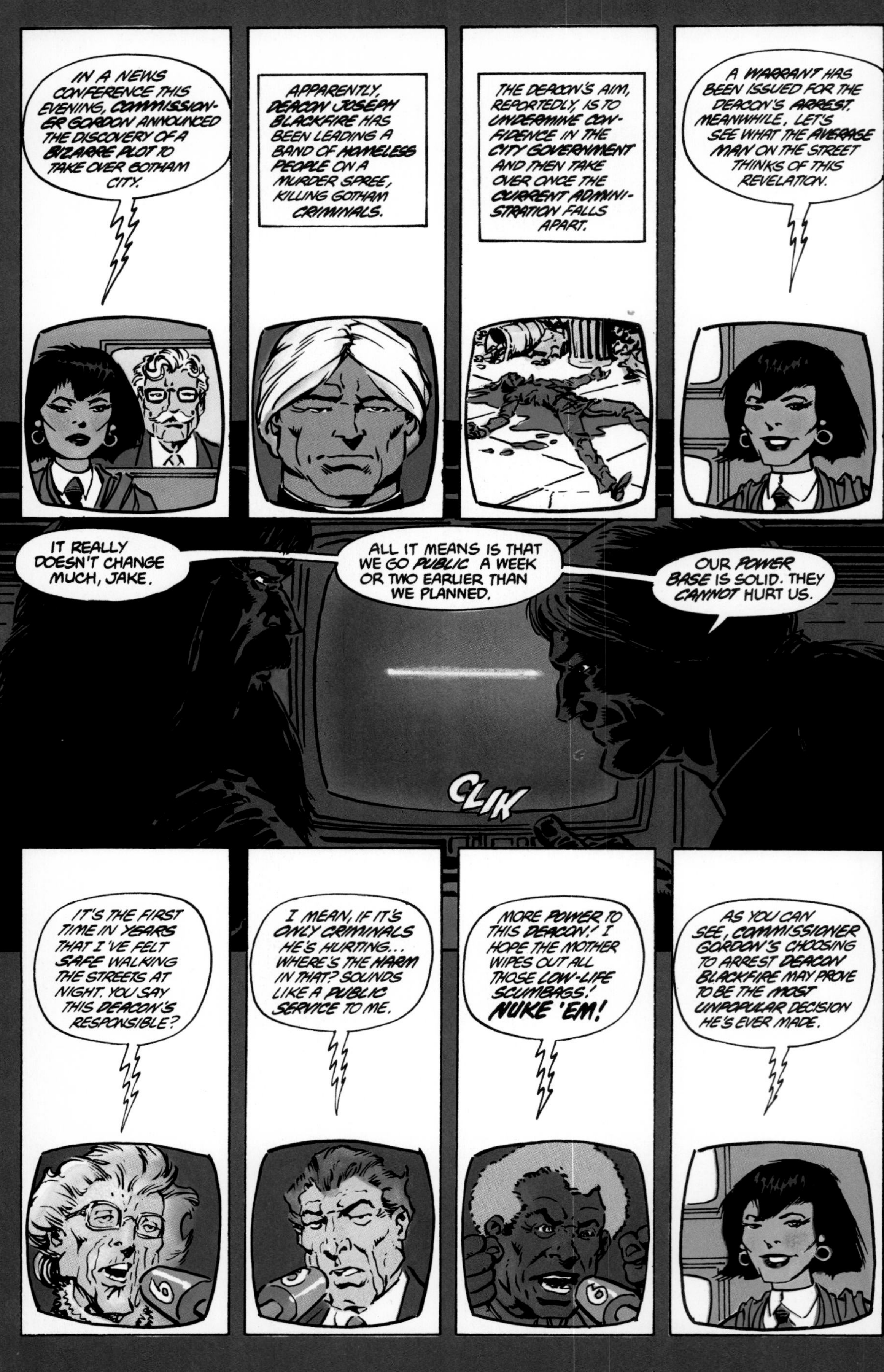
IN A NEWS CONFERENCE THIS EVENING, COMMISSIONER GORDON ANNOUNCED THE DISCOVERY OF A BIZARRE PLOT TO TAKE OVER GOTHAM CITY.
APPARENTLY, DEACON JOSEPH BLACKFIRE HAS BEEN LEADING A BAND OF HOMELESS PEOPLE ON A MURDER SPREE, KILLING GOTHAM CRIMINALS.
THE DEACON'S AIM, REPORTEDLY, IS TO UNDERMINE CONFIDENCE IN THE CITY GOVERNMENT AND THEN TAKE OVER ONCE THE CURRENT ADMINISTRATION FALLS APART.
A WARRANT HAS BEEN ISSUED FOR THE DEACON'S ARREST. MEANWHILE, LET'S SEE WHAT THE AVERAGE MAN ON THE STREET THINKS OF THIS REVELATION.
IT REALLY DOESN'T CHANGE MUCH, JAKE.
ALL IT MEANS IS THAT WE GO PUBLIC A WEEK OR TWO EARLIER THAN WE PLANNED.
OUR POWER BASE IS SOLID. THEY CANNOT HURT US.
CLIK
IT'S THE FIRST TIME IN YEARS THAT I'VE FELT SAFE WALKING THE STREETS AT NIGHT. YOU SAY THIS DEACON'S RESPONSIBLE?
I MEAN, IF IT'S ONLY CRIMINALS HE'S HURTING... WHERE'S THE HARM IN THAT? SOUNDS LIKE A PUBLIC SERVICE TO ME.
MORE POWER TO THIS DEACON! I HOPE THE MOTHER WIPES OUT ALL THOSE LOW-LIFE SCUMBAGS! NUKE 'EM!
AS YOU CAN SEE, COMMISSIONER GORDON'S CHOOSING TO ARREST DEACON BLACKFIRE MAY PROVE TO BE THE MOST UNPOPULAR DECISION HE'S EVER MADE.

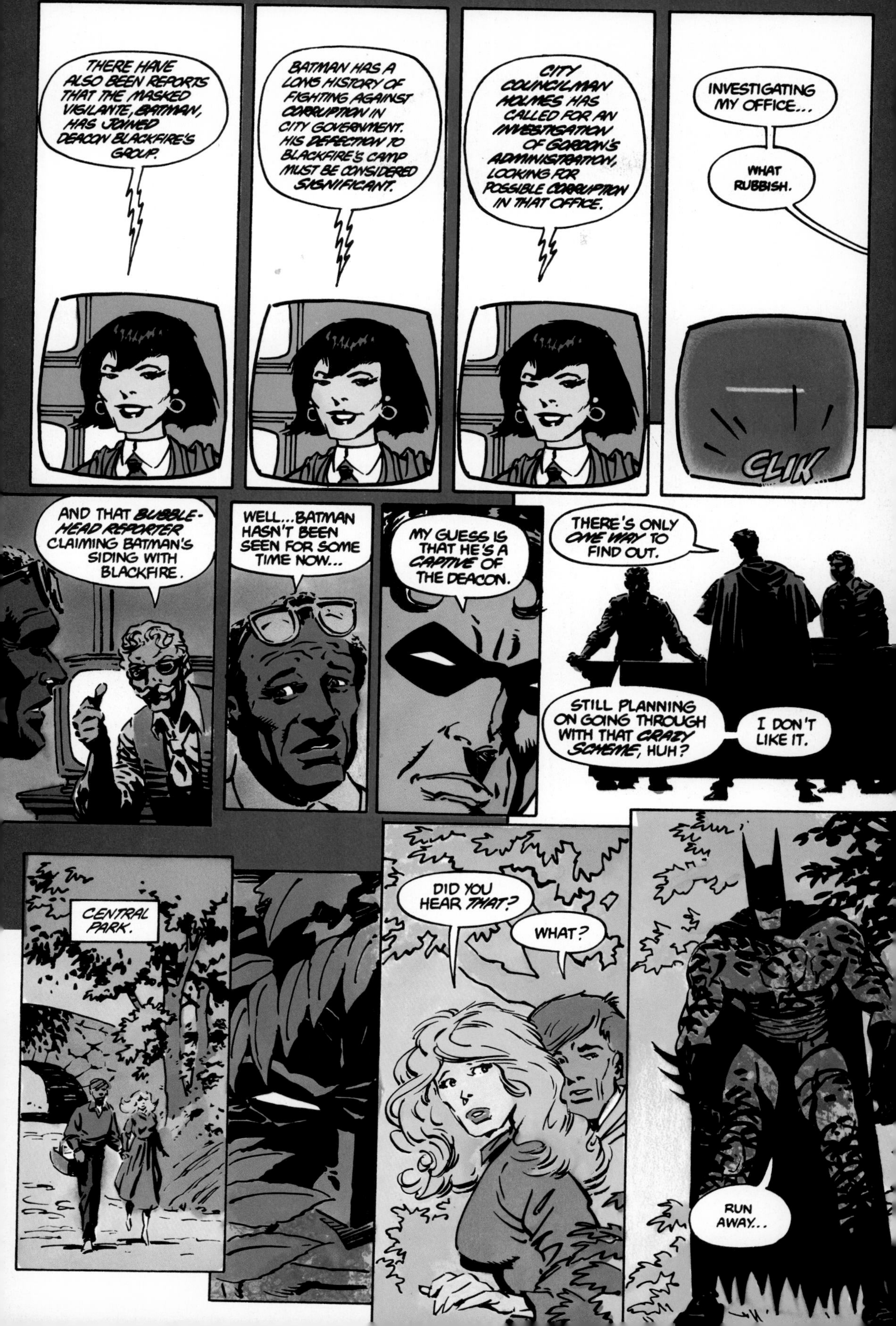
THERE HAVE ALSO BEEN REPORTS THAT THE MASKED VIGILANTE, BATMAN, HAS JOINED DEACON BLACKFIRE'S GROUP.
BATMAN HAS A LONG HISTORY OF FIGHTING AGAINST CORRUPTION IN CITY GOVERNMENT. HIS DEFECTION TO BLACKFIRE'S CAMP MUST BE CONSIDERED SIGNIFICANT.
CITY COUNCILMAN HOLMES HAS CALLED FOR AN INVESTIGATION OF GORDON'S ADMINISTRATION, LOOKING FOR POSSIBLE CORRUPTION IN THAT OFFICE.
INVESTIGATING MY OFFICE...
WHAT RUBBISH.
CLIK
AND THAT BUBBLE-HEAD REPORTER CLAIMING BATMAN'S SIDING WITH BLACKFIRE.
WELL...BATMAN HASN'T BEEN SEEN FOR SOME TIME NOW...
MY GUESS IS THAT HE'S A CAPTIVE OF THE DEACON.
THERE'S ONLY ONE WAY TO FIND OUT.
STILL PLANNING ON GOING THROUGH WITH THAT CRAZY SCHEME, HUH?
I DON'T LIKE IT.
CENTRAL PARK.
DID YOU HEAR THAT?
WHAT?
RUN AWAY...

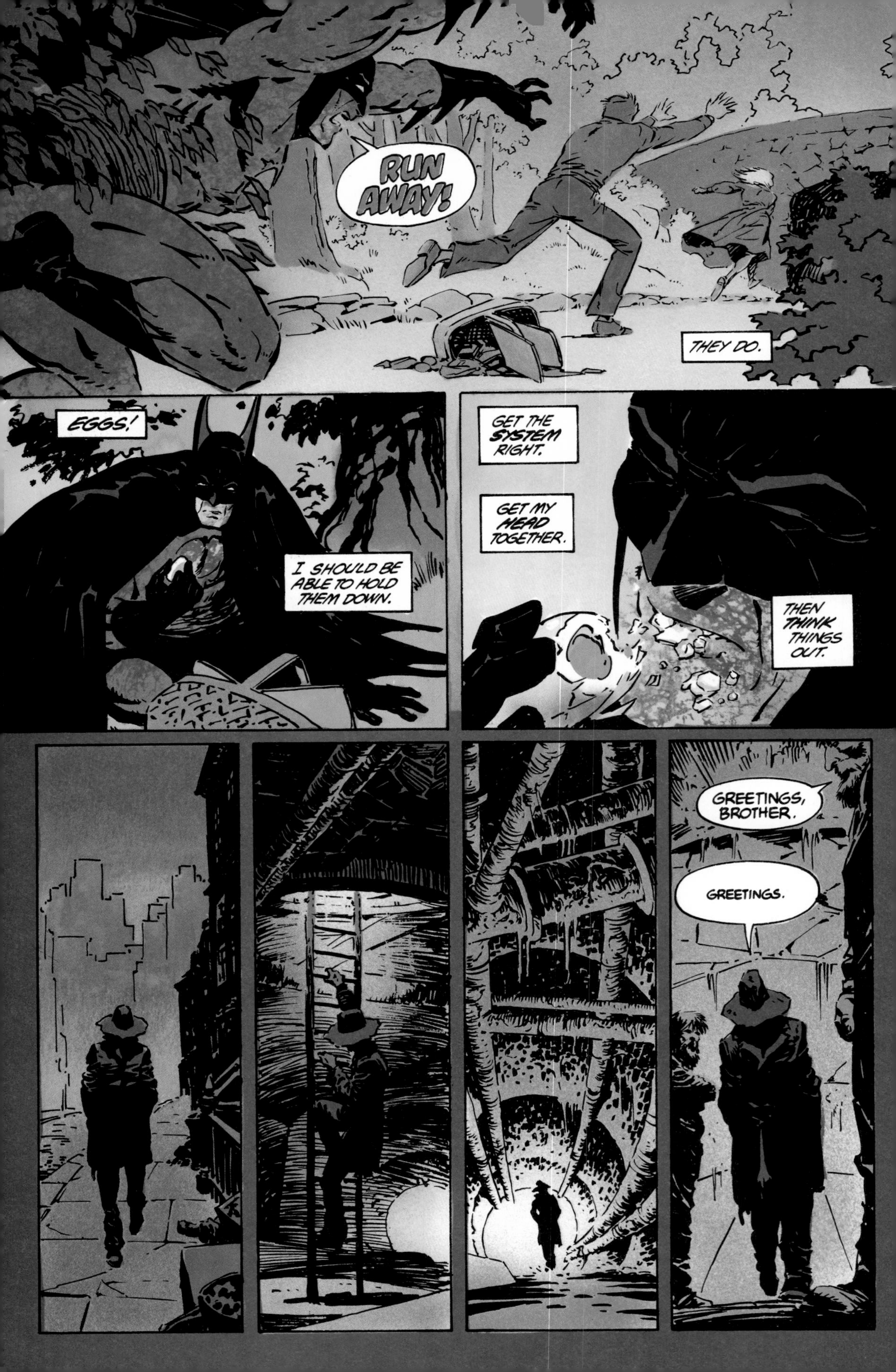
RUN AWAY!
THEY DO.
EGGS!
I SHOULD BE ABLE TO HOLD THEM DOWN.
GET THE SYSTEM RIGHT.
GET MY HEAD TOGETHER.
THEN THINK THINGS OUT.
GREETINGS, BROTHER.
GREETINGS.

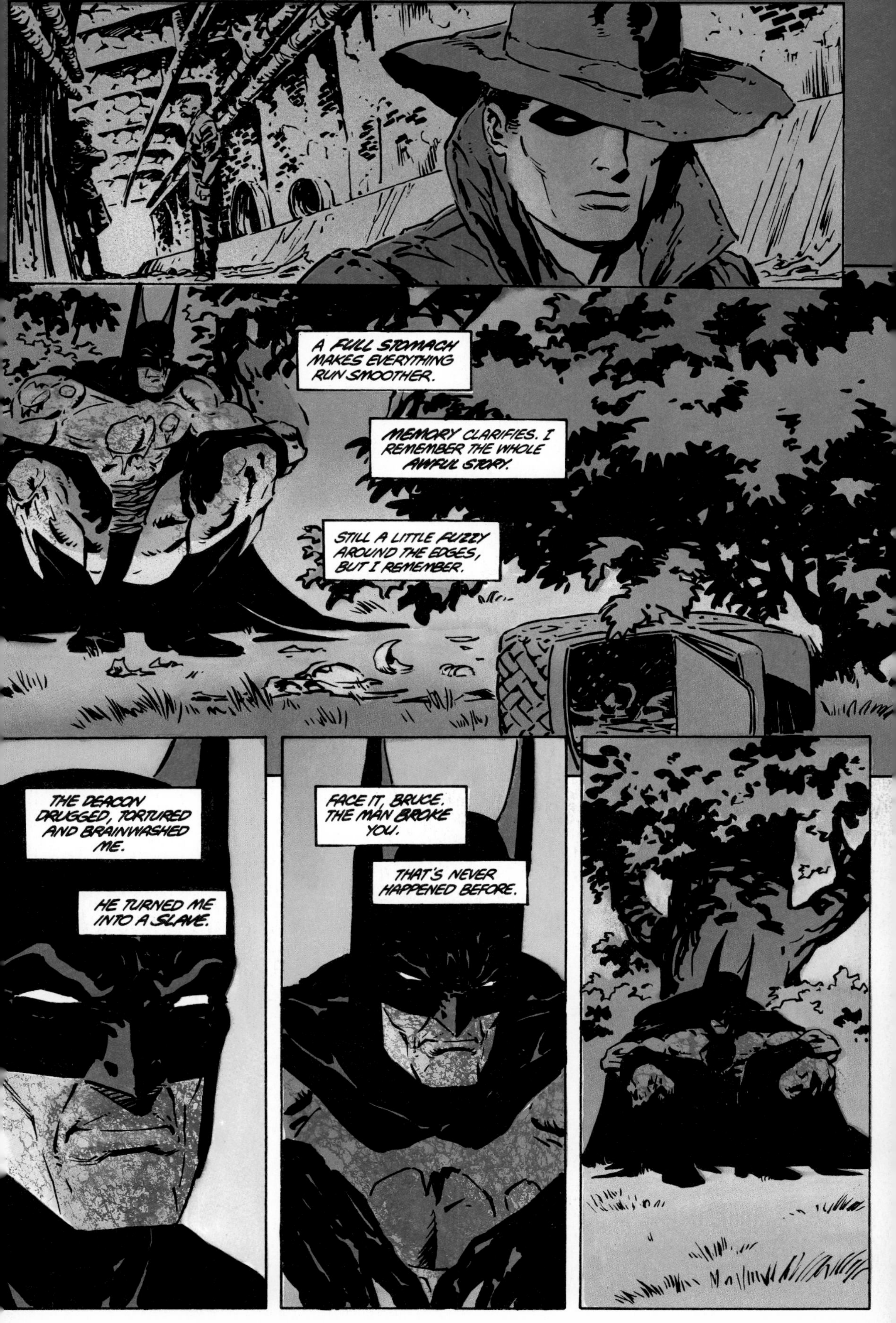
A FULL STOMACH MAKES EVERYTHING RUN SMOOTHER.
MEMORY CLARIFIES. I REMEMBER THE WHOLE AWFUL STORY.
STILL A LITTLE FUZZY AROUND THE EDGES, BUT I REMEMBER.
THE DEACON DRUGGED, TORTURED AND BRAINWASHED ME.
HE TURNED ME INTO A SLAVE.
FACE IT, BRUCE. THE MAN BROKE YOU.
THAT'S NEVER HAPPENED BEFORE.

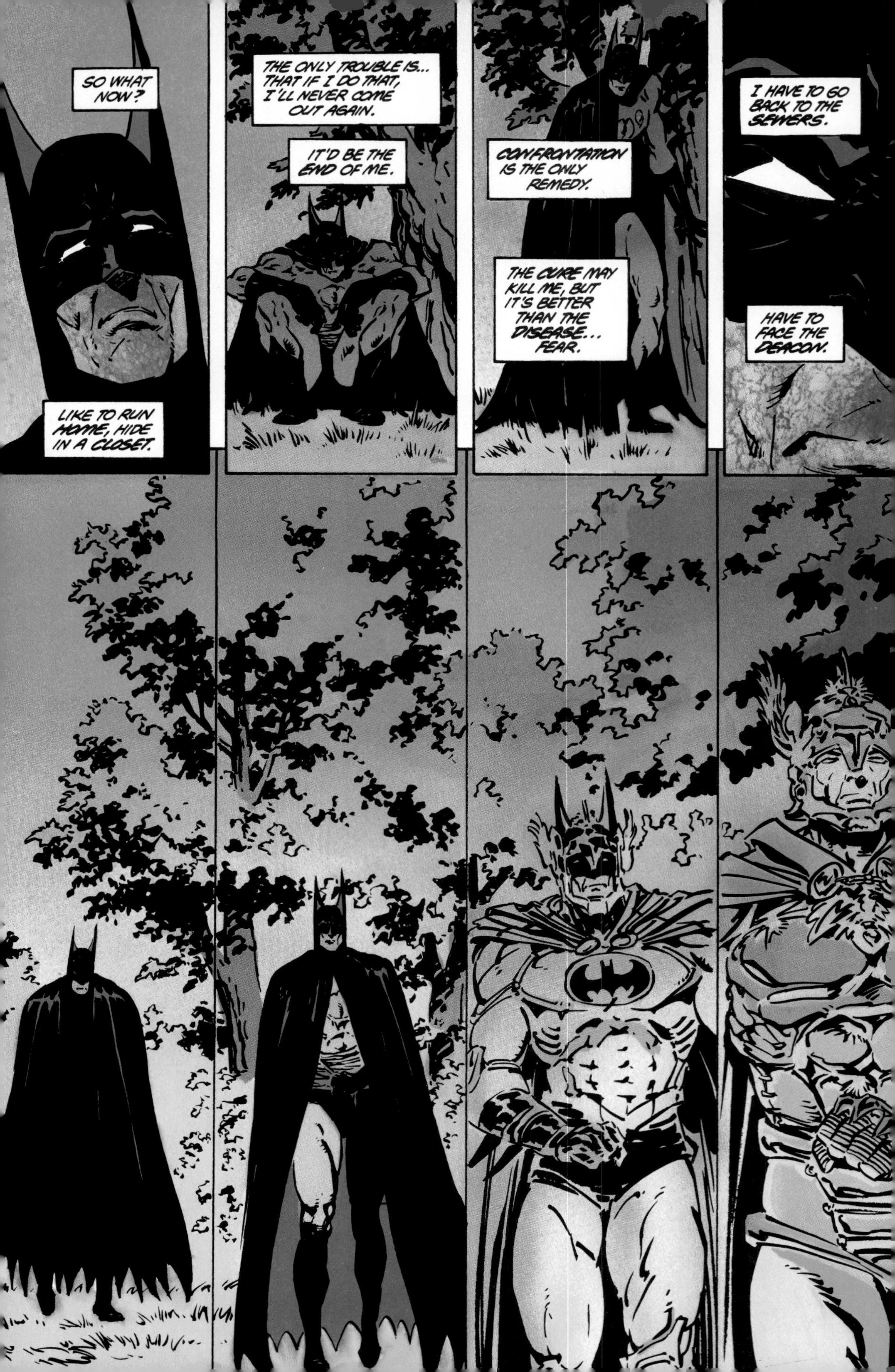
SO WHAT NOW?
LIKE TO RUN HOME, HIDE IN A CLOSET.
THE ONLY TROUBLE IS... THAT IF I DO THAT, I'LL NEVER COME OUT AGAIN.
IT'D BE THE END OF ME.
CONFRONTATION IS THE ONLY REMEDY.
THE CURE MAY KILL ME, BUT IT'S BETTER THAN THE DISEASE... FEAR.
I HAVE TO GO BACK TO THE SEWERS.
HAVE TO FACE THE DEACON.

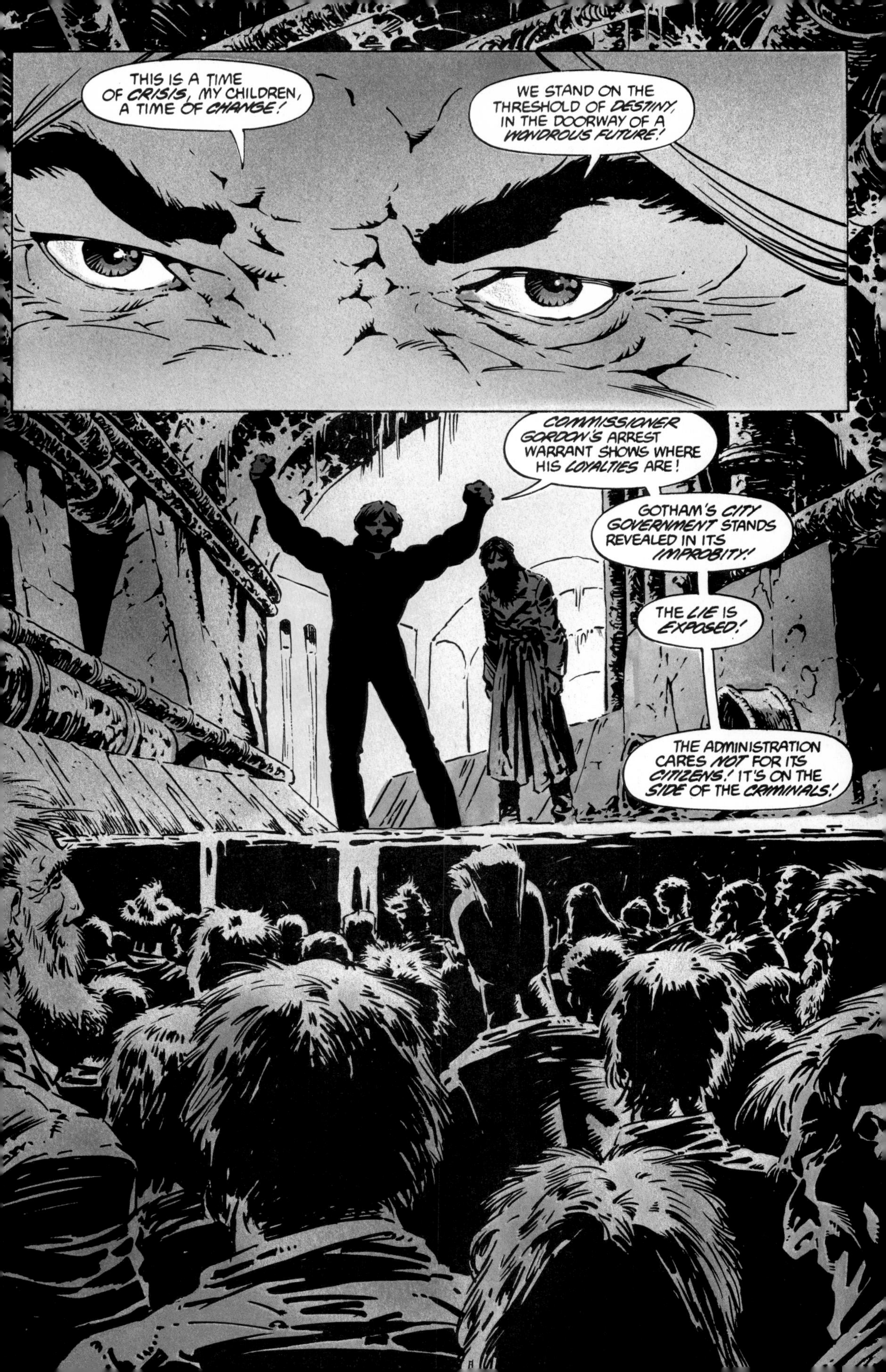
THIS IS A TIME OF CRISIS, MY CHILDREN, A TIME OF CHANGE!
WE STAND ON THE THRESHOLD OF DESTINY, IN THE DOORWAY OF A WONDROUS FUTURE!
COMMISSIONER GORDON'S ARREST WARRANT SHOWS WHERE HIS LOYALTIES ARE!
GOTHAM'S CITY GOVERNMENT STANDS REVEALED IN ITS IMPROBITY!
THE LIE IS EXPOSED!
THE ADMINISTRATION CARES NOT FOR ITS CITIZENS! IT'S ON THE SIDE OF THE CRIMINALS!

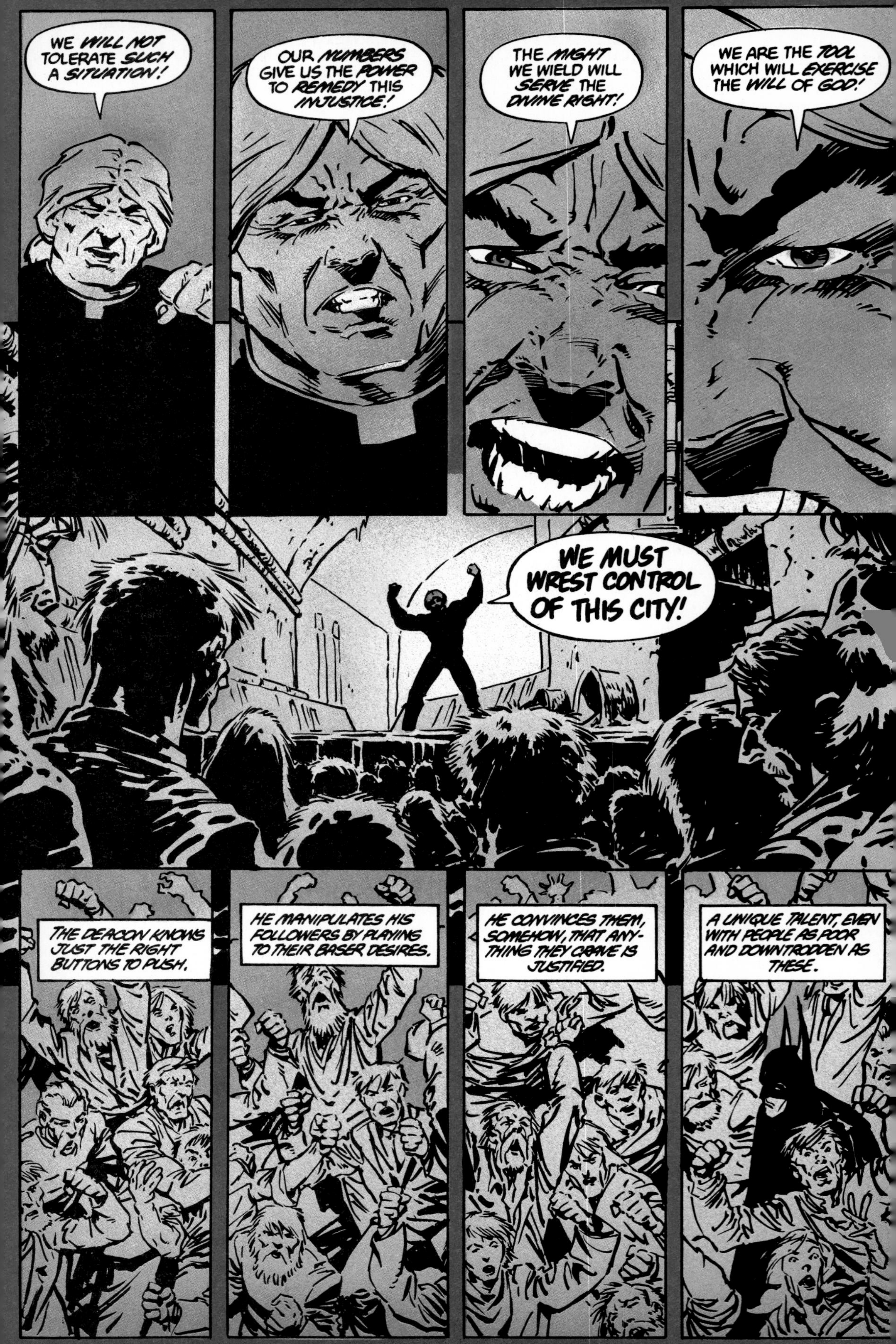
WE WILL NOT TOLERATE SUCH A SITUATION!
OUR NUMBERS GIVE US THE POWER TO REMEDY THIS INJUSTICE!
THE MIGHT WE WIELD WILL SERVE THE DIVINE RIGHT!
WE ARE THE TOOL WHICH WILL EXERCISE THE WILL OF GOD!
WE MUST WREST CONTROL OF THIS CITY!
THE DEACON KNOWS JUST THE RIGHT BUTTONS TO PUSH.
HE MANIPULATES HIS FOLLOWERS BY PLAYING TO THEIR BASER DESIRES.
HE CONVINCES THEM, SOMEHOW, THAT ANY-THING THEY CRAVE IS JUSTIFIED.
A UNIQUE TALENT, EVEN WITH PEOPLE AS POOR AND DOWNTRODDEN AS THESE.

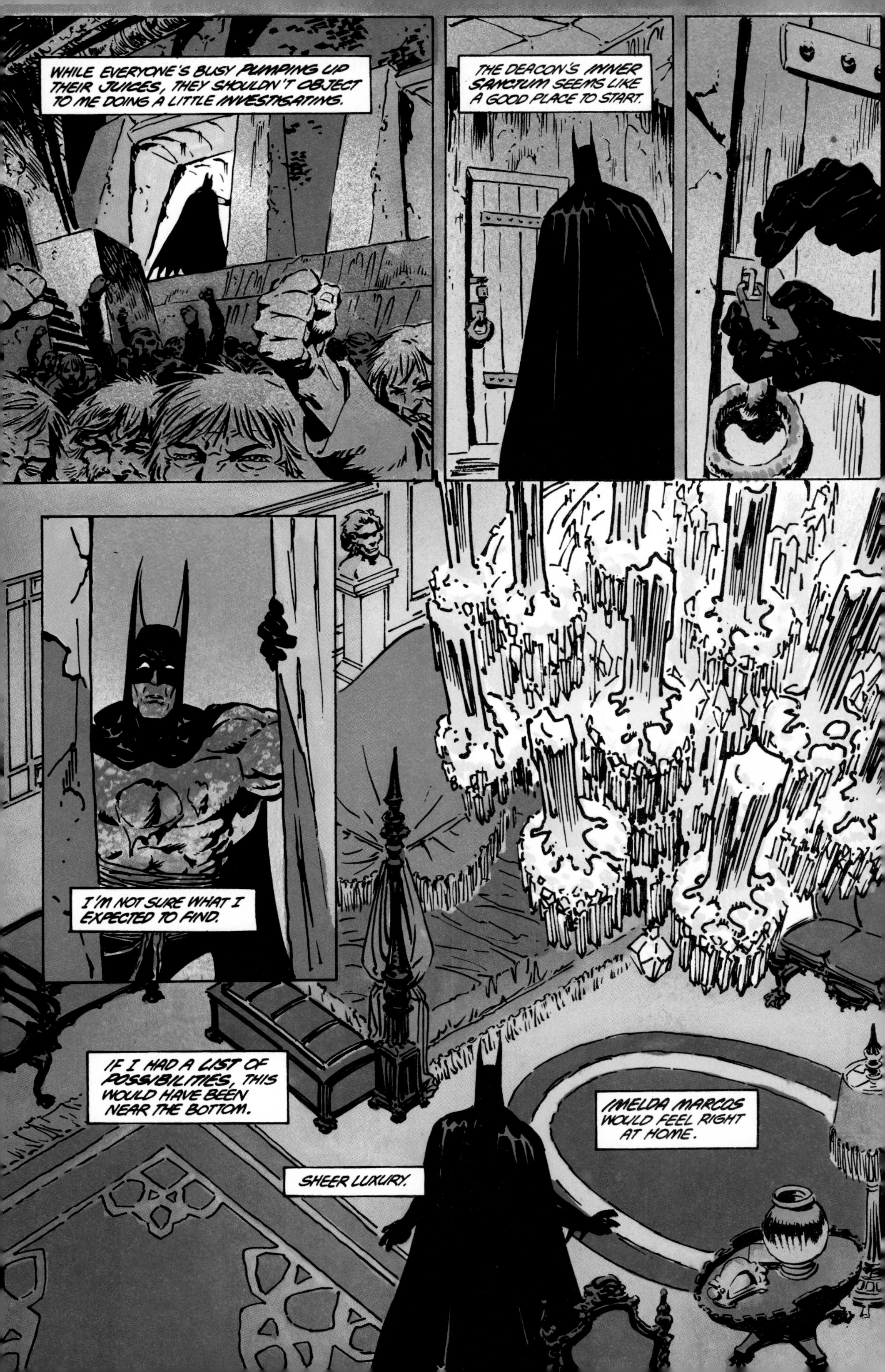
WHILE EVERYONE'S BUSY PUMPING UP THEIR JUICES, THEY SHOULDN'T OBJECT TO ME DOING A LITTLE INVESTIGATING.
THE DEACON'S INNER SANCTUM SEEMS LIKE A GOOD PLACE TO START.
I'M NOT SURE WHAT I EXPECTED TO FIND.
IF I HAD A LIST OF POSSIBILITIES, THIS WOULD HAVE BEEN NEAR THE BOTTOM.
SHEER LUXURY.
IMELDA MARCOS WOULD FEEL RIGHT AT HOME.

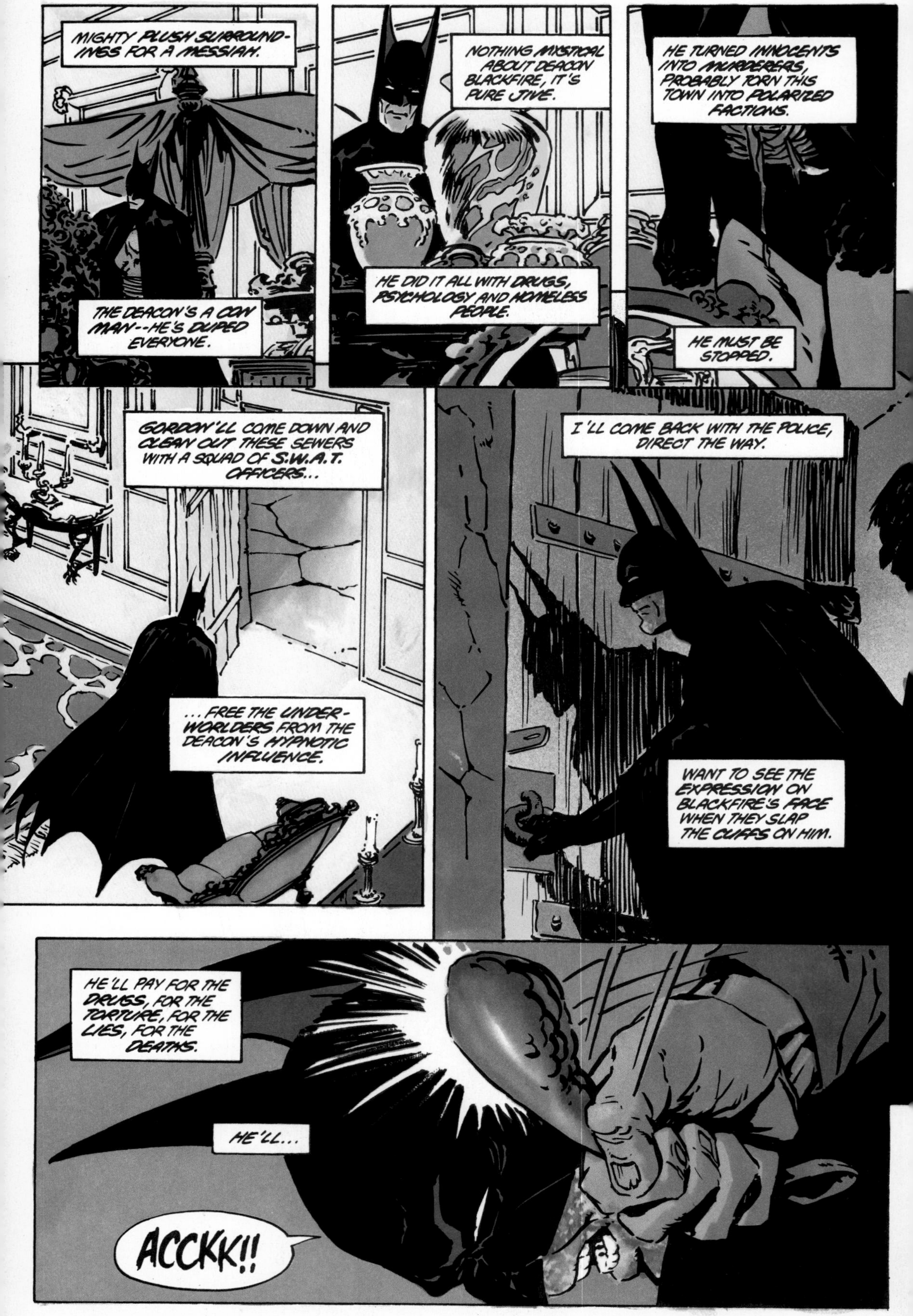
MIGHTY PLUSH SURROUNDINGS FOR A MESSIAH.
THE DEACON'S A CON MAN--HE'S DUPED EVERYONE.
NOTHING MYSTICAL ABOUT DEACON BLACKFIRE, IT'S PURE JIVE.
HE DID IT ALL WITH DRUGS, PSYCHOLOGY AND HOMELESS PEOPLE.
HE TURNED INNOCENTS INTO MURDERERS, PROBABLY TORN THIS TOWN INTO POLARIZED FACTIONS.
HE MUST BE STOPPED.
GORDON'LL COME DOWN AND CLEAN OUT THESE SEWERS WITH A SQUAD OF S.W.A.T. OFFICERS...
...FREE THE UNDERWORLDERS FROM THE DEACON'S HYPNOTIC INFLUENCE.
I'LL COME BACK WITH THE POLICE, DIRECT THE WAY.
WANT TO SEE THE EXPRESSION ON BLACKFIRE'S FACE WHEN THEY SLAP THE CUFFS ON HIM.
HE'LL PAY FOR THE DRUGS, FOR THE TORTURE, FOR THE LIES, FOR THE DEATHS.
HE'LL...
ACCKK!!

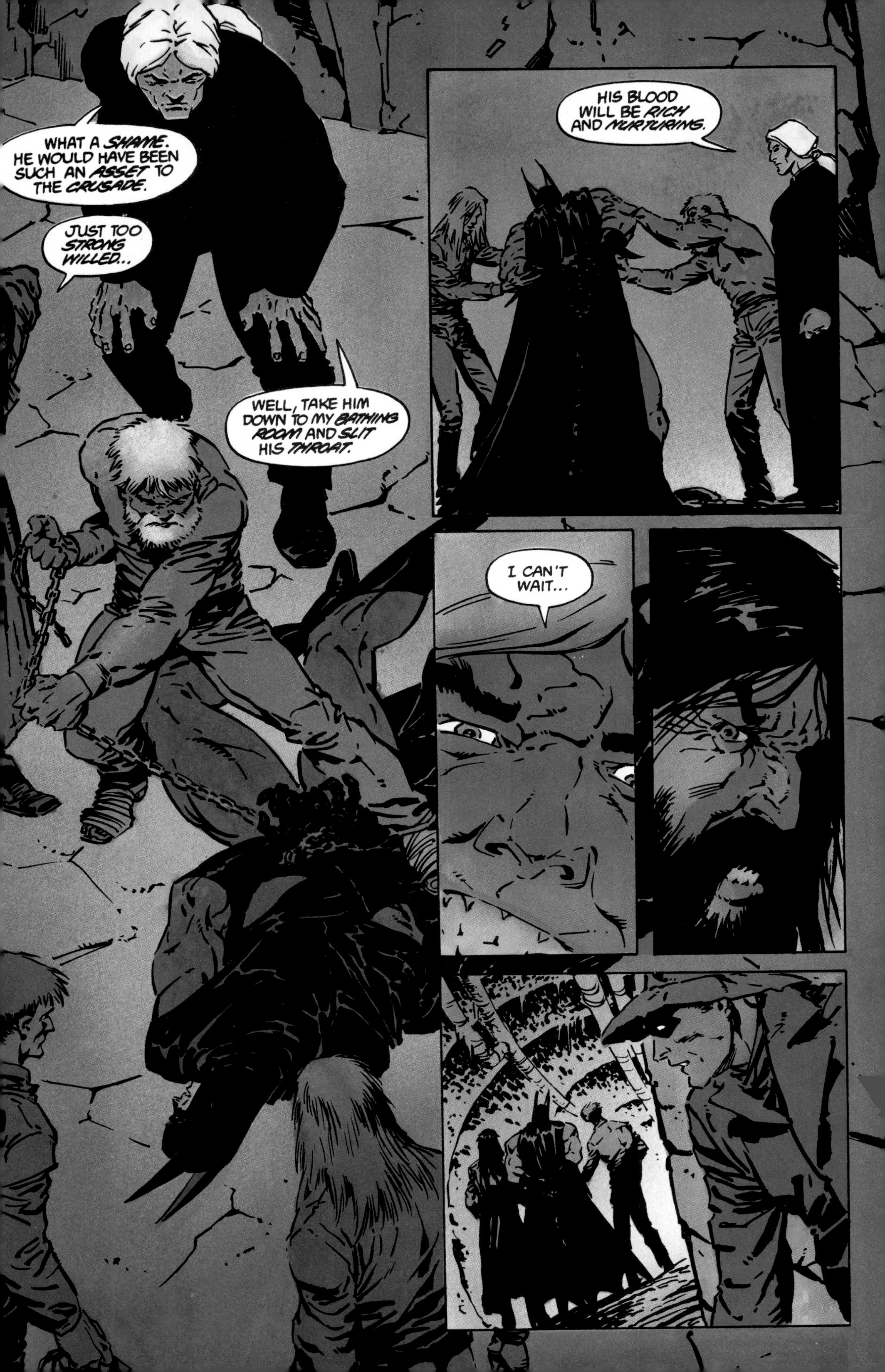
WHAT A SHAME. HE WOULD HAVE BEEN SUCH AN ASSET TO THE CRUSADE.
JUST TOO STRONG WILLED...
WELL, TAKE HIM DOWN TO MY BATHING ROOM AND SLIT HIS THROAT.
HIS BLOOD WILL BE RICH AND NURTURING.
I CAN'T WAIT...

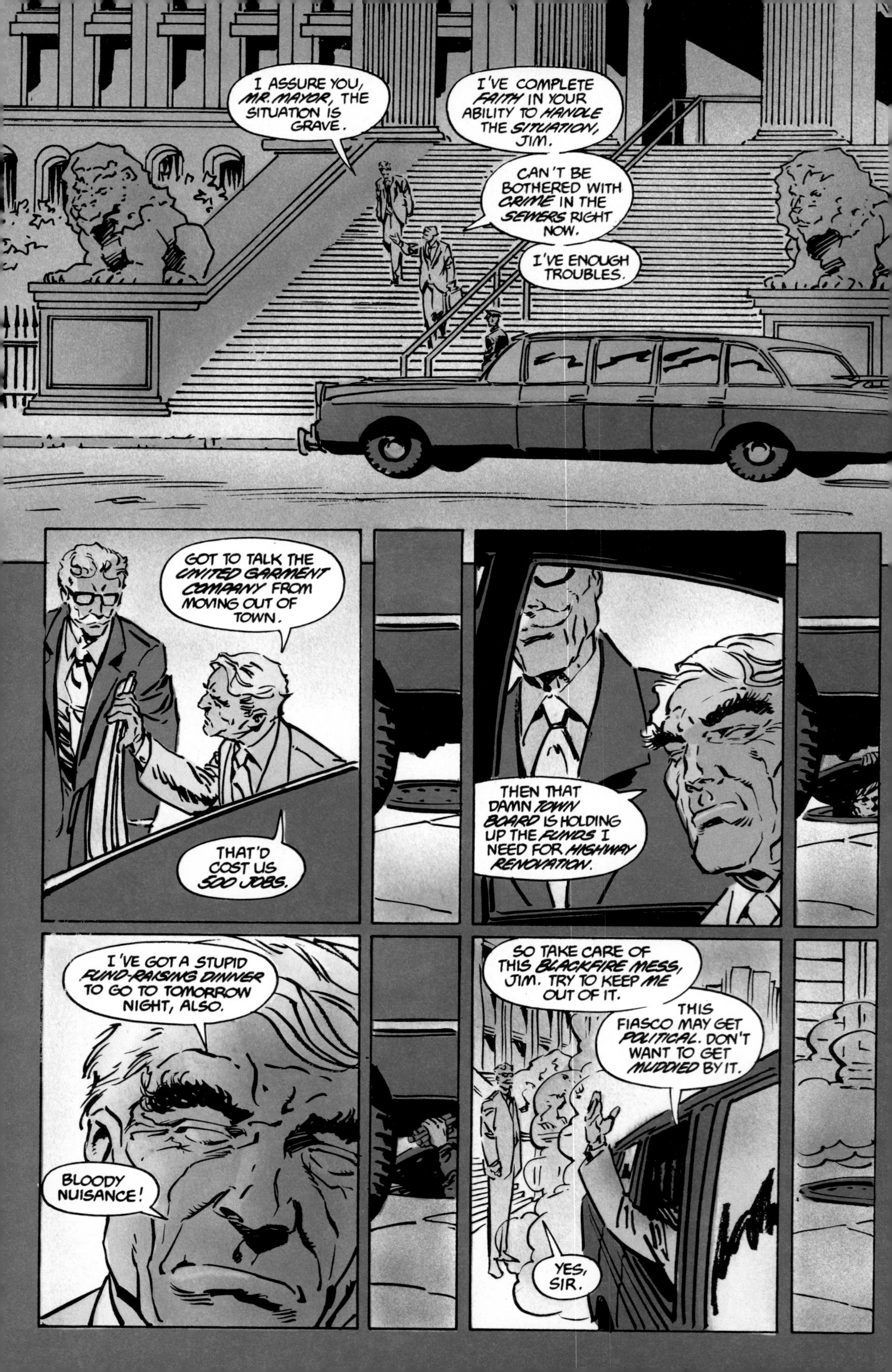
I ASSURE YOU, MR. MAYOR, THE SITUATION IS GRAVE.
I'VE COMPLETE FAITH IN YOUR ABILITY TO HANDLE THE SITUATION, JIM.
CAN'T BE BOTHERED WITH CRIME IN THE SEWERS RIGHT NOW.
I'VE ENOUGH TROUBLES.
GOT TO TALK THE UNITED GARMENT COMPANY FROM MOVING OUT OF TOWN.
THAT'D COST US 500 JOBS.
THEN THAT DAMN TOWN BOARD IS HOLDING UP THE FUNDS I NEED FOR HIGHWAY RENOVATION.
I'VE GOT A STUPID FUND-RAISING DINNER TO GO TO TOMORROW NIGHT, ALSO.
BLOODY NUISANCE!
SO TAKE CARE OF THIS BLACKFIRE MESS, JIM. TRY TO KEEP ME OUT OF IT.
THIS FIASCO MAY GET POLITICAL. DON'T WANT TO GET MUDDIED BY IT.
YES, SIR.

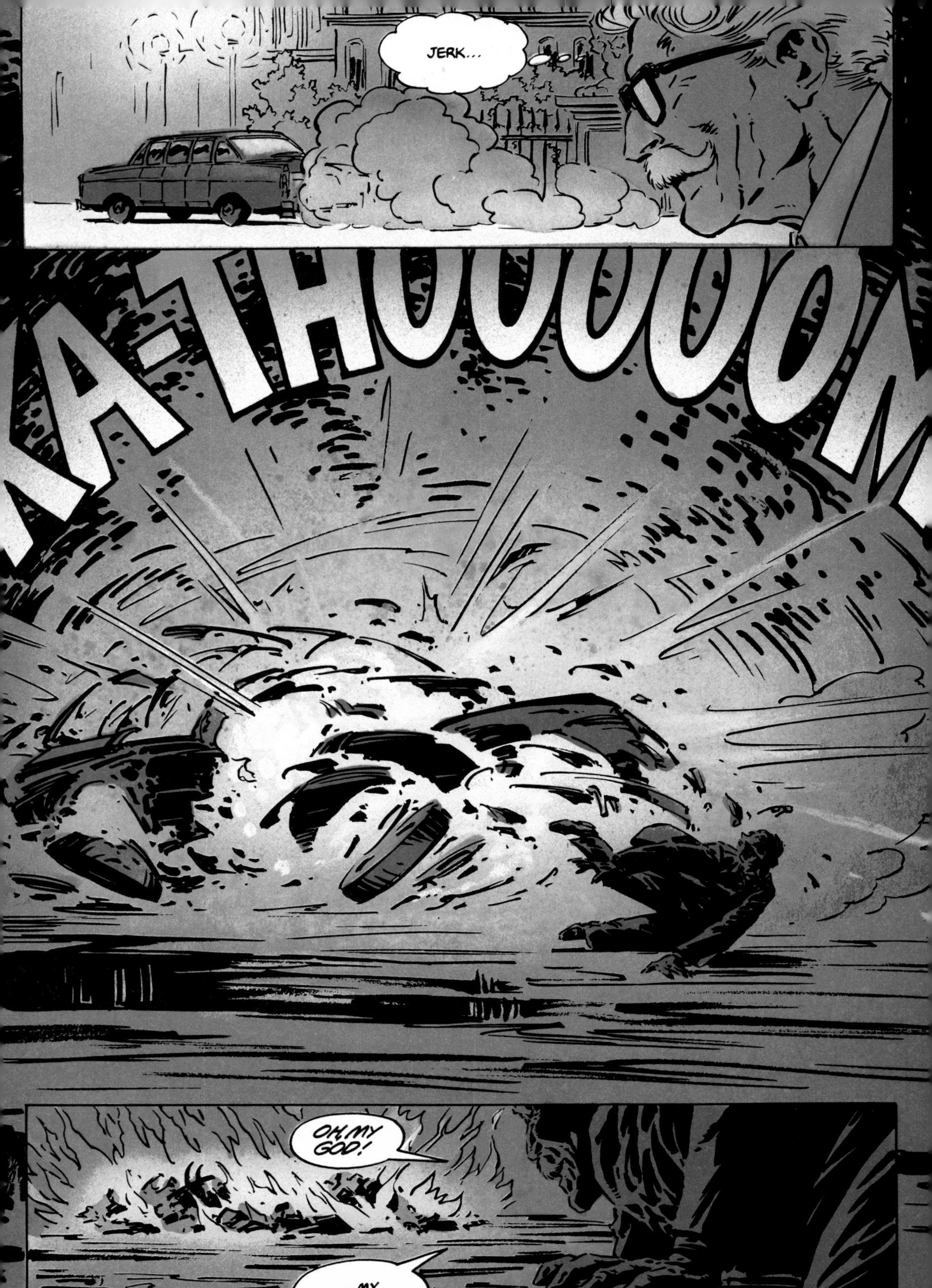
JERK...
KA-THOOOOOM
OH, MY GOD!
...MY GOD...

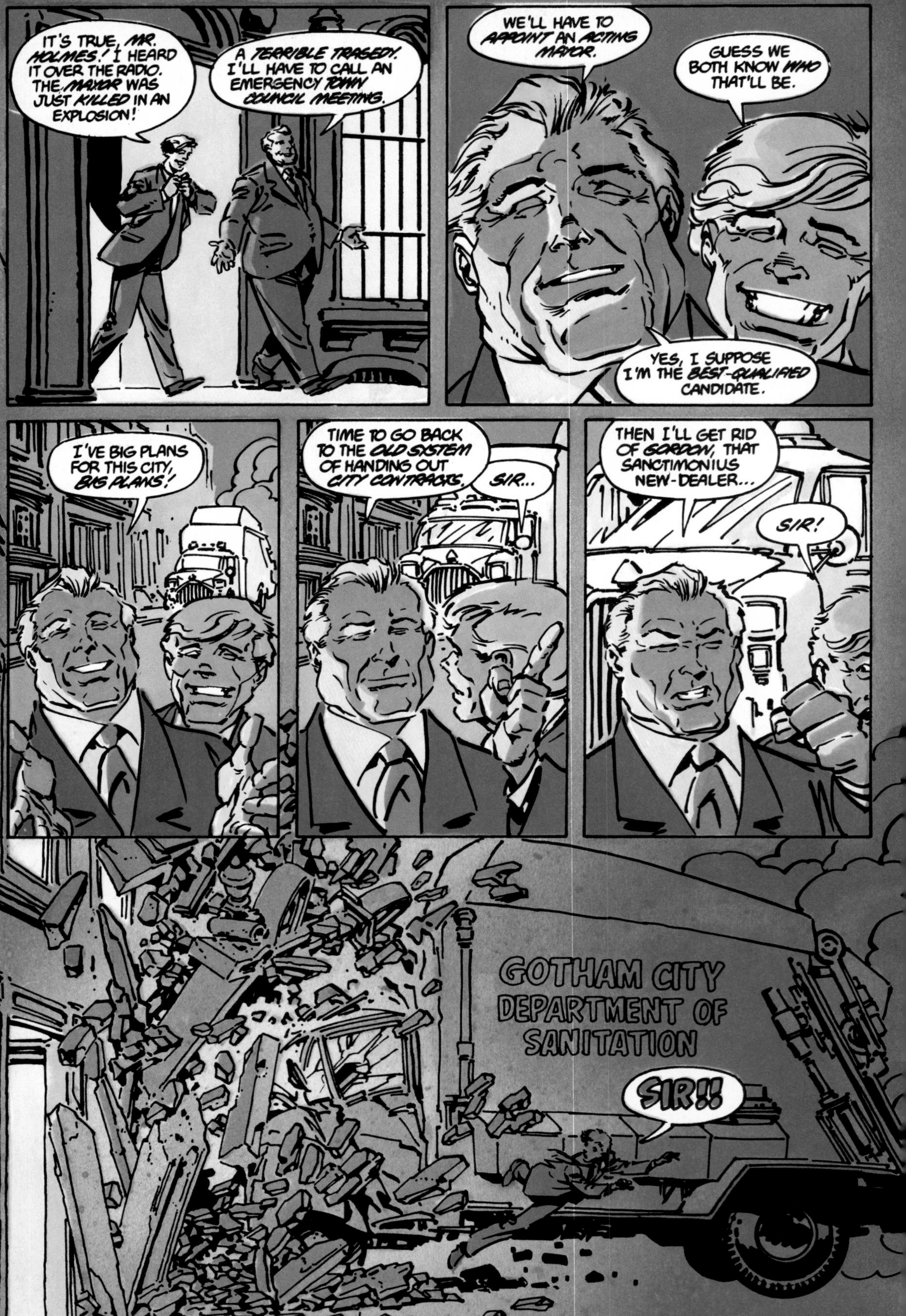
IT'S TRUE, MR. HOLMES! I HEARD IT OVER THE RADIO. THE MAYOR WAS JUST KILLED IN AN EXPLOSION!
A TERRIBLE TRAGEDY. I'LL HAVE TO CALL AN EMERGENCY TOWN COUNCIL MEETING.
WE'LL HAVE TO APPOINT AN ACTING MAYOR.
GUESS WE BOTH KNOW WHO THAT'LL BE.
YES, I SUPPOSE I'M THE BEST-QUALIFIED CANDIDATE.
I'VE BIG PLANS FOR THIS CITY, BIG PLANS!
TIME TO GO BACK TO THE OLD SYSTEM OF HANDING OUT CITY CONTRACTS.
SIR...
THEN I'LL GET RID OF GORDON, THAT SANCTIMONIUS NEW-DEALER...
SIR!
GOTHAM CITY DEPARTMENT OF SANITATION
SIR!!

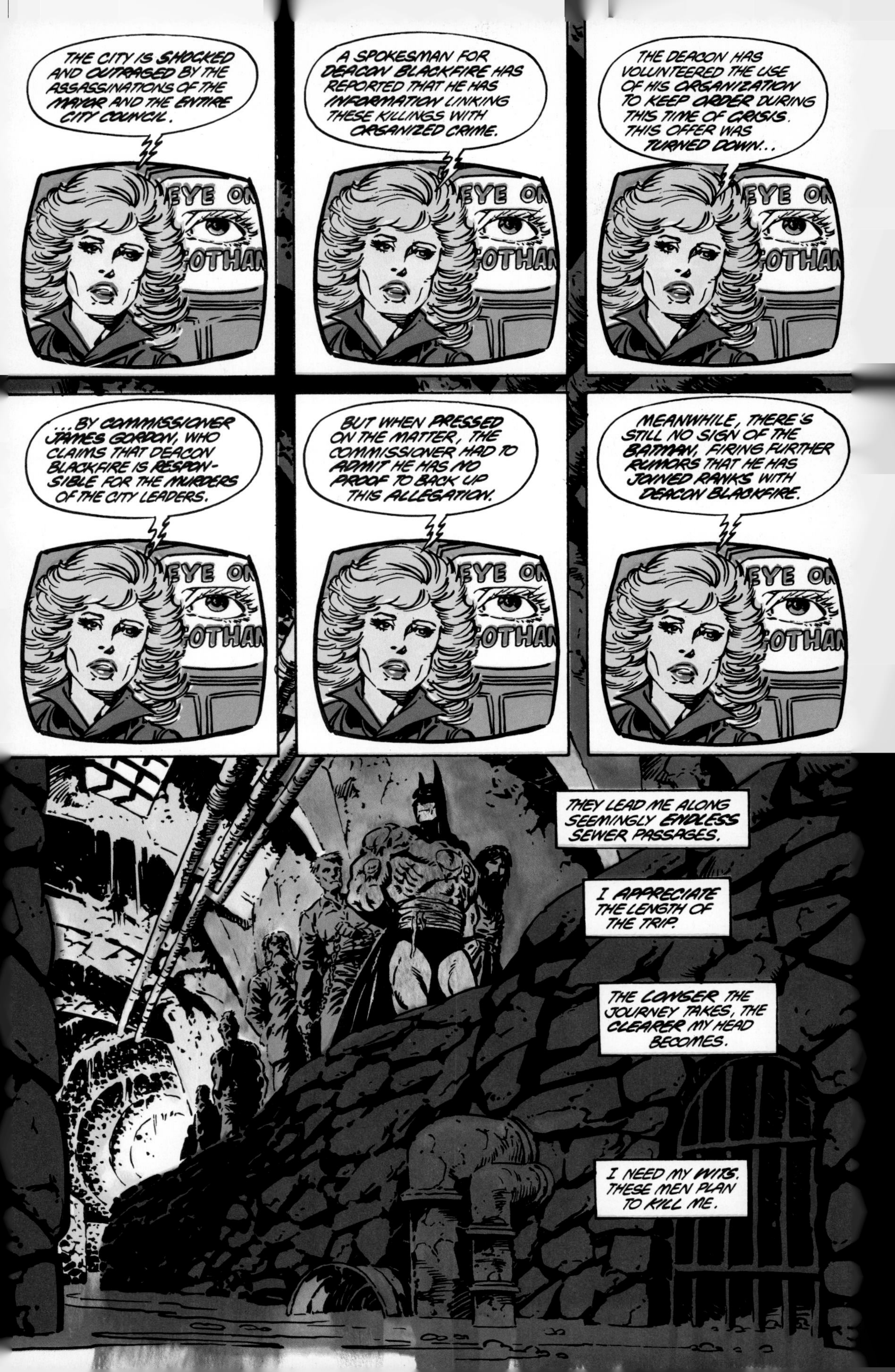

THE CITY IS SHOCKED AND OUTRAGED BY THE ASSASSINATIONS OF THE MAYOR AND THE ENTIRE CITY COUNCIL.
EYE ON GOTHAM
A SPOKESMAN FOR DEACON BLACKFIRE HAS REPORTED THAT HE HAS INFORMATION LINKING THESE KILLINGS WITH ORGANIZED CRIME.
THE DEACON HAS VOLUNTEERED THE USE OF HIS ORGANIZATION TO KEEP ORDER DURING THIS TIME OF CRISIS. THIS OFFER WAS TURNED DOWN...
...BY COMMISSIONER JAMES GORDON, WHO CLAIMS THAT DEACON BLACKFIRE IS RESPONSIBLE FOR THE MURDERS OF THE CITY LEADERS.
BUT WHEN PRESSED ON THE MATTER, THE COMMISSIONER HAD TO ADMIT HE HAS NO PROOF TO BACK UP THIS ALLEGATION.
MEANWHILE, THERE'S STILL NO SIGN OF THE BATMAN, FIRING FURTHER RUMORS THAT HE HAS JOINED RANKS WITH DEACON BLACKFIRE.
THEY LEAD ME ALONG SEEMINGLY ENDLESS SEWER PASSAGES.
I APPRECIATE THE LENGTH OF THE TRIP.
THE LONGER THE JOURNEY TAKES, THE CLEARER MY HEAD BECOMES.
I NEED MY WITS. THESE MEN PLAN TO KILL ME.

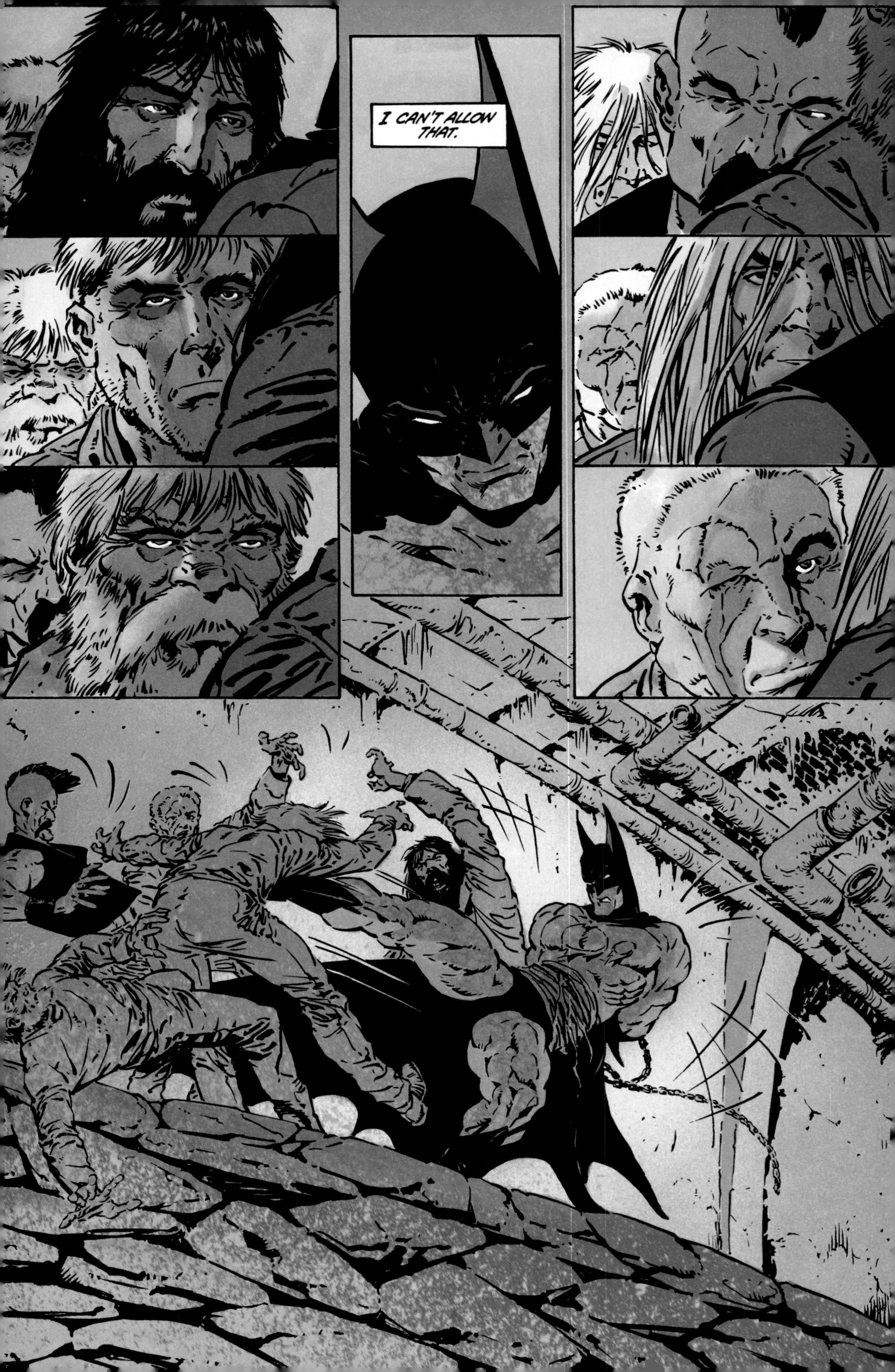
I CAN'T ALLOW THAT.

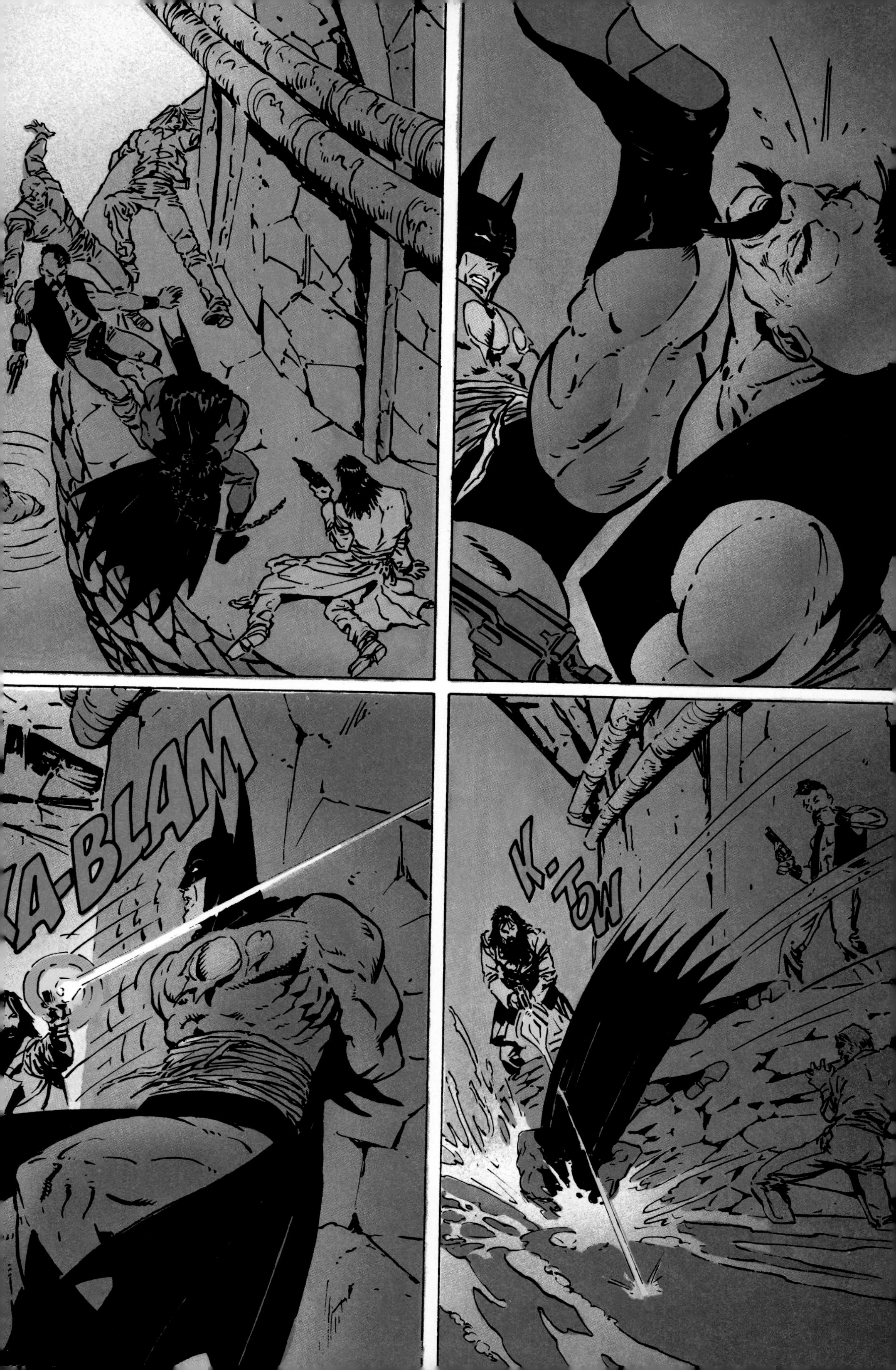
KA-BLAM
K-TOW

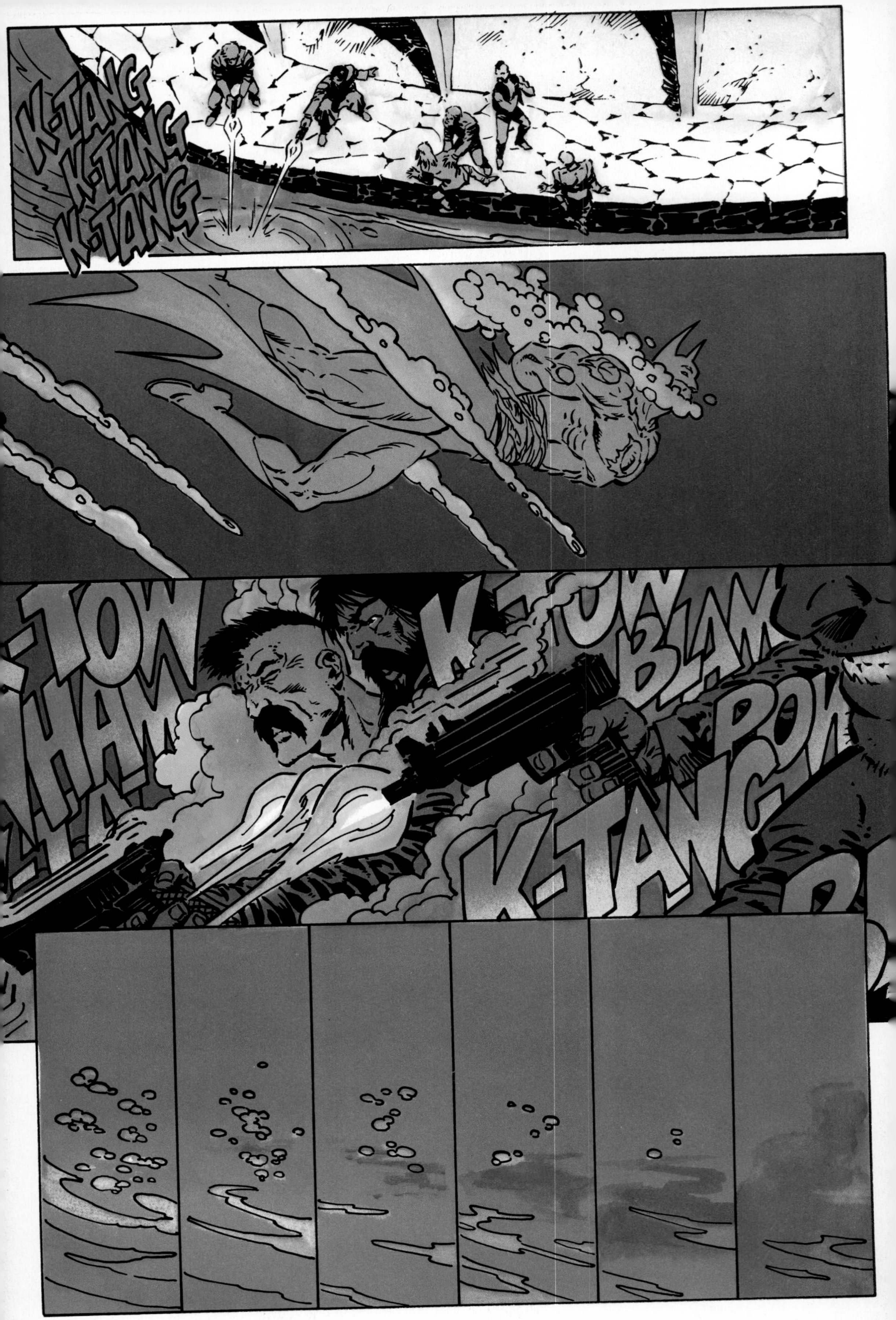
K-TANG
K-TANG
K-TANG
BLAM
POK
K-TANG

DID WE GET HIM?

MUST HAVE.

WHERE'S THE *BODY*?

CURRENT MUST HAVE CARRIED IT AWAY.

THE *BOSS* WANTED US TO TAKE HIM TO THE *BATHING ROOM*.

SO?

HE'S GOING TO BE *MAD* WHEN HE FINDS OUT WHAT HAPPENED.

BIG DEAL!

TO *HELL* WITH THAT *CRAZY BASTARD*. I'LL HANDLE IT.

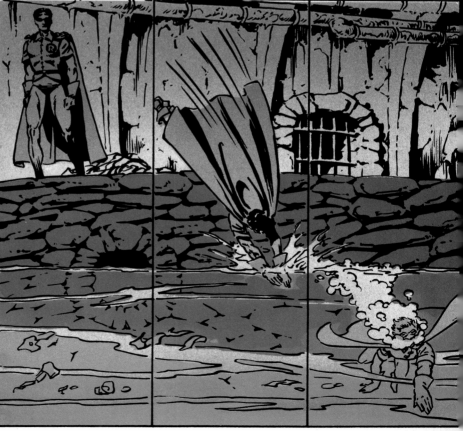

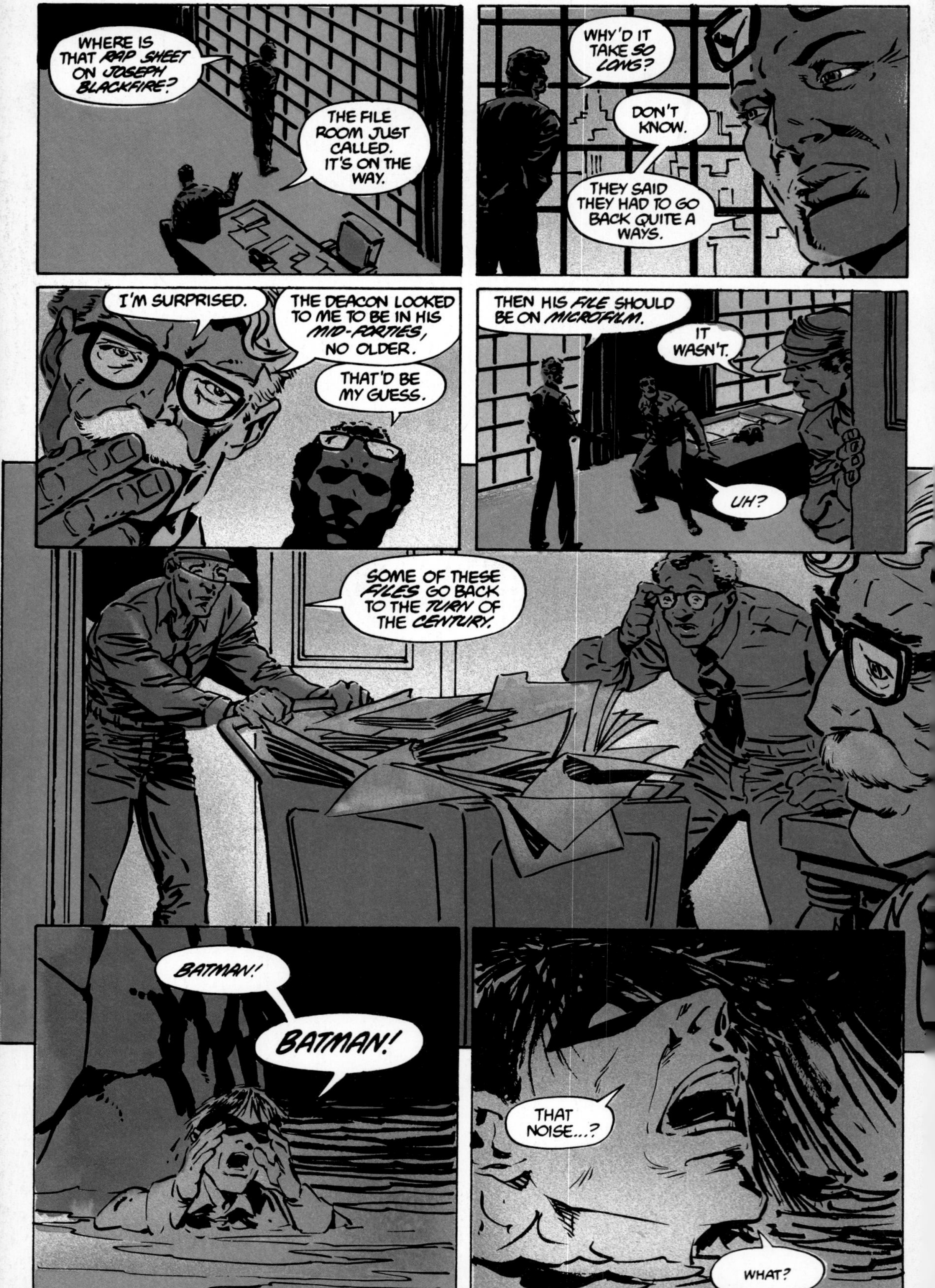
WHERE IS THAT RAP SHEET ON JOSEPH BLACKFIRE?
THE FILE ROOM JUST CALLED. IT'S ON THE WAY.
WHY'D IT TAKE SO LONG?
DON'T KNOW.
THEY SAID THEY HAD TO GO BACK QUITE A WAYS.
I'M SURPRISED.
THE DEACON LOOKED TO ME TO BE IN HIS MID-FORTIES, NO OLDER.
THAT'D BE MY GUESS.
THEN HIS FILE SHOULD BE ON MICROFILM.
IT WASN'T.
UH?
SOME OF THESE FILES GO BACK TO THE TURN OF THE CENTURY.
BATMAN!
BATMAN!
THAT NOISE...?
WHAT?

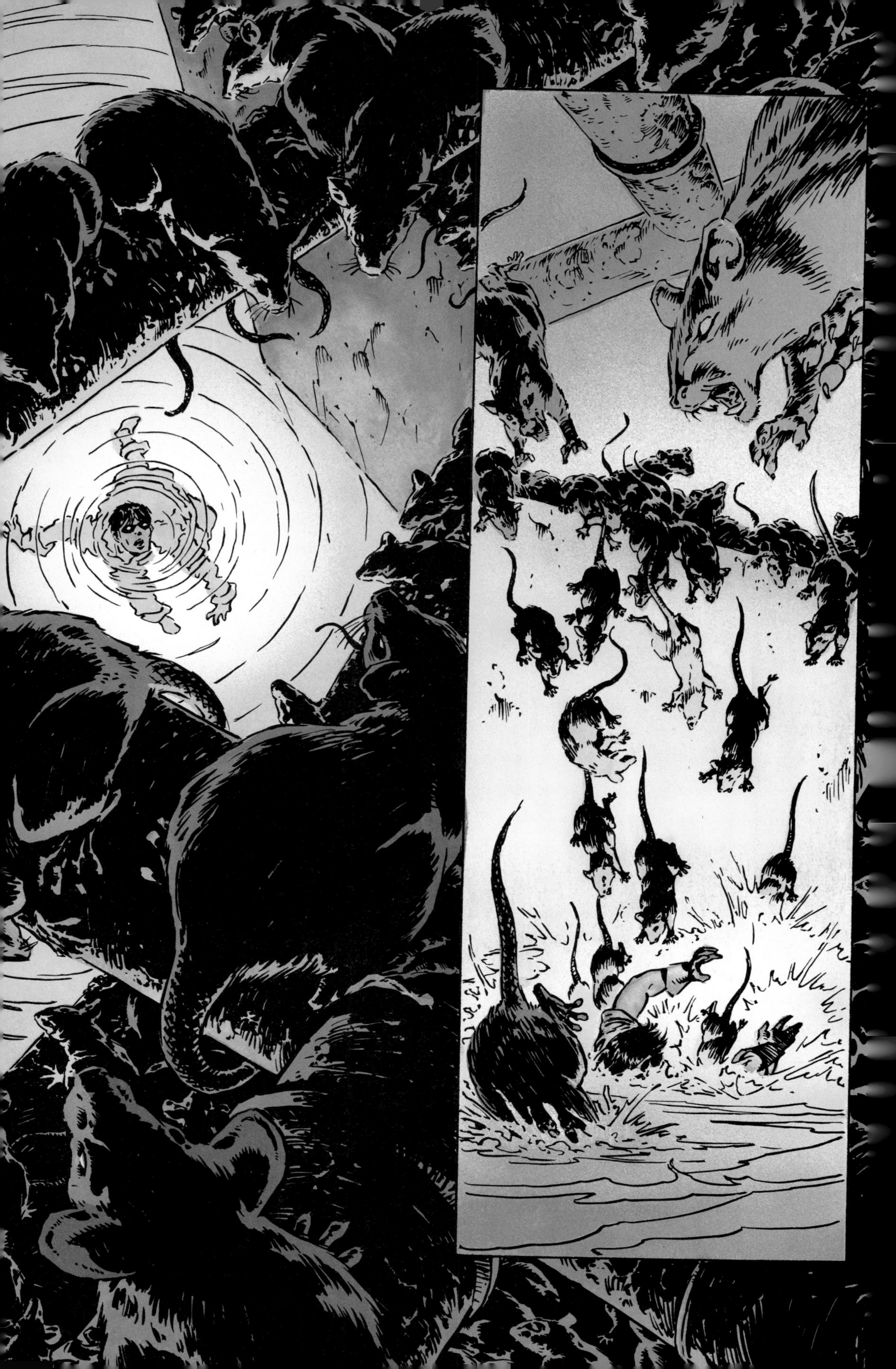

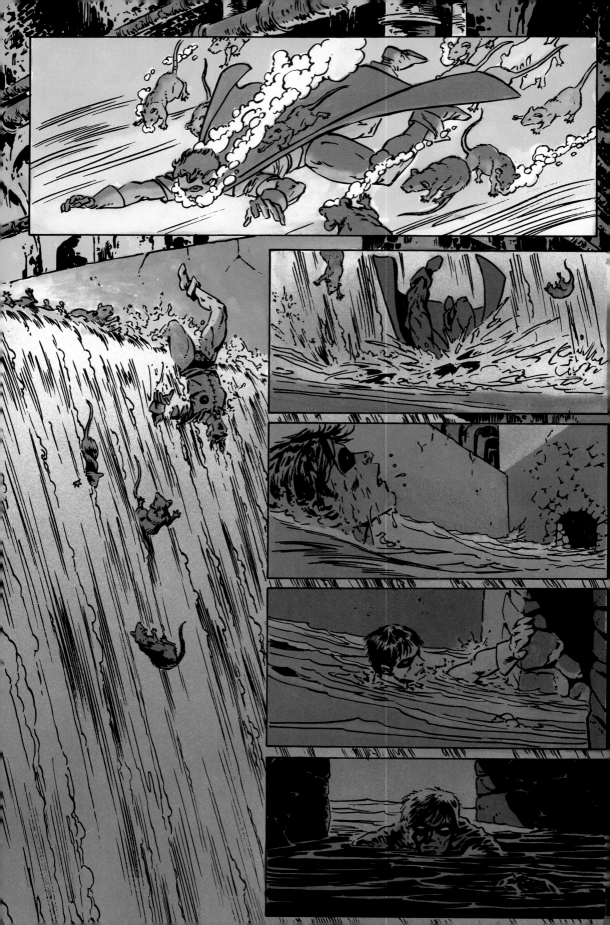

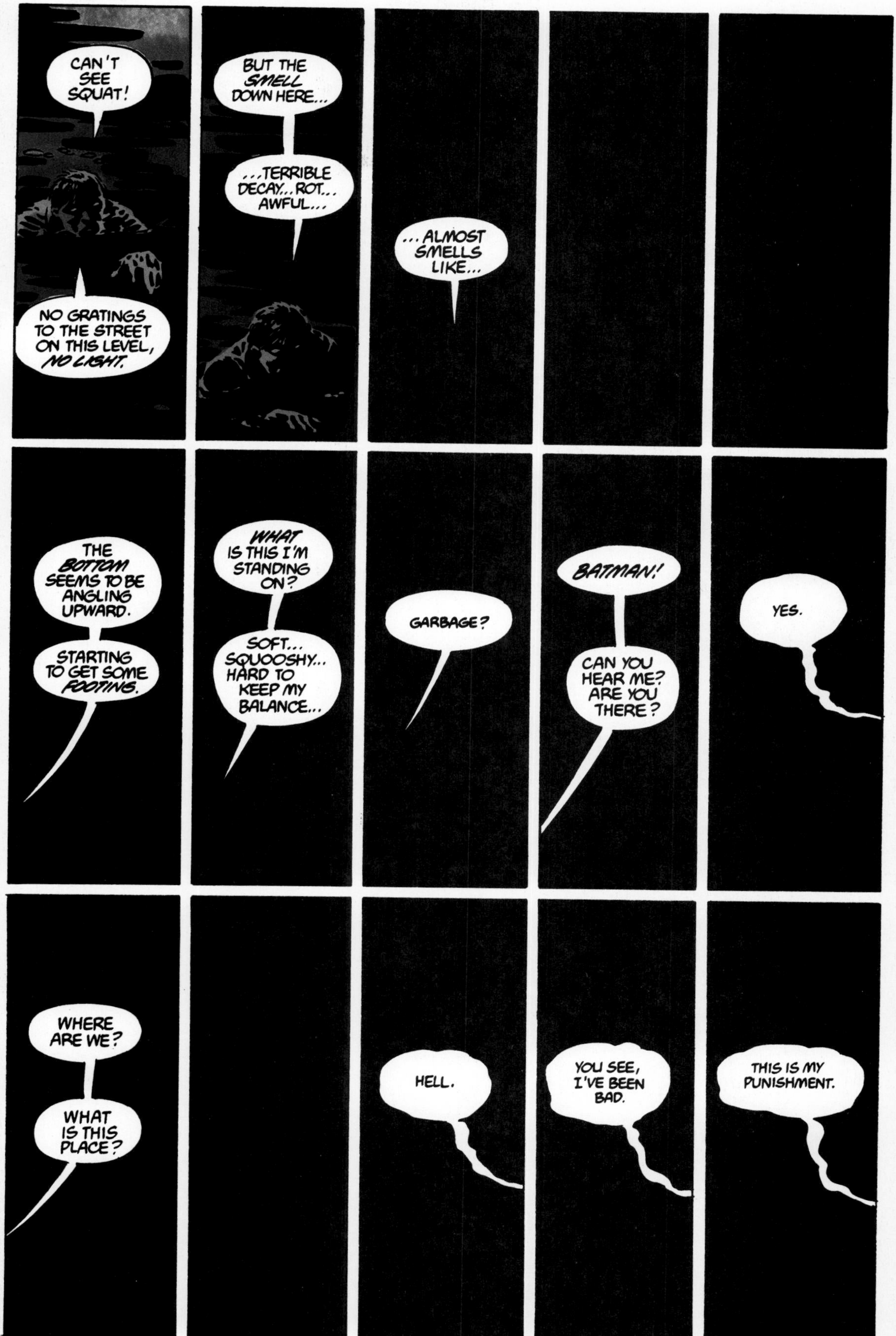

CAN'T SEE SQUAT!
NO GRATINGS TO THE STREET ON THIS LEVEL, NO LIGHT.
BUT THE SMELL DOWN HERE...
...TERRIBLE DECAY...ROT... AWFUL...
...ALMOST SMELLS LIKE...
THE BOTTOM SEEMS TO BE ANGLING UPWARD.
STARTING TO GET SOME FOOTING.
WHAT IS THIS I'M STANDING ON?
SOFT... SQUOOSHY... HARD TO KEEP MY BALANCE...
GARBAGE?
BATMAN!
CAN YOU HEAR ME? ARE YOU THERE?
YES.
WHERE ARE WE?
WHAT IS THIS PLACE?
HELL.
YOU SEE, I'VE BEEN BAD.
THIS IS MY PUNISHMENT.

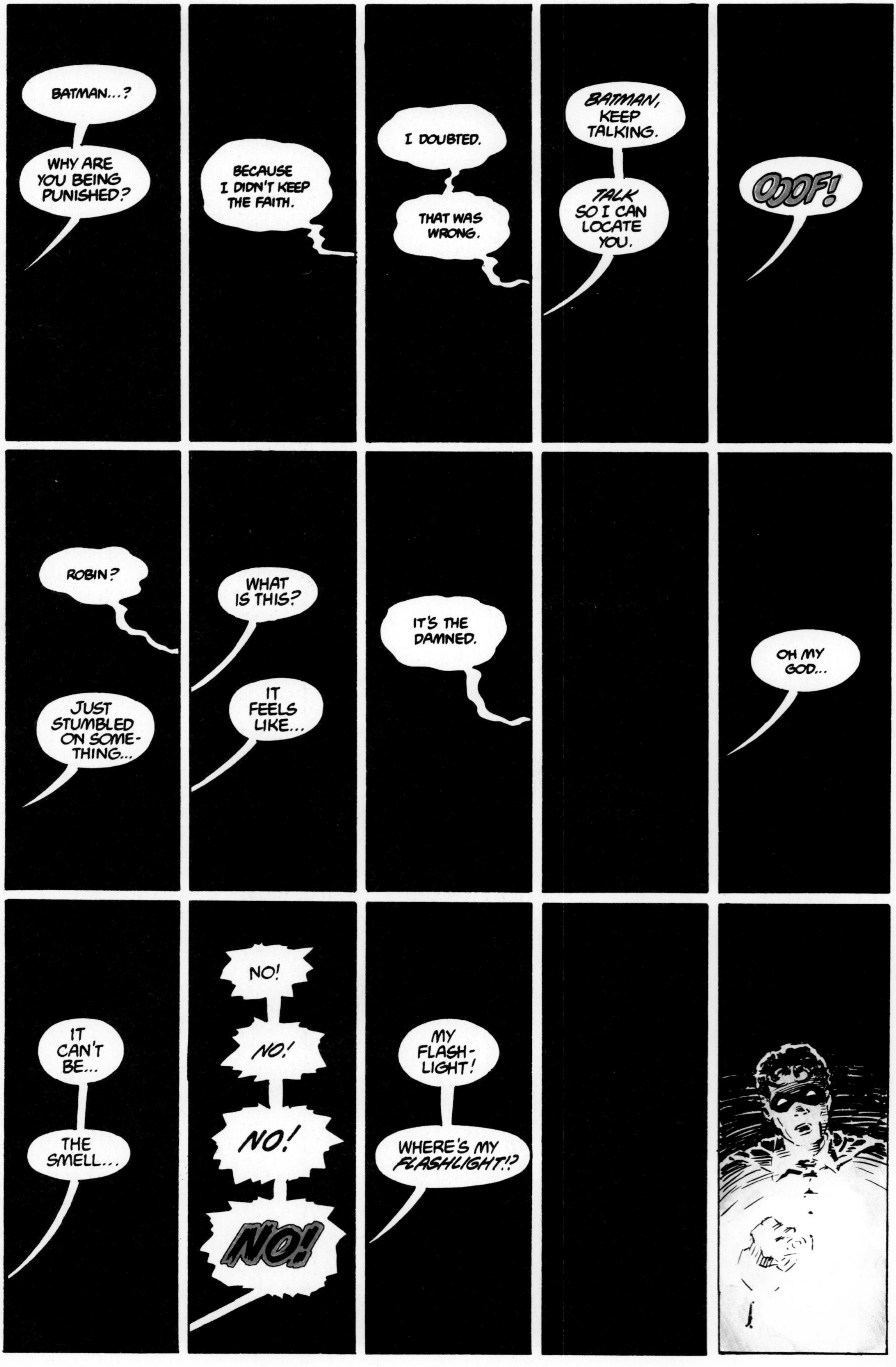
BATMAN...?
WHY ARE YOU BEING PUNISHED?
BECAUSE I DIDN'T KEEP THE FAITH.
I DOUBTED.
THAT WAS WRONG.
BATMAN, KEEP TALKING.
TALK SO I CAN LOCATE YOU.
OOOF!
ROBIN?
JUST STUMBLED ON SOME-THING...
WHAT IS THIS?
IT FEELS LIKE...
IT'S THE DAMNED.
OH MY GOD...
IT CAN'T BE...
THE SMELL...
NO!
NO!
NO!
NO!
MY FLASH-LIGHT!
WHERE'S MY FLASHLIGHT!?

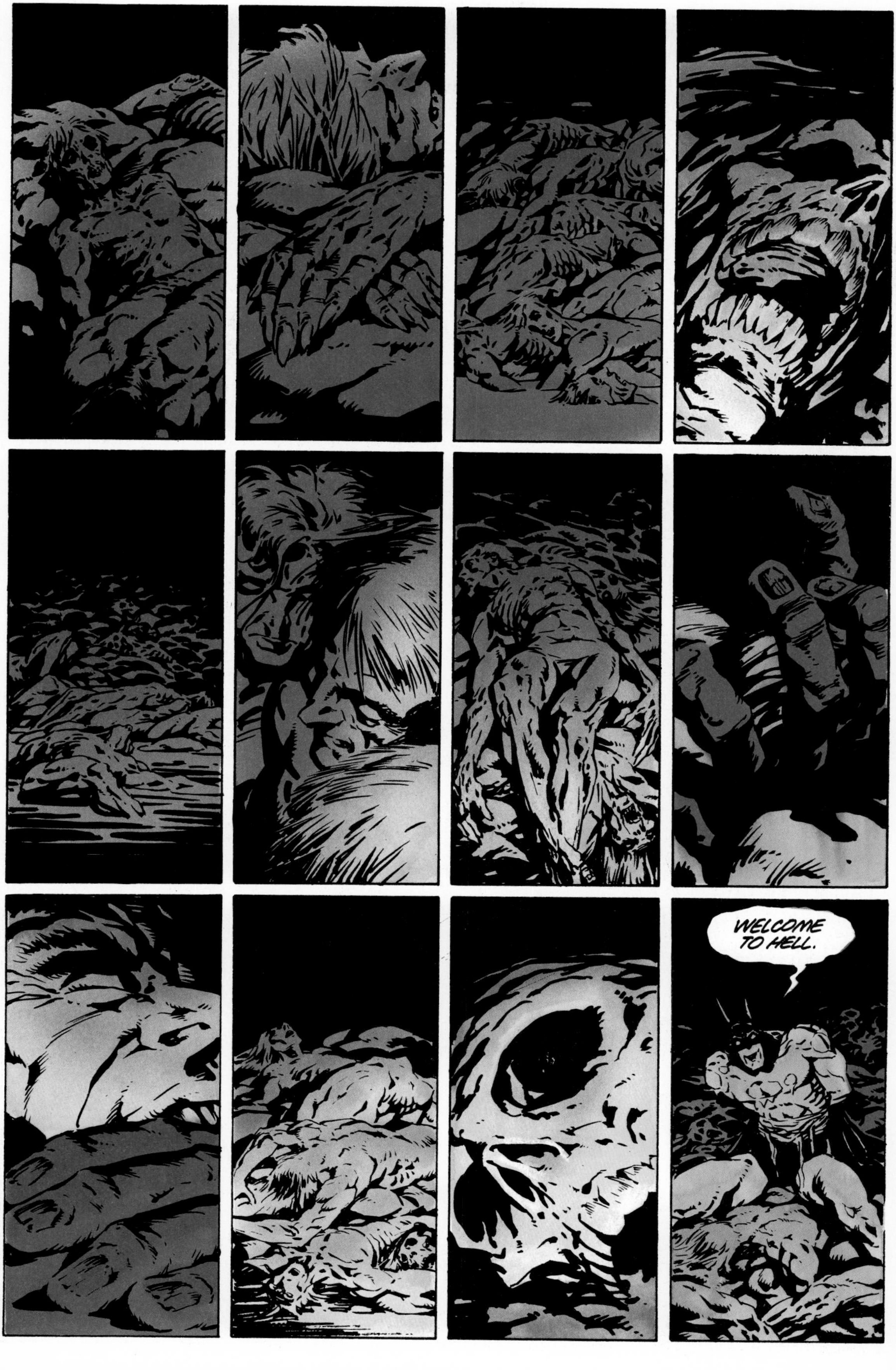
WELCOME TO HELL.

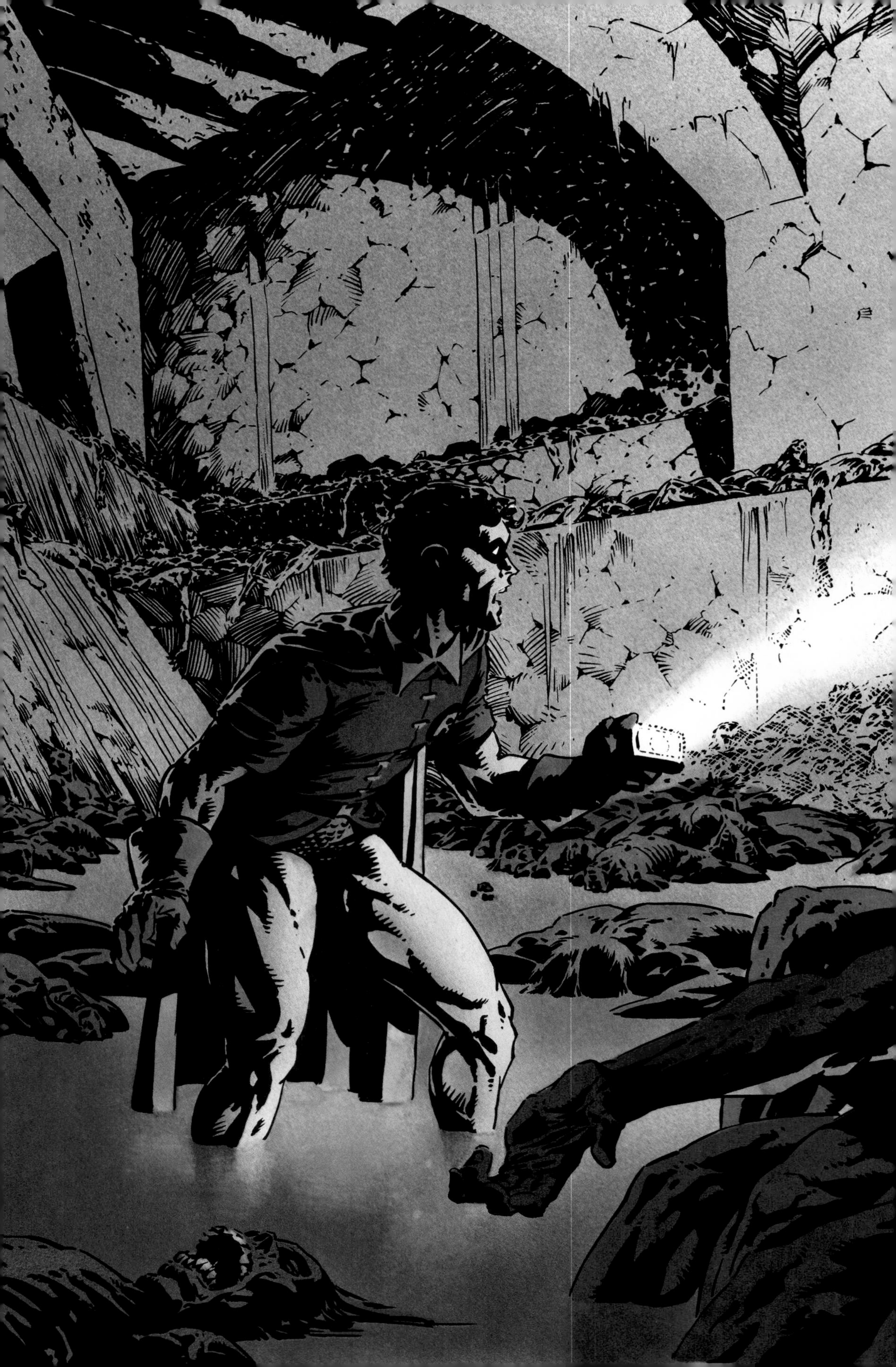

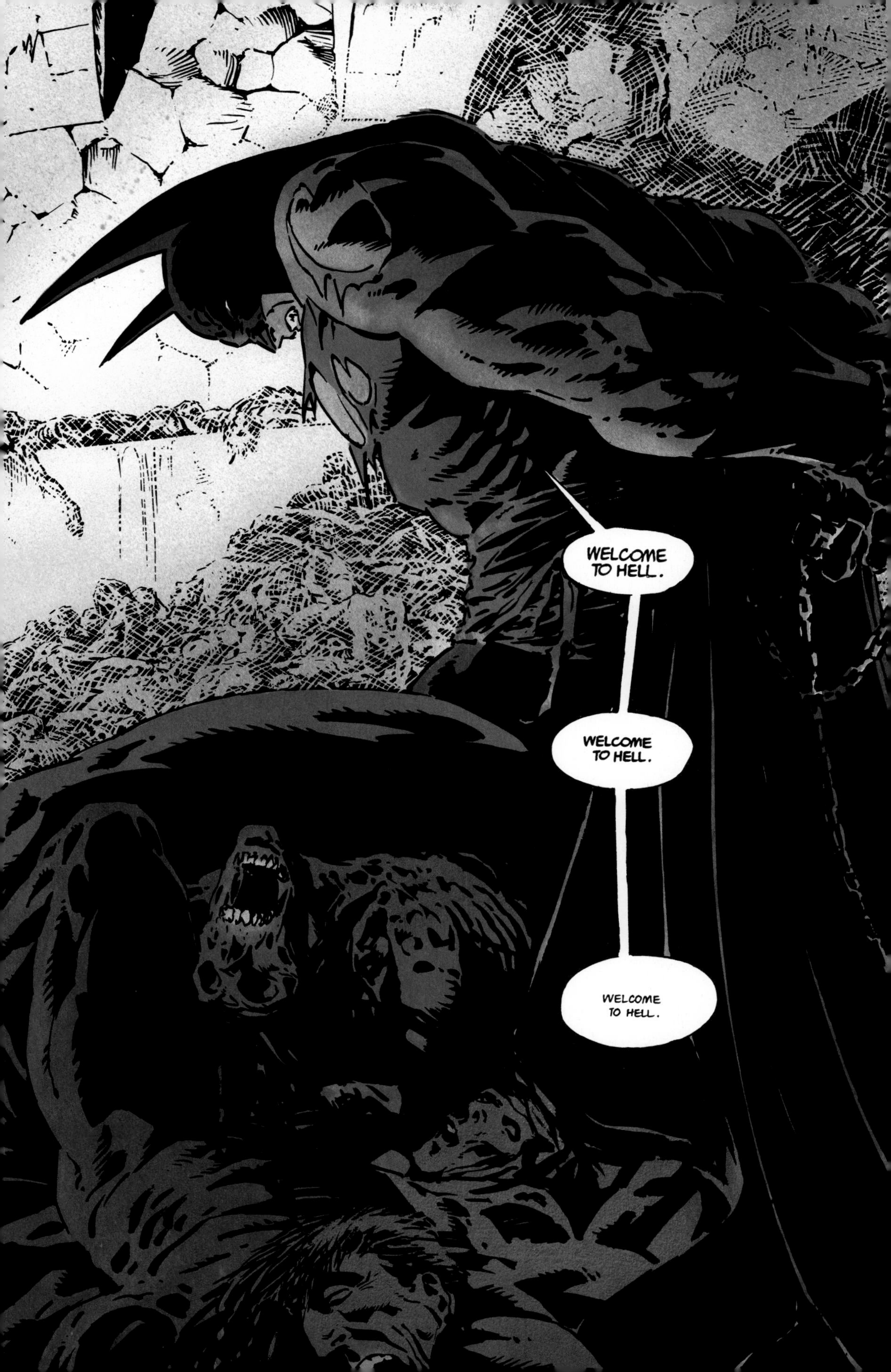
WELCOME TO HELL.
WELCOME TO HELL.
WELCOME TO HELL.

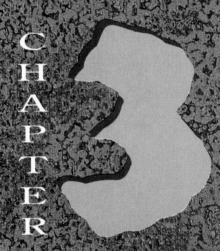

CHAPTER 3

ESCAPE

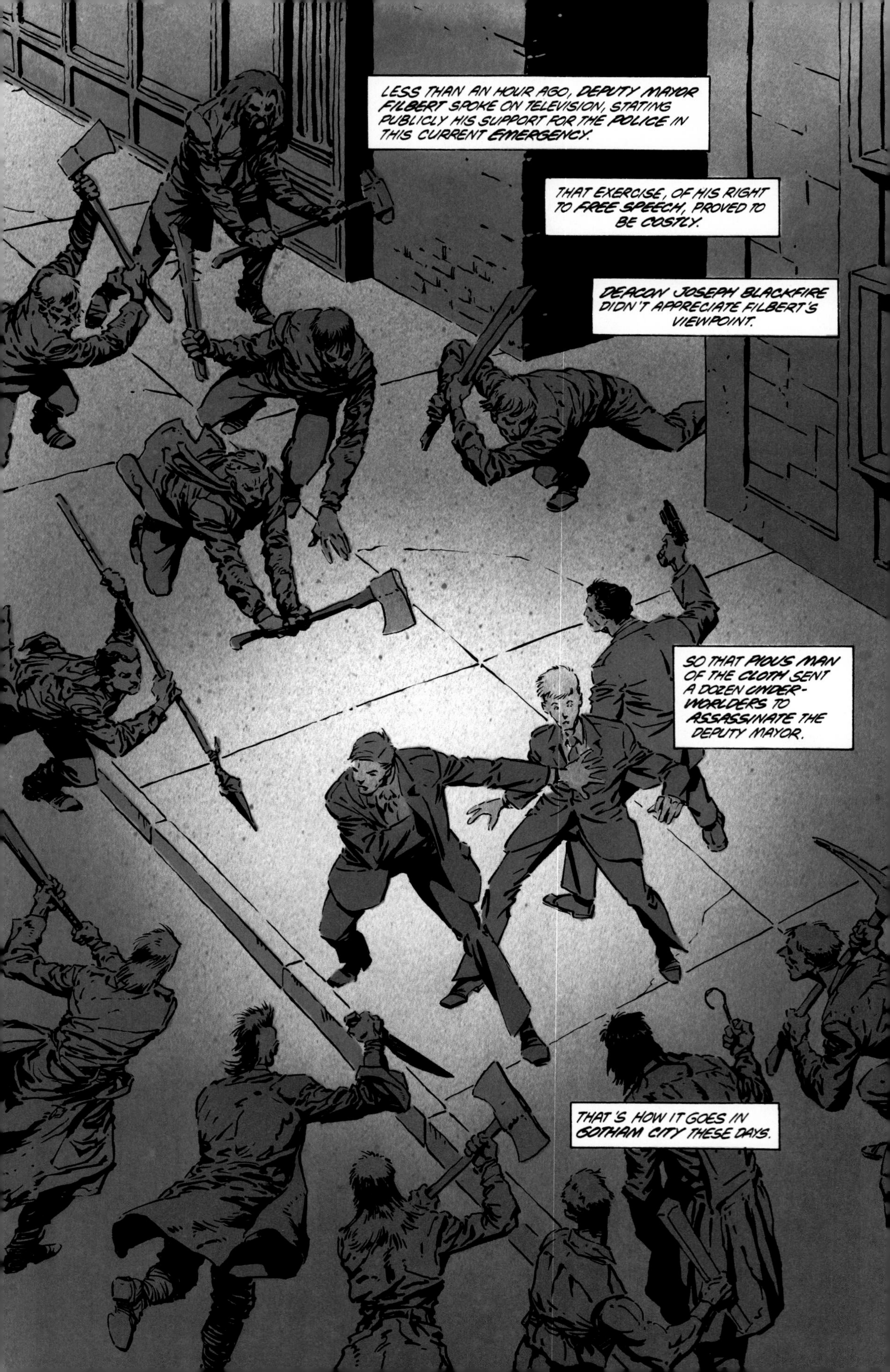
LESS THAN AN HOUR AGO, DEPUTY MAYOR FILBERT SPOKE ON TELEVISION, STATING PUBLICLY HIS SUPPORT FOR THE POLICE IN THIS CURRENT EMERGENCY.
THAT EXERCISE, OF HIS RIGHT TO FREE SPEECH, PROVED TO BE COSTLY.
DEACON JOSEPH BLACKFIRE DIDN'T APPRECIATE FILBERT'S VIEWPOINT.
SO THAT PIOUS MAN OF THE CLOTH SENT A DOZEN UNDER-WORLDERS TO ASSASSINATE THE DEPUTY MAYOR.
THAT'S HOW IT GOES IN GOTHAM CITY THESE DAYS.

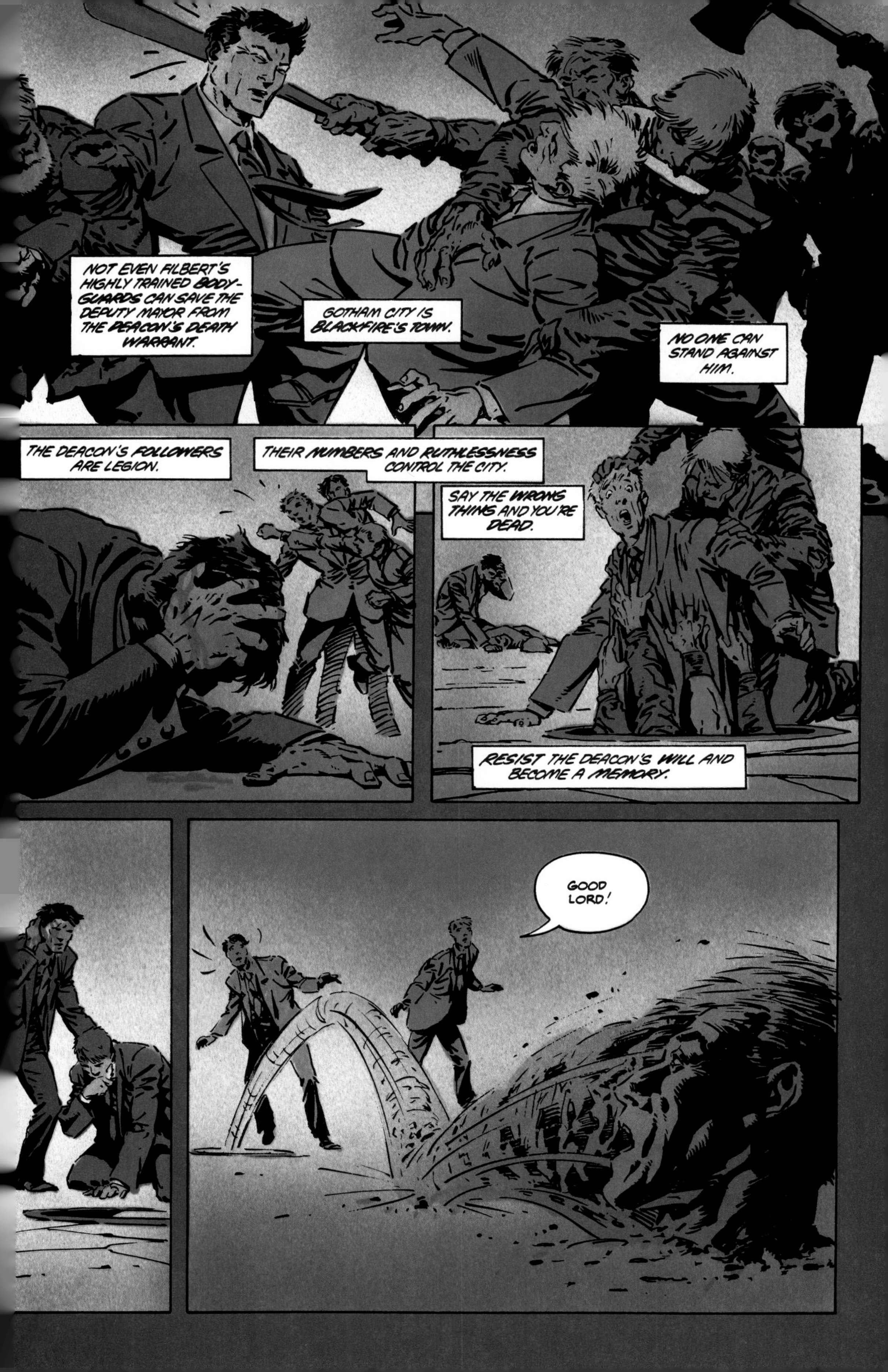

NOT EVEN FILBERT'S HIGHLY TRAINED BODY-GUARDS CAN SAVE THE DEPUTY MAYOR FROM THE DEACON'S DEATH WARRANT.
GOTHAM CITY IS BLACKFIRE'S TOWN.
NO ONE CAN STAND AGAINST HIM.
THE DEACON'S FOLLOWERS ARE LEGION.
THEIR NUMBERS AND RUTHLESSNESS CONTROL THE CITY.
SAY THE WRONG THING AND YOU'RE DEAD.
RESIST THE DEACON'S WILL AND BECOME A MEMORY.
GOOD LORD!

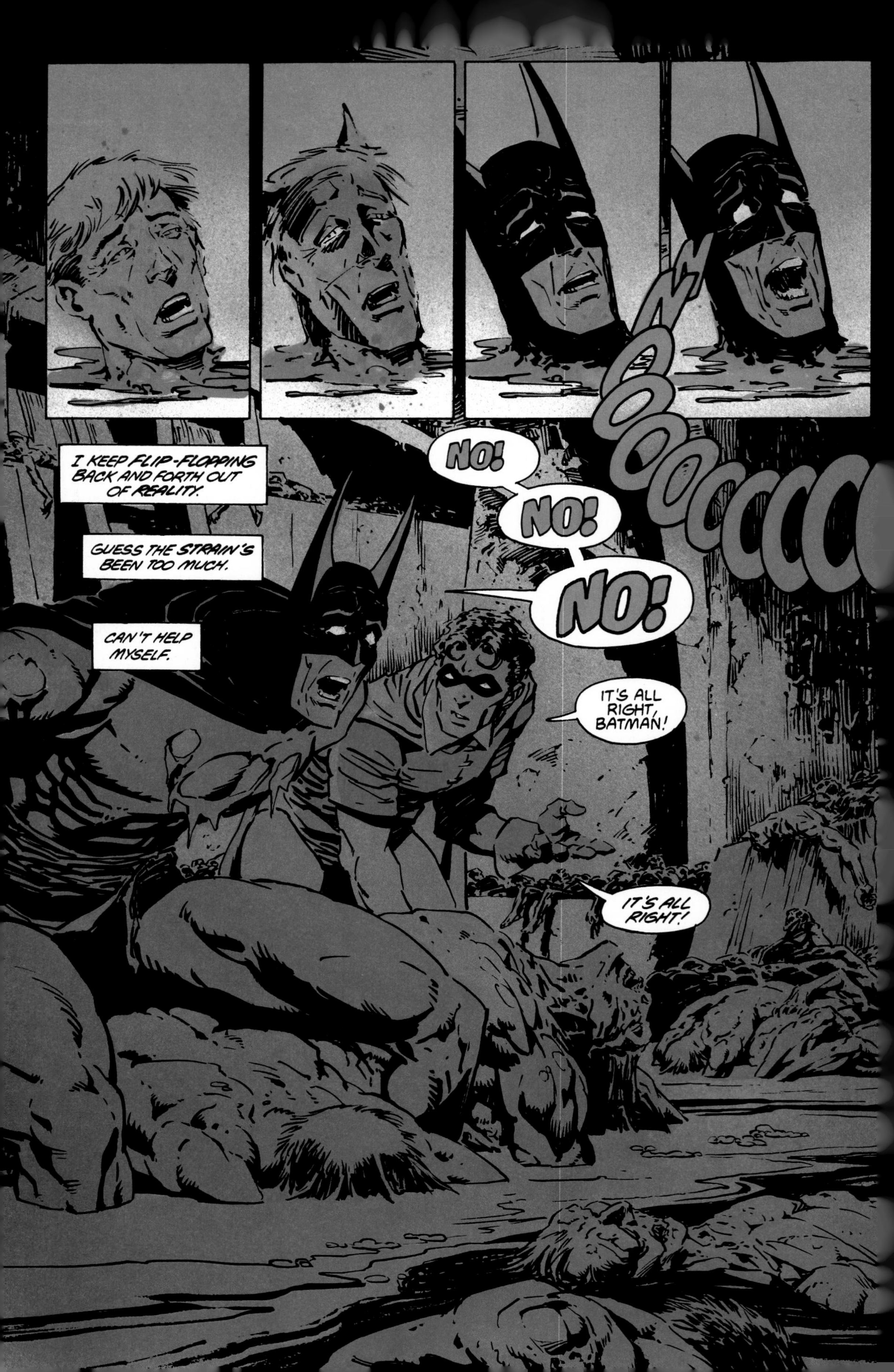

NOOOOOCCCCC
I KEEP FLIP-FLOPPING BACK AND FORTH OUT OF REALITY.
GUESS THE STRAIN'S BEEN TOO MUCH.
CAN'T HELP MYSELF.
NO!
NO!
NO!
IT'S ALL RIGHT, BATMAN!
IT'S ALL RIGHT!

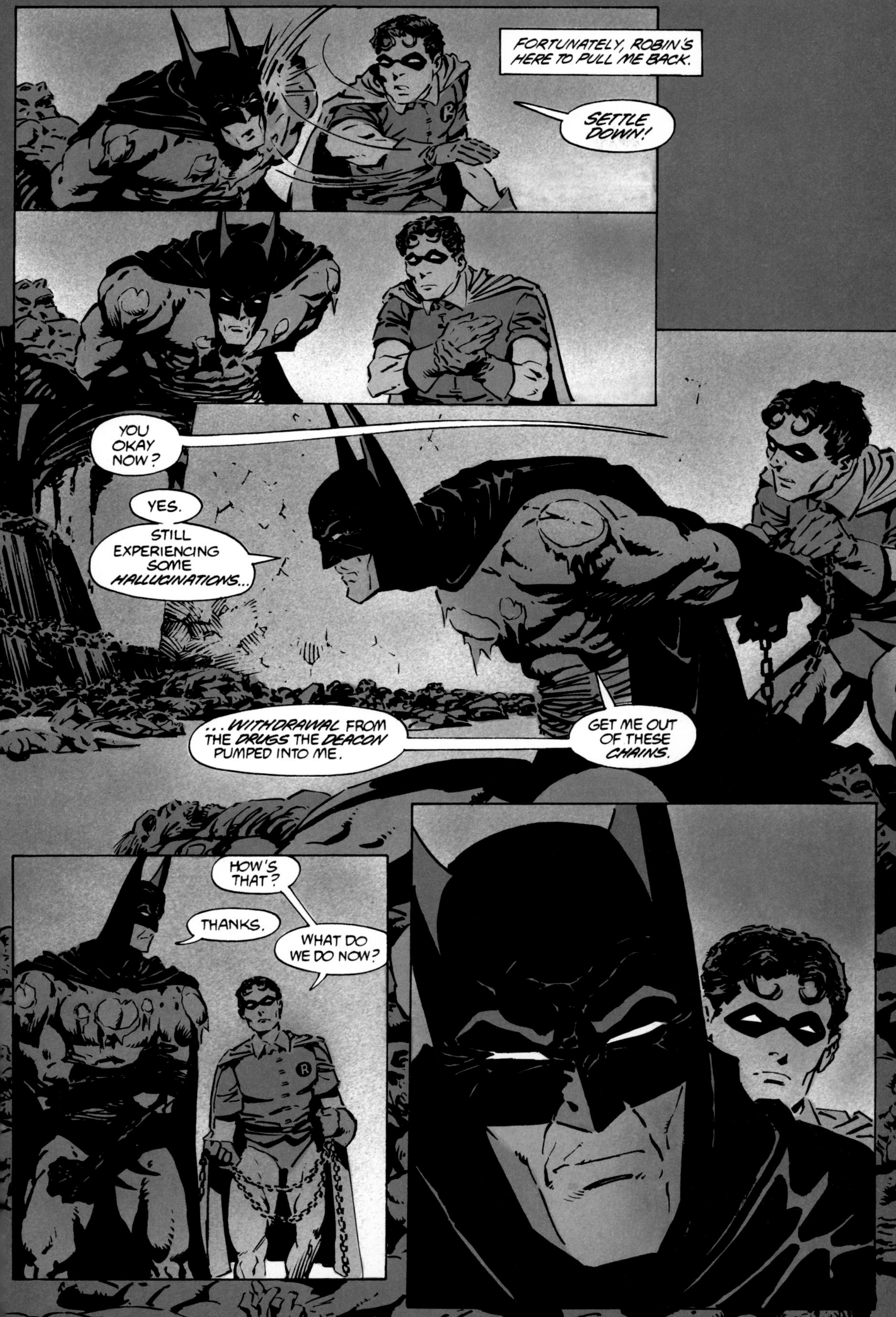
FORTUNATELY, ROBIN'S HERE TO PULL ME BACK.
SETTLE DOWN!
YOU OKAY NOW?
YES.
STILL EXPERIENCING SOME HALLUCINATIONS...
...WITHDRAWAL FROM THE DRUGS THE DEACON PUMPED INTO ME.
GET ME OUT OF THESE CHAINS.
HOW'S THAT?
THANKS.
WHAT DO WE DO NOW?

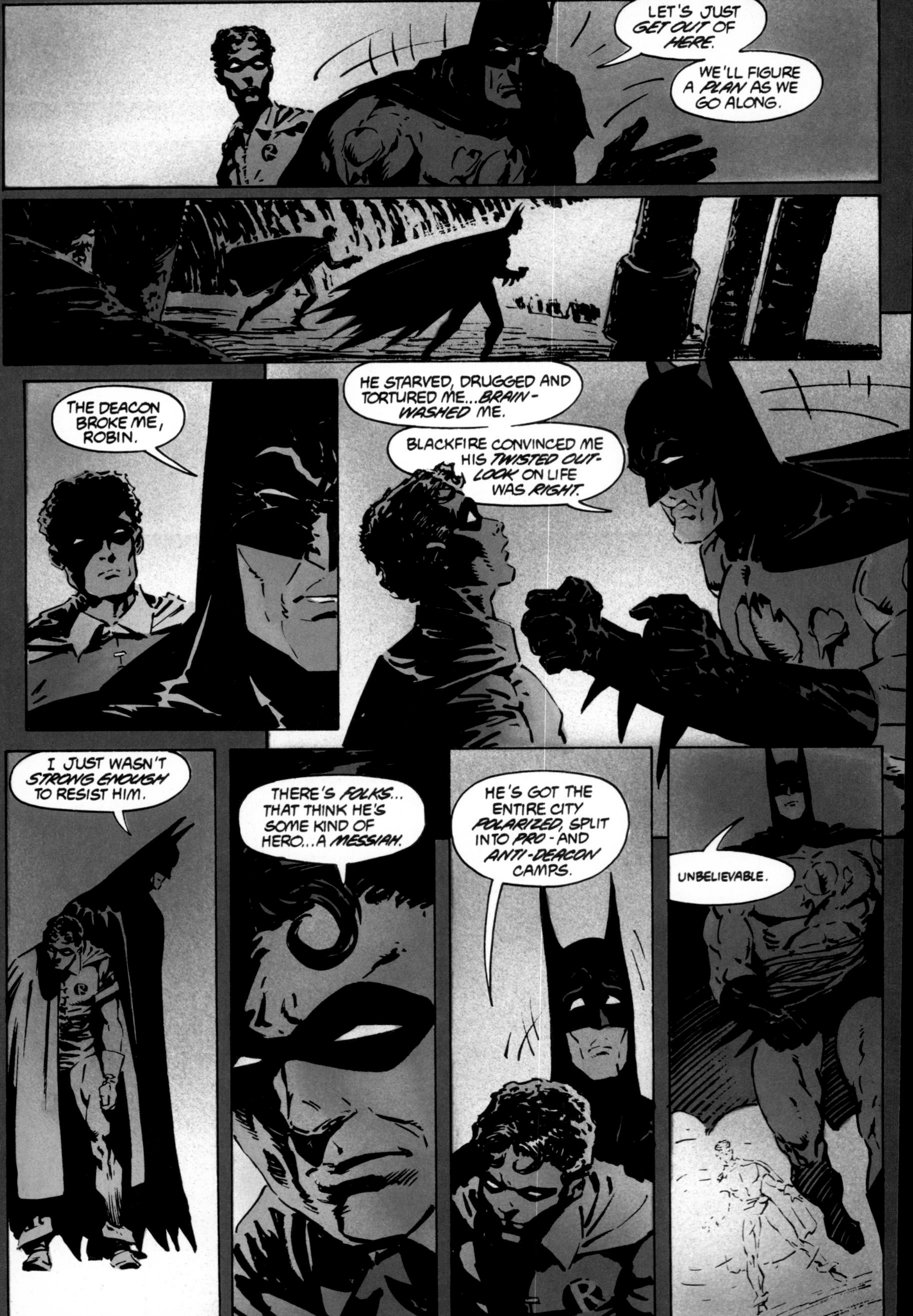
LET'S JUST GET OUT OF HERE.
WE'LL FIGURE A PLAN AS WE GO ALONG.
THE DEACON BROKE ME, ROBIN.
HE STARVED, DRUGGED AND TORTURED ME...BRAIN-WASHED ME.
BLACKFIRE CONVINCED ME HIS TWISTED OUT-LOOK ON LIFE WAS RIGHT.
I JUST WASN'T STRONG ENOUGH TO RESIST HIM.
THERE'S FOLKS... THAT THINK HE'S SOME KIND OF HERO...A MESSIAH.
HE'S GOT THE ENTIRE CITY POLARIZED, SPLIT INTO PRO- AND ANTI-DEACON CAMPS.
UNBELIEVABLE.

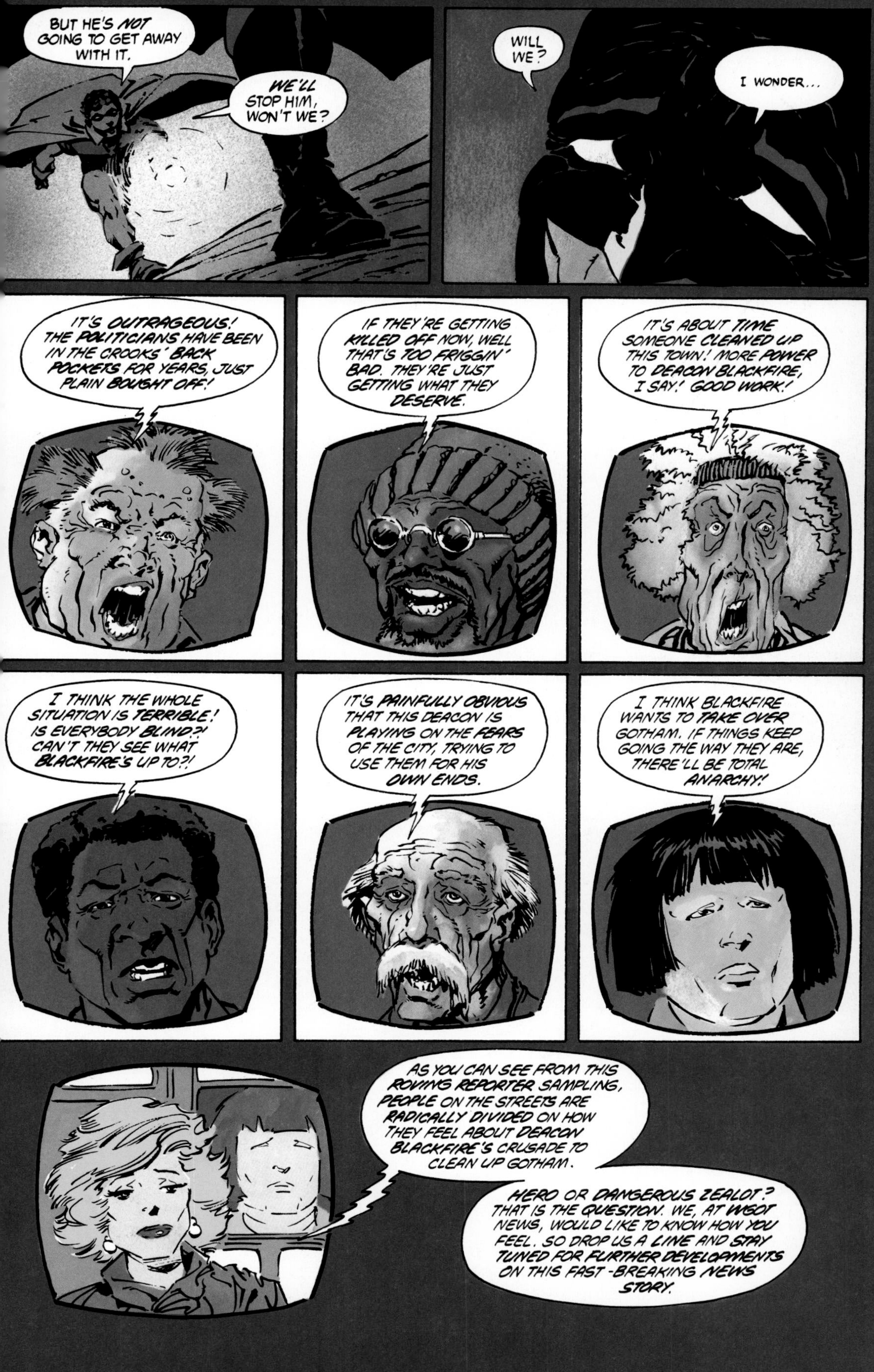
BUT HE'S NOT GOING TO GET AWAY WITH IT.
WE'LL STOP HIM, WON'T WE?
WILL WE?
I WONDER...
IT'S OUTRAGEOUS! THE POLITICIANS HAVE BEEN IN THE CROOKS' BACK POCKETS FOR YEARS, JUST PLAIN BOUGHT OFF!
IF THEY'RE GETTING KILLED OFF NOW, WELL THAT'S TOO FRIGGIN' BAD. THEY'RE JUST GETTING WHAT THEY DESERVE.
IT'S ABOUT TIME SOMEONE CLEANED UP THIS TOWN! MORE POWER TO DEACON BLACKFIRE, I SAY! GOOD WORK!
I THINK THE WHOLE SITUATION IS TERRIBLE! IS EVERYBODY BLIND?! CAN'T THEY SEE WHAT BLACKFIRE'S UP TO?!
IT'S PAINFULLY OBVIOUS THAT THIS DEACON IS PLAYING ON THE FEARS OF THE CITY, TRYING TO USE THEM FOR HIS OWN ENDS.
I THINK BLACKFIRE WANTS TO TAKE OVER GOTHAM. IF THINGS KEEP GOING THE WAY THEY ARE, THERE'LL BE TOTAL ANARCHY!
AS YOU CAN SEE FROM THIS ROVING REPORTER SAMPLING, PEOPLE ON THE STREETS ARE RADICALLY DIVIDED ON HOW THEY FEEL ABOUT DEACON BLACKFIRE'S CRUSADE TO CLEAN UP GOTHAM.
HERO OR DANGEROUS ZEALOT? THAT IS THE QUESTION. WE, AT WGOT NEWS, WOULD LIKE TO KNOW HOW YOU FEEL. SO DROP US A LINE AND STAY TUNED FOR FURTHER DEVELOPMENTS ON THIS FAST-BREAKING NEWS STORY.

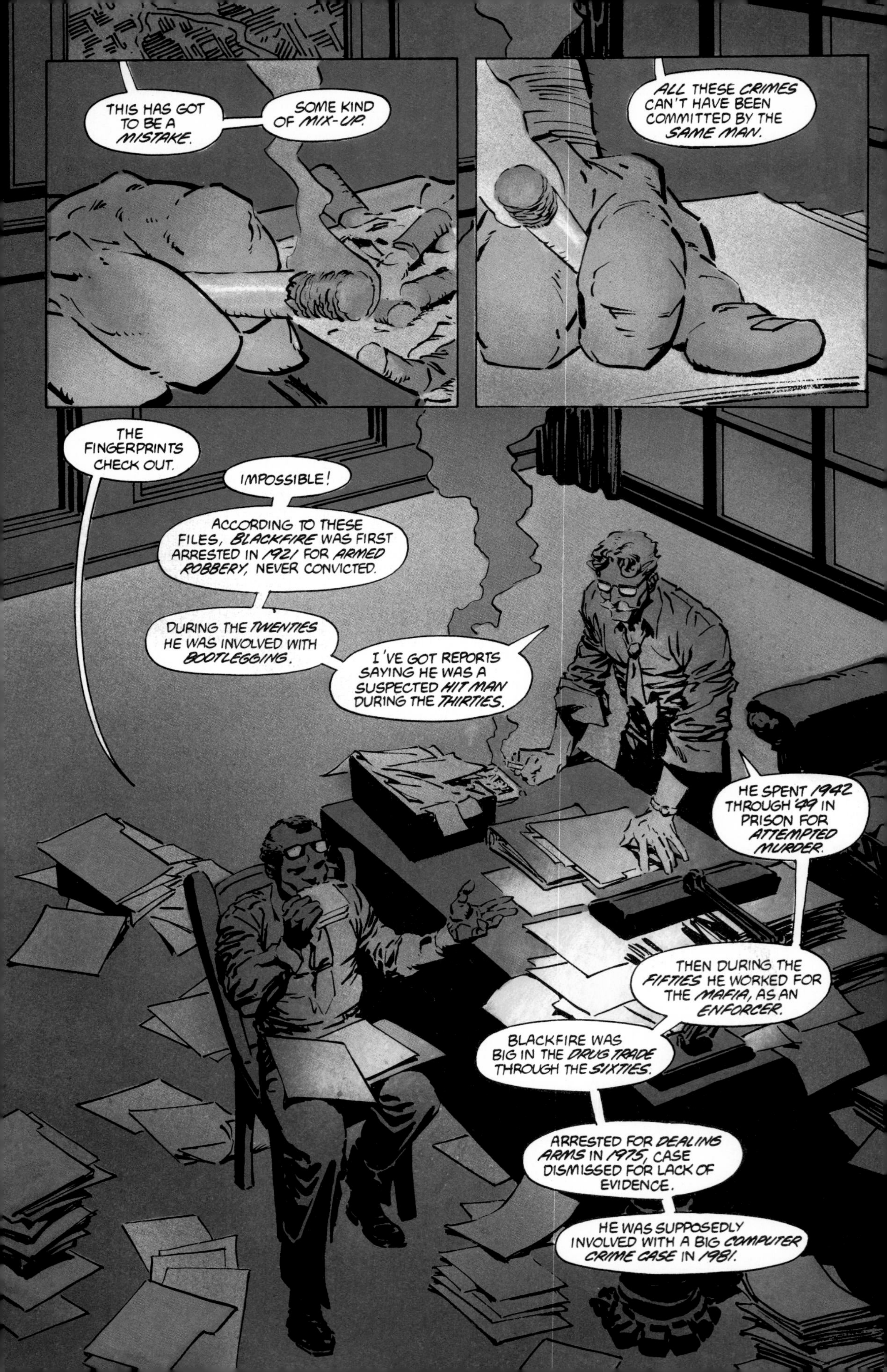
THIS HAS GOT TO BE A MISTAKE.
SOME KIND OF MIX-UP.
ALL THESE CRIMES CAN'T HAVE BEEN COMMITTED BY THE SAME MAN.
THE FINGERPRINTS CHECK OUT.
IMPOSSIBLE!
ACCORDING TO THESE FILES, BLACKFIRE WAS FIRST ARRESTED IN 1921 FOR ARMED ROBBERY, NEVER CONVICTED.
DURING THE TWENTIES HE WAS INVOLVED WITH BOOTLEGGING.
I'VE GOT REPORTS SAYING HE WAS A SUSPECTED HIT MAN DURING THE THIRTIES.
HE SPENT 1942 THROUGH '49 IN PRISON FOR ATTEMPTED MURDER.
THEN DURING THE FIFTIES HE WORKED FOR THE MAFIA, AS AN ENFORCER.
BLACKFIRE WAS BIG IN THE DRUG TRADE THROUGH THE SIXTIES.
ARRESTED FOR DEALING ARMS IN 1975, CASE DISMISSED FOR LACK OF EVIDENCE.
HE WAS SUPPOSEDLY INVOLVED WITH A BIG COMPUTER CRIME CASE IN 1981.

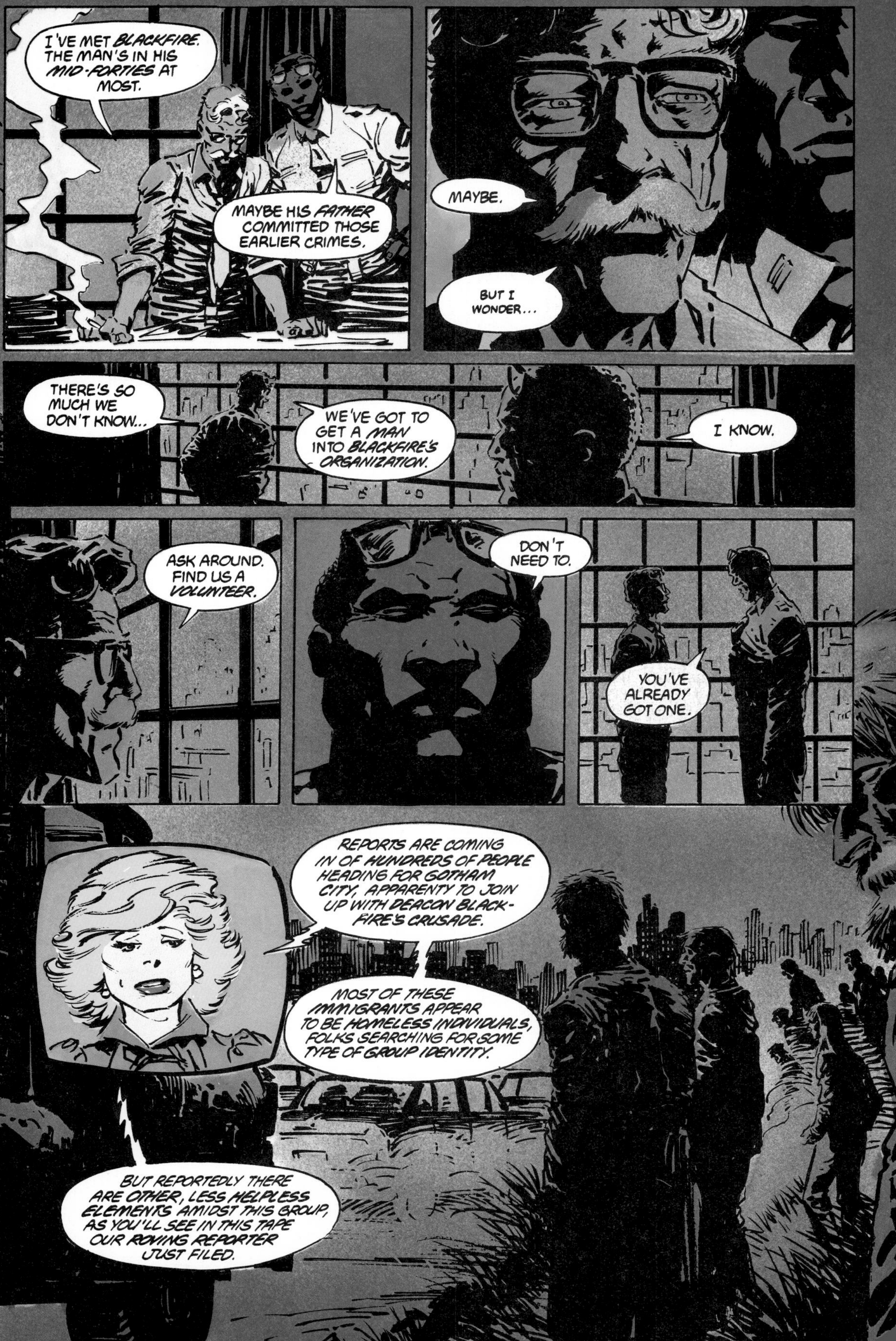

I'VE MET BLACKFIRE. THE MAN'S IN HIS MID-FORTIES AT MOST.
MAYBE HIS FATHER COMMITTED THOSE EARLIER CRIMES.
MAYBE.
BUT I WONDER...
THERE'S SO MUCH WE DON'T KNOW...
WE'VE GOT TO GET A MAN INTO BLACKFIRE'S ORGANIZATION.
I KNOW.
ASK AROUND. FIND US A VOLUNTEER.
DON'T NEED TO.
YOU'VE ALREADY GOT ONE.
REPORTS ARE COMING IN OF HUNDREDS OF PEOPLE HEADING FOR GOTHAM CITY, APPARENTLY TO JOIN UP WITH DEACON BLACK-FIRE'S CRUSADE.
MOST OF THESE IMMIGRANTS APPEAR TO BE HOMELESS INDIVIDUALS, FOLKS SEARCHING FOR SOME TYPE OF GROUP IDENTITY.
BUT REPORTEDLY THERE ARE OTHER, LESS HELPLESS ELEMENTS AMIDST THIS GROUP, AS YOU'LL SEE IN THIS TAPE OUR ROVING REPORTER JUST FILED.

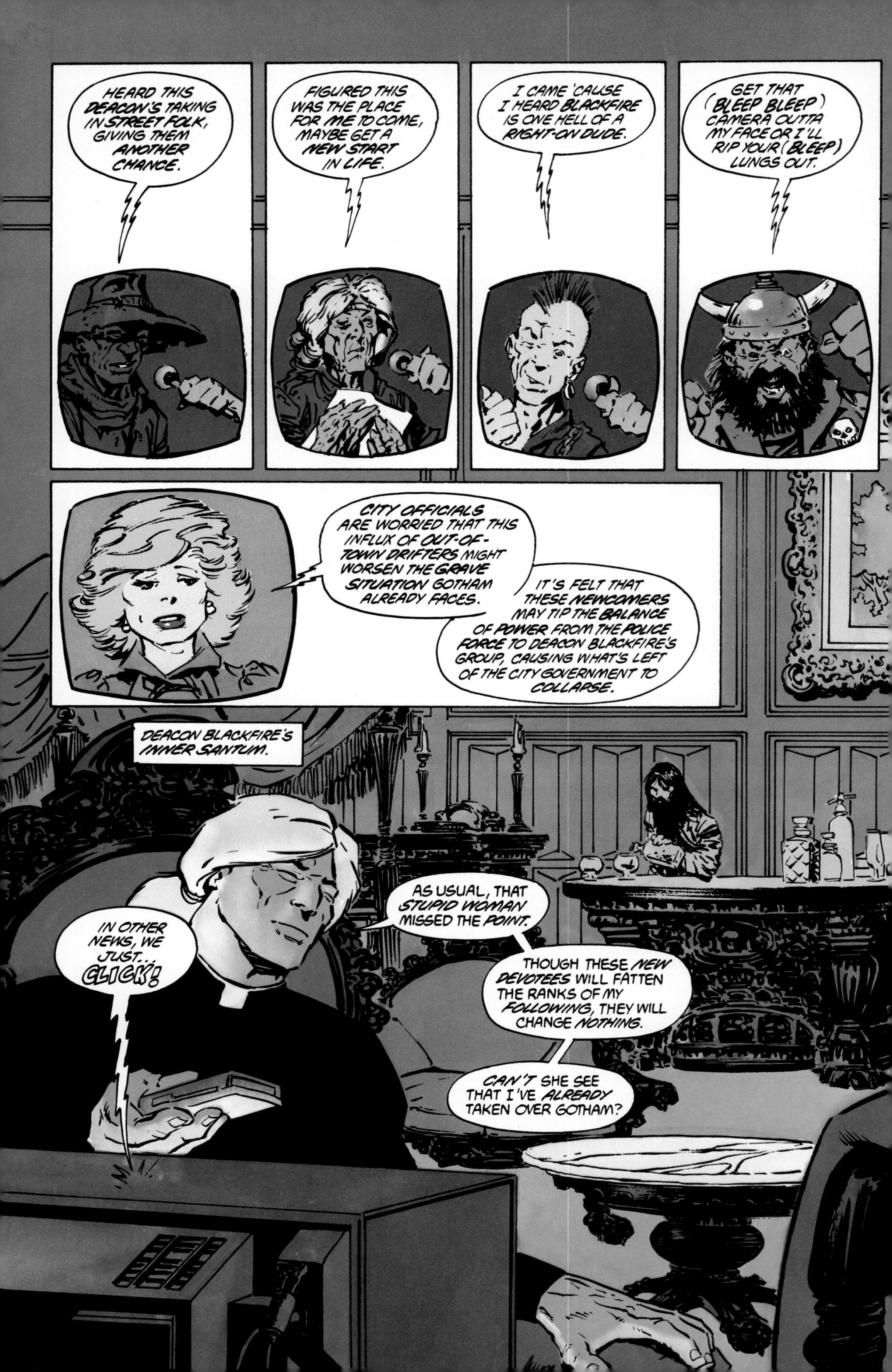

HEARD THIS DEACON'S TAKING IN STREET FOLK, GIVING THEM ANOTHER CHANCE.
FIGURED THIS WAS THE PLACE FOR ME TO COME, MAYBE GET A NEW START IN LIFE.
I CAME 'CAUSE I HEARD BLACKFIRE IS ONE HELL OF A RIGHT-ON DUDE.
GET THAT (BLEEP BLEEP) CAMERA OUTTA MY FACE OR I'LL RIP YOUR (BLEEP) LUNGS OUT.
CITY OFFICIALS ARE WORRIED THAT THIS INFLUX OF OUT-OF-TOWN DRIFTERS MIGHT WORSEN THE GRAVE SITUATION GOTHAM ALREADY FACES.
IT'S FELT THAT THESE NEWCOMERS MAY TIP THE BALANCE OF POWER FROM THE POLICE FORCE TO DEACON BLACKFIRE'S GROUP, CAUSING WHAT'S LEFT OF THE CITY GOVERNMENT TO COLLAPSE.
DEACON BLACKFIRE'S INNER SANTUM.
IN OTHER NEWS, WE JUST... CLICK!
AS USUAL, THAT STUPID WOMAN MISSED THE POINT.
THOUGH THESE NEW DEVOTEES WILL FATTEN THE RANKS OF MY FOLLOWING, THEY WILL CHANGE NOTHING.
CAN'T SHE SEE THAT I'VE ALREADY TAKEN OVER GOTHAM?

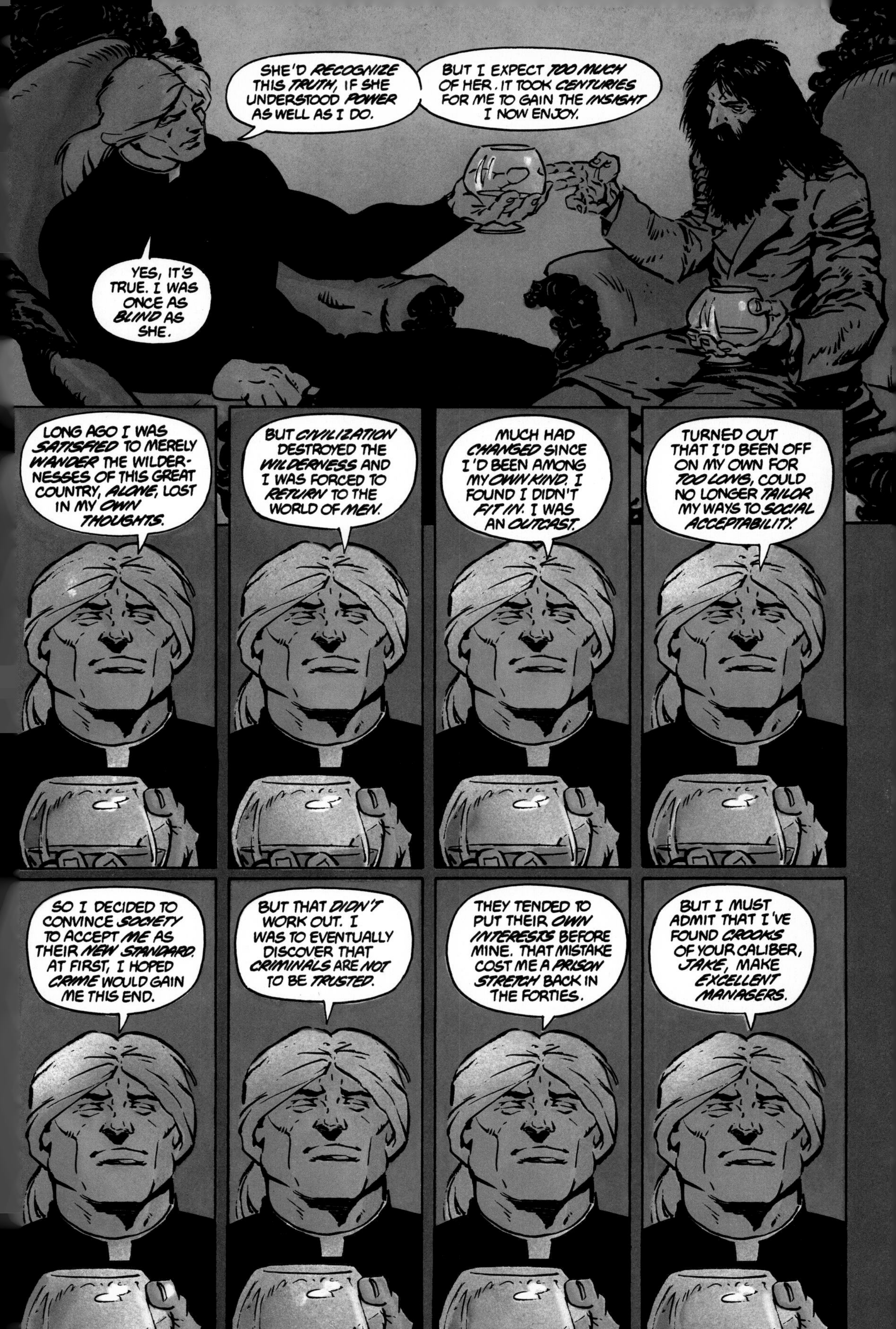
SHE'D RECOGNIZE THIS TRUTH, IF SHE UNDERSTOOD POWER AS WELL AS I DO.
BUT I EXPECT TOO MUCH OF HER. IT TOOK CENTURIES FOR ME TO GAIN THE INSIGHT I NOW ENJOY.
YES, IT'S TRUE. I WAS ONCE AS BLIND AS SHE.
LONG AGO I WAS SATISFIED TO MERELY WANDER THE WILDERNESSES OF THIS GREAT COUNTRY, ALONE, LOST IN MY OWN THOUGHTS.
BUT CIVILIZATION DESTROYED THE WILDERNESS AND I WAS FORCED TO RETURN TO THE WORLD OF MEN.
MUCH HAD CHANGED SINCE I'D BEEN AMONG MY OWN KIND. I FOUND I DIDN'T FIT IN. I WAS AN OUTCAST.
TURNED OUT THAT I'D BEEN OFF ON MY OWN FOR TOO LONG, COULD NO LONGER TAILOR MY WAYS TO SOCIAL ACCEPTABILITY.
SO I DECIDED TO CONVINCE SOCIETY TO ACCEPT ME AS THEIR NEW STANDARD. AT FIRST, I HOPED CRIME WOULD GAIN ME THIS END.
BUT THAT DIDN'T WORK OUT. I WAS TO EVENTUALLY DISCOVER THAT CRIMINALS ARE NOT TO BE TRUSTED.
THEY TENDED TO PUT THEIR OWN INTERESTS BEFORE MINE. THAT MISTAKE COST ME A PRISON STRETCH BACK IN THE FORTIES.
BUT I MUST ADMIT THAT I'VE FOUND CROOKS OF YOUR CALIBER, JAKE, MAKE EXCELLENT MANAGERS.

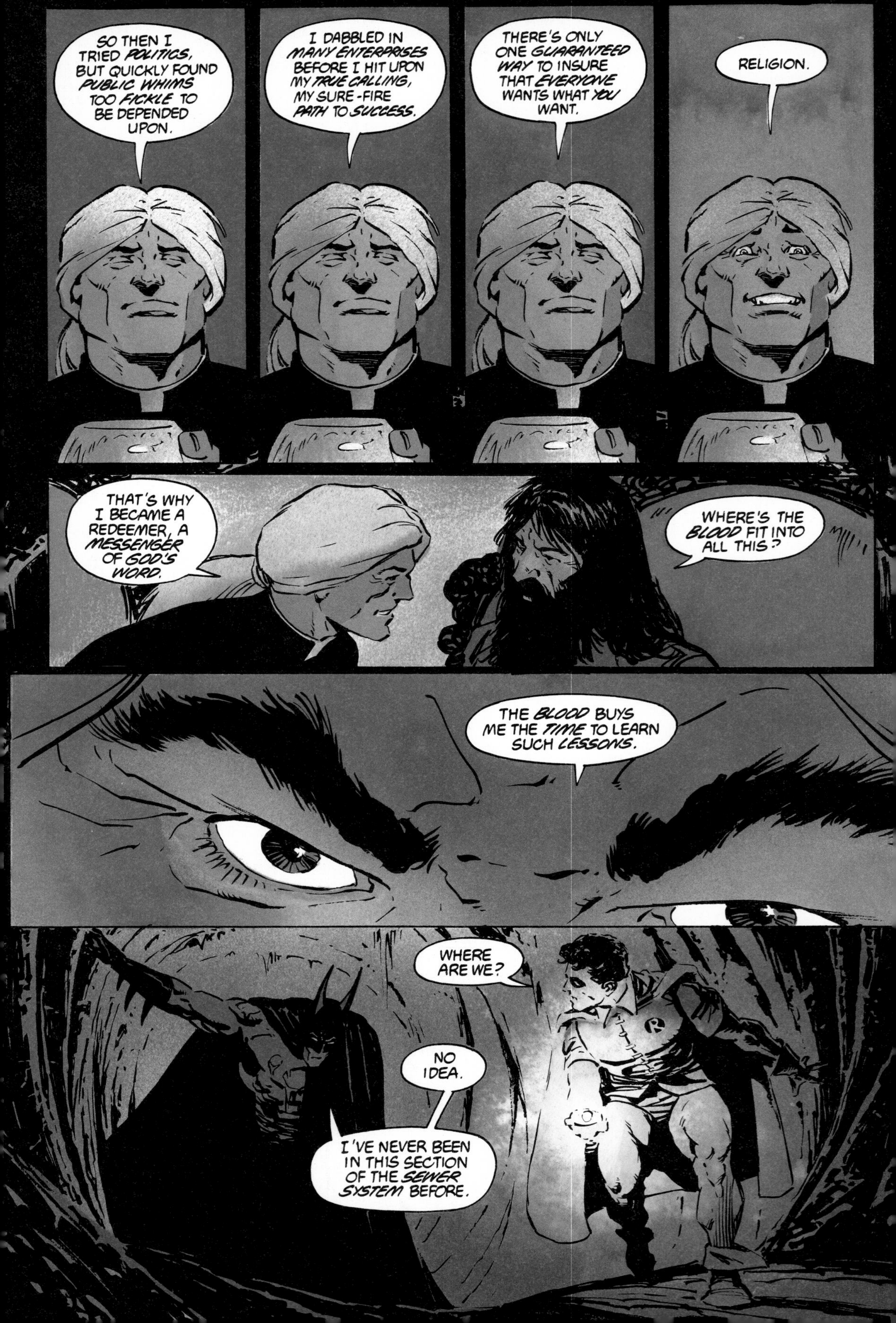
SO THEN I TRIED POLITICS, BUT QUICKLY FOUND PUBLIC WHIMS TOO FICKLE TO BE DEPENDED UPON.
I DABBLED IN MANY ENTERPRISES BEFORE I HIT UPON MY TRUE CALLING, MY SURE-FIRE PATH TO SUCCESS.
THERE'S ONLY ONE GUARANTEED WAY TO INSURE THAT EVERYONE WANTS WHAT YOU WANT.
RELIGION.
THAT'S WHY I BECAME A REDEEMER, A MESSENGER OF GOD'S WORD.
WHERE'S THE BLOOD FIT INTO ALL THIS?
THE BLOOD BUYS ME THE TIME TO LEARN SUCH LESSONS.
WHERE ARE WE?
NO IDEA.
I'VE NEVER BEEN IN THIS SECTION OF THE SEWER SYSTEM BEFORE.

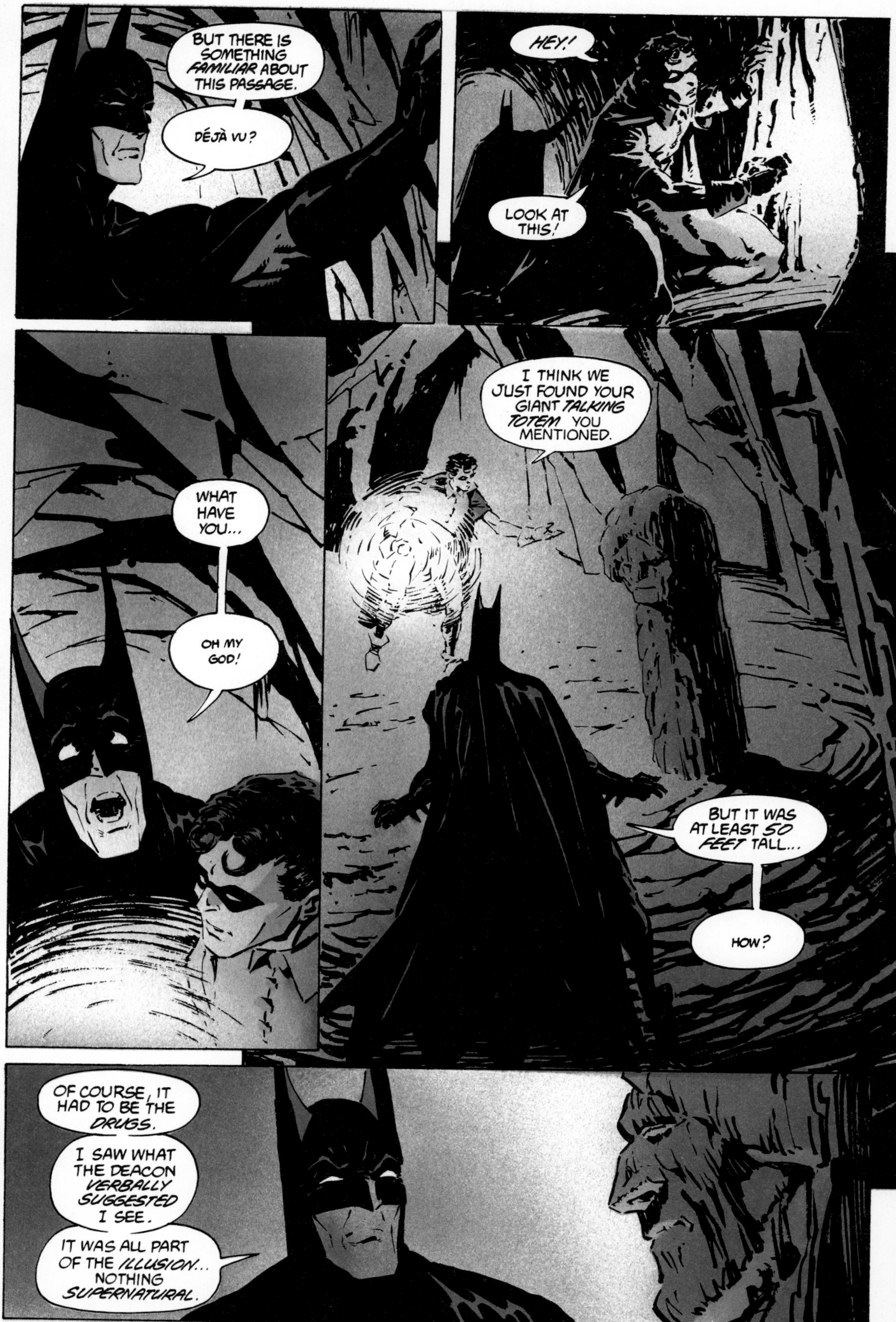
BUT THERE IS SOMETHING FAMILIAR ABOUT THIS PASSAGE.
DÉJÀ VU?
HEY!
LOOK AT THIS!
WHAT HAVE YOU...
OH MY GOD!
I THINK WE JUST FOUND YOUR GIANT TALKING TOTEM YOU MENTIONED.
BUT IT WAS AT LEAST 50 FEET TALL...
HOW?
OF COURSE, IT HAD TO BE THE DRUGS.
I SAW WHAT THE DEACON VERBALLY SUGGESTED I SEE.
IT WAS ALL PART OF THE ILLUSION... NOTHING SUPERNATURAL.

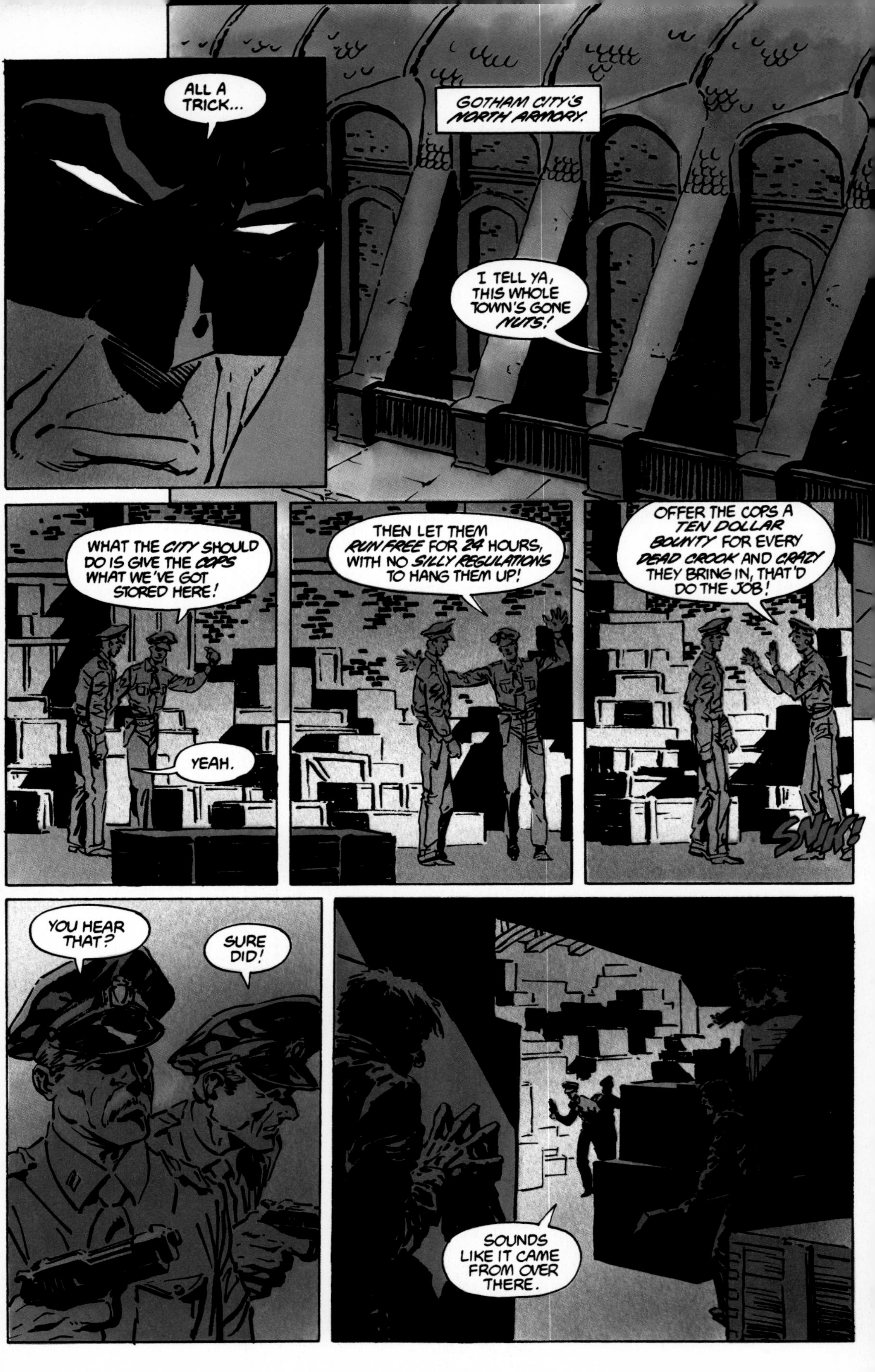

ALL A TRICK...
GOTHAM CITY'S NORTH ARMORY.
I TELL YA, THIS WHOLE TOWN'S GONE NUTS!
WHAT THE CITY SHOULD DO IS GIVE THE COPS WHAT WE'VE GOT STORED HERE!
YEAH.
THEN LET THEM RUN FREE FOR 24 HOURS, WITH NO SILLY REGULATIONS TO HANG THEM UP!
OFFER THE COPS A TEN DOLLAR BOUNTY FOR EVERY DEAD CROOK AND CRAZY THEY BRING IN, THAT'D DO THE JOB!
SNIK!
YOU HEAR THAT?
SURE DID!
SOUNDS LIKE IT CAME FROM OVER THERE.

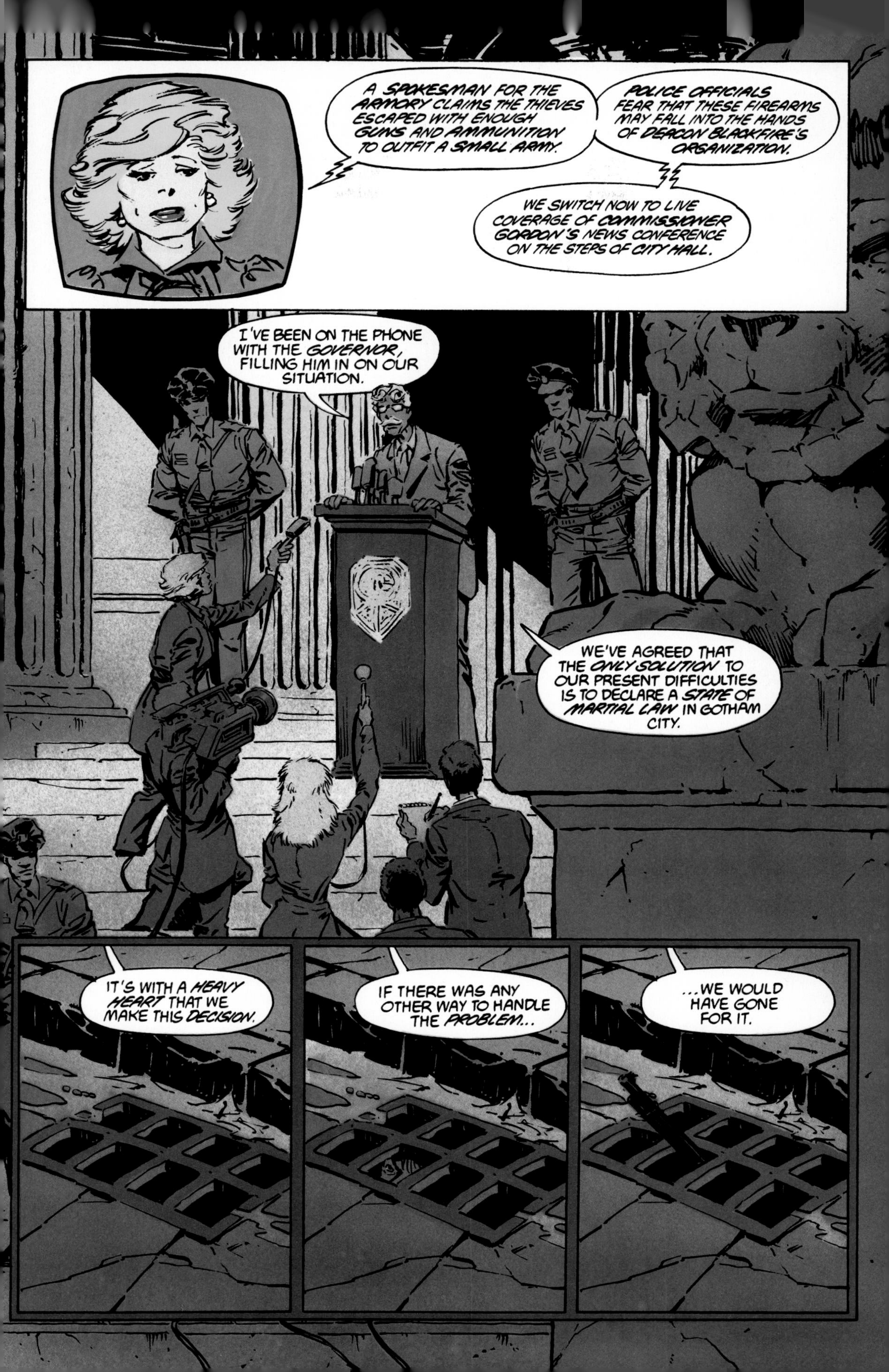
A SPOKESMAN FOR THE ARMORY CLAIMS THE THIEVES ESCAPED WITH ENOUGH GUNS AND AMMUNITION TO OUTFIT A SMALL ARMY.
POLICE OFFICIALS FEAR THAT THESE FIREARMS MAY FALL INTO THE HANDS OF DEACON BLACKFIRE'S ORGANIZATION.
WE SWITCH NOW TO LIVE COVERAGE OF COMMISSIONER GORDON'S NEWS CONFERENCE ON THE STEPS OF CITY HALL.
I'VE BEEN ON THE PHONE WITH THE GOVERNOR, FILLING HIM IN ON OUR SITUATION.
WE'VE AGREED THAT THE ONLY SOLUTION TO OUR PRESENT DIFFICULTIES IS TO DECLARE A STATE OF MARTIAL LAW IN GOTHAM CITY.
IT'S WITH A HEAVY HEART THAT WE MAKE THIS DECISION.
IF THERE WAS ANY OTHER WAY TO HANDLE THE PROBLEM...
...WE WOULD HAVE GONE FOR IT.

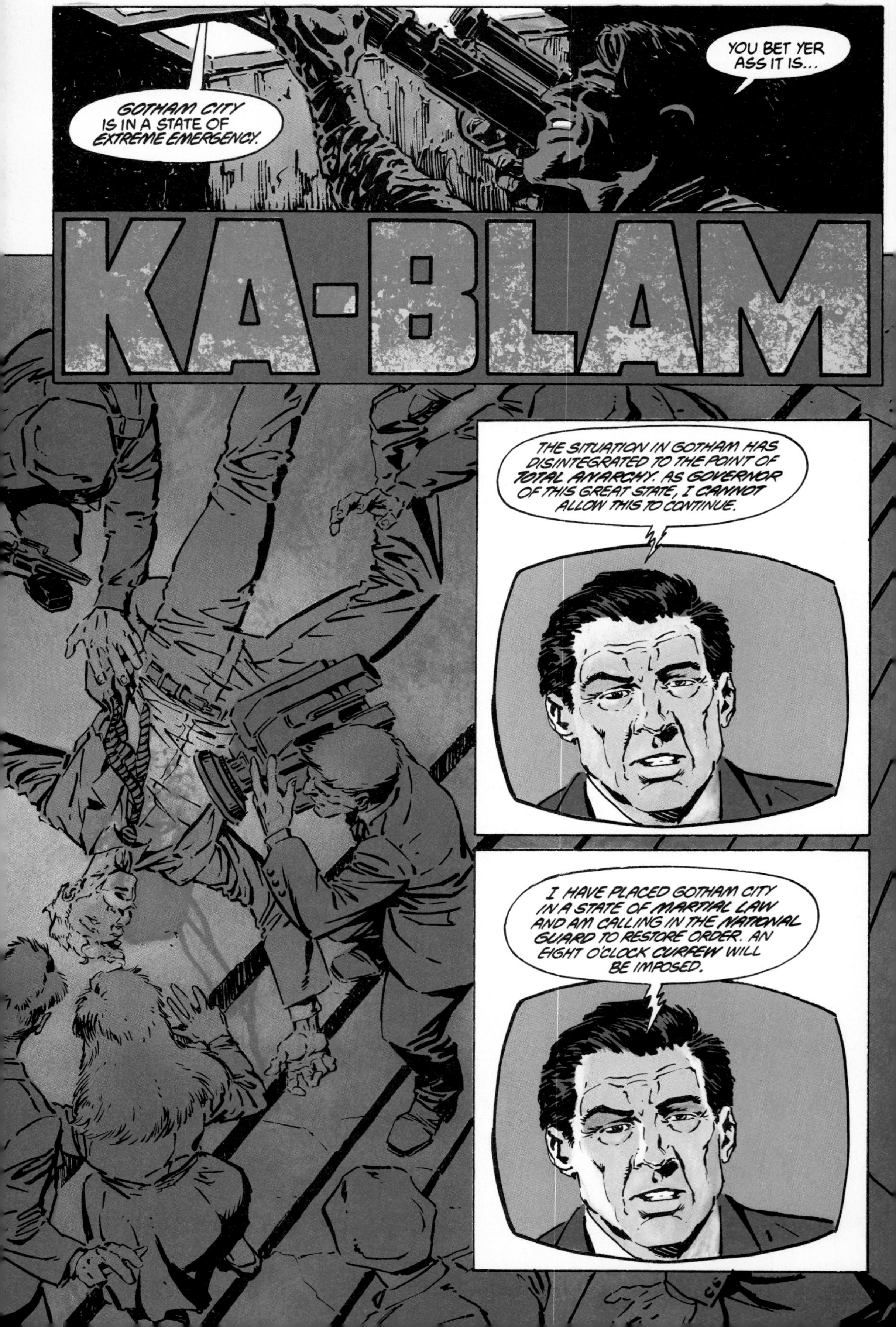
GOTHAM CITY IS IN A STATE OF EXTREME EMERGENCY.
YOU BET YER ASS IT IS...
KA-BLAM
THE SITUATION IN GOTHAM HAS DISINTEGRATED TO THE POINT OF TOTAL ANARCHY. AS GOVERNOR OF THIS GREAT STATE, I CANNOT ALLOW THIS TO CONTINUE.
I HAVE PLACED GOTHAM CITY IN A STATE OF MARTIAL LAW AND AM CALLING IN THE NATIONAL GUARD TO RESTORE ORDER. AN EIGHT O'CLOCK CURFEW WILL BE IMPOSED.

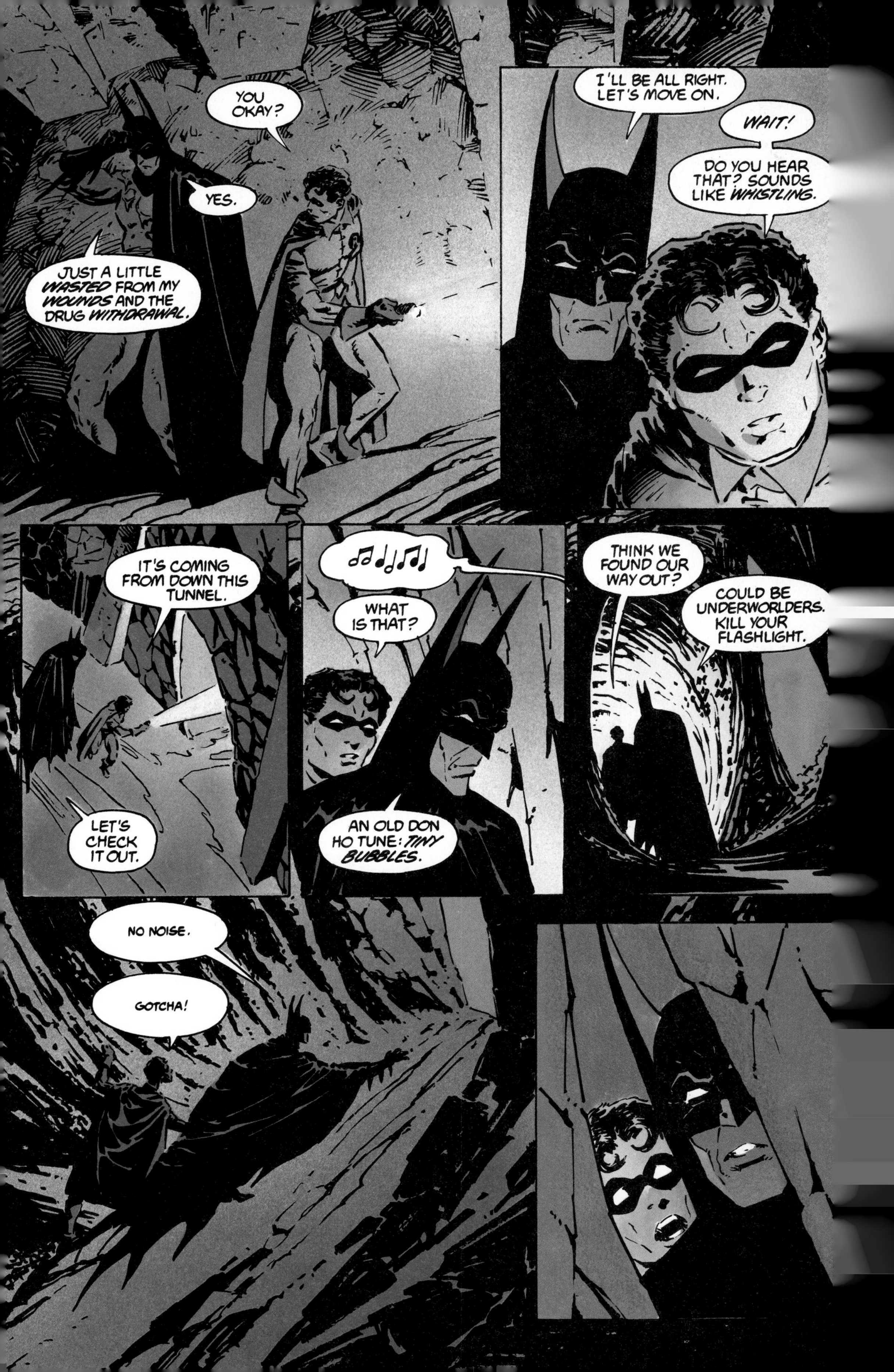
YOU OKAY?
YES.
JUST A LITTLE WASTED FROM MY WOUNDS AND THE DRUG WITHDRAWAL.
I'LL BE ALL RIGHT. LET'S MOVE ON.
WAIT!
DO YOU HEAR THAT? SOUNDS LIKE WHISTLING.
IT'S COMING FROM DOWN THIS TUNNEL.
LET'S CHECK IT OUT.
♫♩♩♫♩
WHAT IS THAT?
AN OLD DON HO TUNE: TINY BUBBLES.
THINK WE FOUND OUR WAY OUT?
COULD BE UNDERWORLDERS. KILL YOUR FLASHLIGHT.
NO NOISE.
GOTCHA!

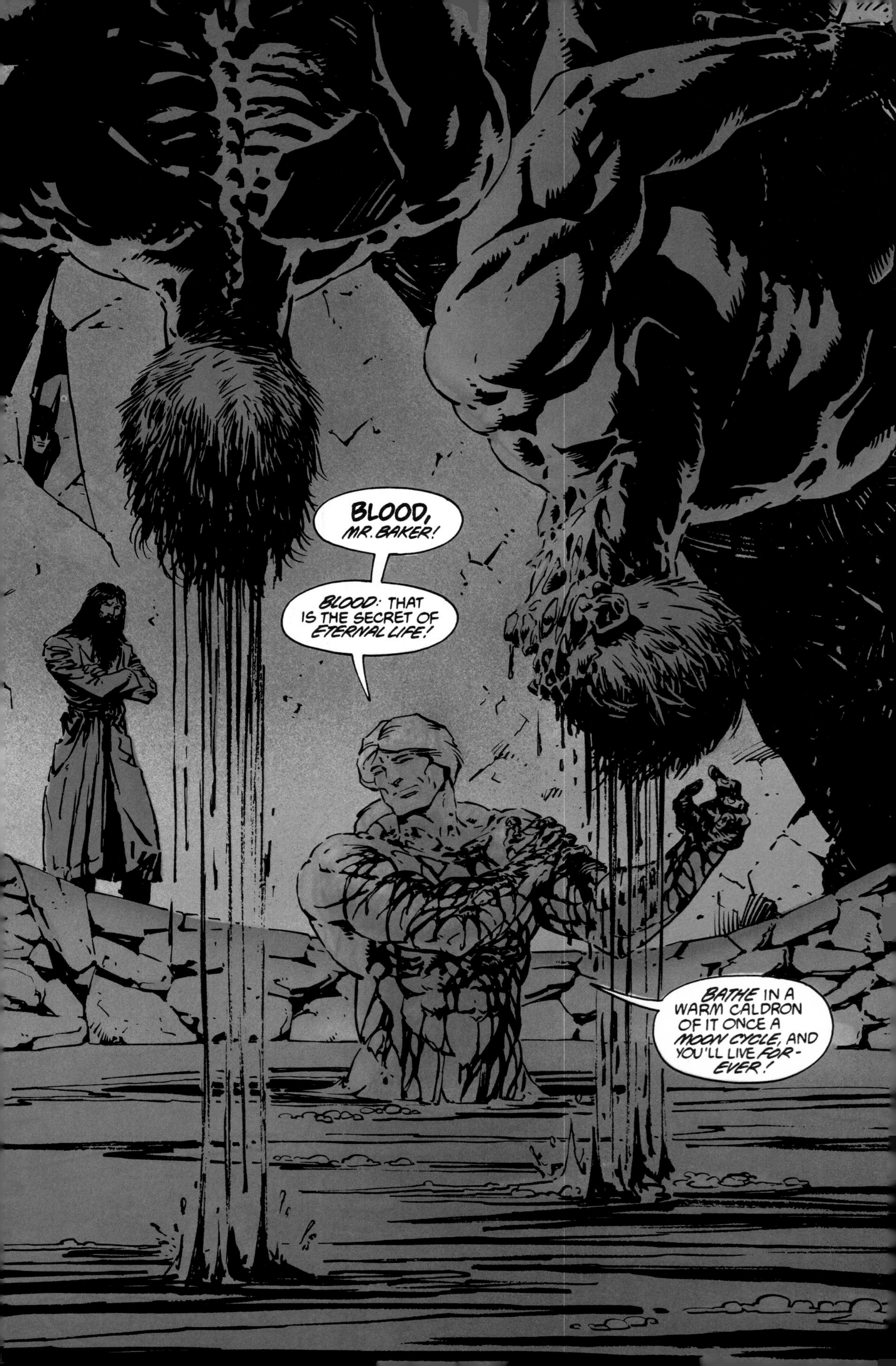
BLOOD, MR. BAKER!
BLOOD: THAT IS THE SECRET OF ETERNAL LIFE!
BATHE IN A WARM CALDRON OF IT ONCE A MOON CYCLE, AND YOU'LL LIVE FOR-EVER!

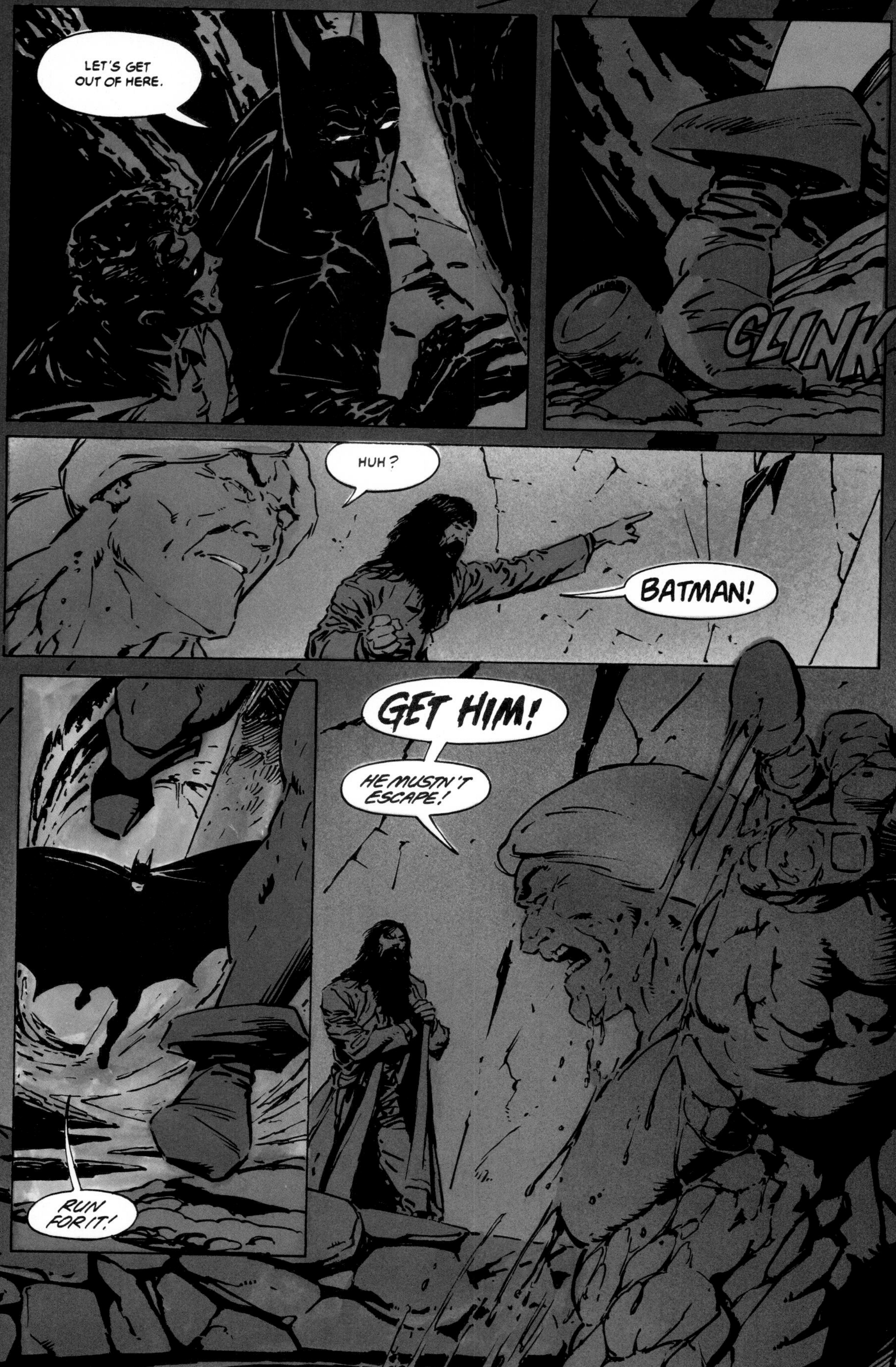
LET'S GET OUT OF HERE.
CLINK
HUH?
BATMAN!
GET HIM!
HE MUSTN'T ESCAPE!
RUN FOR IT!

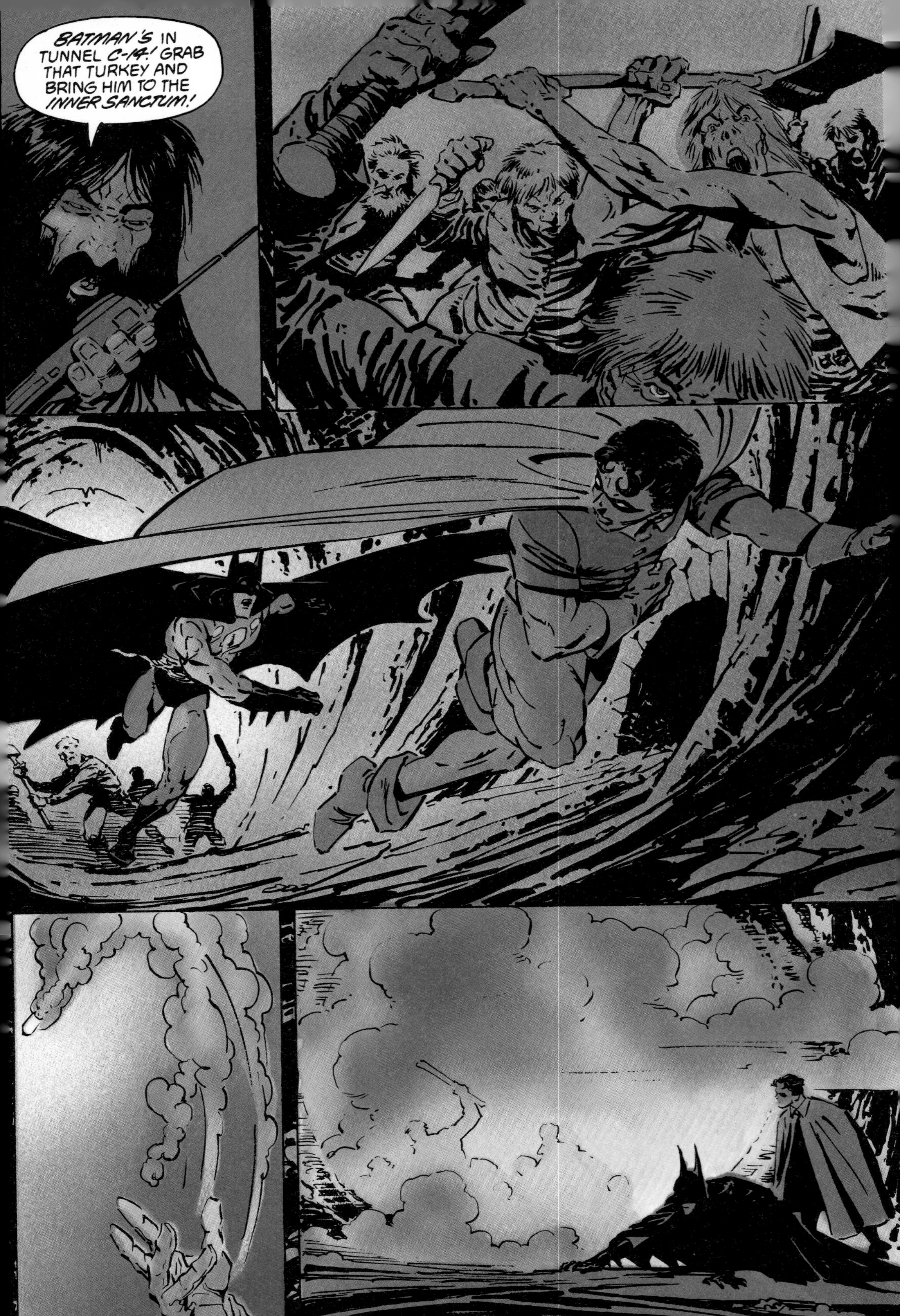
BATMAN'S IN TUNNEL C-14! GRAB THAT TURKEY AND BRING HIM TO THE INNER SANCTUM!

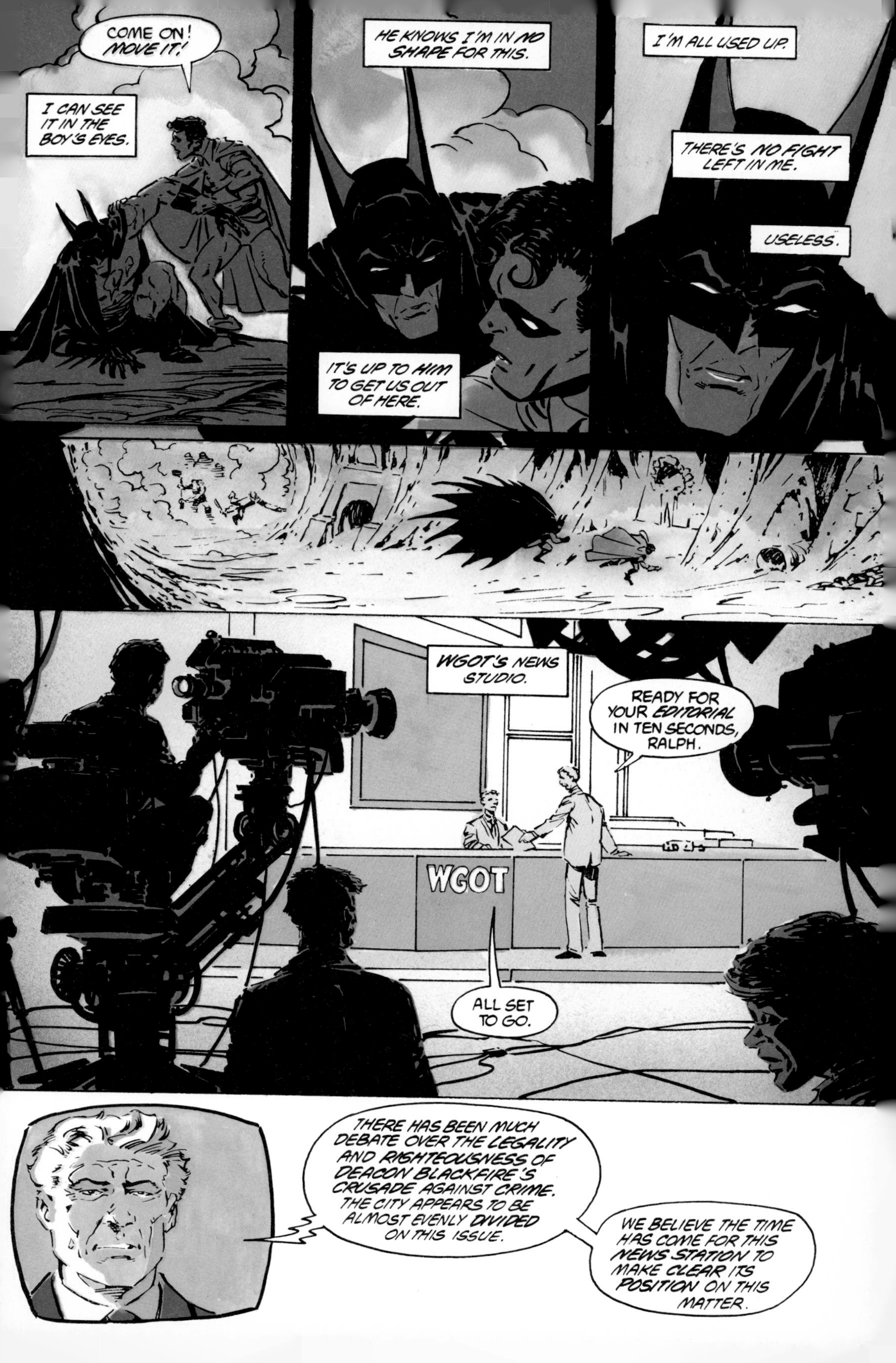
COME ON! MOVE IT!
I CAN SEE IT IN THE BOY'S EYES.
HE KNOWS I'M IN NO SHAPE FOR THIS.
IT'S UP TO HIM TO GET US OUT OF HERE.
I'M ALL USED UP.
THERE'S NO FIGHT LEFT IN ME.
USELESS.
WGOT'S NEWS STUDIO.
READY FOR YOUR EDITORIAL IN TEN SECONDS, RALPH.
WGOT
ALL SET TO GO.
THERE HAS BEEN MUCH DEBATE OVER THE LEGALITY AND RIGHTEOUSNESS OF DEACON BLACKFIRE'S CRUSADE AGAINST CRIME. THE CITY APPEARS TO BE ALMOST EVENLY DIVIDED ON THIS ISSUE.
WE BELIEVE THE TIME HAS COME FOR THIS NEWS STATION TO MAKE CLEAR ITS POSITION ON THIS MATTER.

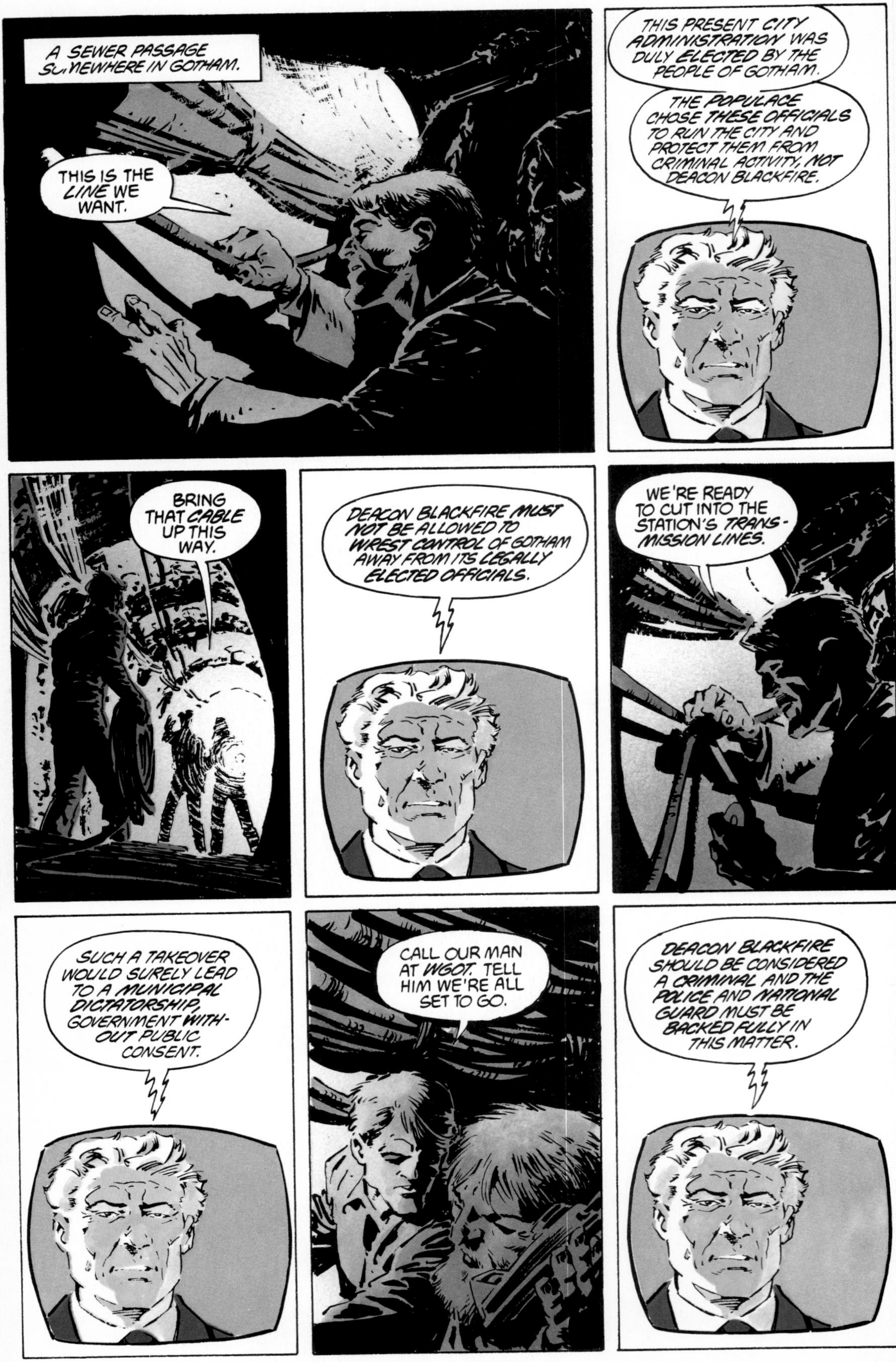
A SEWER PASSAGE SOMEWHERE IN GOTHAM.
THIS IS THE LINE WE WANT.
THIS PRESENT CITY ADMINISTRATION WAS DULY ELECTED BY THE PEOPLE OF GOTHAM.
THE POPULACE CHOSE THESE OFFICIALS TO RUN THE CITY AND PROTECT THEM FROM CRIMINAL ACTIVITY, NOT DEACON BLACKFIRE.
BRING THAT CABLE UP THIS WAY.
DEACON BLACKFIRE MUST NOT BE ALLOWED TO WREST CONTROL OF GOTHAM AWAY FROM ITS LEGALLY ELECTED OFFICIALS.
WE'RE READY TO CUT INTO THE STATION'S TRANS-MISSION LINES.
SUCH A TAKEOVER WOULD SURELY LEAD TO A MUNICIPAL DICTATORSHIP, GOVERNMENT WITH-OUT PUBLIC CONSENT.
CALL OUR MAN AT WGOT. TELL HIM WE'RE ALL SET TO GO.
DEACON BLACKFIRE SHOULD BE CONSIDERED A CRIMINAL AND THE POLICE AND NATIONAL GUARD MUST BE BACKED FULLY IN THIS MATTER.

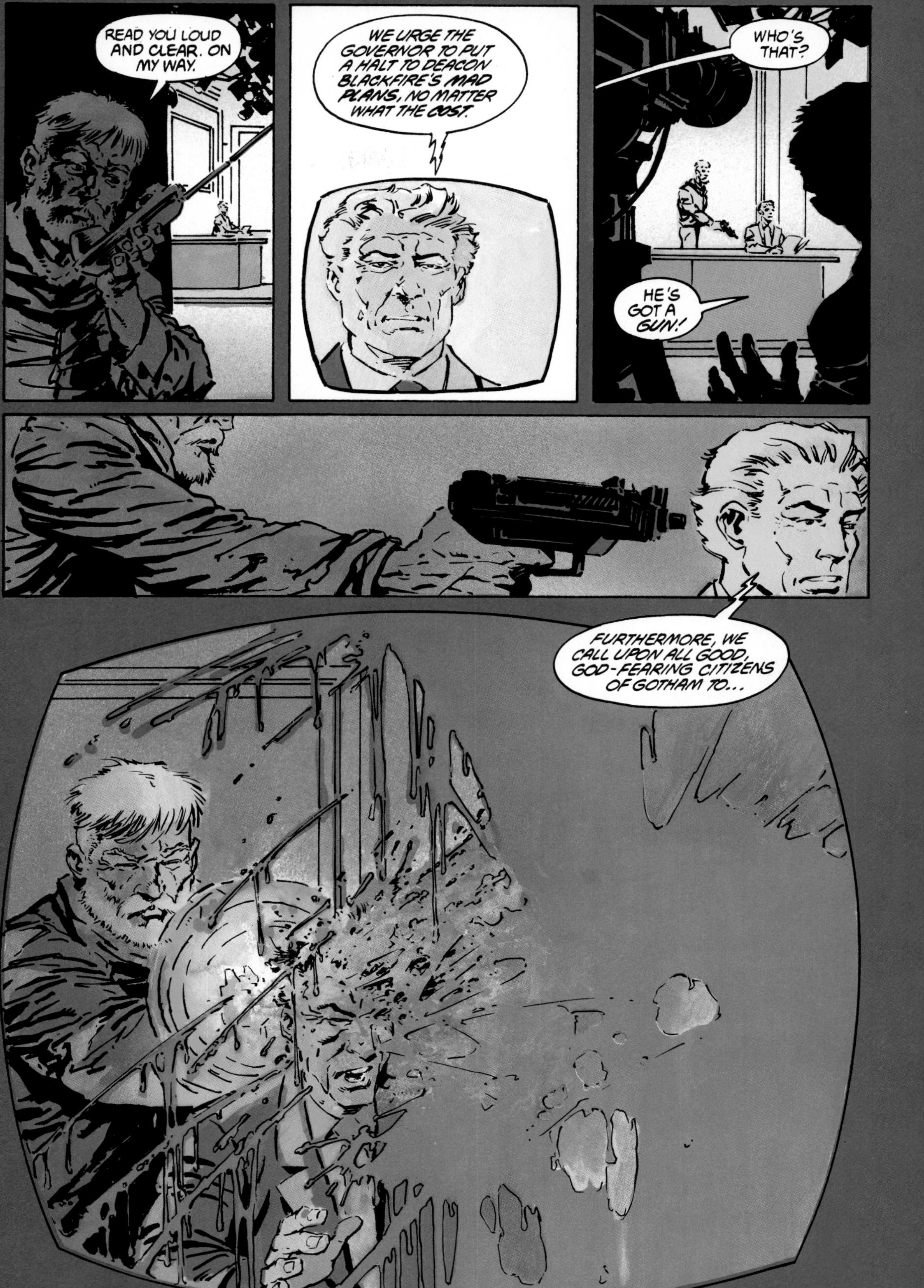
READ YOU LOUD AND CLEAR. ON MY WAY.
WE URGE THE GOVERNOR TO PUT A HALT TO DEACON BLACKFIRE'S MAD PLANS, NO MATTER WHAT THE COST.
WHO'S THAT?
HE'S GOT A GUN!
FURTHERMORE, WE CALL UPON ALL GOOD, GOD-FEARING CITIZENS OF GOTHAM TO...

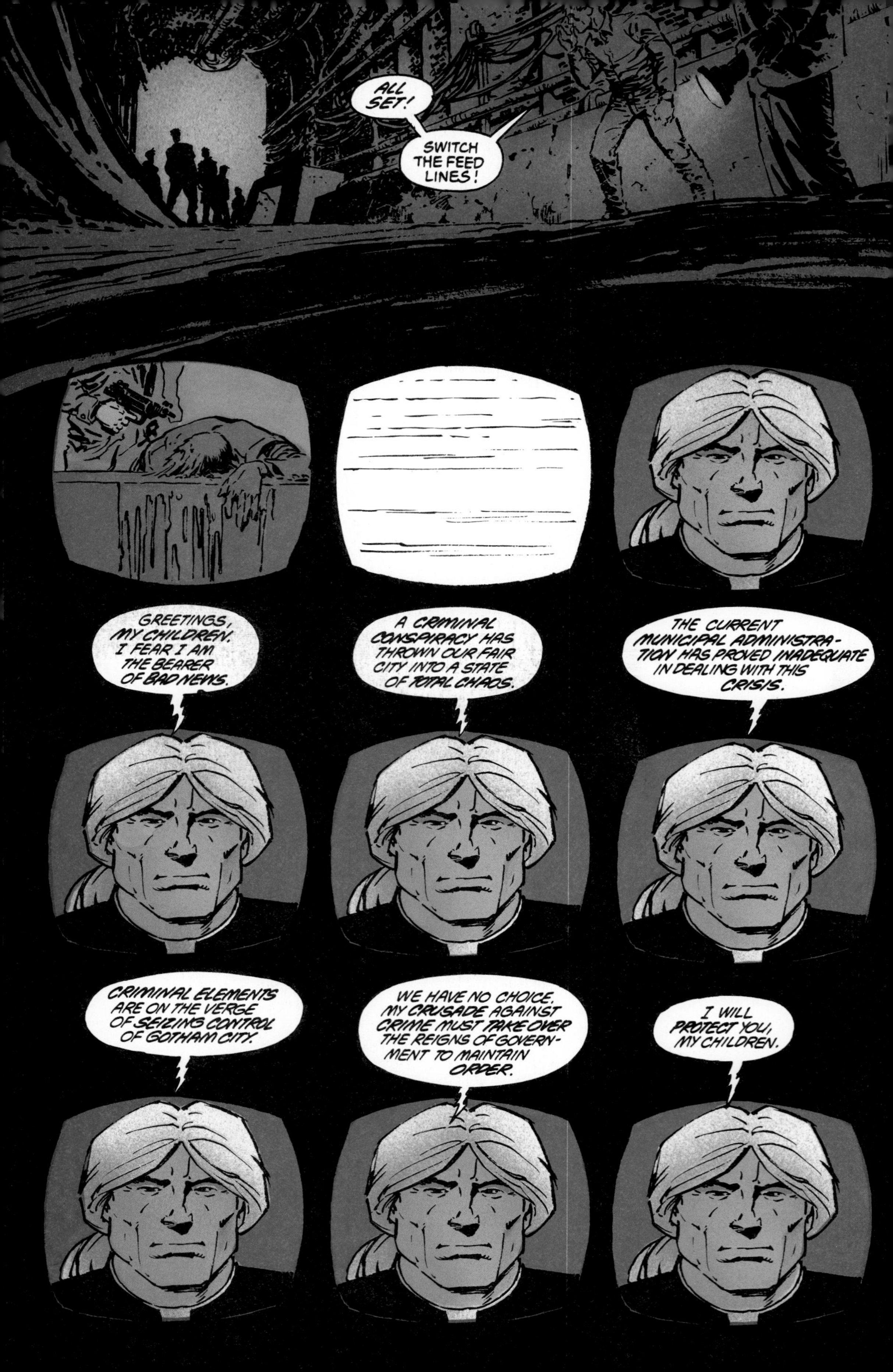
ALL SET!
SWITCH THE FEED LINES!
GREETINGS, MY CHILDREN. I FEAR I AM THE BEARER OF BAD NEWS.
A CRIMINAL CONSPIRACY HAS THROWN OUR FAIR CITY INTO A STATE OF TOTAL CHAOS.
THE CURRENT MUNICIPAL ADMINISTRATION HAS PROVED INADEQUATE IN DEALING WITH THIS CRISIS.
CRIMINAL ELEMENTS ARE ON THE VERGE OF SEIZING CONTROL OF GOTHAM CITY.
WE HAVE NO CHOICE. MY CRUSADE AGAINST CRIME MUST TAKE OVER THE REIGNS OF GOVERNMENT TO MAINTAIN ORDER.
I WILL PROTECT YOU, MY CHILDREN.

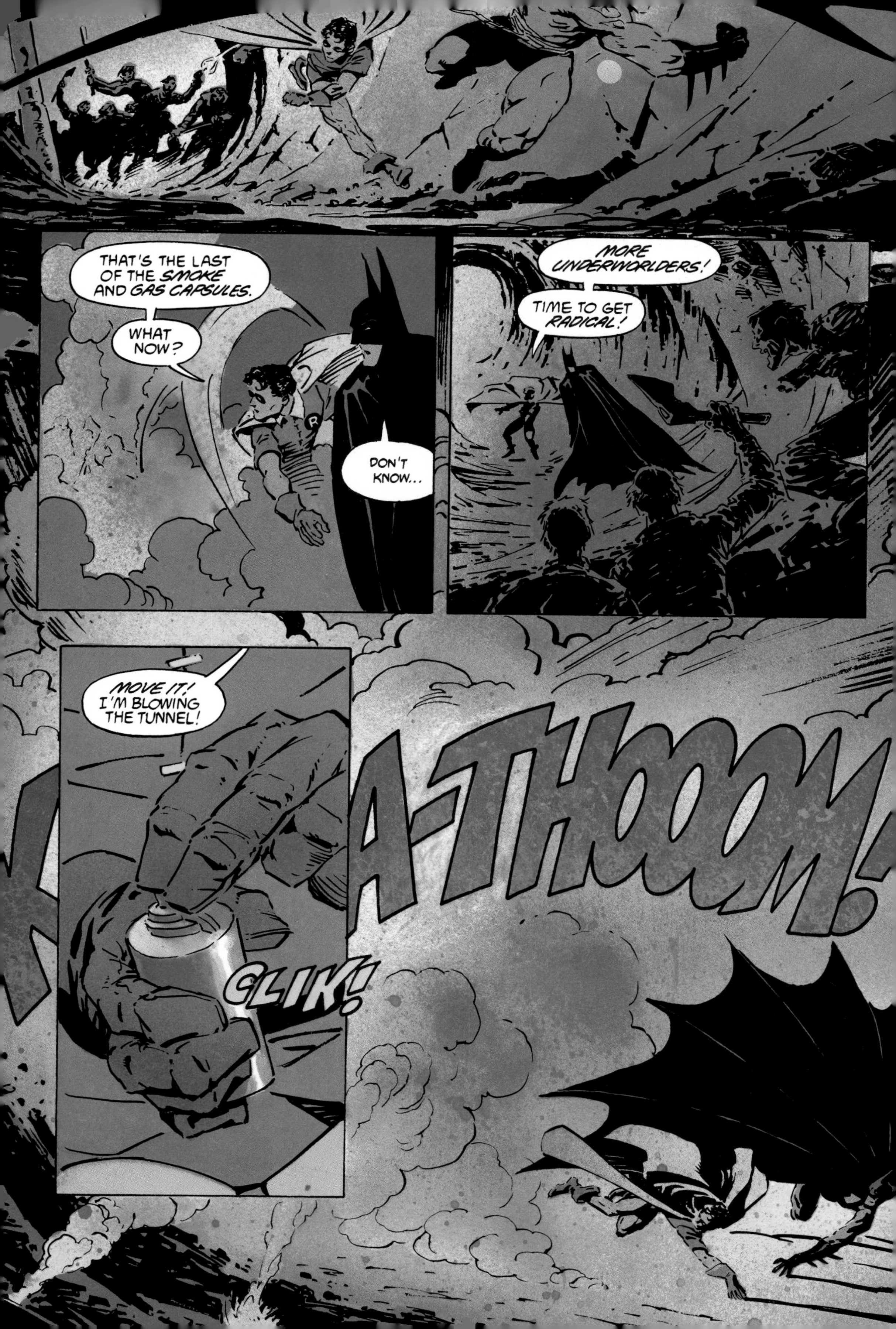
THAT'S THE LAST OF THE SMOKE AND GAS CAPSULES.
WHAT NOW?
DON'T KNOW...
MORE UNDERWORLDERS!
TIME TO GET RADICAL!
MOVE IT! I'M BLOWING THE TUNNEL!
CLIK!
A-THOOOM!

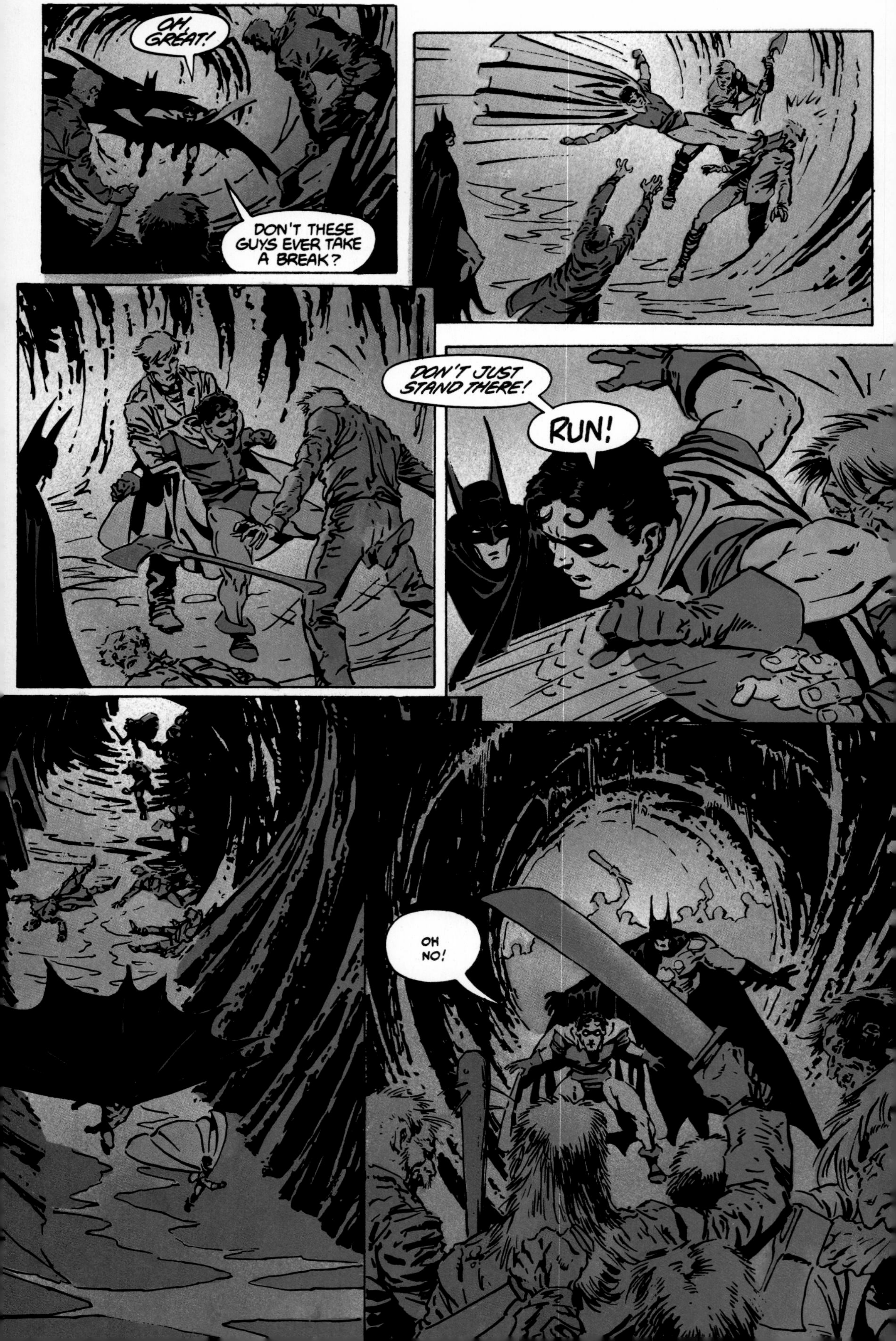
OH, GREAT!
DON'T THESE GUYS EVER TAKE A BREAK?
DON'T JUST STAND THERE!
RUN!
OH NO!

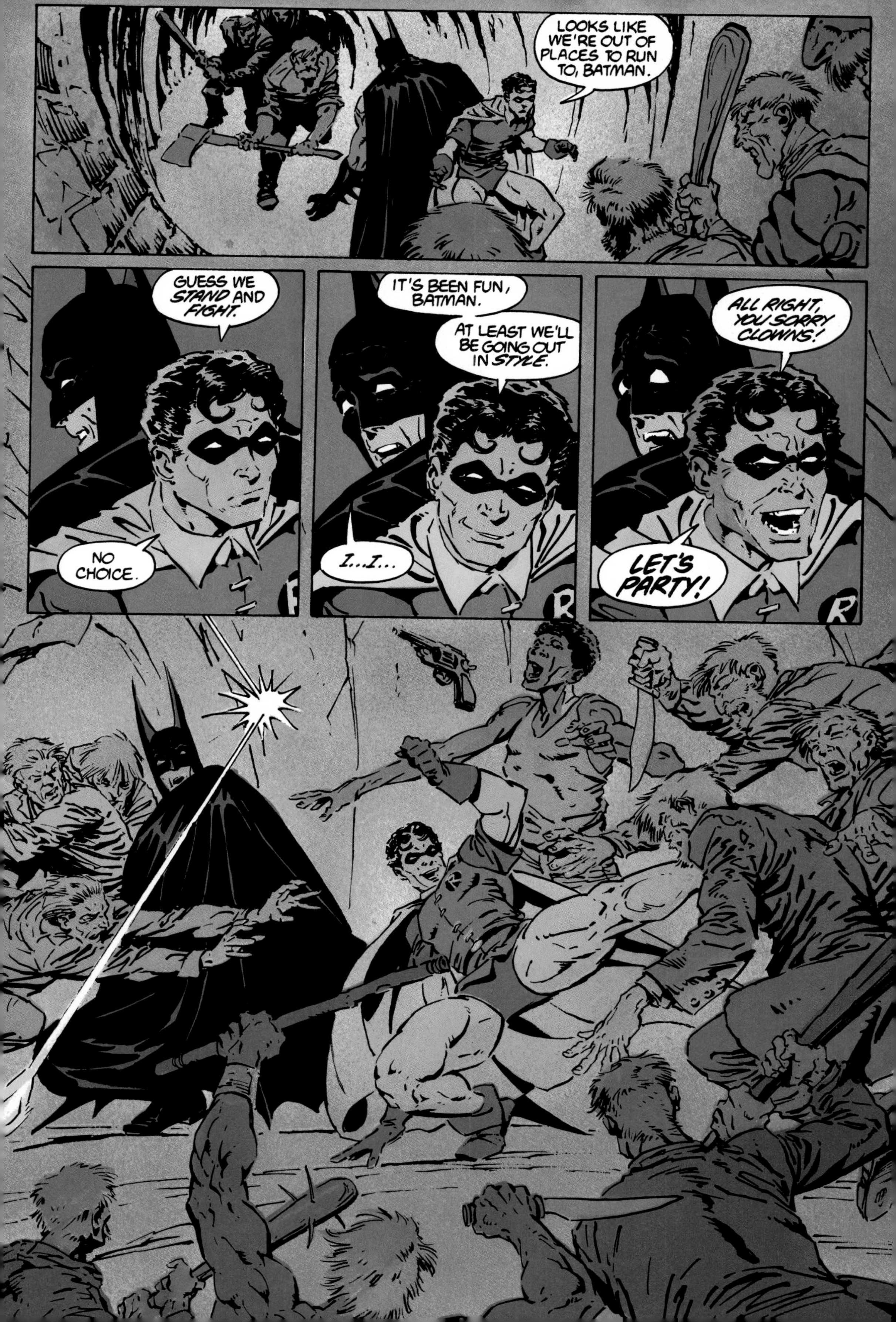

LOOKS LIKE WE'RE OUT OF PLACES TO RUN TO, BATMAN.
GUESS WE STAND AND FIGHT.
NO CHOICE.
IT'S BEEN FUN, BATMAN.
AT LEAST WE'LL BE GOING OUT IN STYLE.
I...I...
ALL RIGHT, YOU SORRY CLOWNS!
LET'S PARTY!

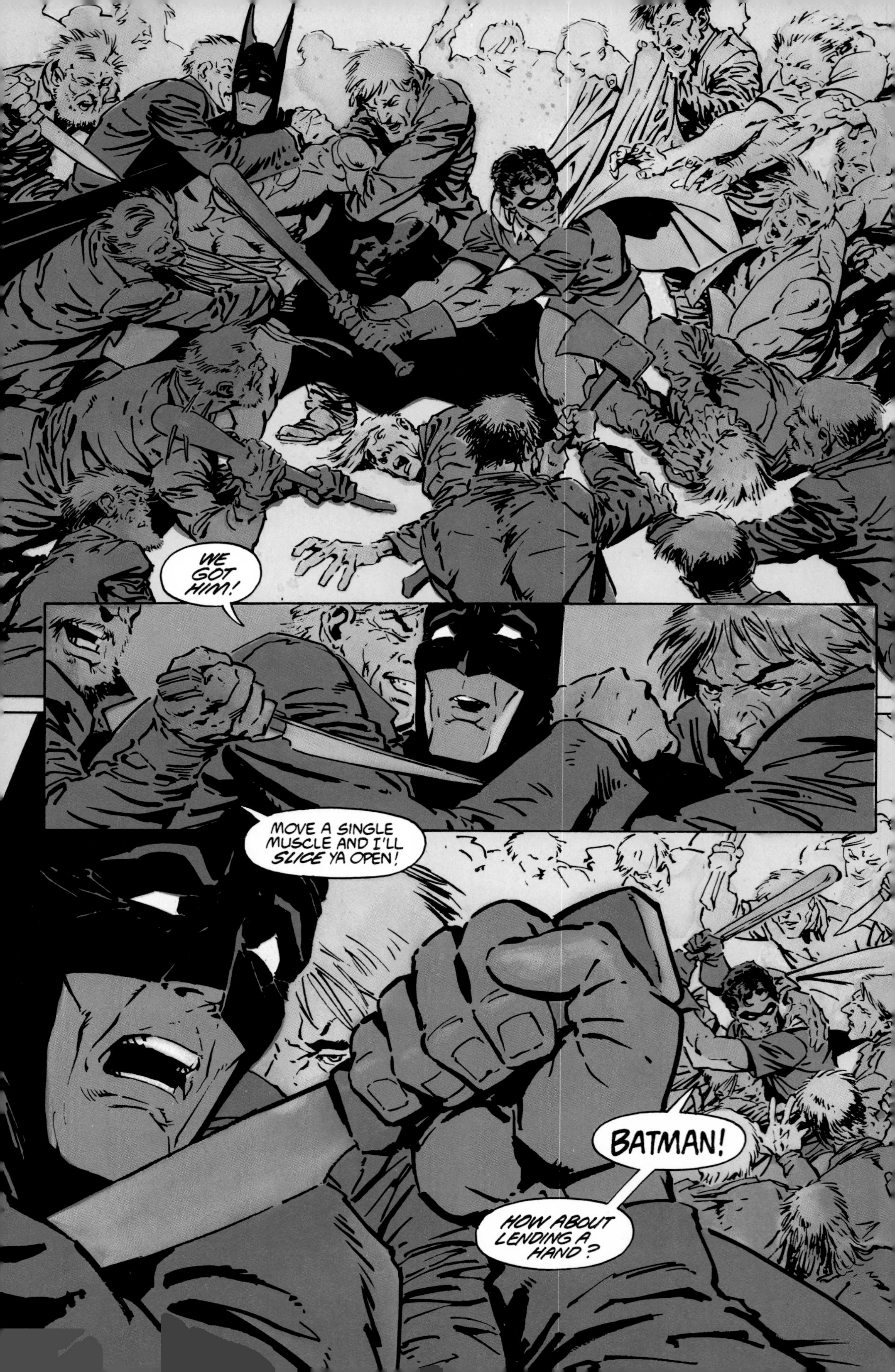
WE GOT HIM!
MOVE A SINGLE MUSCLE AND I'LL SLICE YA OPEN!
BATMAN!
HOW ABOUT LENDING A HAND?

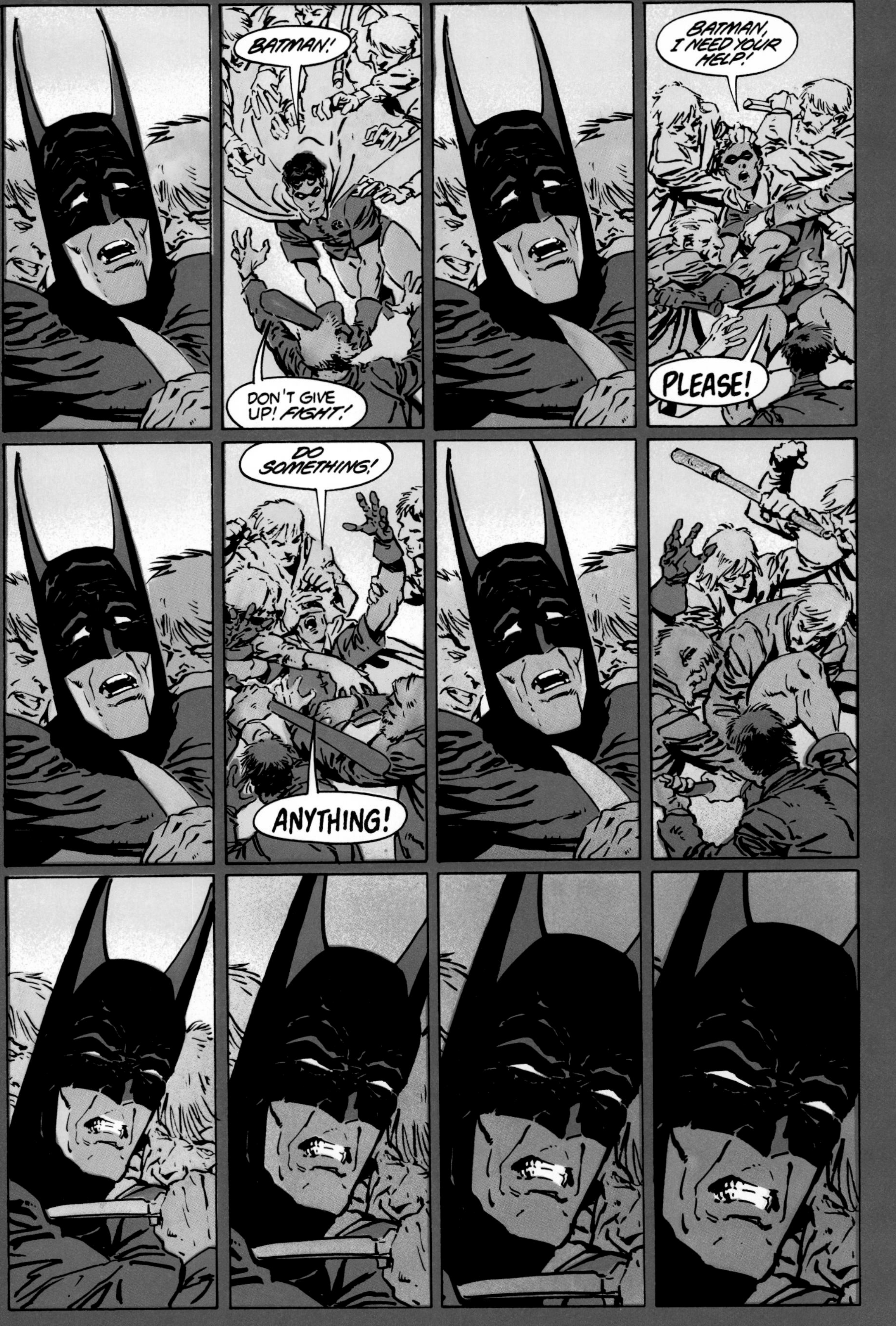
BATMAN!
DON'T GIVE UP! FIGHT!
BATMAN, I NEED YOUR HELP!
PLEASE!
DO SOMETHING!
ANYTHING!

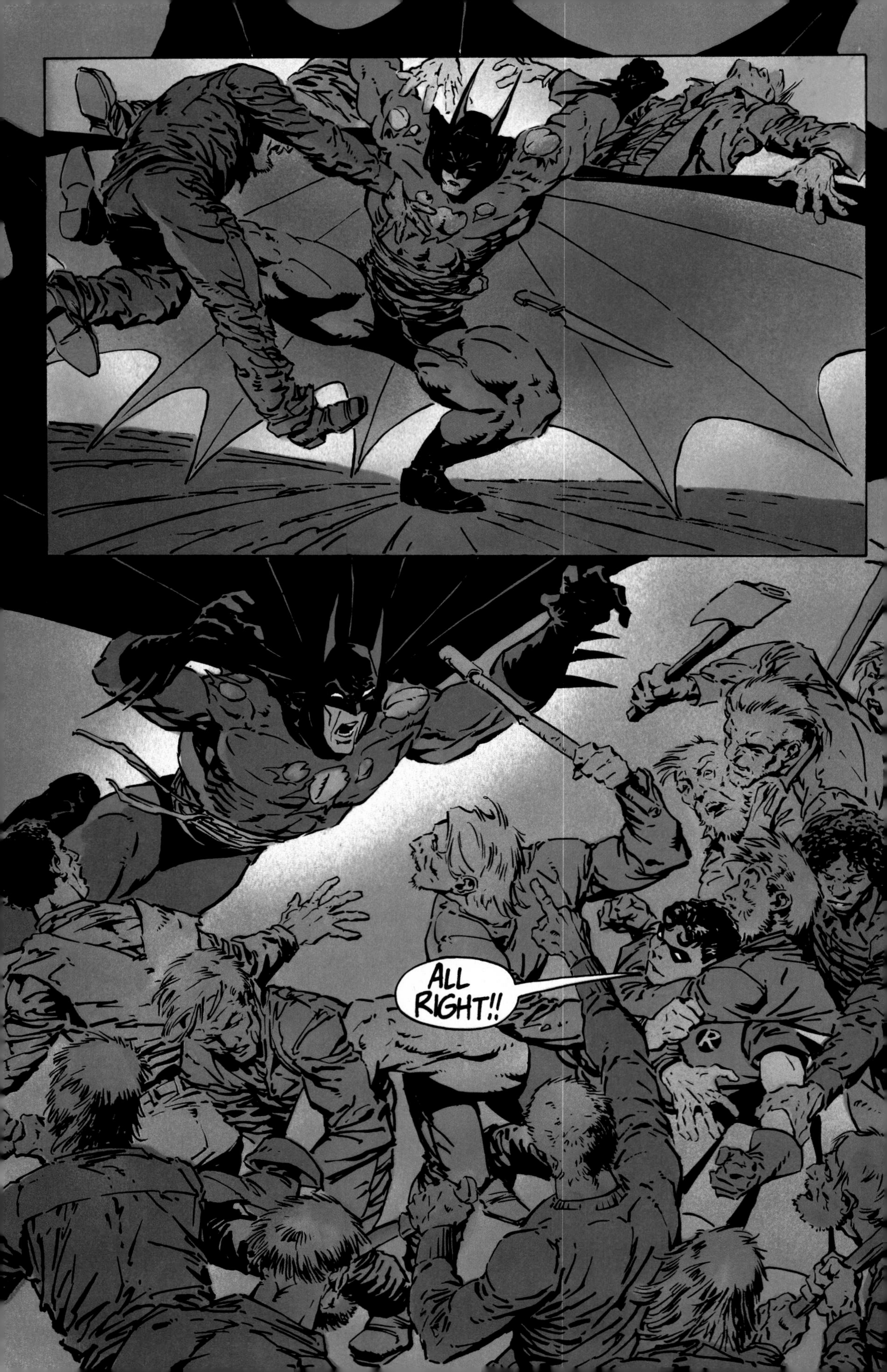
ALL RIGHT!!

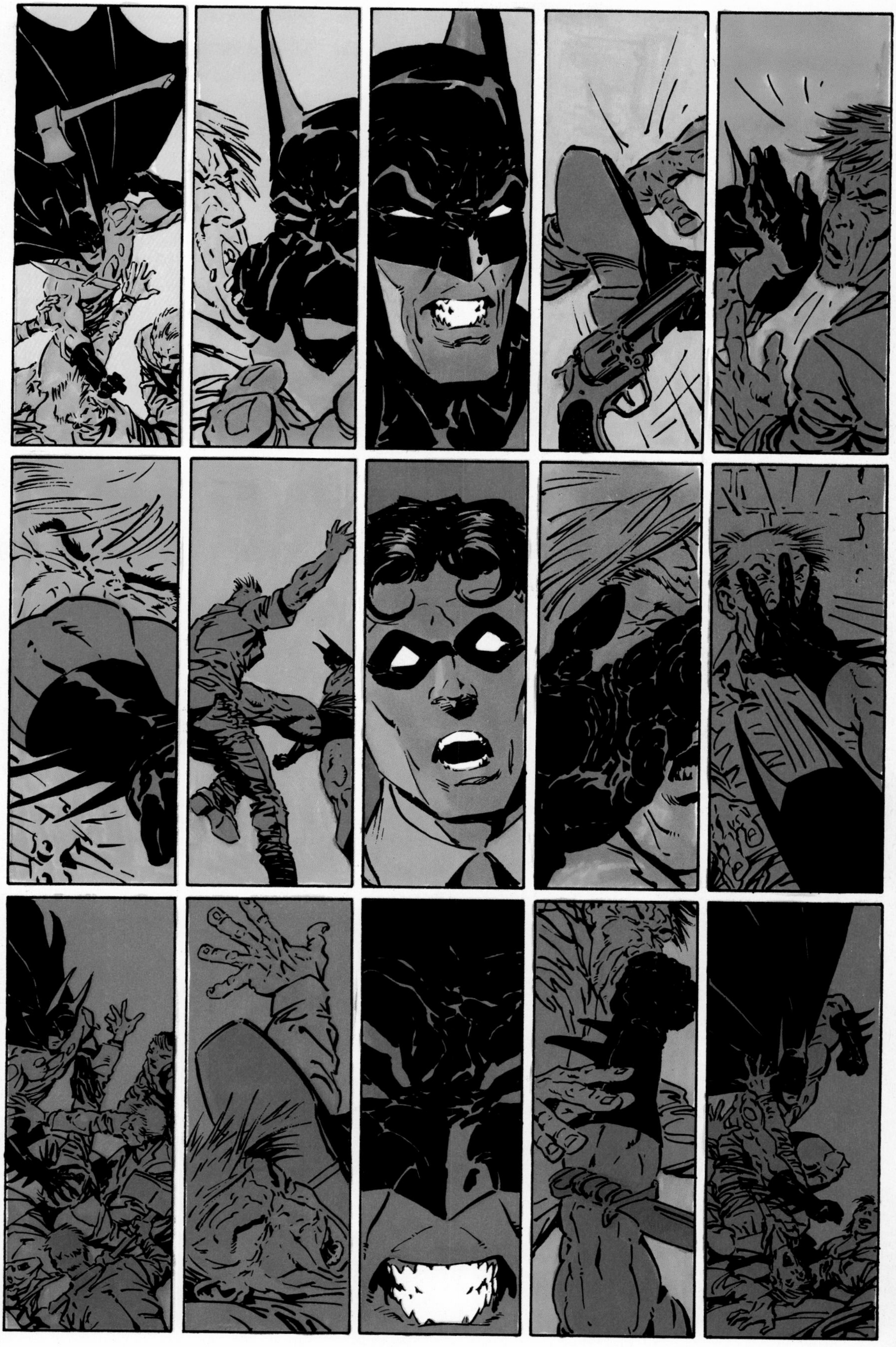

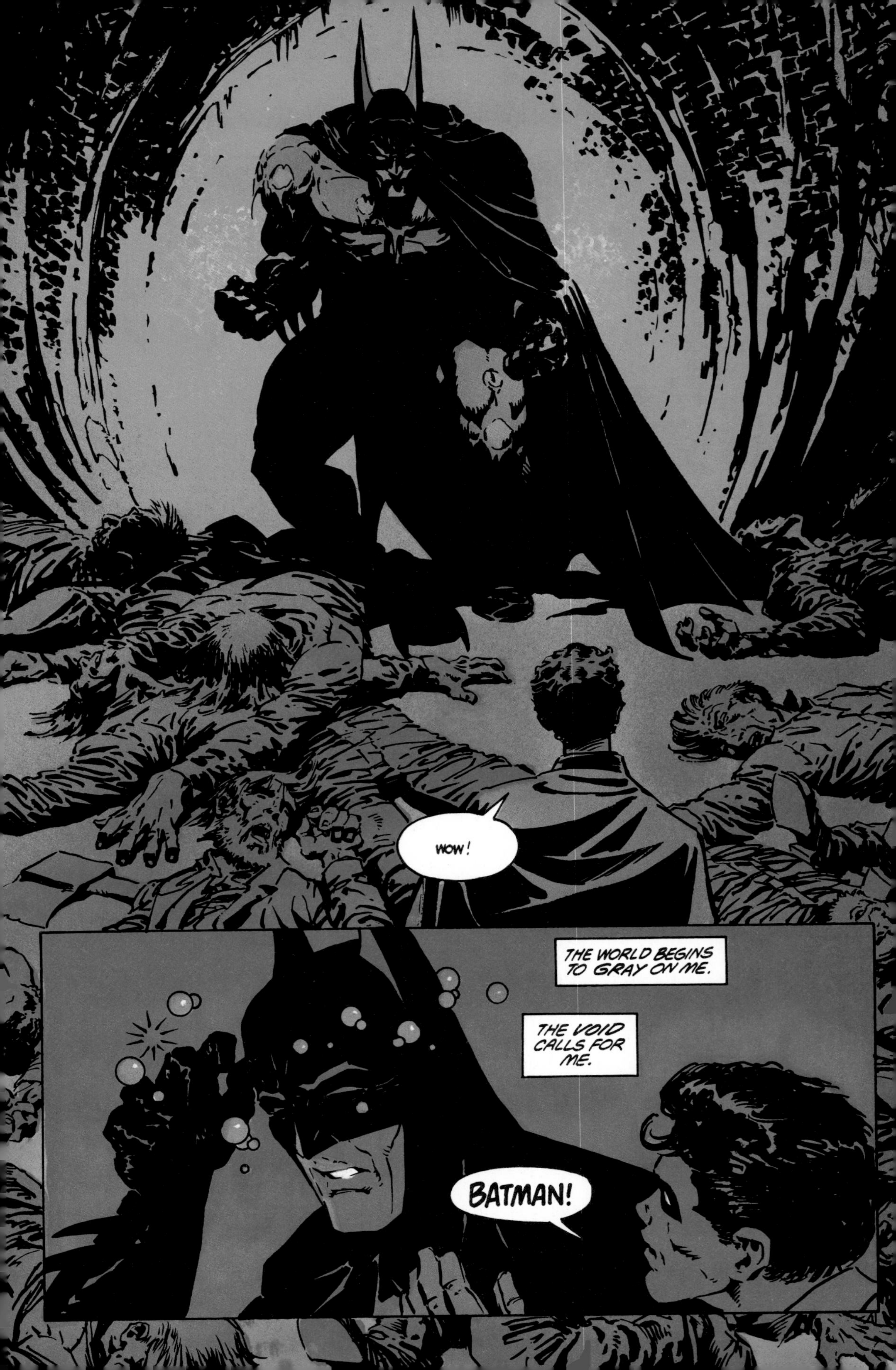
WOW!
THE WORLD BEGINS TO GRAY ON ME.
THE VOID CALLS FOR ME.
BATMAN!

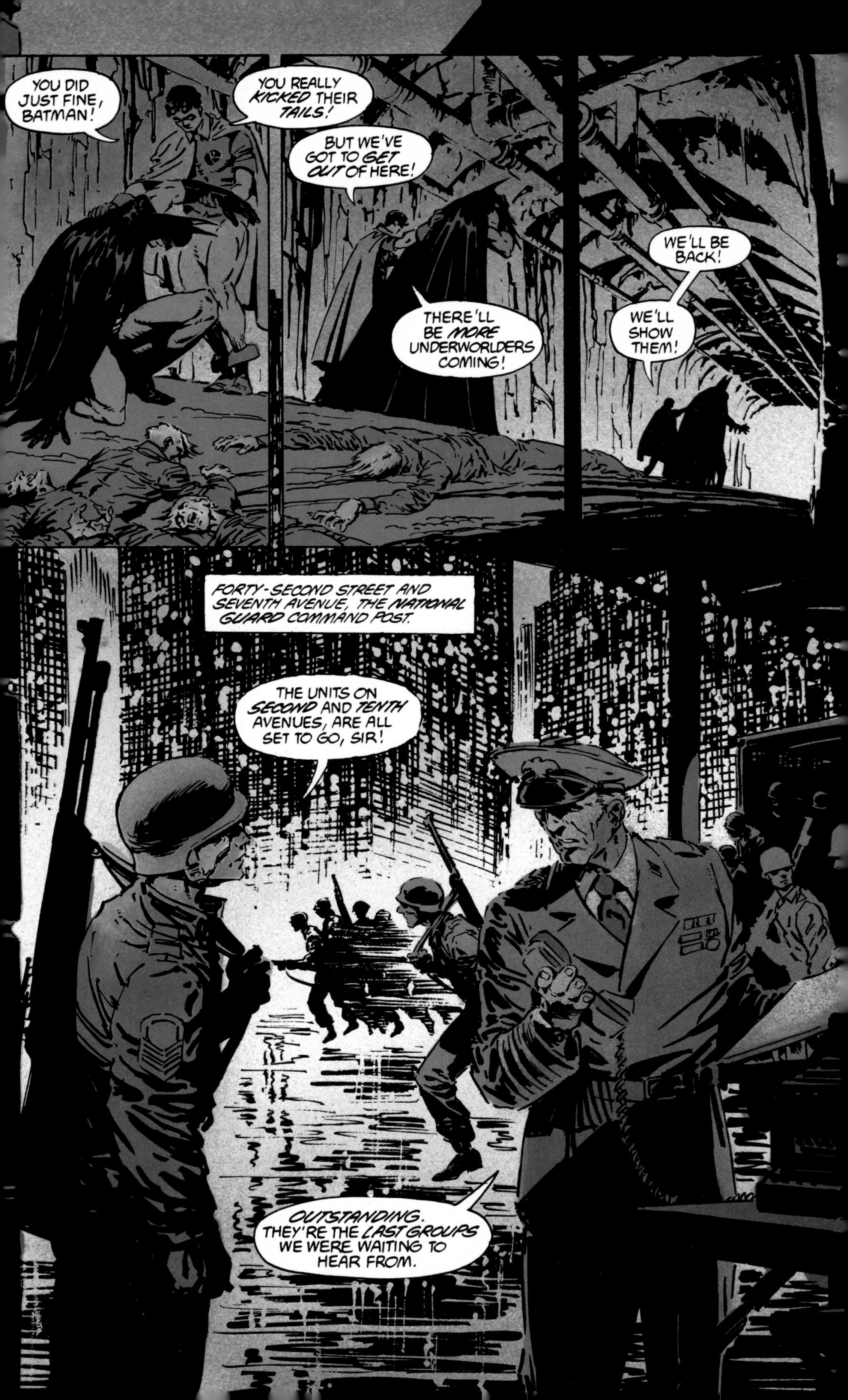
YOU DID JUST FINE, BATMAN!
YOU REALLY KICKED THEIR TAILS!
BUT WE'VE GOT TO GET OUT OF HERE!
THERE'LL BE MORE UNDERWORLDERS COMING!
WE'LL BE BACK!
WE'LL SHOW THEM!
FORTY-SECOND STREET AND SEVENTH AVENUE, THE NATIONAL GUARD COMMAND POST.
THE UNITS ON SECOND AND TENTH AVENUES, ARE ALL SET TO GO, SIR!
OUTSTANDING. THEY'RE THE LAST GROUPS WE WERE WAITING TO HEAR FROM.

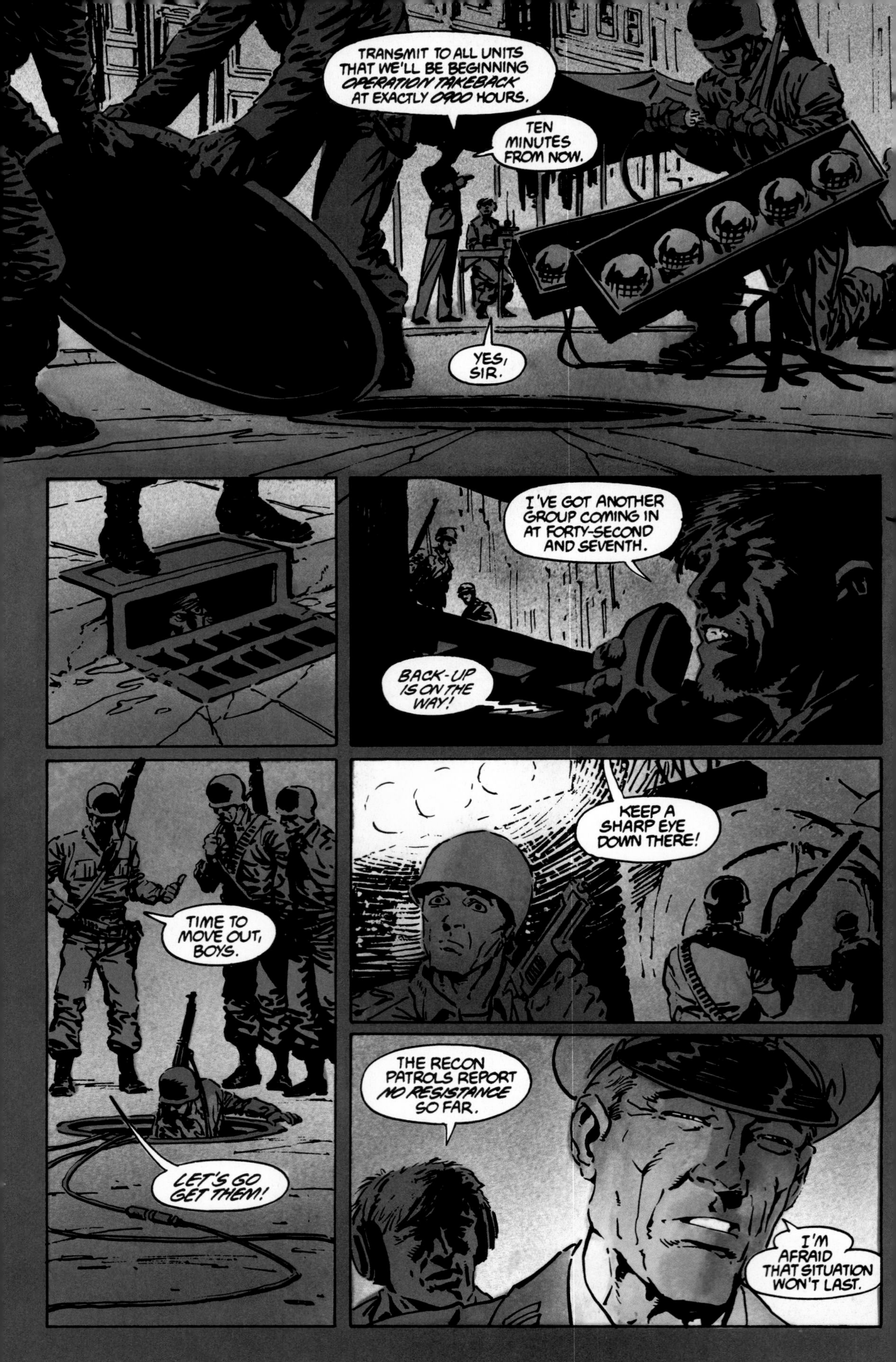
TRANSMIT TO ALL UNITS THAT WE'LL BE BEGINNING *OPERATION TAKEBACK* AT EXACTLY *0900* HOURS.
TEN MINUTES FROM NOW.
YES, SIR.
I'VE GOT ANOTHER GROUP COMING IN AT FORTY-SECOND AND SEVENTH.
BACK-UP IS ON THE WAY!
TIME TO MOVE OUT, BOYS.
LET'S GO GET THEM!
KEEP A SHARP EYE DOWN THERE!
THE RECON PATROLS REPORT *NO RESISTANCE* SO FAR.
I'M AFRAID THAT SITUATION WON'T LAST.

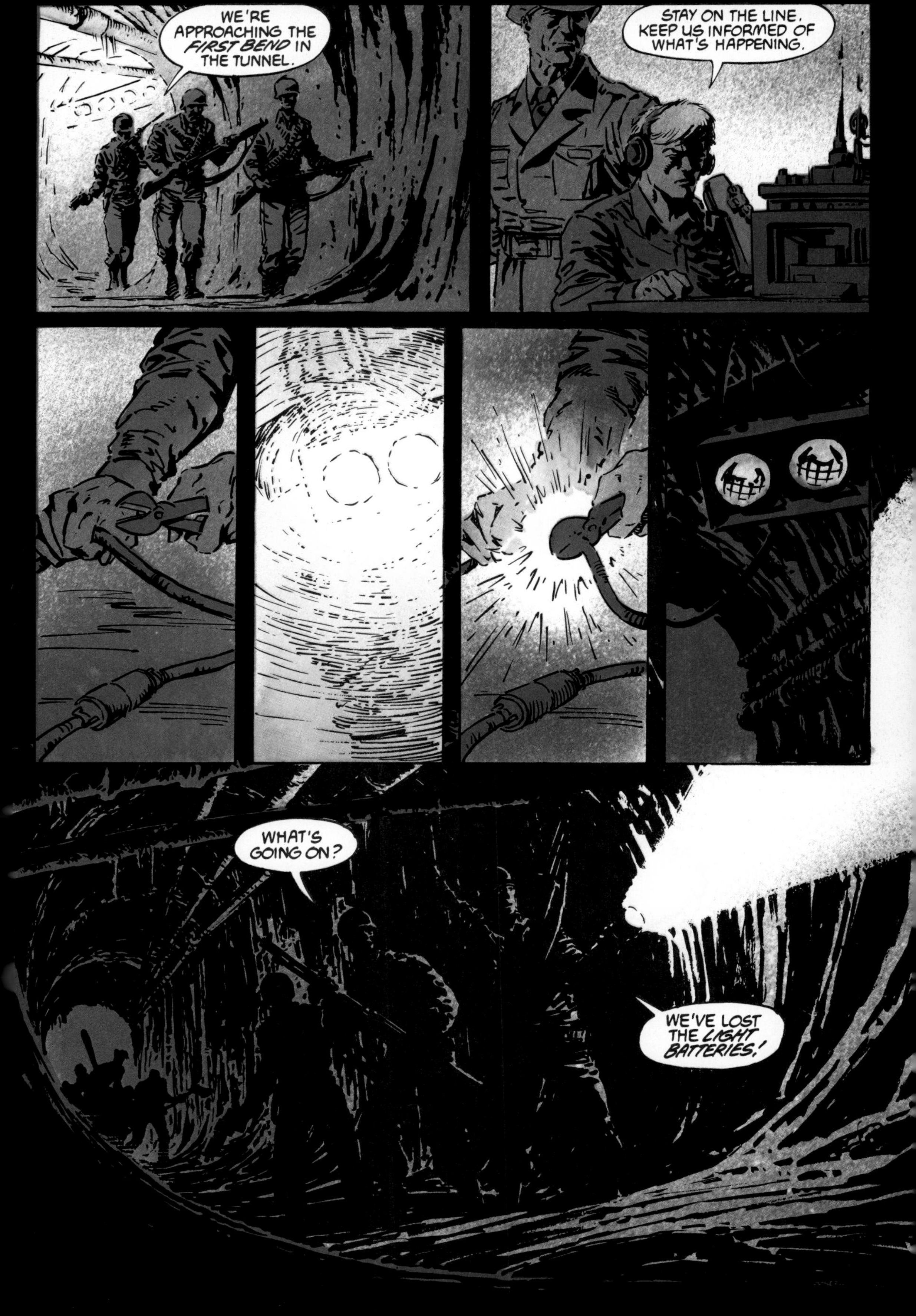

WE'RE APPROACHING THE *FIRST BEND* IN THE TUNNEL.
STAY ON THE LINE. KEEP US INFORMED OF WHAT'S HAPPENING.
WHAT'S GOING ON?
WE'VE LOST THE *LIGHT BATTERIES!*

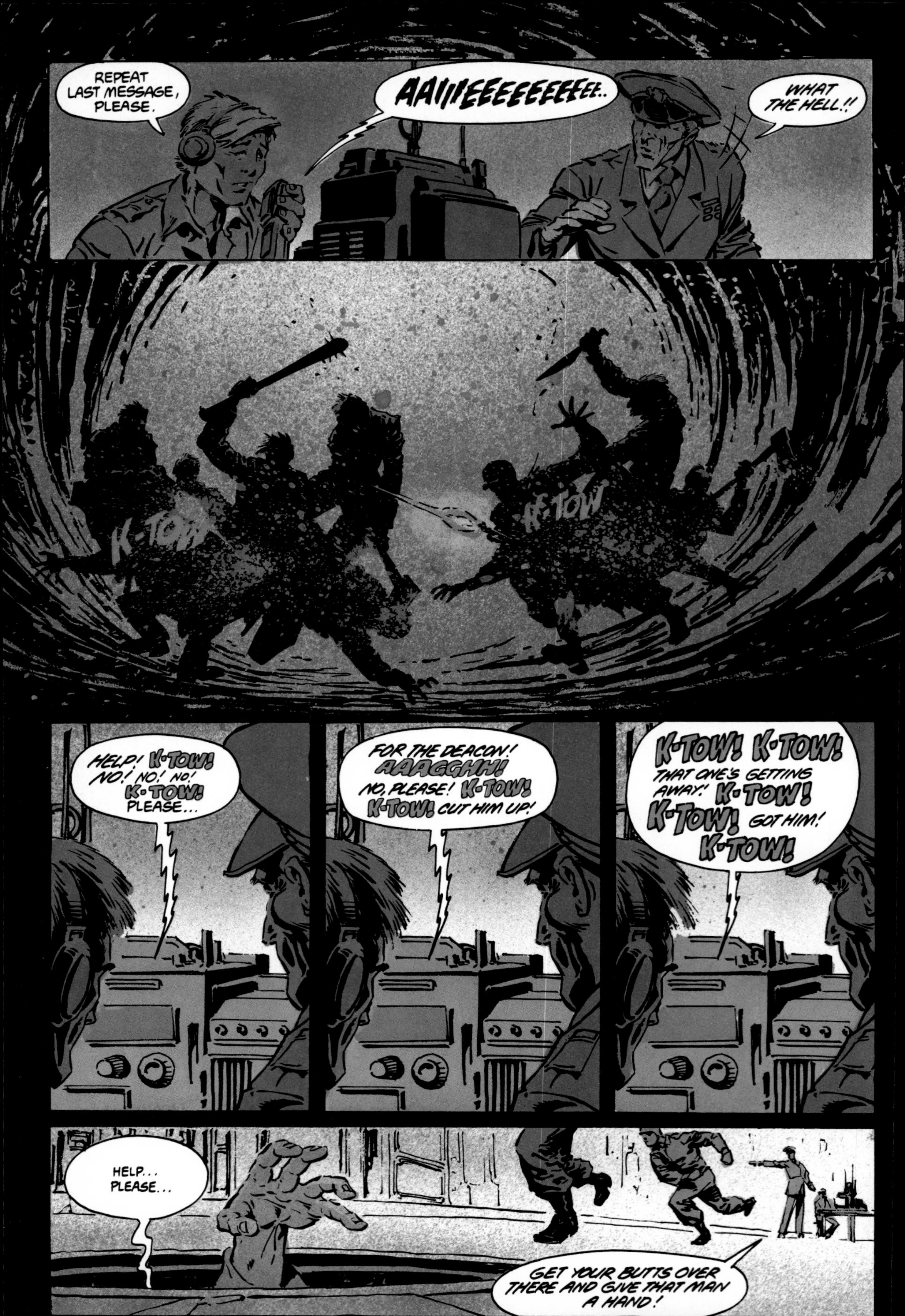
REPEAT LAST MESSAGE, PLEASE.
AAIIIEEEEEEEEEEEE..
WHAT THE HELL!!
K-TOW
K-TOW
HELP! K-TOW! NO! NO! NO! K-TOW! PLEASE...
FOR THE DEACON! AAAAGGHH! NO, PLEASE! K-TOW! K-TOW! CUT HIM UP!
K-TOW! K-TOW! THAT ONE'S GETTING AWAY! K-TOW! K-TOW! GOT HIM! K-TOW!
HELP... PLEASE...
GET YOUR BUTTS OVER THERE AND GIVE THAT MAN A HAND!

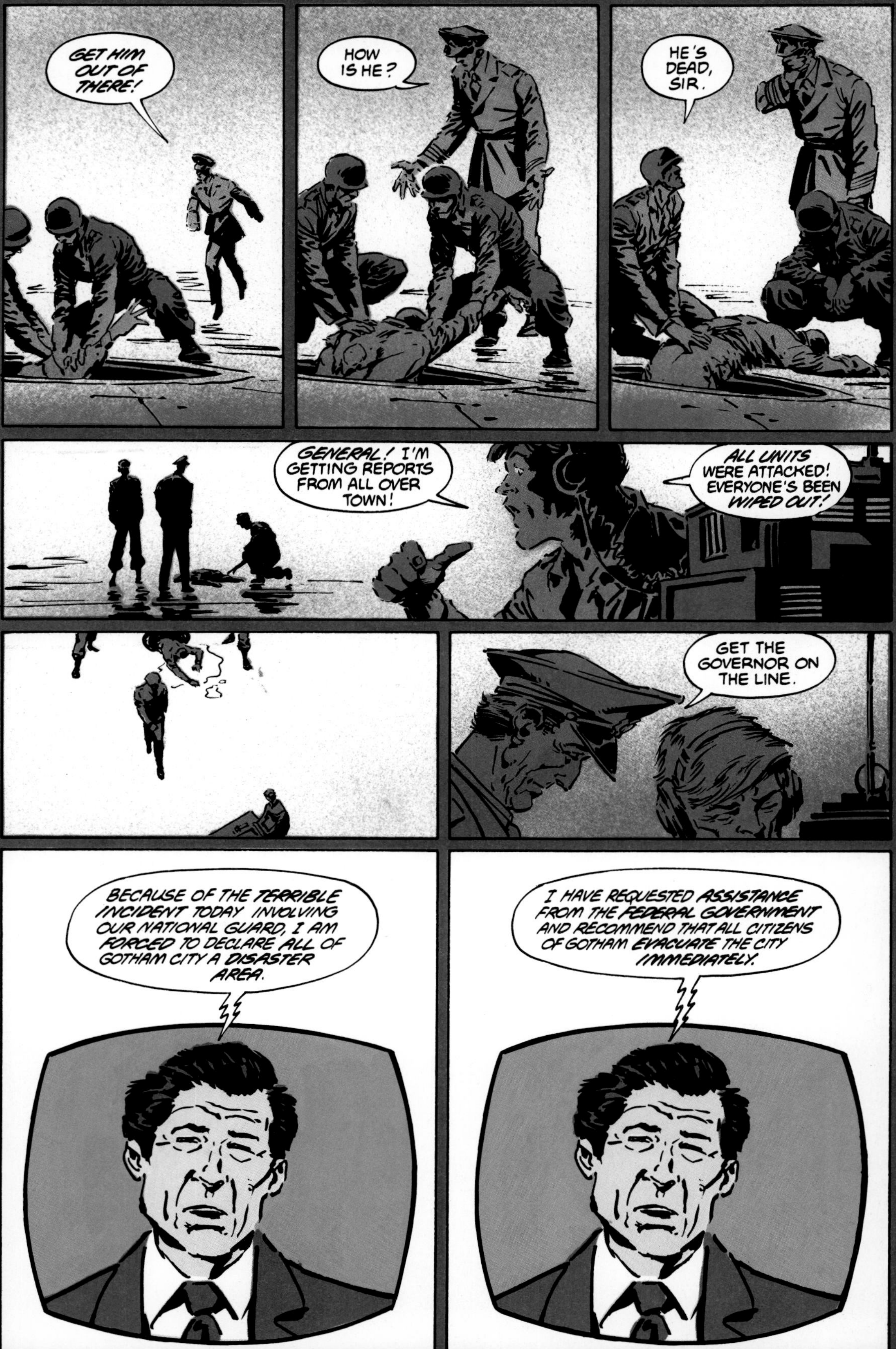
GET HIM OUT OF THERE!
HOW IS HE?
HE'S DEAD, SIR.
GENERAL! I'M GETTING REPORTS FROM ALL OVER TOWN!
ALL UNITS WERE ATTACKED! EVERYONE'S BEEN WIPED OUT!
GET THE GOVERNOR ON THE LINE.
BECAUSE OF THE TERRIBLE INCIDENT TODAY INVOLVING OUR NATIONAL GUARD, I AM FORCED TO DECLARE ALL OF GOTHAM CITY A DISASTER AREA.
I HAVE REQUESTED ASSISTANCE FROM THE FEDERAL GOVERNMENT AND RECOMMEND THAT ALL CITIZENS OF GOTHAM EVACUATE THE CITY IMMEDIATELY.

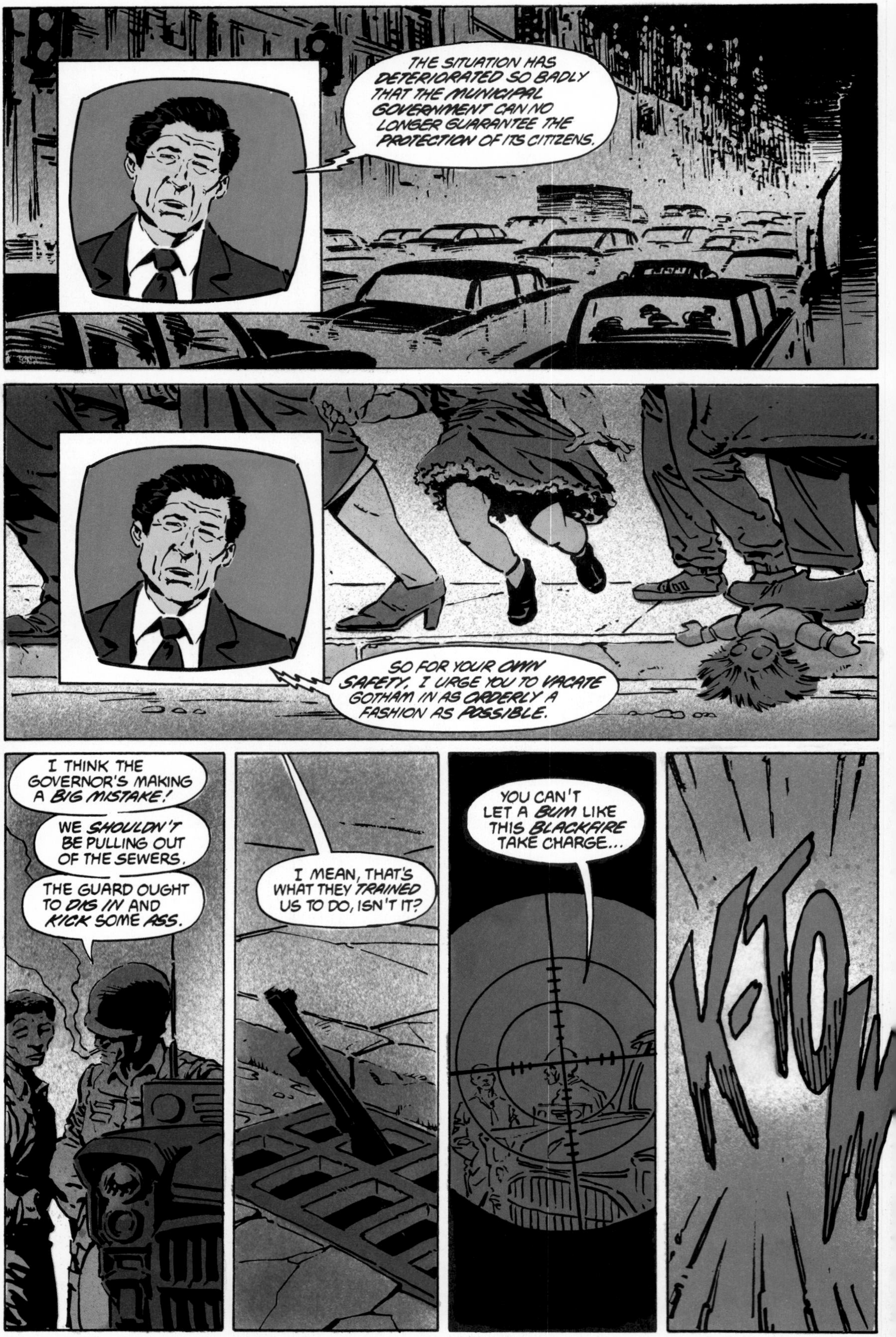
THE SITUATION HAS DETERIORATED SO BADLY THAT THE MUNICIPAL GOVERNMENT CAN NO LONGER GUARANTEE THE PROTECTION OF ITS CITIZENS.
SO FOR YOUR OWN SAFETY, I URGE YOU TO VACATE GOTHAM IN AS ORDERLY A FASHION AS POSSIBLE.
I THINK THE GOVERNOR'S MAKING A BIG MISTAKE!
WE SHOULDN'T BE PULLING OUT OF THE SEWERS.
THE GUARD OUGHT TO DIG IN AND KICK SOME ASS.
I MEAN, THAT'S WHAT THEY TRAINED US TO DO, ISN'T IT?
YOU CAN'T LET A BUM LIKE THIS BLACKFIRE TAKE CHARGE...
K-TOW

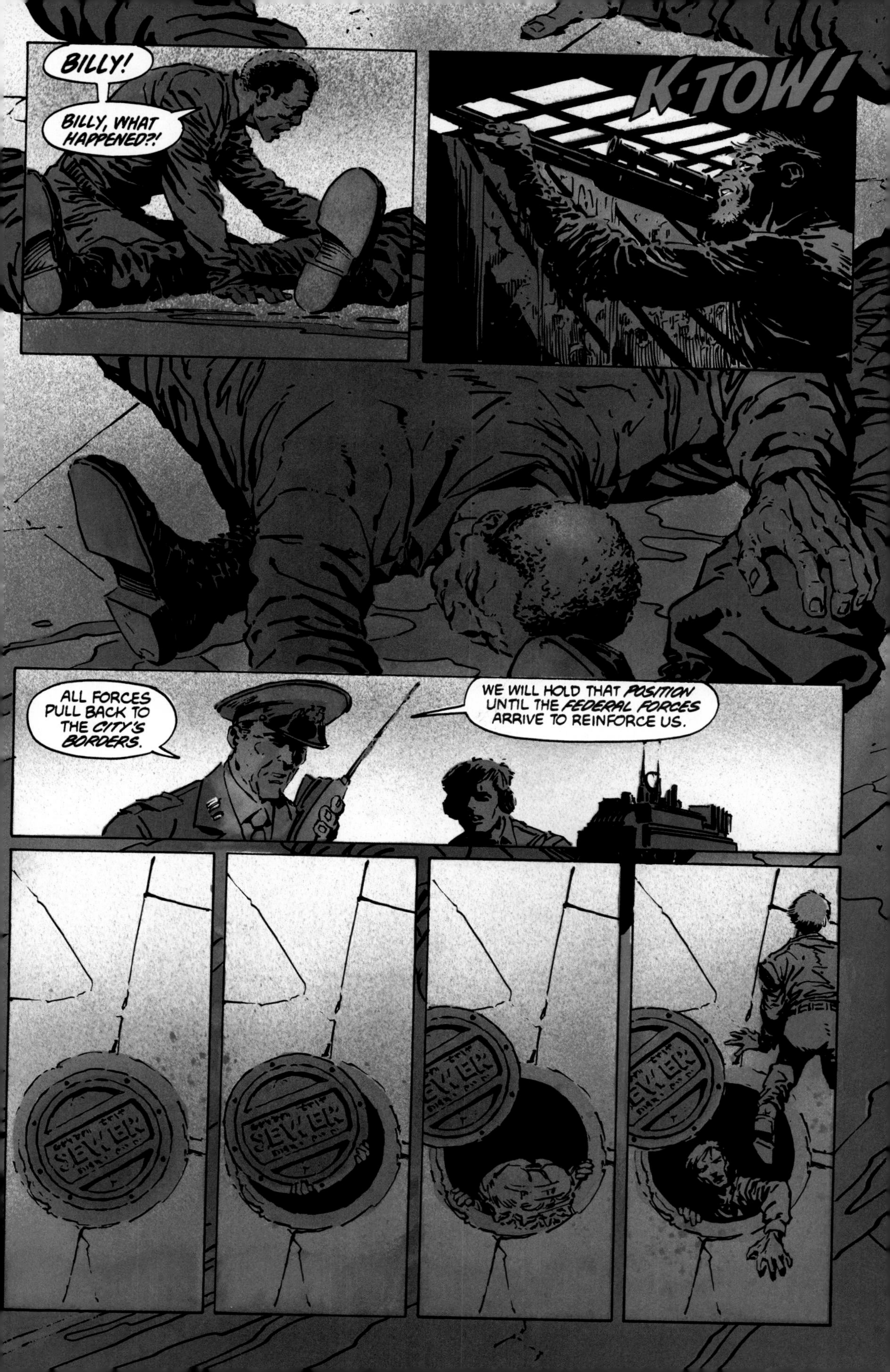
BILLY!
BILLY, WHAT HAPPENED?!
K-TOW!
ALL FORCES PULL BACK TO THE CITY'S BORDERS.
WE WILL HOLD THAT POSITION UNTIL THE FEDERAL FORCES ARRIVE TO REINFORCE US.
SEWER
SEWER
SEWER
SEWER

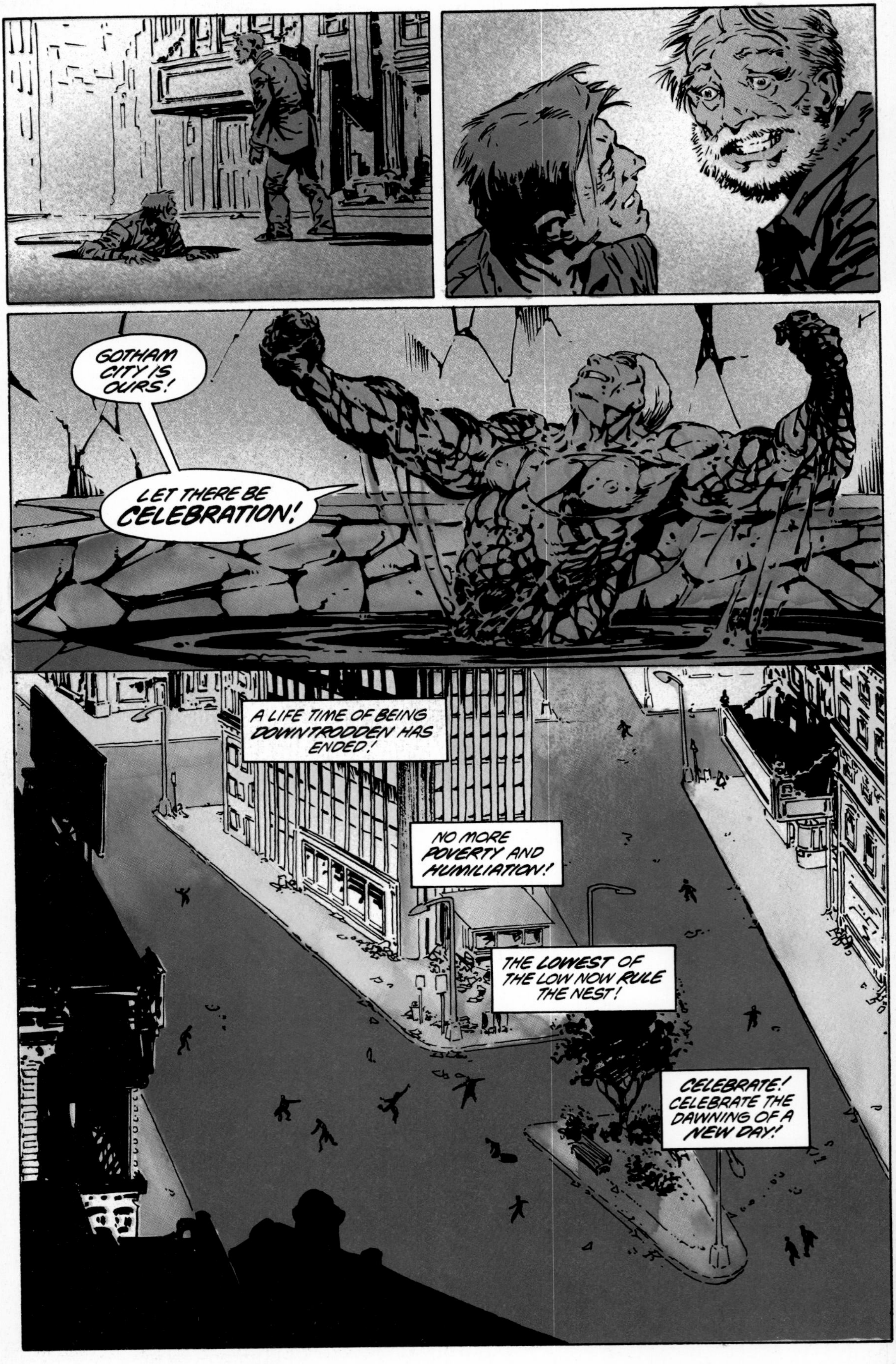
GOTHAM CITY IS OURS!
LET THERE BE CELEBRATION!
A LIFE TIME OF BEING DOWNTRODDEN HAS ENDED!
NO MORE POVERTY AND HUMILIATION!
THE LOWEST OF THE LOW NOW RULE THE NEST!
CELEBRATE! CELEBRATE THE DAWNING OF A NEW DAY!

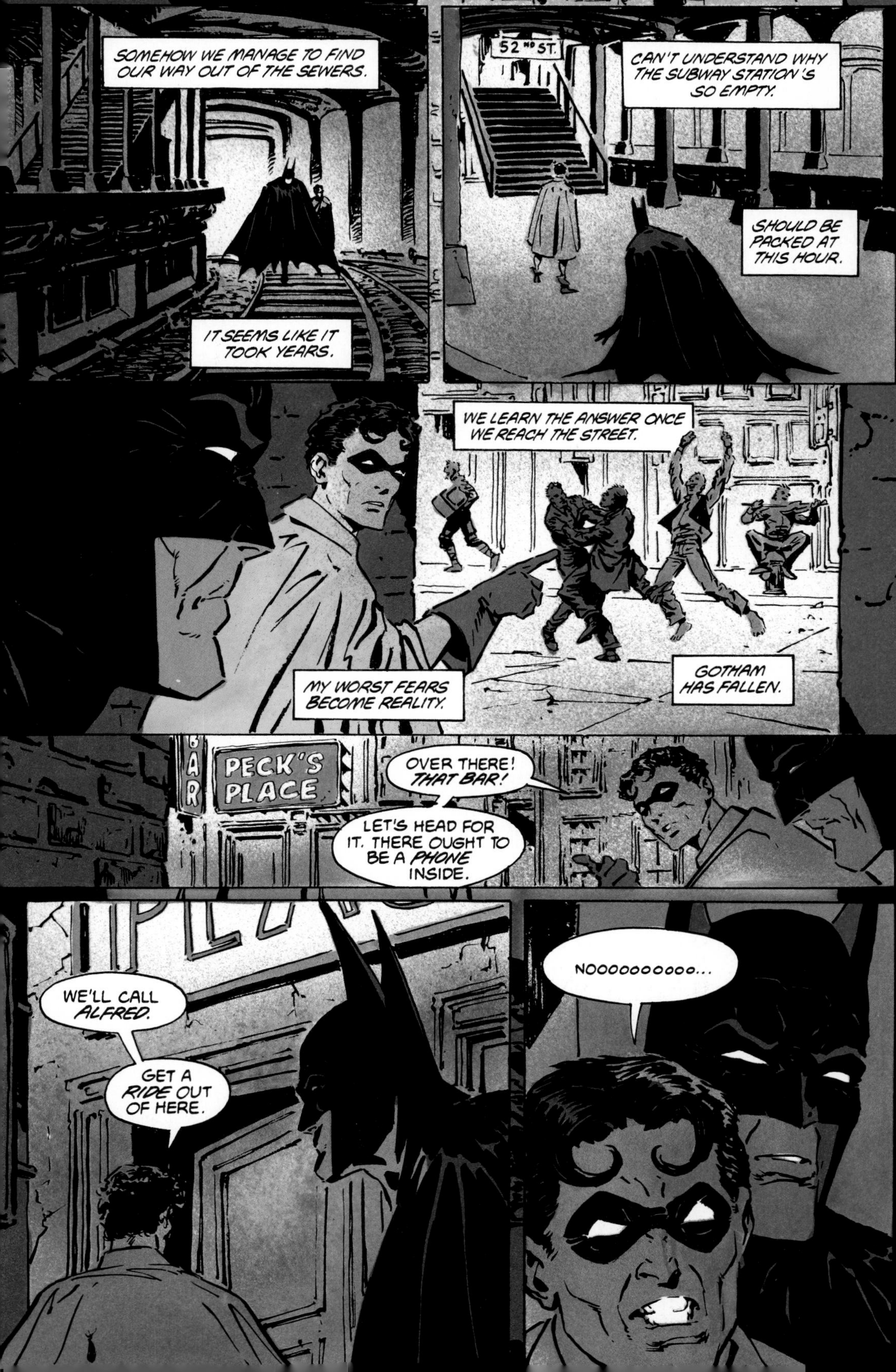
SOMEHOW WE MANAGE TO FIND OUR WAY OUT OF THE SEWERS.
IT SEEMS LIKE IT TOOK YEARS.
52ND ST.
CAN'T UNDERSTAND WHY THE SUBWAY STATION'S SO EMPTY.
SHOULD BE PACKED AT THIS HOUR.
WE LEARN THE ANSWER ONCE WE REACH THE STREET.
MY WORST FEARS BECOME REALITY.
GOTHAM HAS FALLEN.
BAR
PECK'S PLACE
OVER THERE! THAT BAR!
LET'S HEAD FOR IT. THERE OUGHT TO BE A PHONE INSIDE.
WE'LL CALL ALFRED.
GET A RIDE OUT OF HERE.
NOOOOOOOOOO...

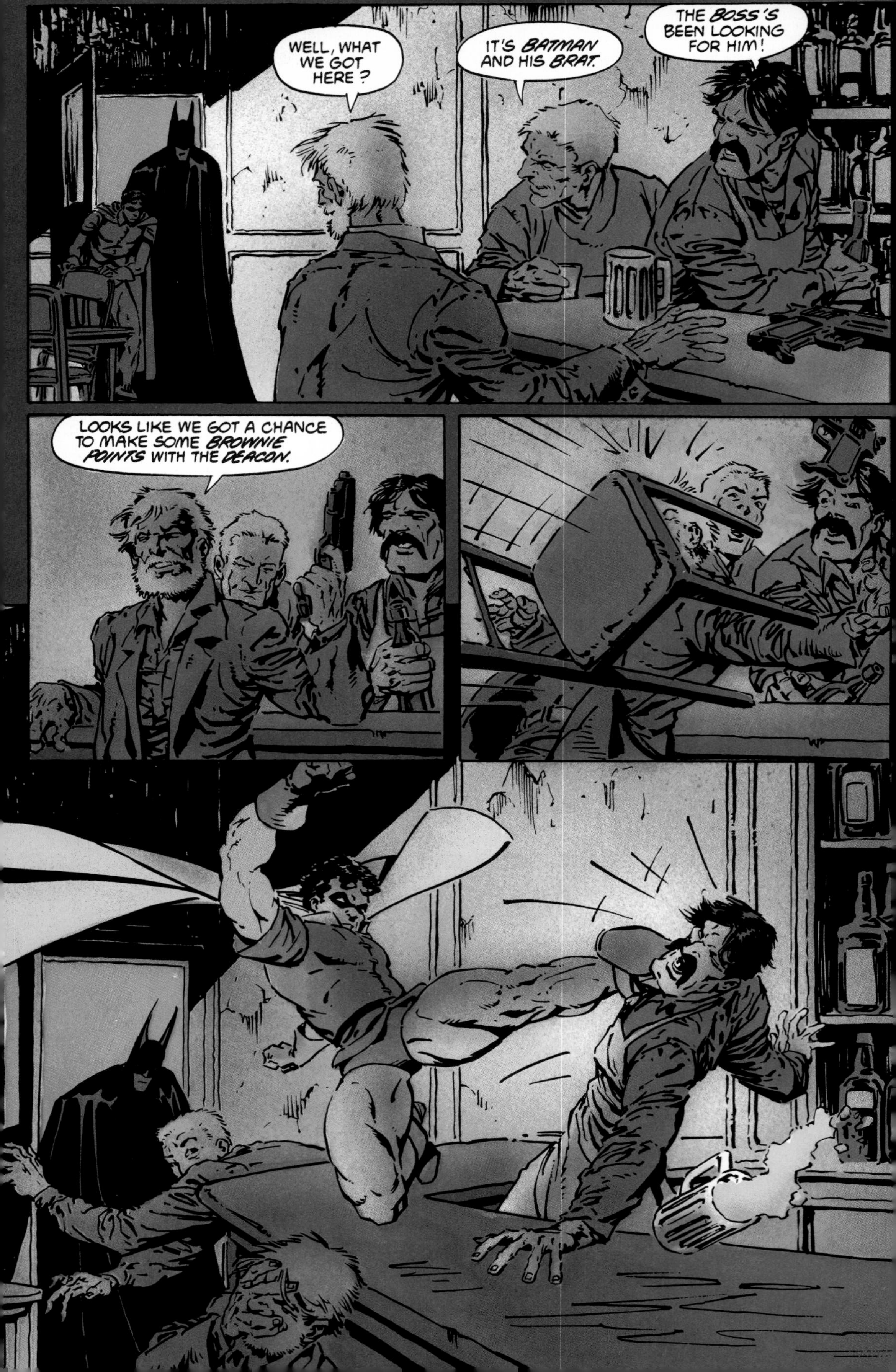
WELL, WHAT WE GOT HERE ?
IT'S *BATMAN* AND HIS *BRAT.*
THE *BOSS*'S BEEN LOOKING FOR HIM!
LOOKS LIKE WE GOT A CHANCE TO MAKE SOME *BROWNIE POINTS* WITH THE *DEACON.*

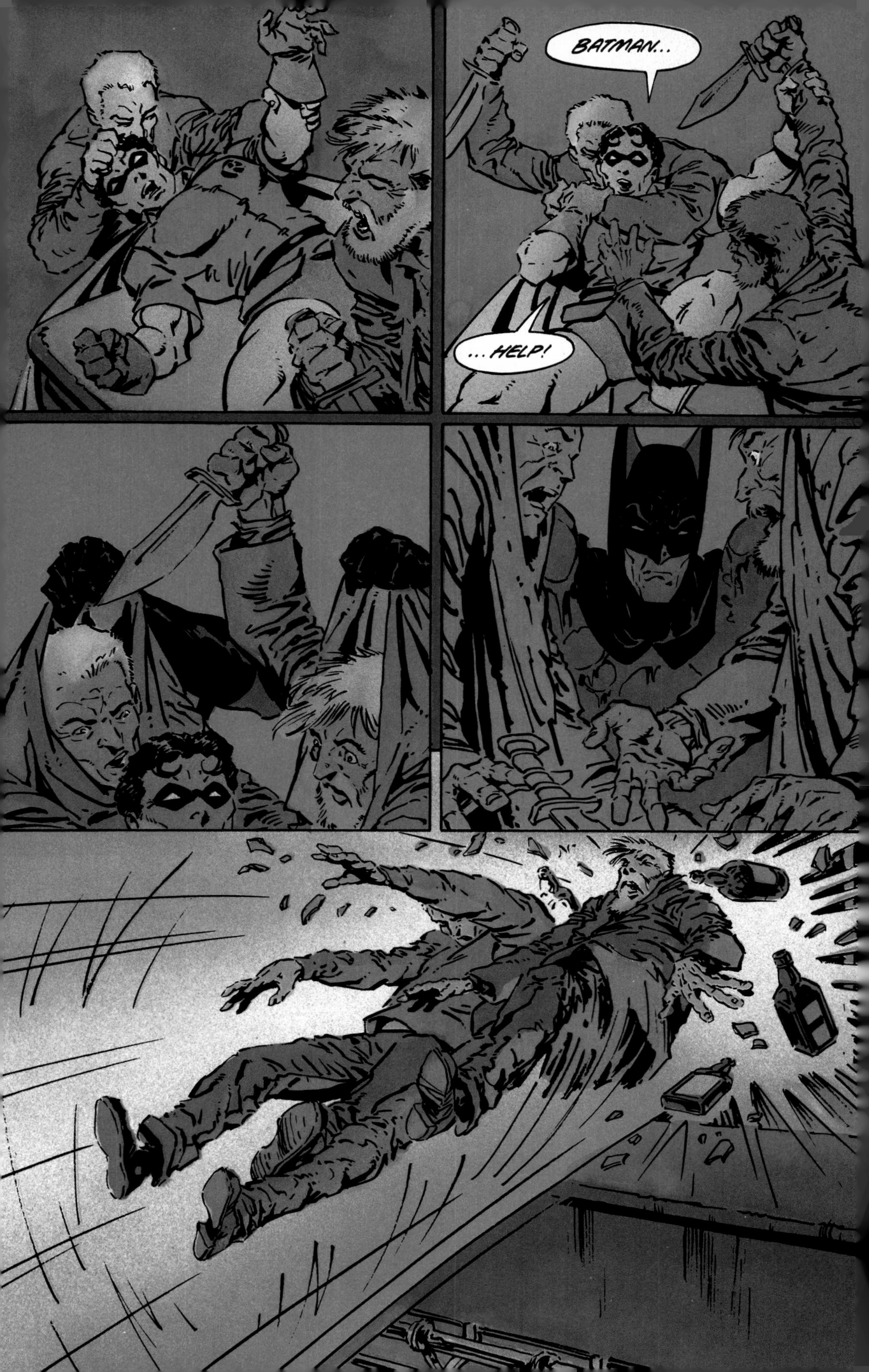
BATMAN...
...HELP!

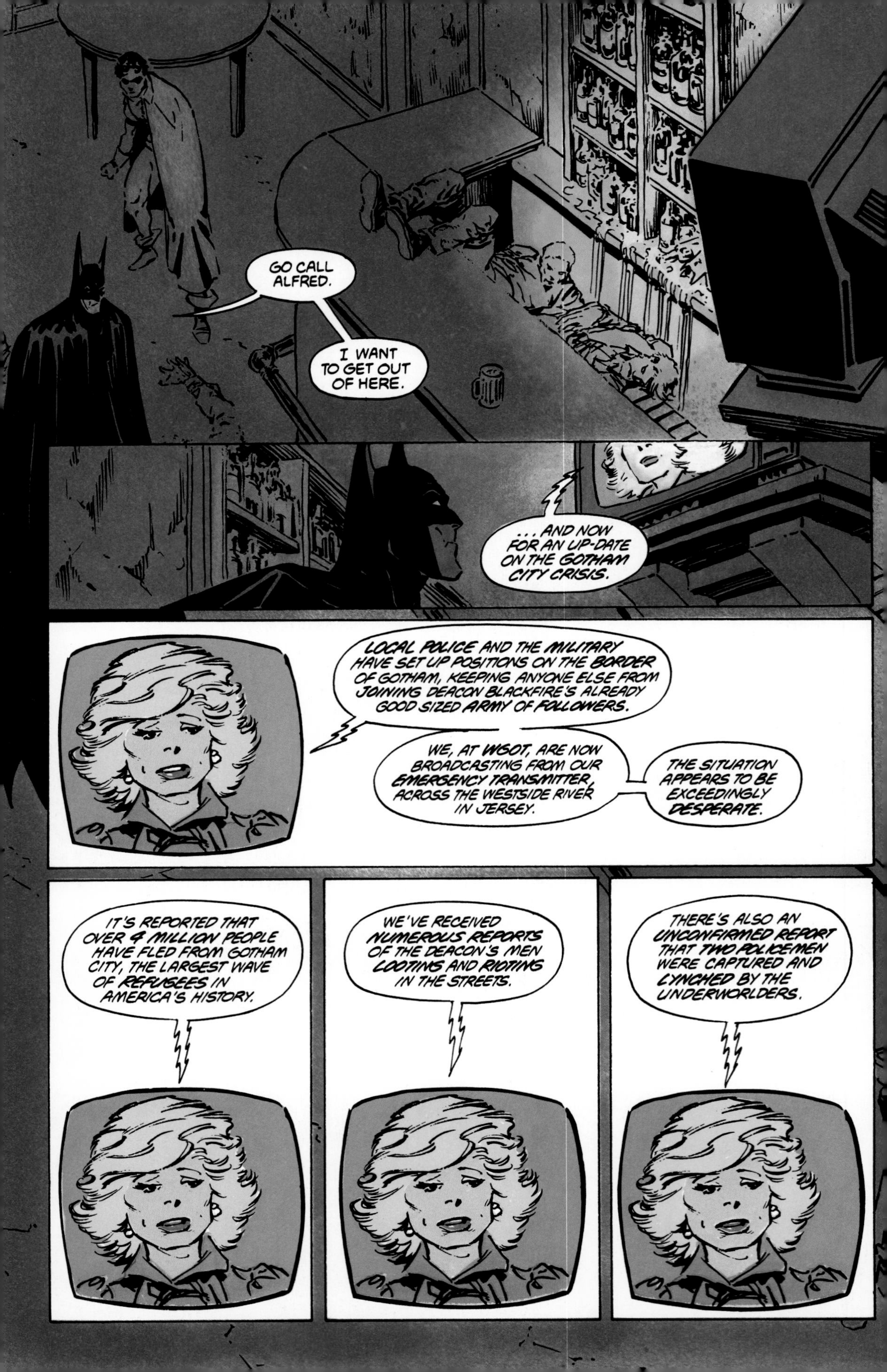
GO CALL ALFRED.
I WANT TO GET OUT OF HERE.
...AND NOW FOR AN UP-DATE ON THE GOTHAM CITY CRISIS.
LOCAL POLICE AND THE MILITARY HAVE SET UP POSITIONS ON THE BORDER OF GOTHAM, KEEPING ANYONE ELSE FROM JOINING DEACON BLACKFIRE'S ALREADY GOOD SIZED ARMY OF FOLLOWERS.
WE, AT WSOT, ARE NOW BROADCASTING FROM OUR EMERGENCY TRANSMITTER, ACROSS THE WESTSIDE RIVER IN JERSEY.
THE SITUATION APPEARS TO BE EXCEEDINGLY DESPERATE.
IT'S REPORTED THAT OVER 4 MILLION PEOPLE HAVE FLED FROM GOTHAM CITY, THE LARGEST WAVE OF REFUGEES IN AMERICA'S HISTORY.
WE'VE RECEIVED NUMEROUS REPORTS OF THE DEACON'S MEN LOOTING AND RIOTING IN THE STREETS.
THERE'S ALSO AN UNCONFIRMED REPORT THAT TWO POLICEMEN WERE CAPTURED AND LYNCHED BY THE UNDERWORLDERS.

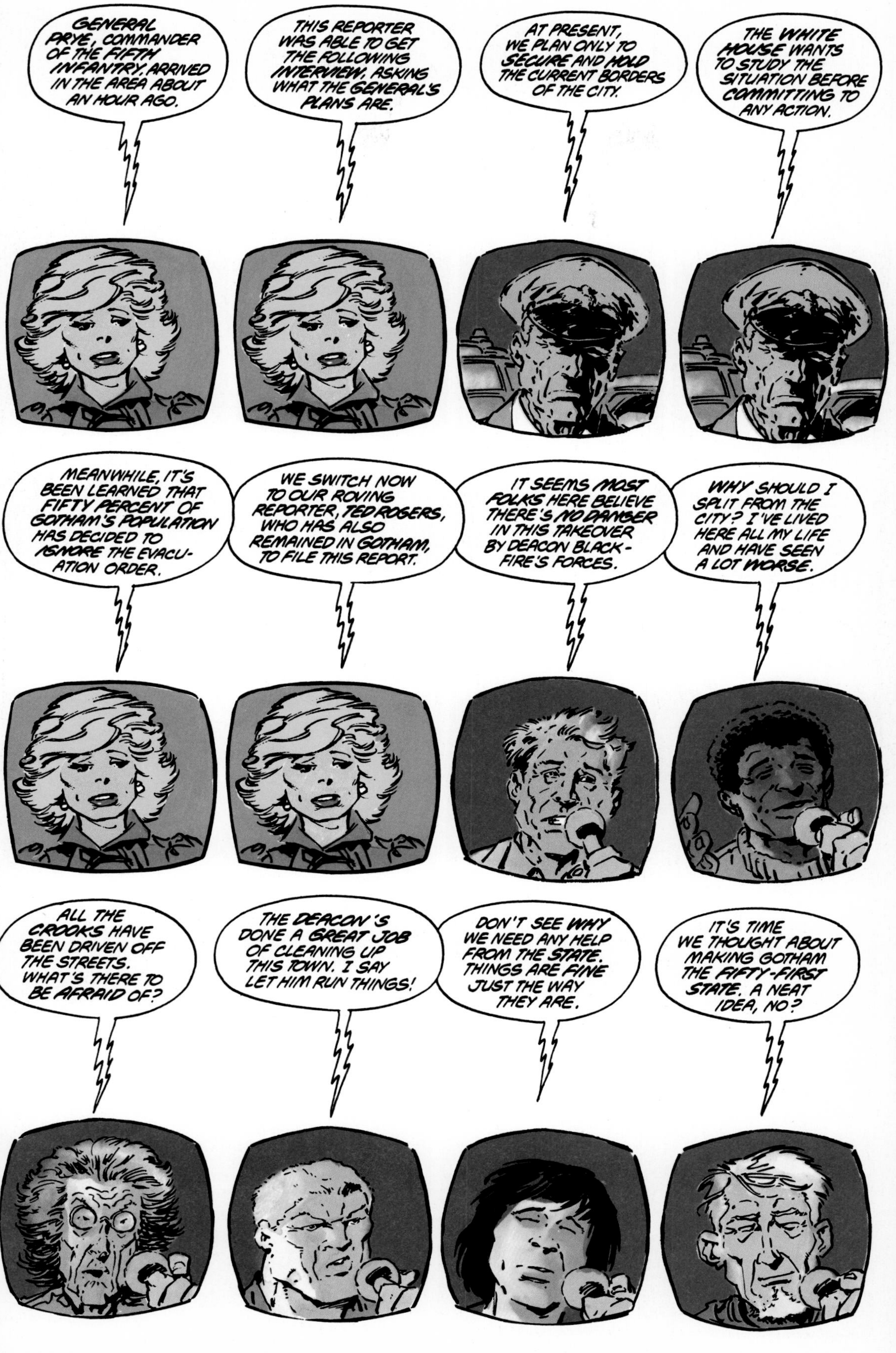
GENERAL PRYE, COMMANDER OF THE FIFTH INFANTRY, ARRIVED IN THE AREA ABOUT AN HOUR AGO.
THIS REPORTER WAS ABLE TO GET THE FOLLOWING INTERVIEW, ASKING WHAT THE GENERAL'S PLANS ARE.
AT PRESENT, WE PLAN ONLY TO SECURE AND HOLD THE CURRENT BORDERS OF THE CITY.
THE WHITE HOUSE WANTS TO STUDY THE SITUATION BEFORE COMMITTING TO ANY ACTION.
MEANWHILE, IT'S BEEN LEARNED THAT FIFTY PERCENT OF GOTHAM'S POPULATION HAS DECIDED TO IGNORE THE EVACU-ATION ORDER.
WE SWITCH NOW TO OUR ROVING REPORTER, TED ROGERS, WHO HAS ALSO REMAINED IN GOTHAM, TO FILE THIS REPORT.
IT SEEMS MOST FOLKS HERE BELIEVE THERE'S NO DANGER IN THIS TAKEOVER BY DEACON BLACK-FIRE'S FORCES.
WHY SHOULD I SPLIT FROM THE CITY? I'VE LIVED HERE ALL MY LIFE AND HAVE SEEN A LOT WORSE.
ALL THE CROOKS HAVE BEEN DRIVEN OFF THE STREETS. WHAT'S THERE TO BE AFRAID OF?
THE DEACON'S DONE A GREAT JOB OF CLEANING UP THIS TOWN. I SAY LET HIM RUN THINGS!
DON'T SEE WHY WE NEED ANY HELP FROM THE STATE. THINGS ARE FINE JUST THE WAY THEY ARE.
IT'S TIME WE THOUGHT ABOUT MAKING GOTHAM THE FIFTY-FIRST STATE. A NEAT IDEA, NO?

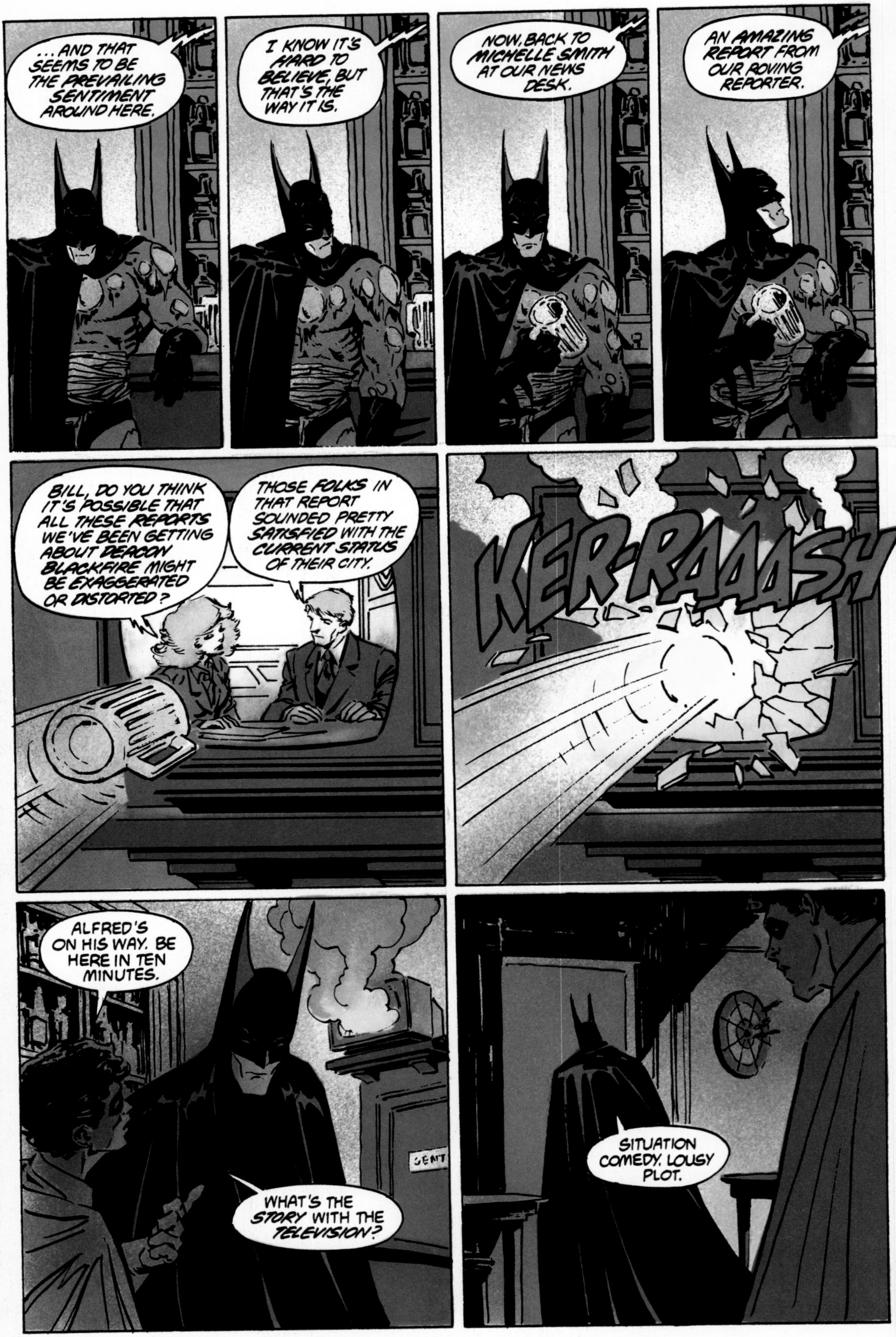
...AND THAT SEEMS TO BE THE PREVAILING SENTIMENT AROUND HERE.
I KNOW IT'S HARD TO BELIEVE, BUT THAT'S THE WAY IT IS.
NOW, BACK TO MICHELLE SMITH AT OUR NEWS DESK.
AN AMAZING REPORT FROM OUR ROVING REPORTER.
BILL, DO YOU THINK IT'S POSSIBLE THAT ALL THESE REPORTS WE'VE BEEN GETTING ABOUT DEACON BLACKFIRE MIGHT BE EXAGGERATED OR DISTORTED?
THOSE FOLKS IN THAT REPORT SOUNDED PRETTY SATISFIED WITH THE CURRENT STATUS OF THEIR CITY.
KER-RAAASH
ALFRED'S ON HIS WAY. BE HERE IN TEN MINUTES.
WHAT'S THE STORY WITH THE TELEVISION?
SITUATION COMEDY. LOUSY PLOT.

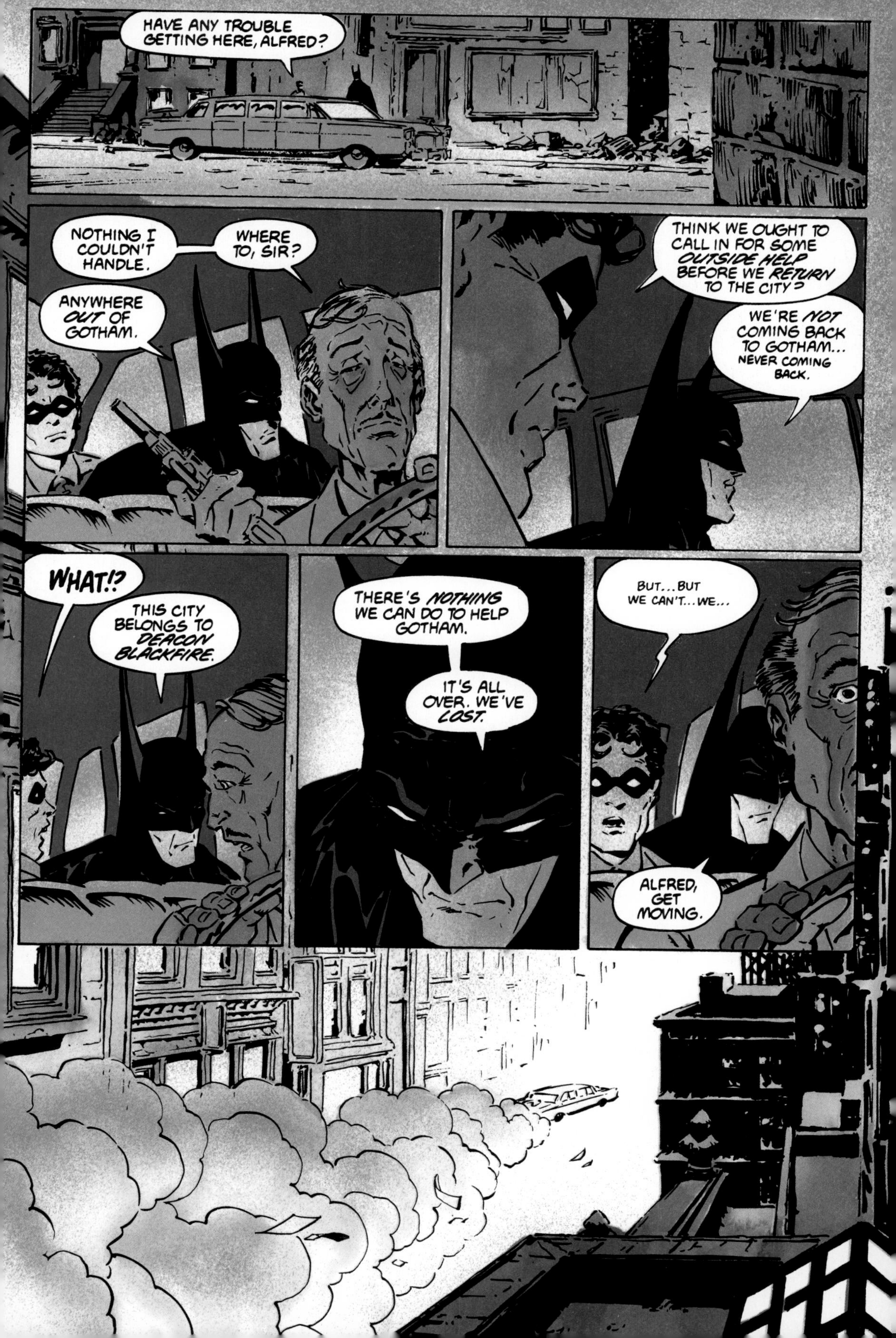

HAVE ANY TROUBLE GETTING HERE, ALFRED?
NOTHING I COULDN'T HANDLE.
WHERE TO, SIR?
ANYWHERE OUT OF GOTHAM.
THINK WE OUGHT TO CALL IN FOR SOME OUTSIDE HELP BEFORE WE RETURN TO THE CITY?
WE'RE NOT COMING BACK TO GOTHAM... NEVER COMING BACK.
WHAT!?
THIS CITY BELONGS TO DEACON BLACKFIRE.
THERE'S NOTHING WE CAN DO TO HELP GOTHAM.
IT'S ALL OVER. WE'VE LOST.
BUT...BUT WE CAN'T...WE...
ALFRED, GET MOVING.

CHAPTER 4

COMBAT

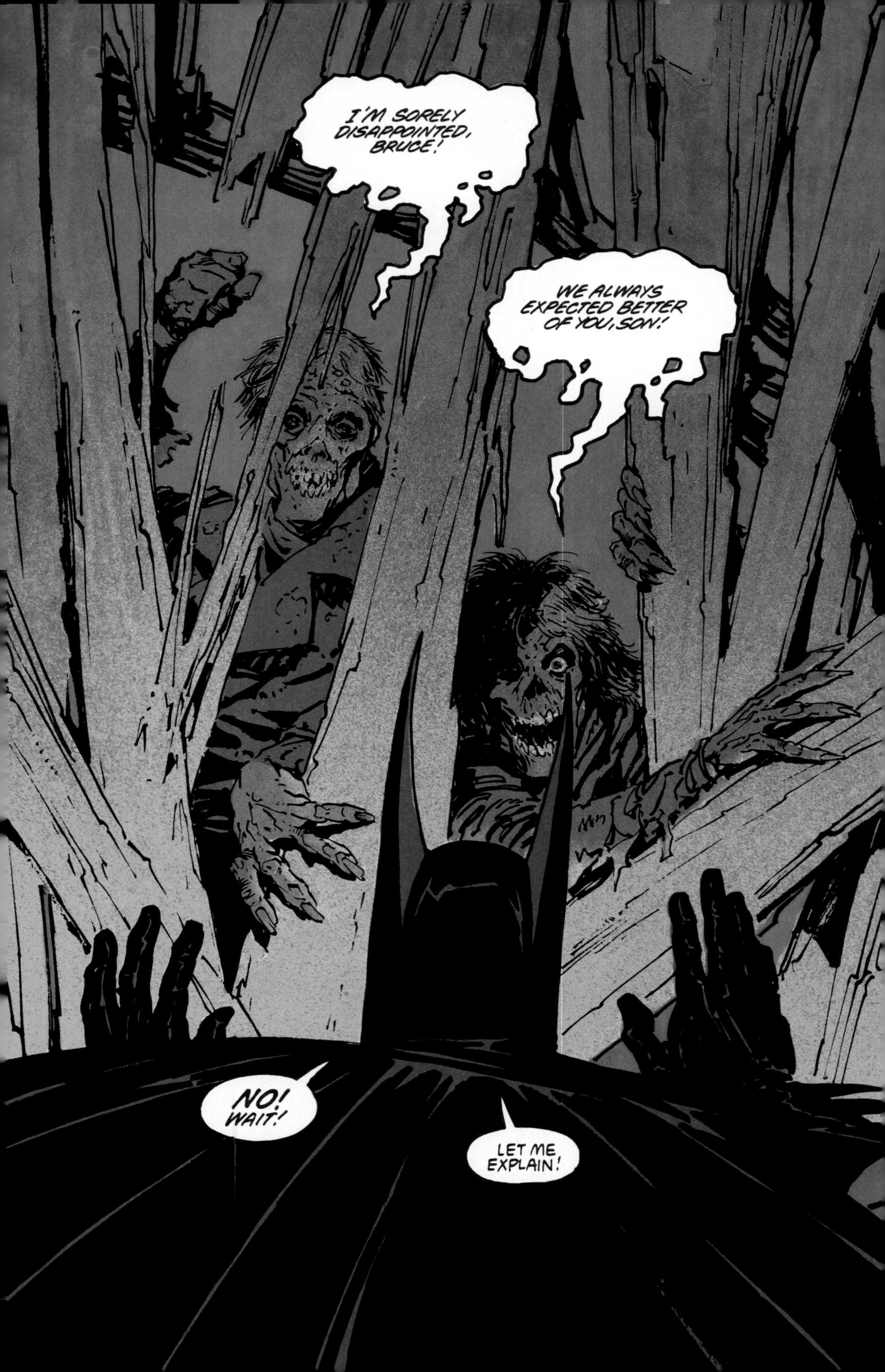
I'M SORELY DISAPPOINTED, BRUCE!
WE ALWAYS EXPECTED BETTER OF YOU, SON!
NO! WAIT!
LET ME EXPLAIN!

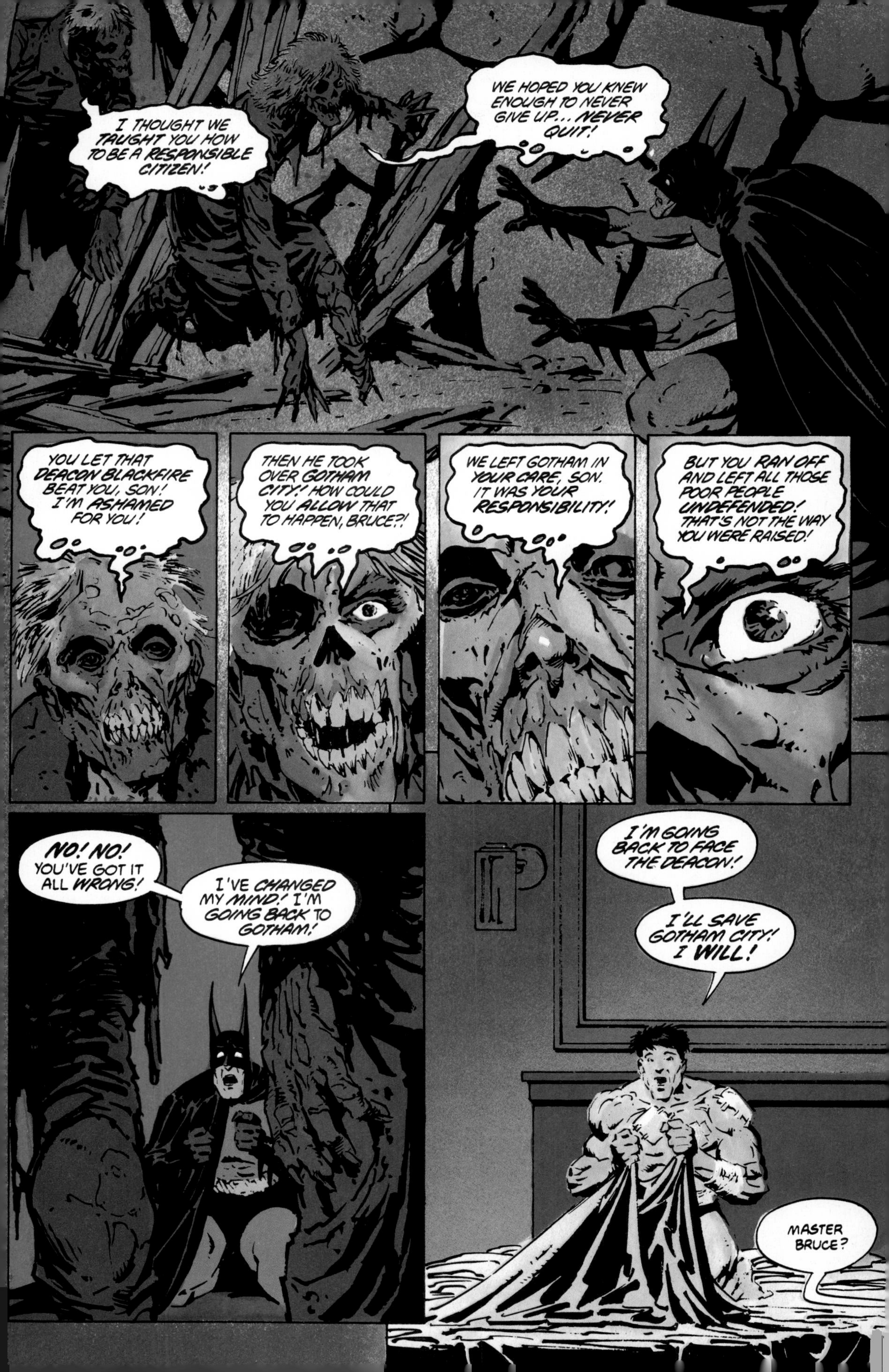
I THOUGHT WE TAUGHT YOU HOW TO BE A RESPONSIBLE CITIZEN!
WE HOPED YOU KNEW ENOUGH TO NEVER GIVE UP... NEVER QUIT!
YOU LET THAT DEACON BLACKFIRE BEAT YOU, SON! I'M ASHAMED FOR YOU!
THEN HE TOOK OVER GOTHAM CITY! HOW COULD YOU ALLOW THAT TO HAPPEN, BRUCE?!
WE LEFT GOTHAM IN YOUR CARE, SON. IT WAS YOUR RESPONSIBILITY!
BUT YOU RAN OFF AND LEFT ALL THOSE POOR PEOPLE UNDEFENDED! THAT'S NOT THE WAY YOU WERE RAISED!
NO! NO! YOU'VE GOT IT ALL WRONG!
I'VE CHANGED MY MIND! I'M GOING BACK TO GOTHAM!
I'M GOING BACK TO FACE THE DEACON!
I'LL SAVE GOTHAM CITY! I WILL!
MASTER BRUCE?

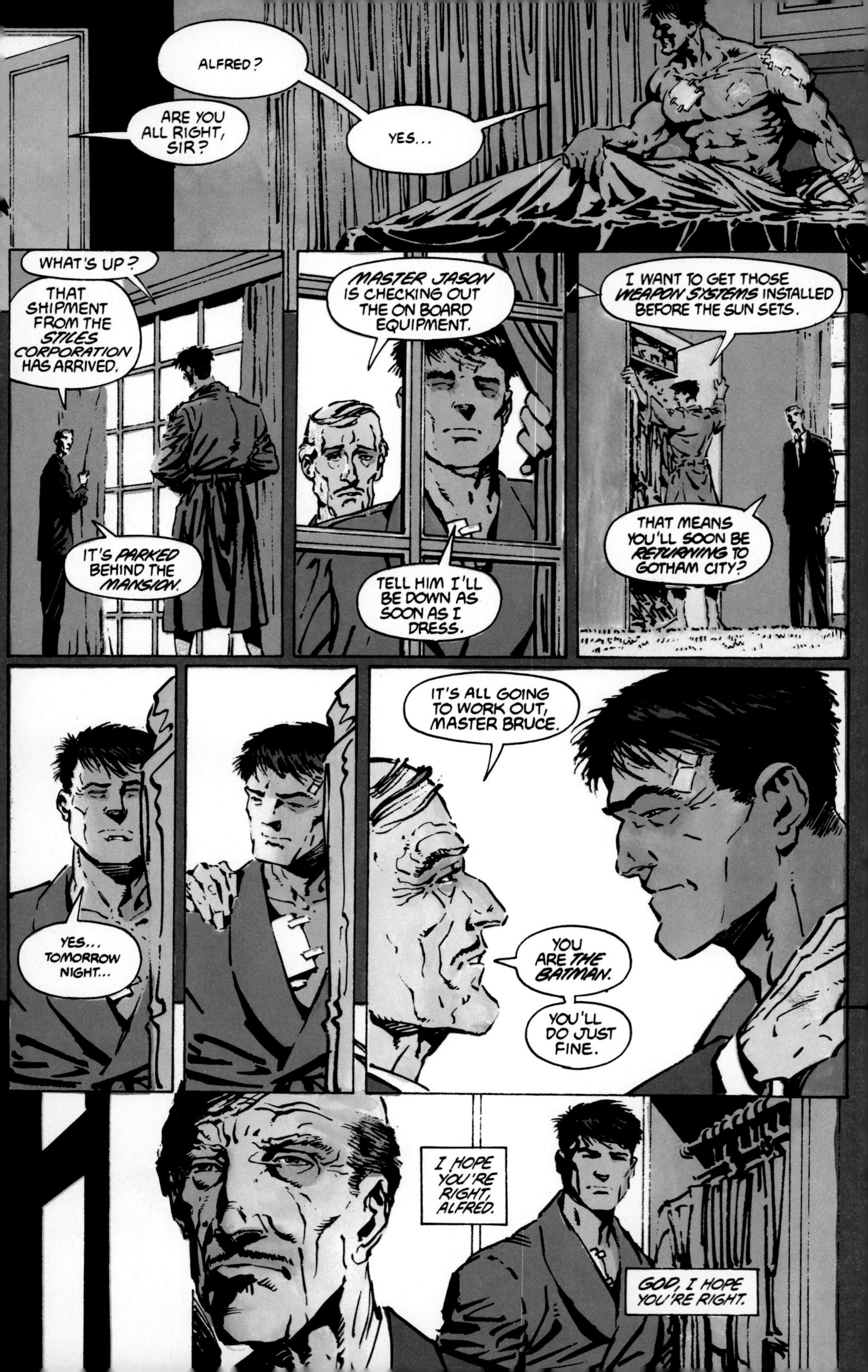
ALFRED?
ARE YOU ALL RIGHT, SIR?
YES...
WHAT'S UP?
THAT SHIPMENT FROM THE STILES CORPORATION HAS ARRIVED.
IT'S PARKED BEHIND THE MANSION.
MASTER JASON IS CHECKING OUT THE ON BOARD EQUIPMENT.
TELL HIM I'LL BE DOWN AS SOON AS I DRESS.
I WANT TO GET THOSE WEAPON SYSTEMS INSTALLED BEFORE THE SUN SETS.
THAT MEANS YOU'LL SOON BE RETURNING TO GOTHAM CITY?
YES... TOMORROW NIGHT...
IT'S ALL GOING TO WORK OUT, MASTER BRUCE.
YOU ARE THE BATMAN.
YOU'LL DO JUST FINE.
I HOPE YOU'RE RIGHT, ALFRED.
GOD, I HOPE YOU'RE RIGHT.

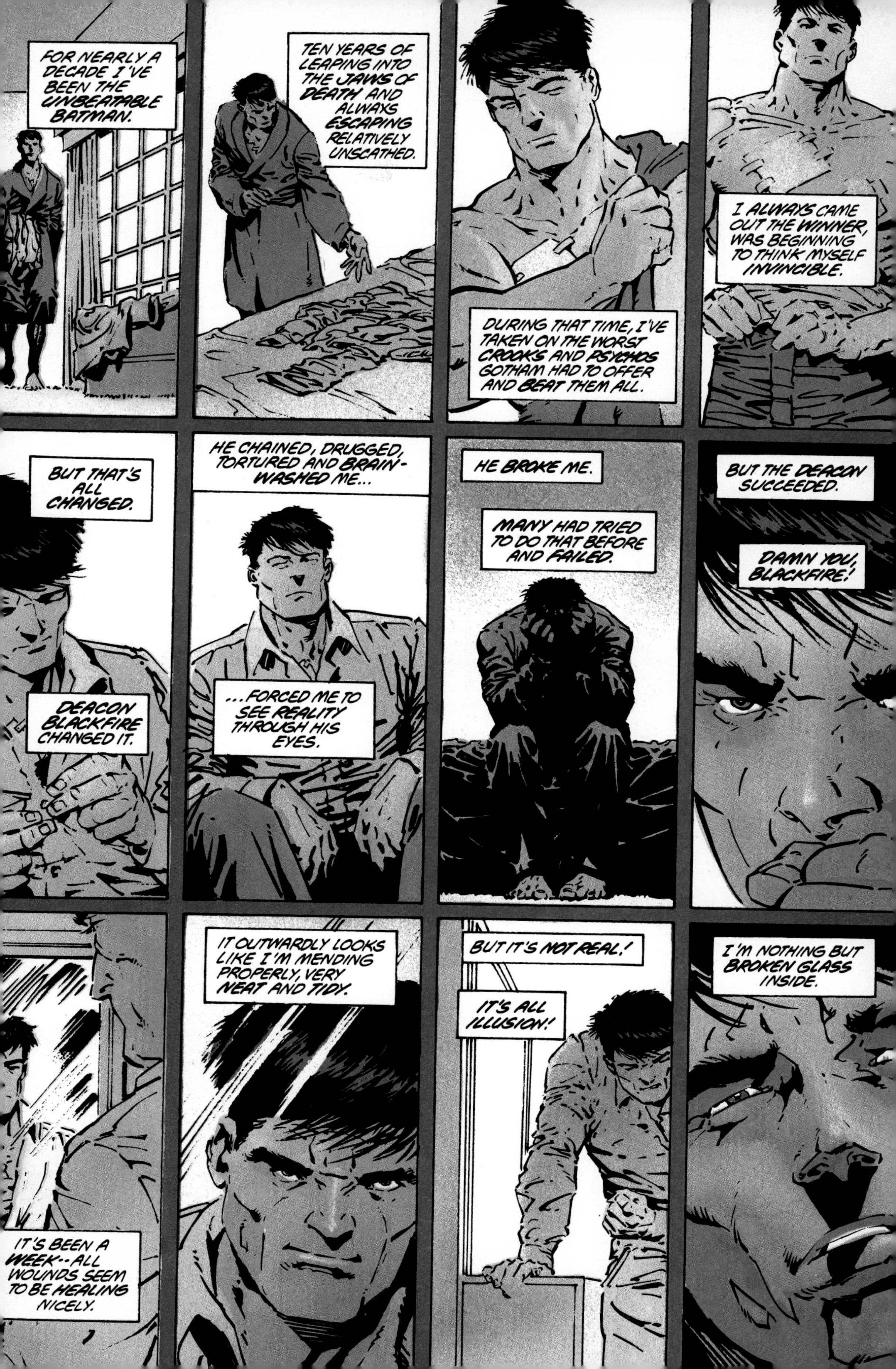
FOR NEARLY A DECADE I'VE BEEN THE UNBEATABLE BATMAN.
TEN YEARS OF LEAPING INTO THE JAWS OF DEATH AND ALWAYS ESCAPING RELATIVELY UNSCATHED.
DURING THAT TIME, I'VE TAKEN ON THE WORST CROOKS AND PSYCHOS GOTHAM HAD TO OFFER AND BEAT THEM ALL.
I ALWAYS CAME OUT THE WINNER, WAS BEGINNING TO THINK MYSELF INVINCIBLE.
BUT THAT'S ALL CHANGED.
DEACON BLACKFIRE CHANGED IT.
HE CHAINED, DRUGGED, TORTURED AND BRAIN-WASHED ME...
...FORCED ME TO SEE REALITY THROUGH HIS EYES.
HE BROKE ME.
MANY HAD TRIED TO DO THAT BEFORE AND FAILED.
BUT THE DEACON SUCCEEDED.
DAMN YOU, BLACKFIRE!
IT'S BEEN A WEEK--ALL WOUNDS SEEM TO BE HEALING NICELY.
IT OUTWARDLY LOOKS LIKE I'M MENDING PROPERLY, VERY NEAT AND TIDY.
BUT IT'S NOT REAL!
IT'S ALL ILLUSION!
I'M NOTHING BUT BROKEN GLASS INSIDE.

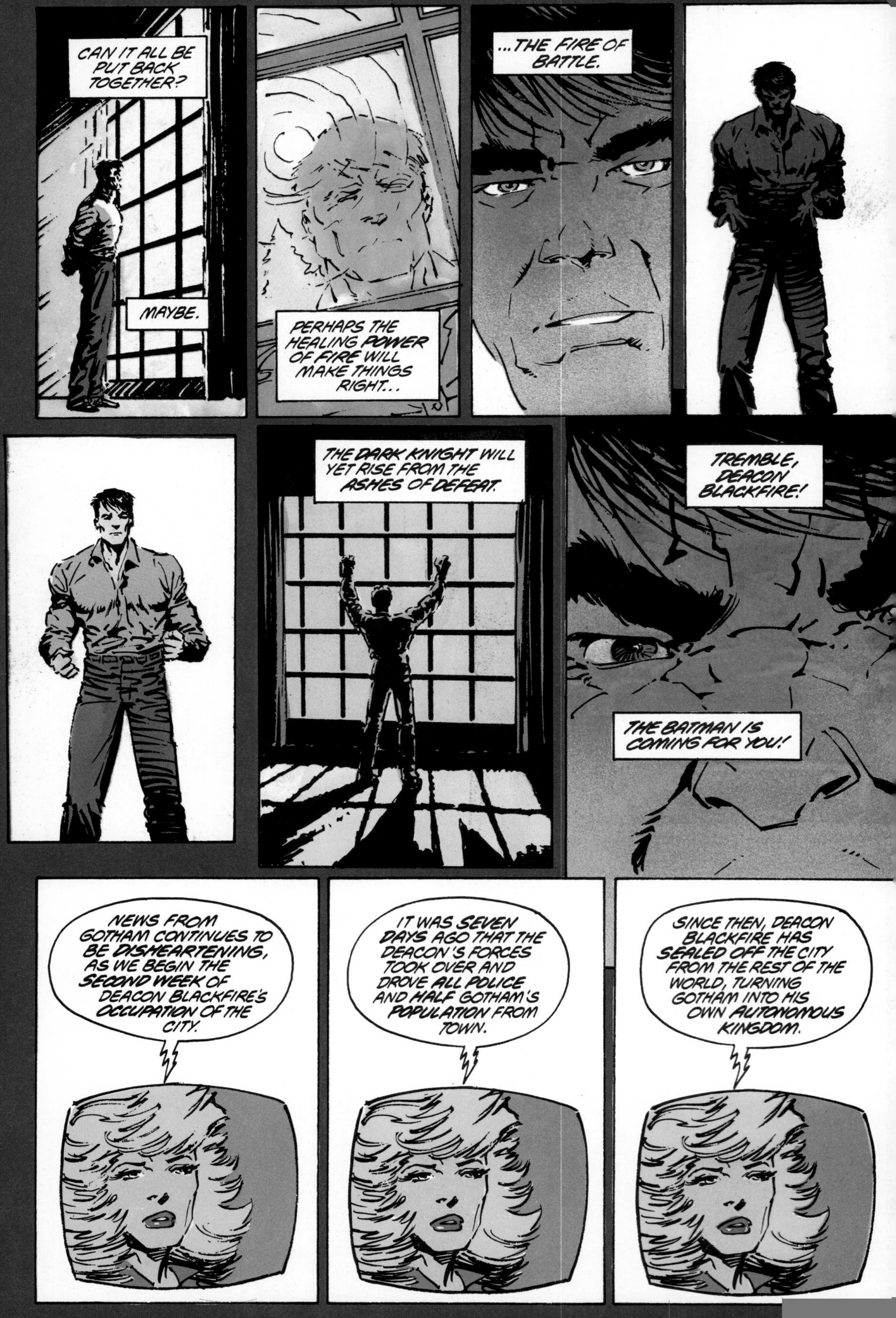
CAN IT ALL BE PUT BACK TOGETHER?
MAYBE.
PERHAPS THE HEALING POWER OF FIRE WILL MAKE THINGS RIGHT...
...THE FIRE OF BATTLE.
THE DARK KNIGHT WILL YET RISE FROM THE ASHES OF DEFEAT.
TREMBLE, DEACON BLACKFIRE!
THE BATMAN IS COMING FOR YOU!
NEWS FROM GOTHAM CONTINUES TO BE DISHEARTENING, AS WE BEGIN THE SECOND WEEK OF DEACON BLACKFIRE'S OCCUPATION OF THE CITY.
IT WAS SEVEN DAYS AGO THAT THE DEACON'S FORCES TOOK OVER AND DROVE ALL POLICE AND HALF GOTHAM'S POPULATION FROM TOWN.
SINCE THEN, DEACON BLACKFIRE HAS SEALED OFF THE CITY FROM THE REST OF THE WORLD, TURNING GOTHAM INTO HIS OWN AUTONOMOUS KINGDOM.

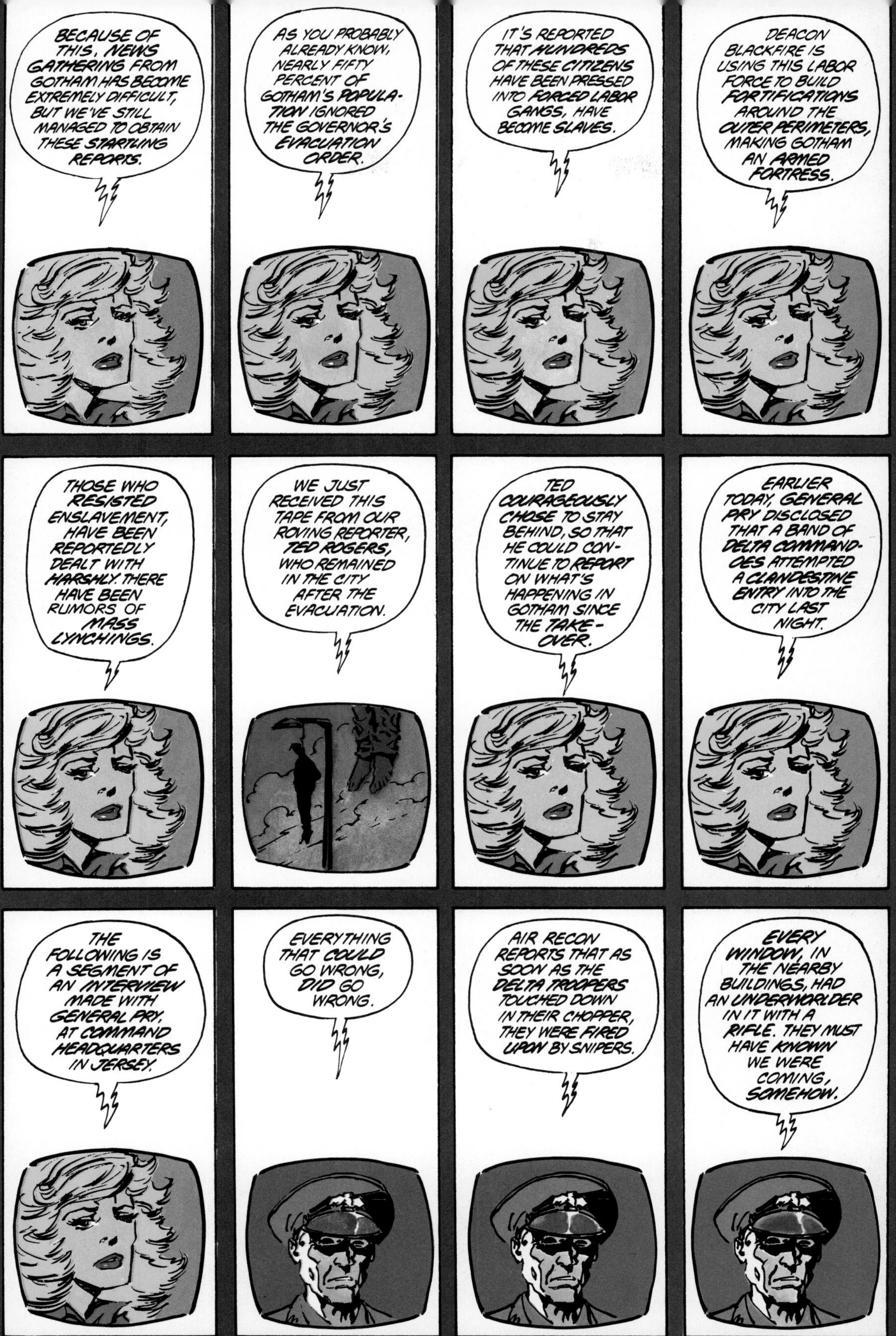

BECAUSE OF THIS, NEWS GATHERING FROM GOTHAM HAS BECOME EXTREMELY DIFFICULT, BUT WE'VE STILL MANAGED TO OBTAIN THESE STARTLING REPORTS.
AS YOU PROBABLY ALREADY KNOW, NEARLY FIFTY PERCENT OF GOTHAM'S POPULATION IGNORED THE GOVERNOR'S EVACUATION ORDER.
IT'S REPORTED THAT HUNDREDS OF THESE CITIZENS HAVE BEEN PRESSED INTO FORCED LABOR GANGS, HAVE BECOME SLAVES.
DEACON BLACKFIRE IS USING THIS LABOR FORCE TO BUILD FORTIFICATIONS AROUND THE OUTER PERIMETERS, MAKING GOTHAM AN ARMED FORTRESS.
THOSE WHO RESISTED ENSLAVEMENT, HAVE BEEN REPORTEDLY DEALT WITH HARSHLY. THERE HAVE BEEN RUMORS OF MASS LYNCHINGS.
WE JUST RECEIVED THIS TAPE FROM OUR ROVING REPORTER, TED ROGERS, WHO REMAINED IN THE CITY AFTER THE EVACUATION.
TED COURAGEOUSLY CHOSE TO STAY BEHIND, SO THAT HE COULD CONTINUE TO REPORT ON WHAT'S HAPPENING IN GOTHAM SINCE THE TAKE-OVER.
EARLIER TODAY, GENERAL PRY DISCLOSED THAT A BAND OF DELTA COMMANDOES ATTEMPTED A CLANDESTINE ENTRY INTO THE CITY LAST NIGHT.
THE FOLLOWING IS A SEGMENT OF AN INTERVIEW MADE WITH GENERAL PRY, AT COMMAND HEADQUARTERS IN JERSEY.
EVERYTHING THAT COULD GO WRONG, DID GO WRONG.
AIR RECON REPORTS THAT AS SOON AS THE DELTA TROOPERS TOUCHED DOWN IN THEIR CHOPPER, THEY WERE FIRED UPON BY SNIPERS.
EVERY WINDOW, IN THE NEARBY BUILDINGS, HAD AN UNDERWORLDER IN IT WITH A RIFLE. THEY MUST HAVE KNOWN WE WERE COMING, SOMEHOW.

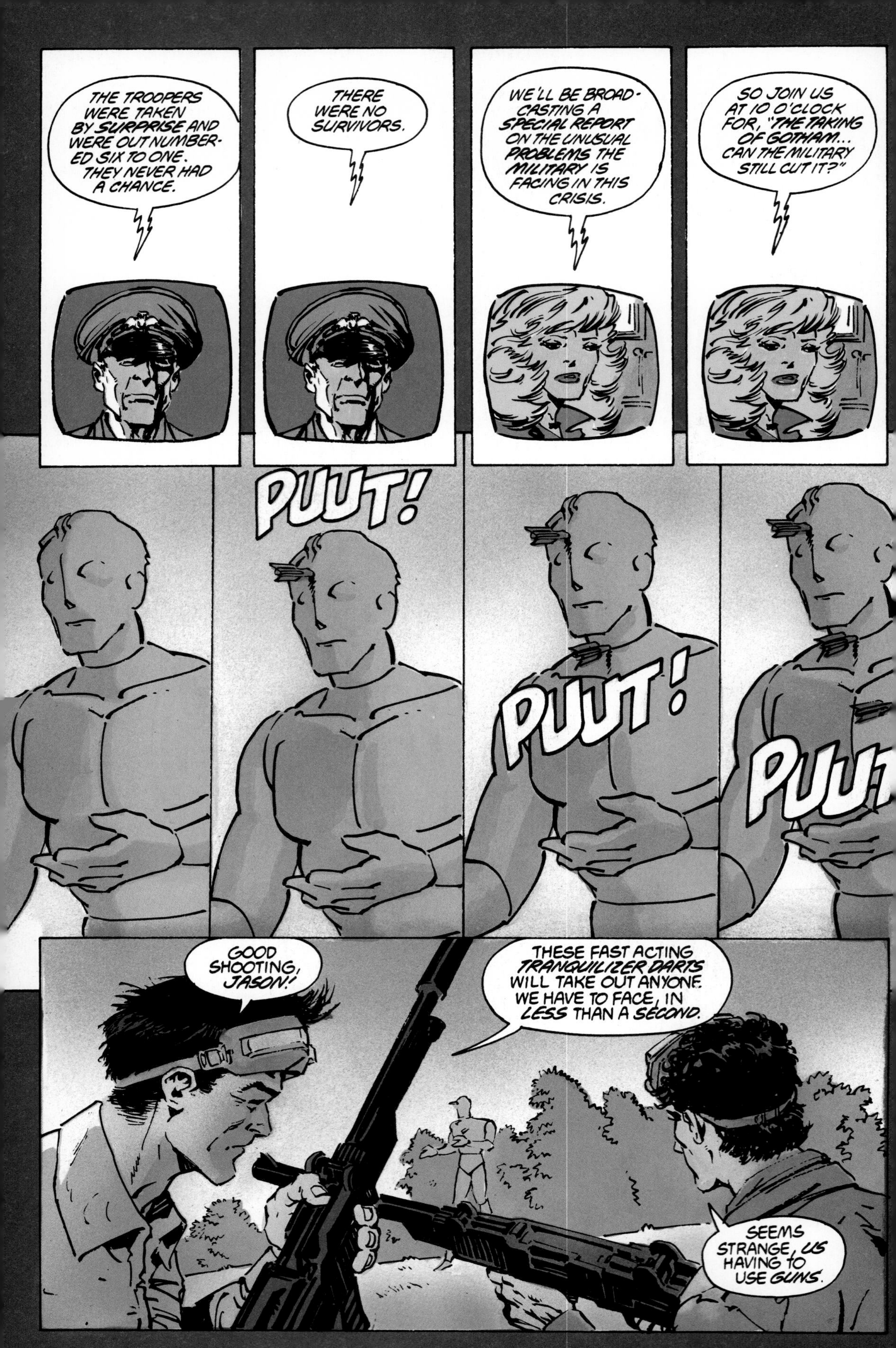
THE TROOPERS WERE TAKEN BY SURPRISE AND WERE OUTNUMBERED SIX TO ONE. THEY NEVER HAD A CHANCE.
THERE WERE NO SURVIVORS.
WE'LL BE BROADCASTING A SPECIAL REPORT ON THE UNUSUAL PROBLEMS THE MILITARY IS FACING IN THIS CRISIS.
SO JOIN US AT 10 O'CLOCK FOR, "THE TAKING OF GOTHAM... CAN THE MILITARY STILL CUT IT?"
PUUT!
PUUT!
GOOD SHOOTING, JASON!
THESE FAST ACTING TRANQUILIZER DARTS WILL TAKE OUT ANYONE WE HAVE TO FACE, IN LESS THAN A SECOND.
SEEMS STRANGE, US HAVING TO USE GUNS.

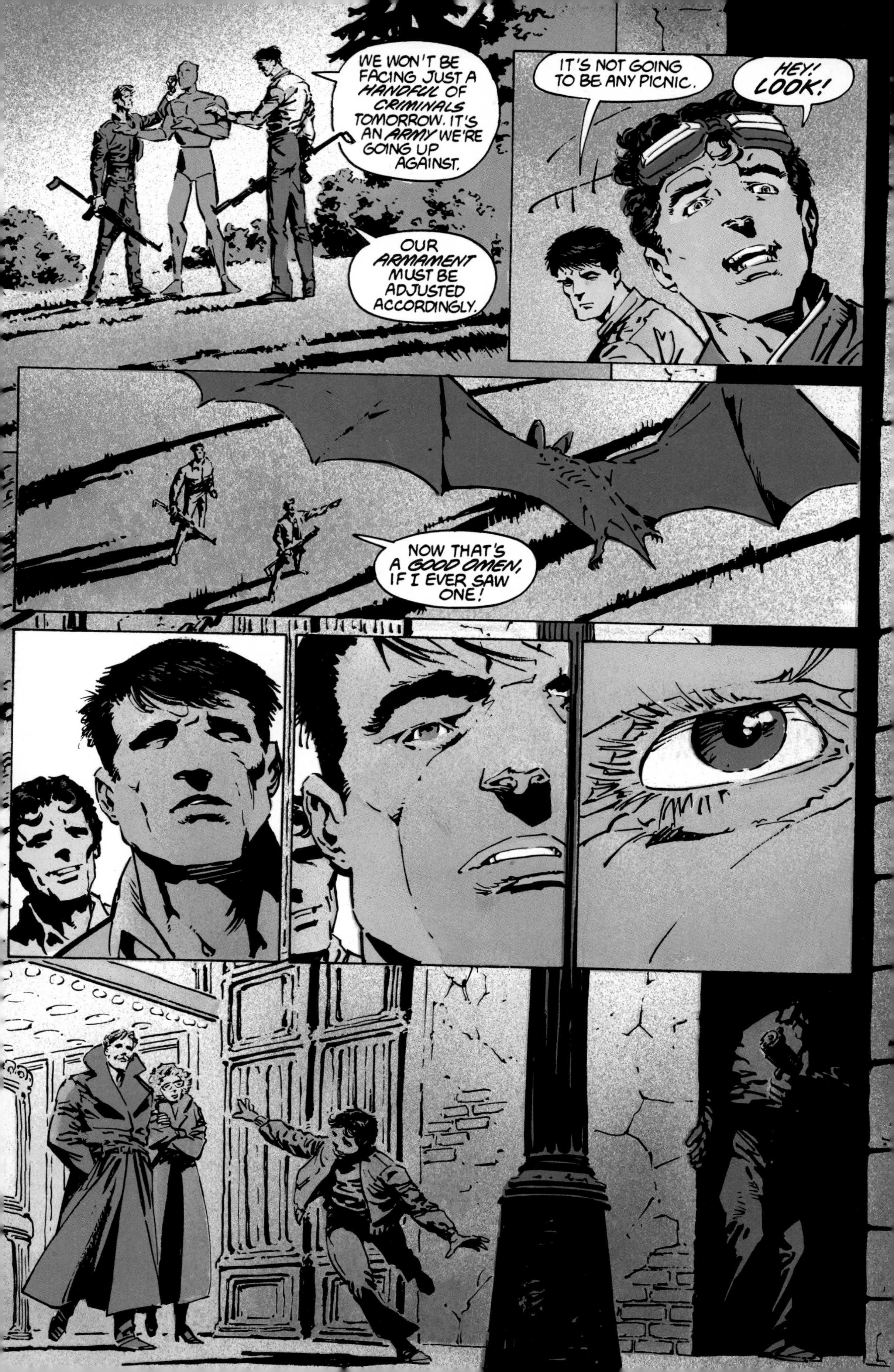
WE WON'T BE FACING JUST A *HANDFUL* OF *CRIMINALS* TOMORROW. IT'S AN *ARMY* WE'RE GOING UP AGAINST.
OUR *ARMAMENT* MUST BE ADJUSTED ACCORDINGLY.
IT'S NOT GOING TO BE ANY PICNIC.
HEY! LOOK!
NOW THAT'S A *GOOD OMEN,* IF I EVER SAW ONE!

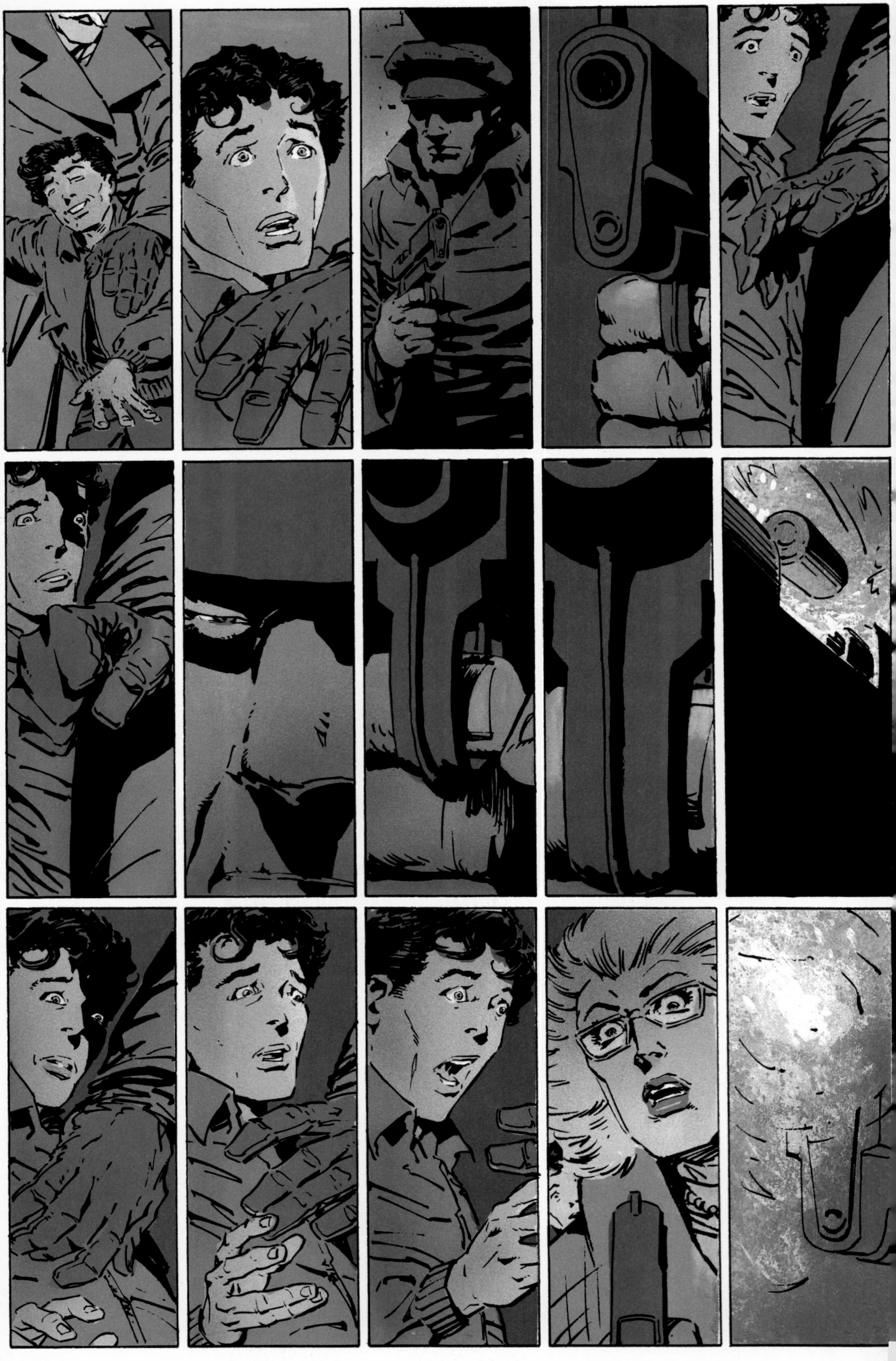

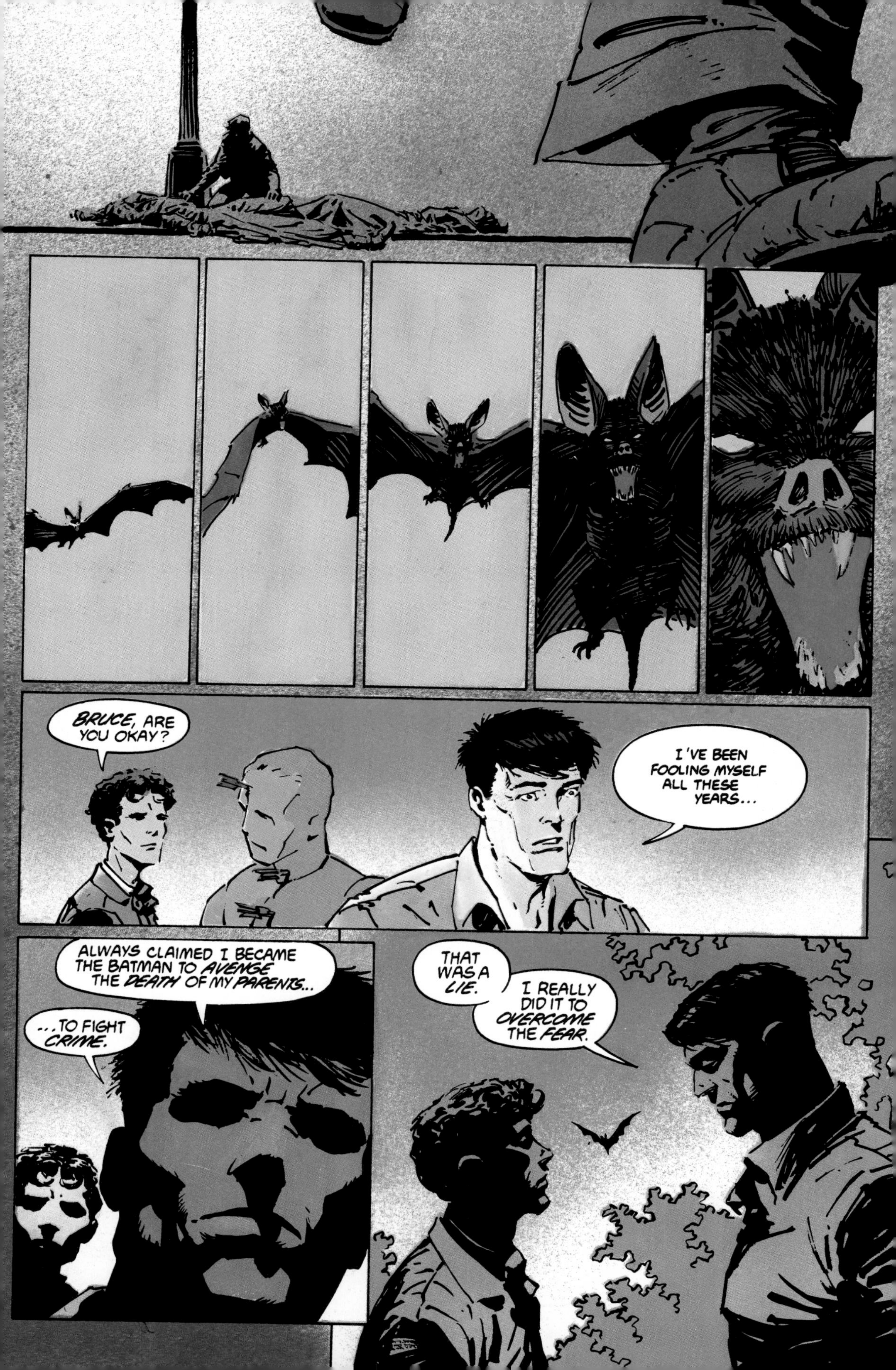
BRUCE, ARE YOU OKAY?
I'VE BEEN FOOLING MYSELF ALL THESE YEARS...
ALWAYS CLAIMED I BECAME THE BATMAN TO AVENGE THE DEATH OF MY PARENTS...
...TO FIGHT CRIME.
THAT WAS A LIE.
I REALLY DID IT TO OVERCOME THE FEAR.

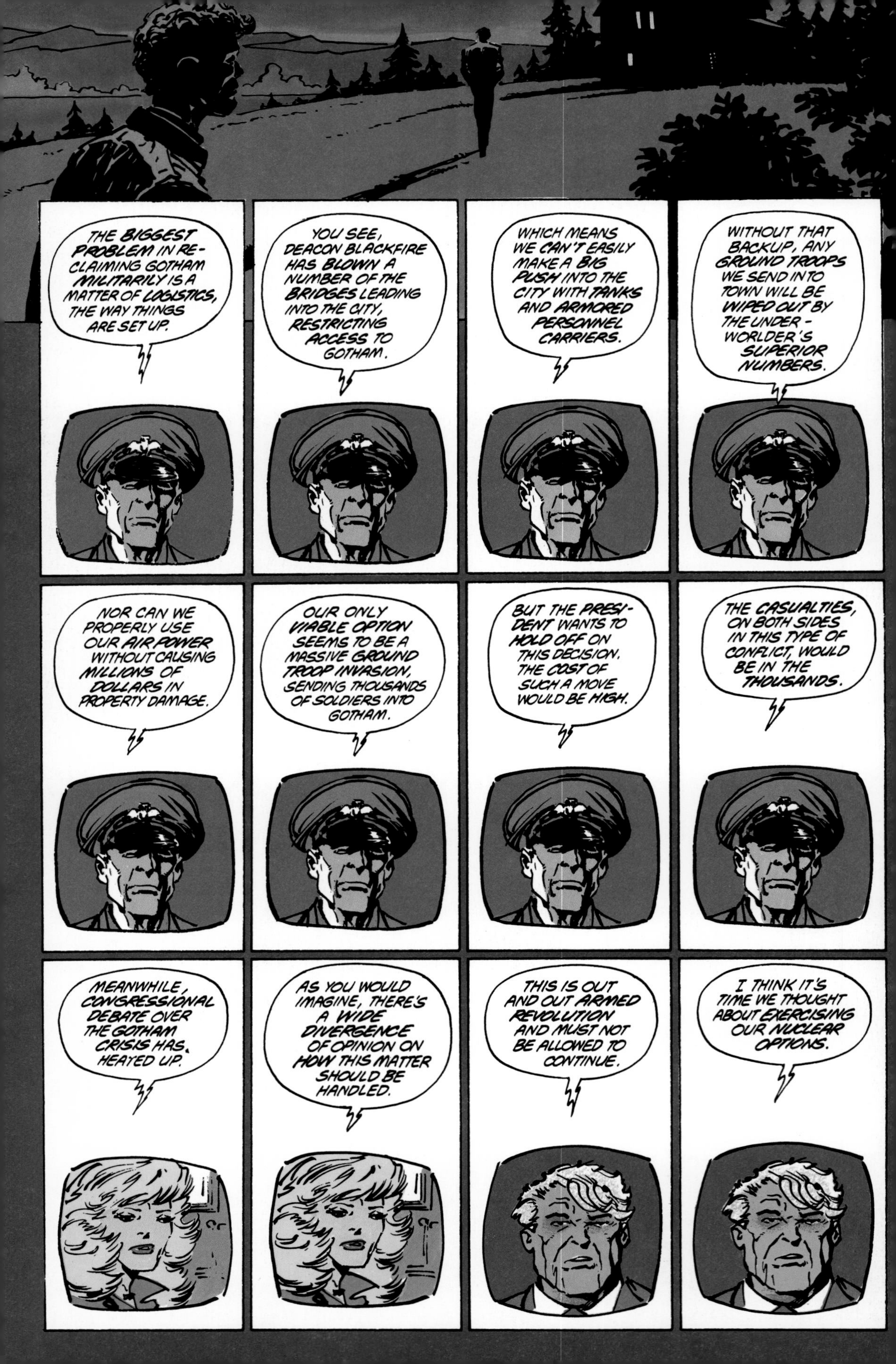
THE BIGGEST PROBLEM IN RE-CLAIMING GOTHAM MILITARILY IS A MATTER OF LOGISTICS, THE WAY THINGS ARE SET UP.
YOU SEE, DEACON BLACKFIRE HAS BLOWN A NUMBER OF THE BRIDGES LEADING INTO THE CITY, RESTRICTING ACCESS TO GOTHAM.
WHICH MEANS WE CAN'T EASILY MAKE A BIG PUSH INTO THE CITY WITH TANKS AND ARMORED PERSONNEL CARRIERS.
WITHOUT THAT BACKUP, ANY GROUND TROOPS WE SEND INTO TOWN WILL BE WIPED OUT BY THE UNDER-WORLDER'S SUPERIOR NUMBERS.
NOR CAN WE PROPERLY USE OUR AIR POWER WITHOUT CAUSING MILLIONS OF DOLLARS IN PROPERTY DAMAGE.
OUR ONLY VIABLE OPTION SEEMS TO BE A MASSIVE GROUND TROOP INVASION, SENDING THOUSANDS OF SOLDIERS INTO GOTHAM.
BUT THE PRESI-DENT WANTS TO HOLD OFF ON THIS DECISION. THE COST OF SUCH A MOVE WOULD BE HIGH.
THE CASUALTIES, ON BOTH SIDES IN THIS TYPE OF CONFLICT, WOULD BE IN THE THOUSANDS.
MEANWHILE, CONGRESSIONAL DEBATE OVER THE GOTHAM CRISIS HAS HEATED UP.
AS YOU WOULD IMAGINE, THERE'S A WIDE DIVERGENCE OF OPINION ON HOW THIS MATTER SHOULD BE HANDLED.
THIS IS OUT AND OUT ARMED REVOLUTION AND MUST NOT BE ALLOWED TO CONTINUE.
I THINK IT'S TIME WE THOUGHT ABOUT EXERCISING OUR NUCLEAR OPTIONS.

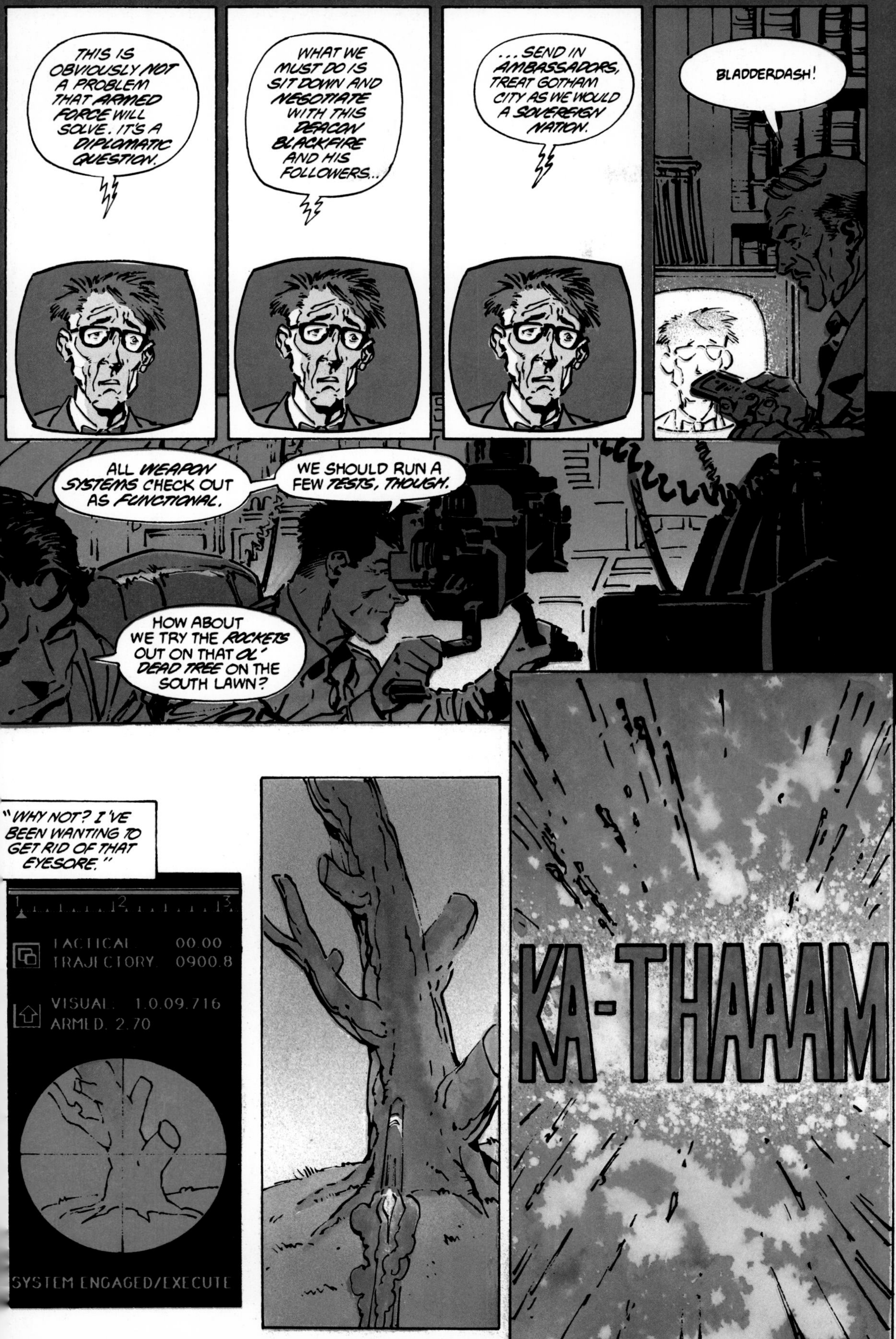
THIS IS OBVIOUSLY NOT A PROBLEM THAT ARMED FORCE WILL SOLVE. IT'S A DIPLOMATIC QUESTION.
WHAT WE MUST DO IS SIT DOWN AND NEGOTIATE WITH THIS DEACON BLACKFIRE AND HIS FOLLOWERS...
...SEND IN AMBASSADORS, TREAT GOTHAM CITY AS WE WOULD A SOVEREIGN NATION.
BLADDERDASH!
ALL WEAPON SYSTEMS CHECK OUT AS FUNCTIONAL.
WE SHOULD RUN A FEW TESTS, THOUGH.
HOW ABOUT WE TRY THE ROCKETS OUT ON THAT OL' DEAD TREE ON THE SOUTH LAWN?
"WHY NOT? I'VE BEEN WANTING TO GET RID OF THAT EYESORE."
TACTICAL 00.00
TRAJECTORY 0900.8
VISUAL 1.0.09.716
ARMED 2.70
SYSTEM ENGAGED/EXECUTE
KA-THAAAM

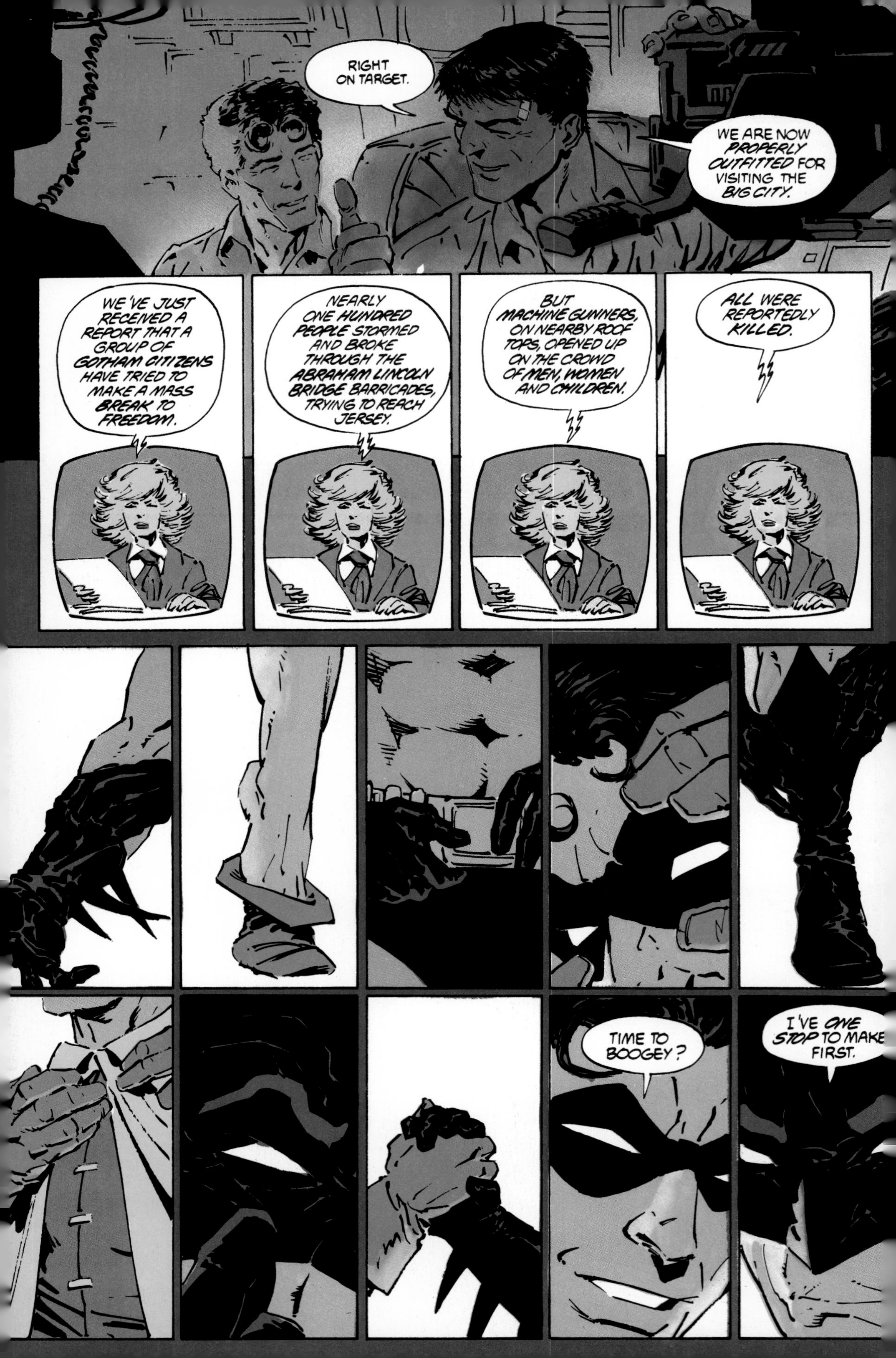
RIGHT ON TARGET.
WE ARE NOW PROPERLY OUTFITTED FOR VISITING THE BIG CITY.
WE'VE JUST RECEIVED A REPORT THAT A GROUP OF GOTHAM CITIZENS HAVE TRIED TO MAKE A MASS BREAK TO FREEDOM.
NEARLY ONE HUNDRED PEOPLE STORMED AND BROKE THROUGH THE ABRAHAM LINCOLN BRIDGE BARRICADES, TRYING TO REACH JERSEY.
BUT MACHINE GUNNERS, ON NEARBY ROOF TOPS, OPENED UP ON THE CROWD OF MEN, WOMEN AND CHILDREN.
ALL WERE REPORTEDLY KILLED.
TIME TO BOOGEY?
I'VE ONE STOP TO MAKE FIRST.

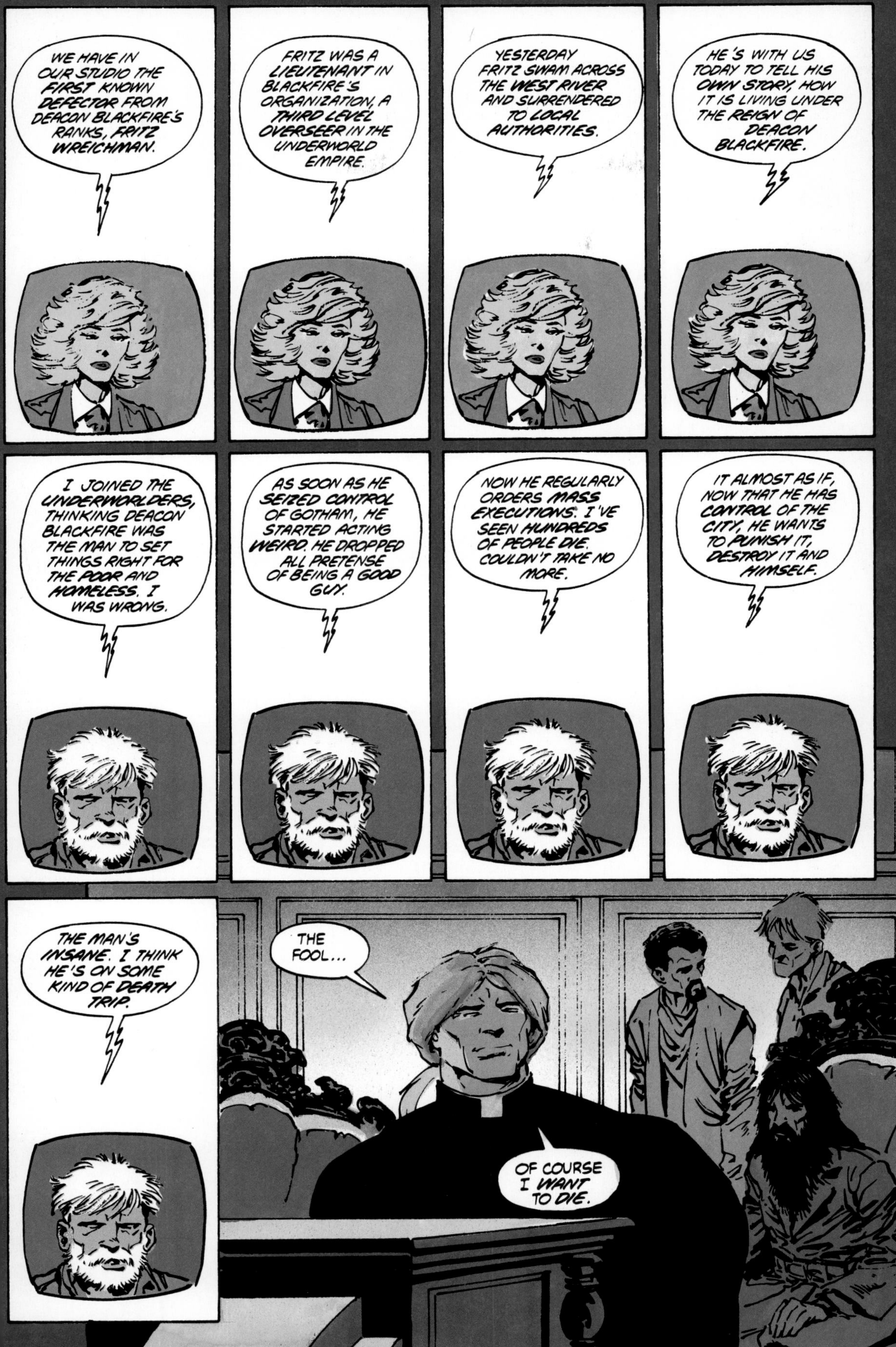
WE HAVE IN OUR STUDIO THE FIRST KNOWN DEFECTOR FROM DEACON BLACKFIRE'S RANKS, FRITZ WREICHMAN.
FRITZ WAS A LIEUTENANT IN BLACKFIRE'S ORGANIZATION, A THIRD LEVEL OVERSEER IN THE UNDERWORLD EMPIRE.
YESTERDAY FRITZ SWAM ACROSS THE WEST RIVER AND SURRENDERED TO LOCAL AUTHORITIES.
HE'S WITH US TODAY TO TELL HIS OWN STORY, HOW IT IS LIVING UNDER THE REIGN OF DEACON BLACKFIRE.
I JOINED THE UNDERWORLDERS, THINKING DEACON BLACKFIRE WAS THE MAN TO SET THINGS RIGHT FOR THE POOR AND HOMELESS. I WAS WRONG.
AS SOON AS HE SEIZED CONTROL OF GOTHAM, HE STARTED ACTING WEIRD. HE DROPPED ALL PRETENSE OF BEING A GOOD GUY.
NOW HE REGULARLY ORDERS MASS EXECUTIONS. I'VE SEEN HUNDREDS OF PEOPLE DIE. COULDN'T TAKE NO MORE.
IT ALMOST AS IF, NOW THAT HE HAS CONTROL OF THE CITY, HE WANTS TO PUNISH IT, DESTROY IT AND HIMSELF.
THE MAN'S INSANE. I THINK HE'S ON SOME KIND OF DEATH TRIP.
THE FOOL...
OF COURSE I WANT TO DIE.

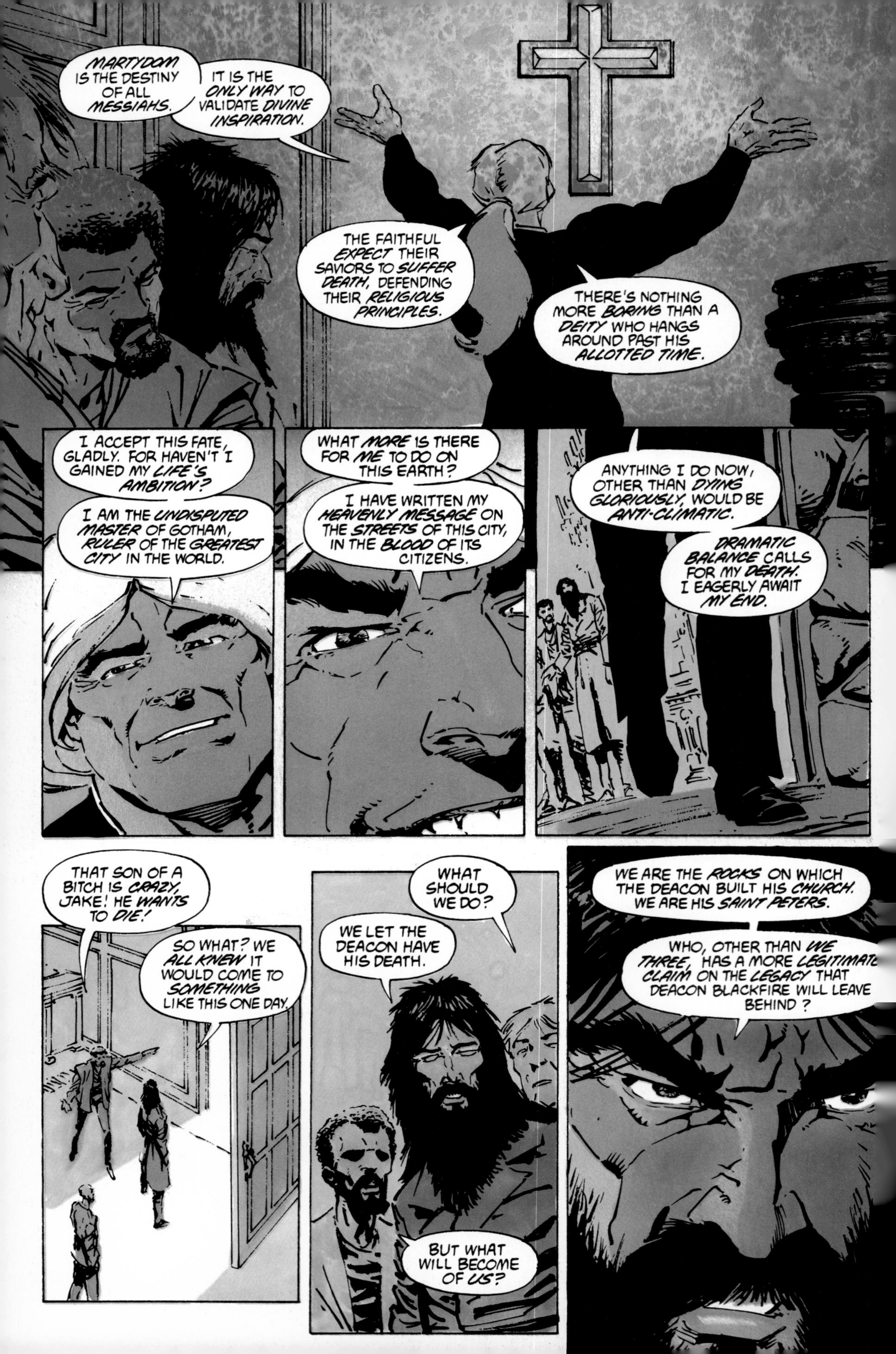
MARTYDOM IS THE DESTINY OF ALL MESSIAHS.
IT IS THE ONLY WAY TO VALIDATE DIVINE INSPIRATION.
THE FAITHFUL EXPECT THEIR SAVIORS TO SUFFER DEATH, DEFENDING THEIR RELIGIOUS PRINCIPLES.
THERE'S NOTHING MORE BORING THAN A DEITY WHO HANGS AROUND PAST HIS ALLOTTED TIME.
I ACCEPT THIS FATE, GLADLY. FOR HAVEN'T I GAINED MY LIFE'S AMBITION?
I AM THE UNDISPUTED MASTER OF GOTHAM, RULER OF THE GREATEST CITY IN THE WORLD.
WHAT MORE IS THERE FOR ME TO DO ON THIS EARTH?
I HAVE WRITTEN MY HEAVENLY MESSAGE ON THE STREETS OF THIS CITY, IN THE BLOOD OF ITS CITIZENS.
ANYTHING I DO NOW, OTHER THAN DYING GLORIOUSLY, WOULD BE ANTI-CLIMATIC.
DRAMATIC BALANCE CALLS FOR MY DEATH. I EAGERLY AWAIT MY END.
THAT SON OF A BITCH IS CRAZY, JAKE! HE WANTS TO DIE!
SO WHAT? WE ALL KNEW IT WOULD COME TO SOMETHING LIKE THIS ONE DAY.
WHAT SHOULD WE DO?
WE LET THE DEACON HAVE HIS DEATH.
BUT WHAT WILL BECOME OF US?
WE ARE THE ROCKS ON WHICH THE DEACON BUILT HIS CHURCH. WE ARE HIS SAINT PETERS.
WHO, OTHER THAN WE THREE, HAS A MORE LEGITIMATE CLAIM ON THE LEGACY THAT DEACON BLACKFIRE WILL LEAVE BEHIND?

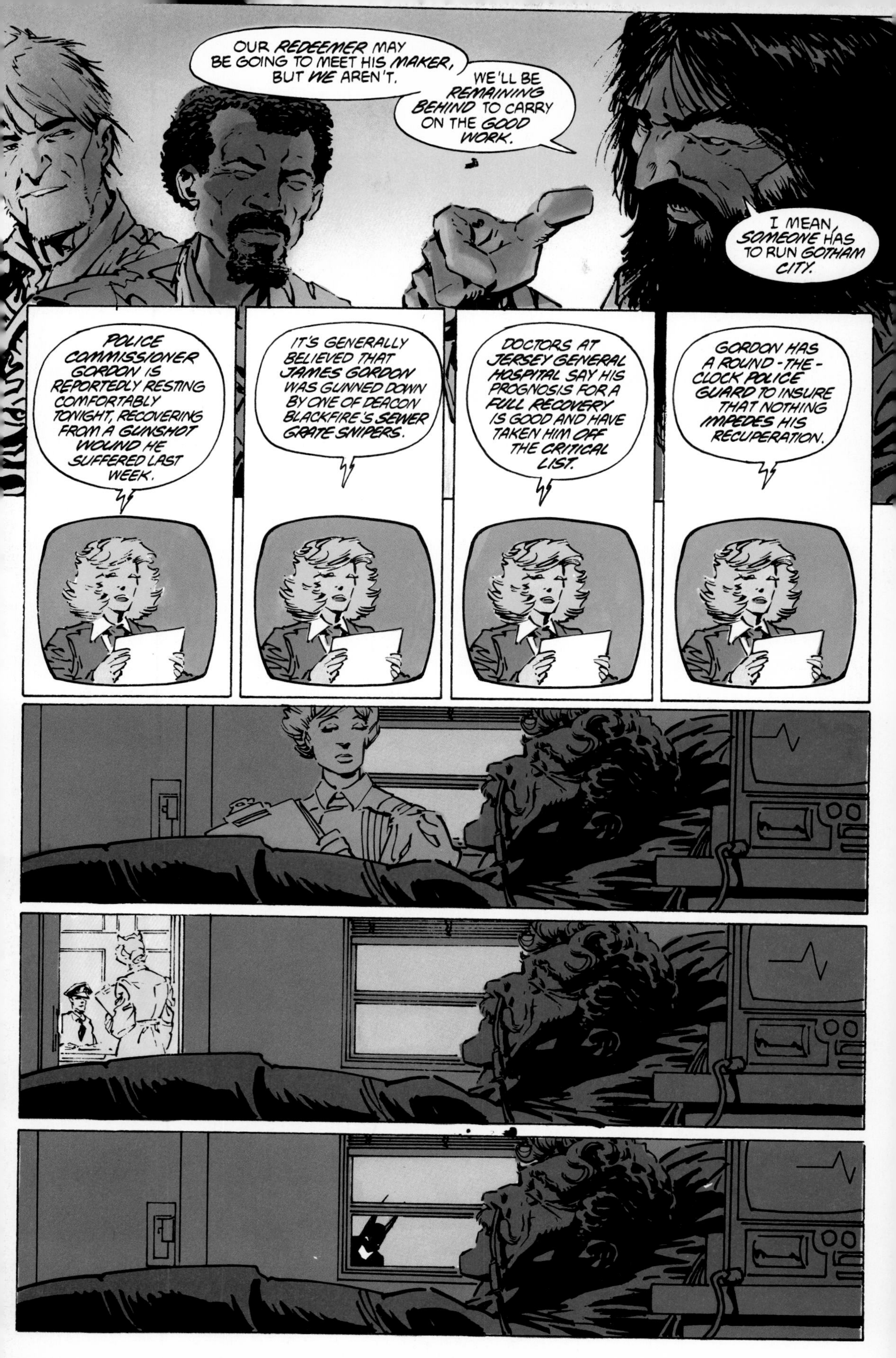

OUR REDEEMER MAY BE GOING TO MEET HIS MAKER, BUT WE AREN'T.
WE'LL BE REMAINING BEHIND TO CARRY ON THE GOOD WORK.
I MEAN, SOMEONE HAS TO RUN GOTHAM CITY.
POLICE COMMISSIONER GORDON IS REPORTEDLY RESTING COMFORTABLY TONIGHT, RECOVERING FROM A GUNSHOT WOUND HE SUFFERED LAST WEEK.
IT'S GENERALLY BELIEVED THAT JAMES GORDON WAS GUNNED DOWN BY ONE OF DEACON BLACKFIRE'S SEWER GRATE SNIPERS.
DOCTORS AT JERSEY GENERAL HOSPITAL SAY HIS PROGNOSIS FOR A FULL RECOVERY IS GOOD AND HAVE TAKEN HIM OFF THE CRITICAL LIST.
GORDON HAS A ROUND-THE-CLOCK POLICE GUARD TO INSURE THAT NOTHING IMPEDES HIS RECUPERATION.

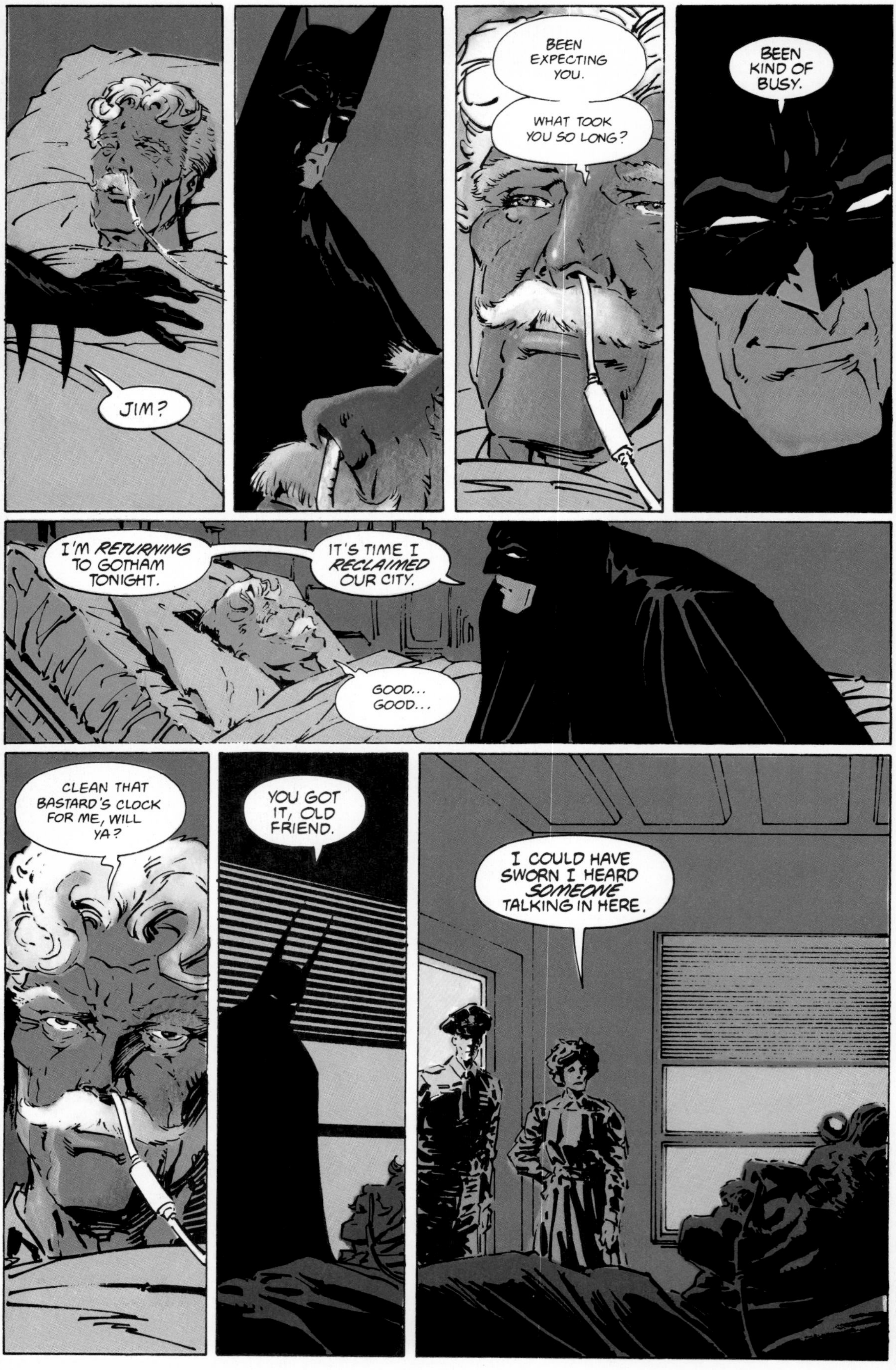
JIM?
BEEN EXPECTING YOU.
WHAT TOOK YOU SO LONG?
BEEN KIND OF BUSY.
I'M *RETURNING* TO GOTHAM TONIGHT.
IT'S TIME I *RECLAIMED* OUR CITY.
GOOD... GOOD...
CLEAN THAT BASTARD'S CLOCK FOR ME, WILL YA?
YOU GOT IT, OLD FRIEND.
I COULD HAVE SWORN I HEARD *SOMEONE* TALKING IN HERE.

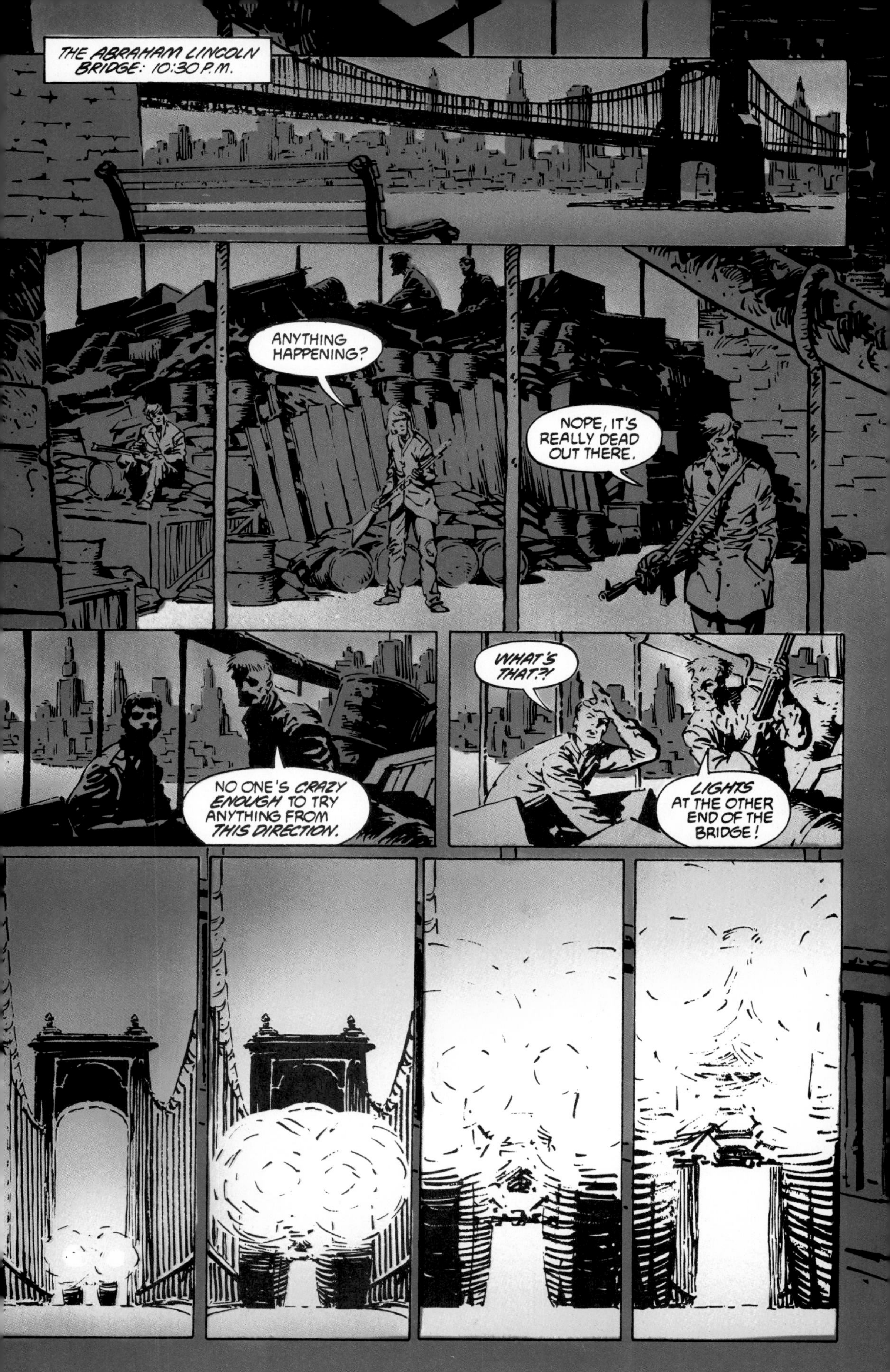
THE ABRAHAM LINCOLN BRIDGE: 10:30 P.M.
ANYTHING HAPPENING?
NOPE, IT'S REALLY DEAD OUT THERE.
NO ONE'S CRAZY ENOUGH TO TRY ANYTHING FROM THIS DIRECTION.
WHAT'S THAT?!
LIGHTS AT THE OTHER END OF THE BRIDGE!

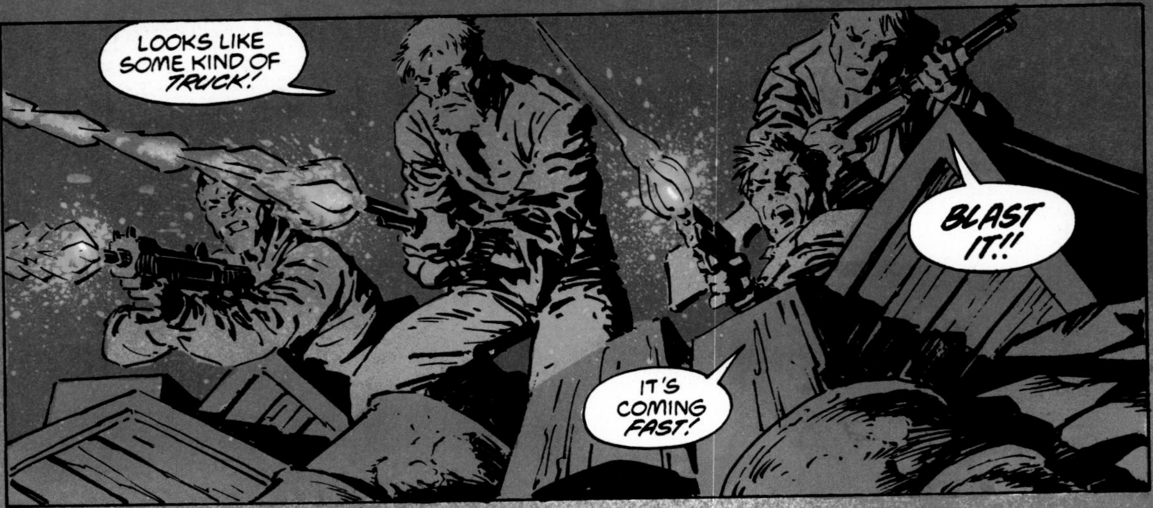
LOOKS LIKE SOME KIND OF TRUCK!
BLAST IT!!
IT'S COMING FAST!

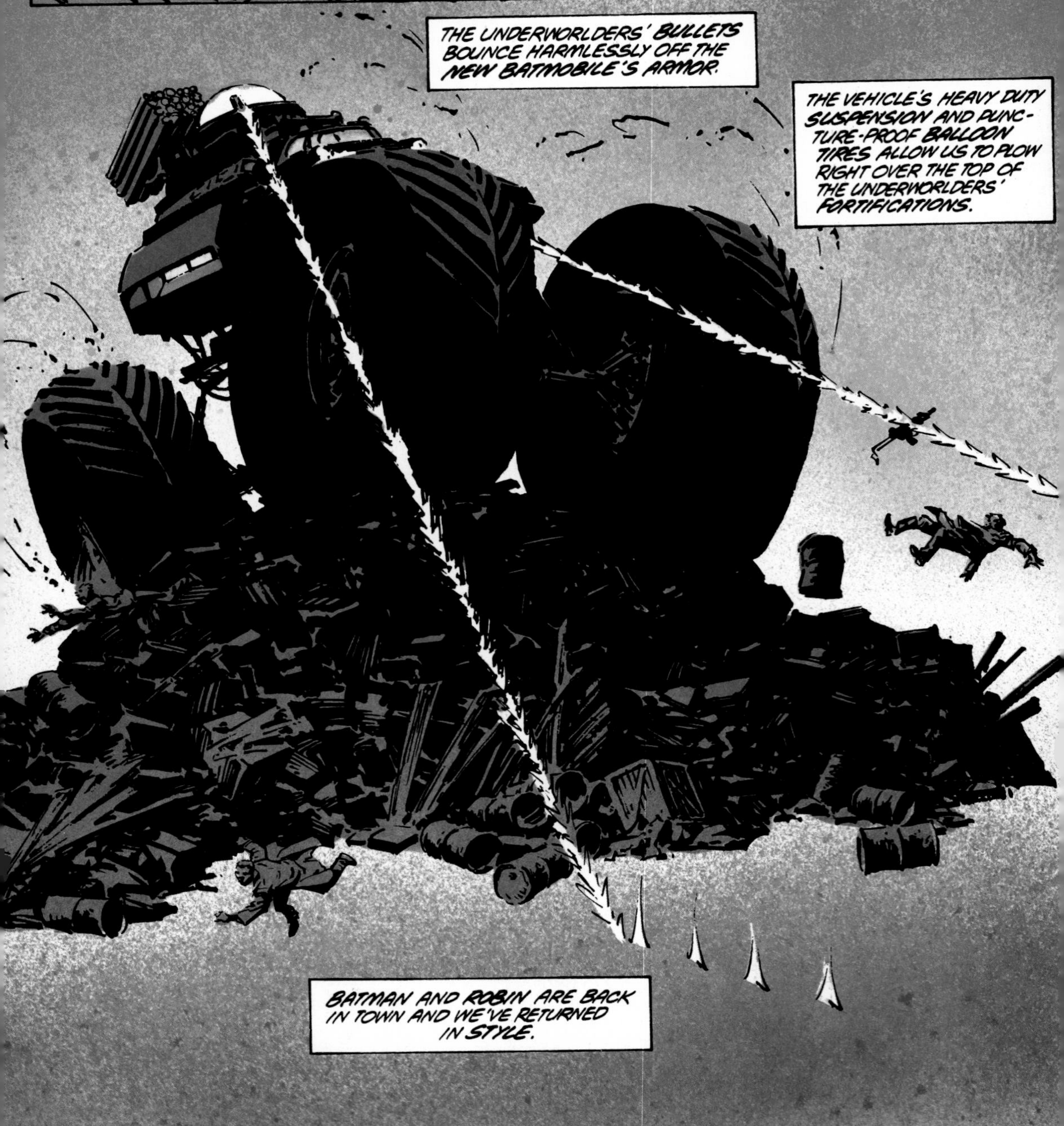
THE UNDERWORLDERS' BULLETS BOUNCE HARMLESSLY OFF THE NEW BATMOBILE'S ARMOR.
THE VEHICLE'S HEAVY DUTY SUSPENSION AND PUNCTURE-PROOF BALLOON TIRES ALLOW US TO PLOW RIGHT OVER THE TOP OF THE UNDERWORLDERS' FORTIFICATIONS.
BATMAN AND ROBIN ARE BACK IN TOWN AND WE'VE RETURNED IN STYLE.

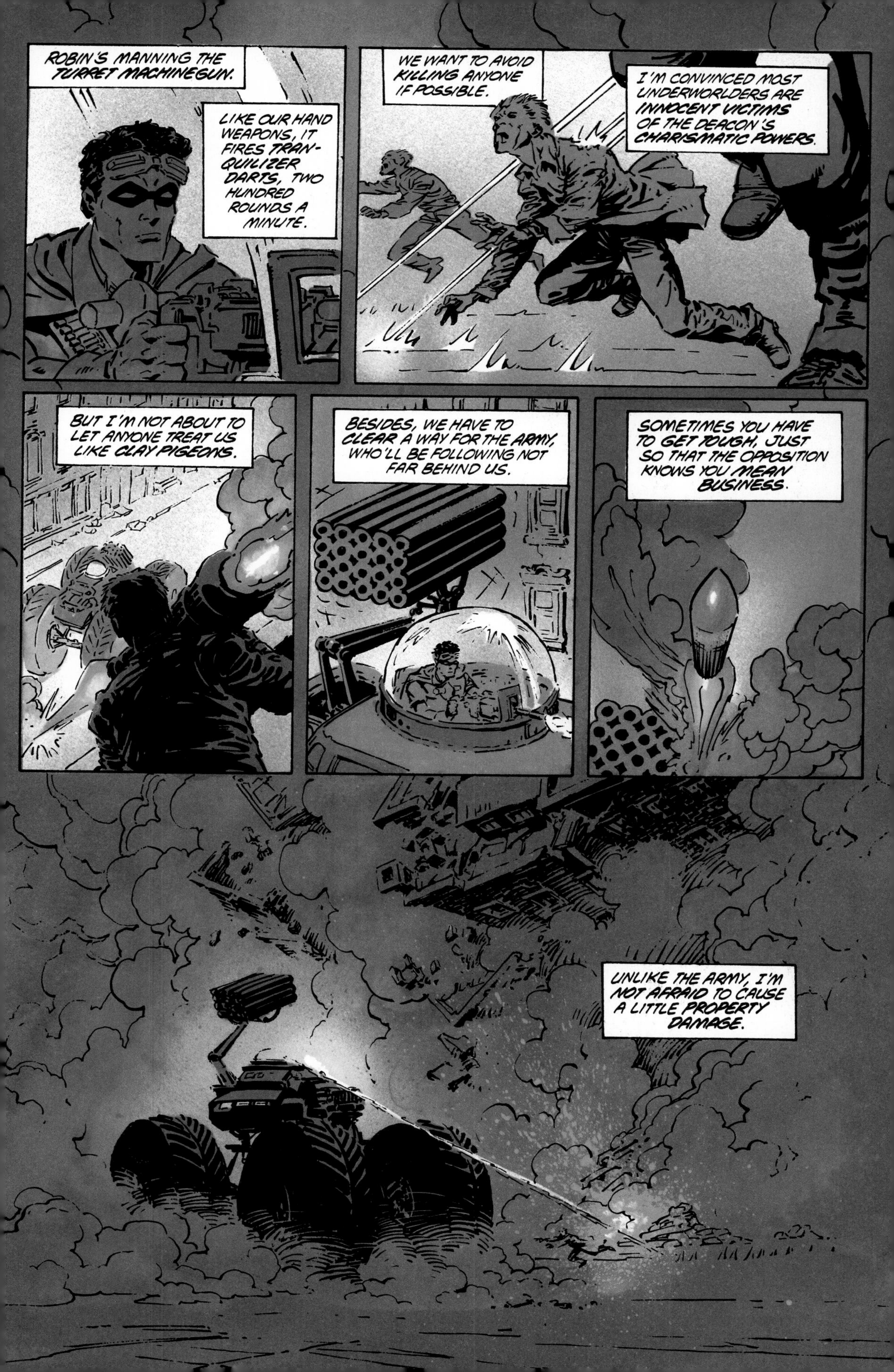

ROBIN'S MANNING THE TURRET MACHINEGUN.
LIKE OUR HAND WEAPONS, IT FIRES TRANQUILIZER DARTS, TWO HUNDRED ROUNDS A MINUTE.
WE WANT TO AVOID KILLING ANYONE IF POSSIBLE.
I'M CONVINCED MOST UNDERWORLDERS ARE INNOCENT VICTIMS OF THE DEACON'S CHARISMATIC POWERS.
BUT I'M NOT ABOUT TO LET ANYONE TREAT US LIKE CLAY PIGEONS.
BESIDES, WE HAVE TO CLEAR A WAY FOR THE ARMY, WHO'LL BE FOLLOWING NOT FAR BEHIND US.
SOMETIMES YOU HAVE TO GET TOUGH, JUST SO THAT THE OPPOSITION KNOWS YOU MEAN BUSINESS.
UNLIKE THE ARMY, I'M NOT AFRAID TO CAUSE A LITTLE PROPERTY DAMAGE.

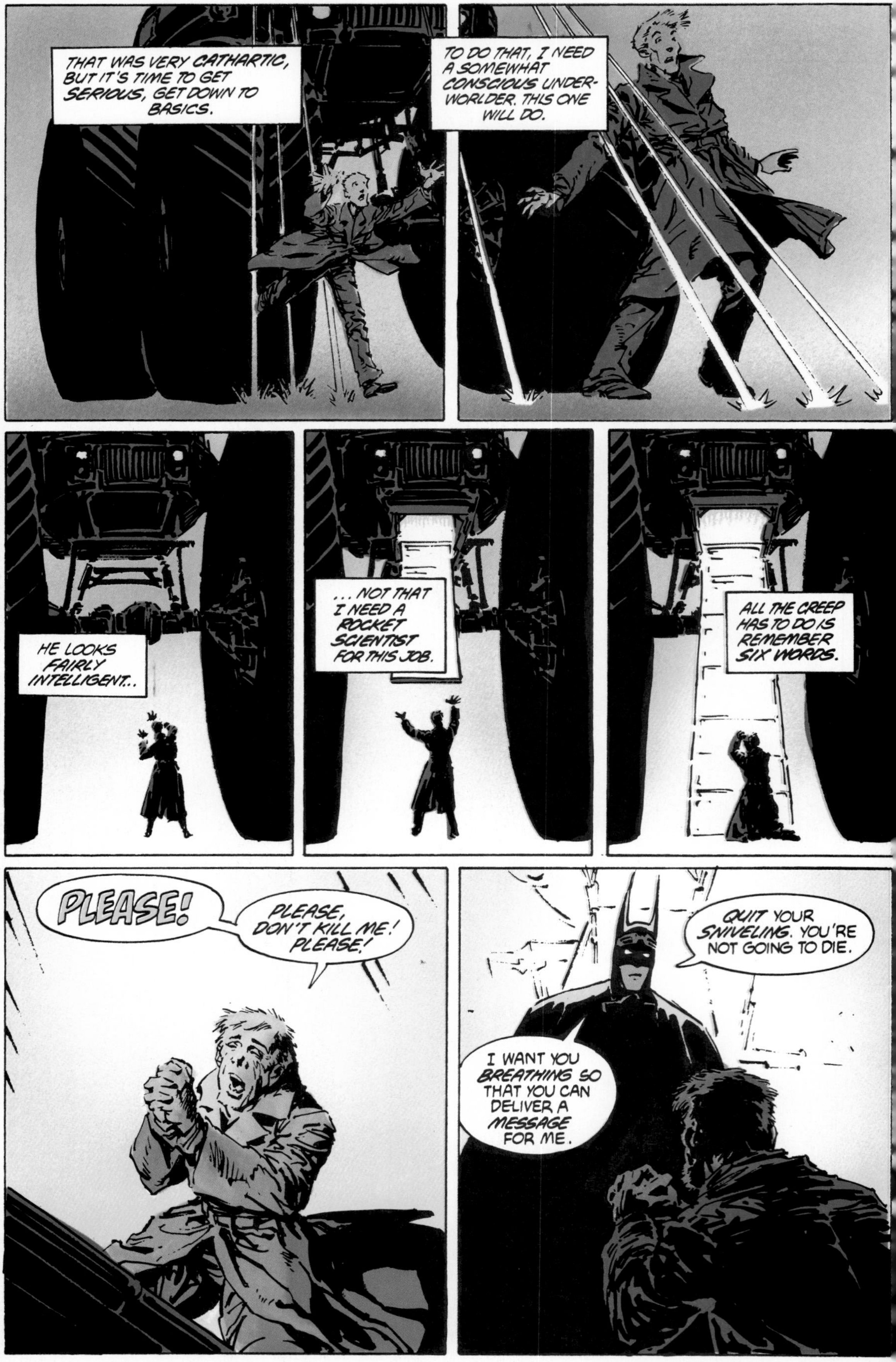
THAT WAS VERY CATHARTIC, BUT IT'S TIME TO GET SERIOUS, GET DOWN TO BASICS.
TO DO THAT, I NEED A SOMEWHAT CONSCIOUS UNDER-WORLDER. THIS ONE WILL DO.
HE LOOKS FAIRLY INTELLIGENT...
...NOT THAT I NEED A ROCKET SCIENTIST FOR THIS JOB.
ALL THE CREEP HAS TO DO IS REMEMBER SIX WORDS.
PLEASE!
PLEASE, DON'T KILL ME! PLEASE!
QUIT YOUR SNIVELING. YOU'RE NOT GOING TO DIE.
I WANT YOU BREATHING SO THAT YOU CAN DELIVER A MESSAGE FOR ME.

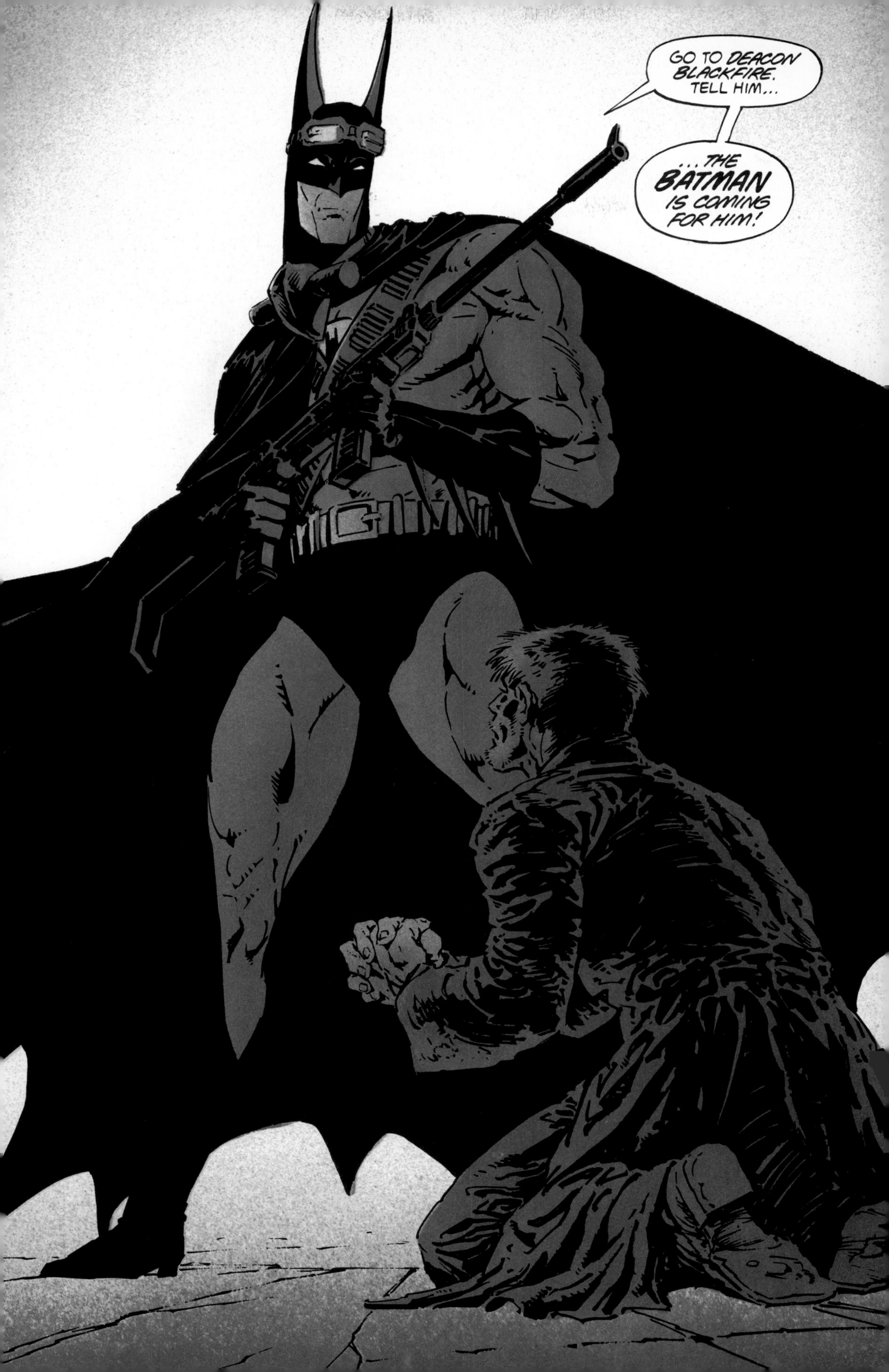
GO TO DEACON BLACKFIRE. TELL HIM...
...THE BATMAN IS COMING FOR HIM!

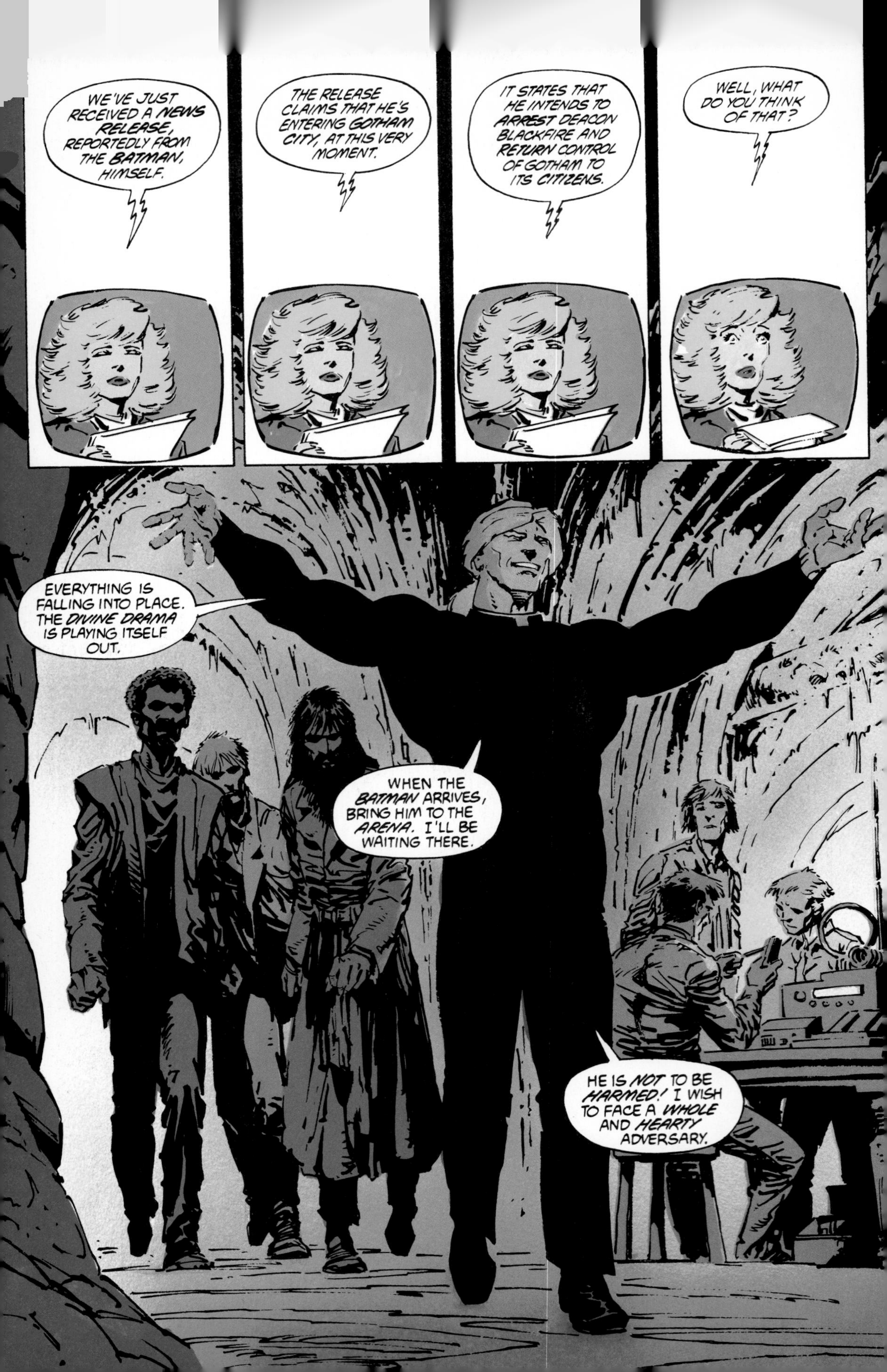
WE'VE JUST RECEIVED A NEWS RELEASE, REPORTEDLY FROM THE BATMAN, HIMSELF.
THE RELEASE CLAIMS THAT HE'S ENTERING GOTHAM CITY, AT THIS VERY MOMENT.
IT STATES THAT HE INTENDS TO ARREST DEACON BLACKFIRE AND RETURN CONTROL OF GOTHAM TO ITS CITIZENS.
WELL, WHAT DO YOU THINK OF THAT?
EVERYTHING IS FALLING INTO PLACE. THE DIVINE DRAMA IS PLAYING ITSELF OUT.
WHEN THE BATMAN ARRIVES, BRING HIM TO THE ARENA. I'LL BE WAITING THERE.
HE IS NOT TO BE HARMED! I WISH TO FACE A WHOLE AND HEARTY ADVERSARY.

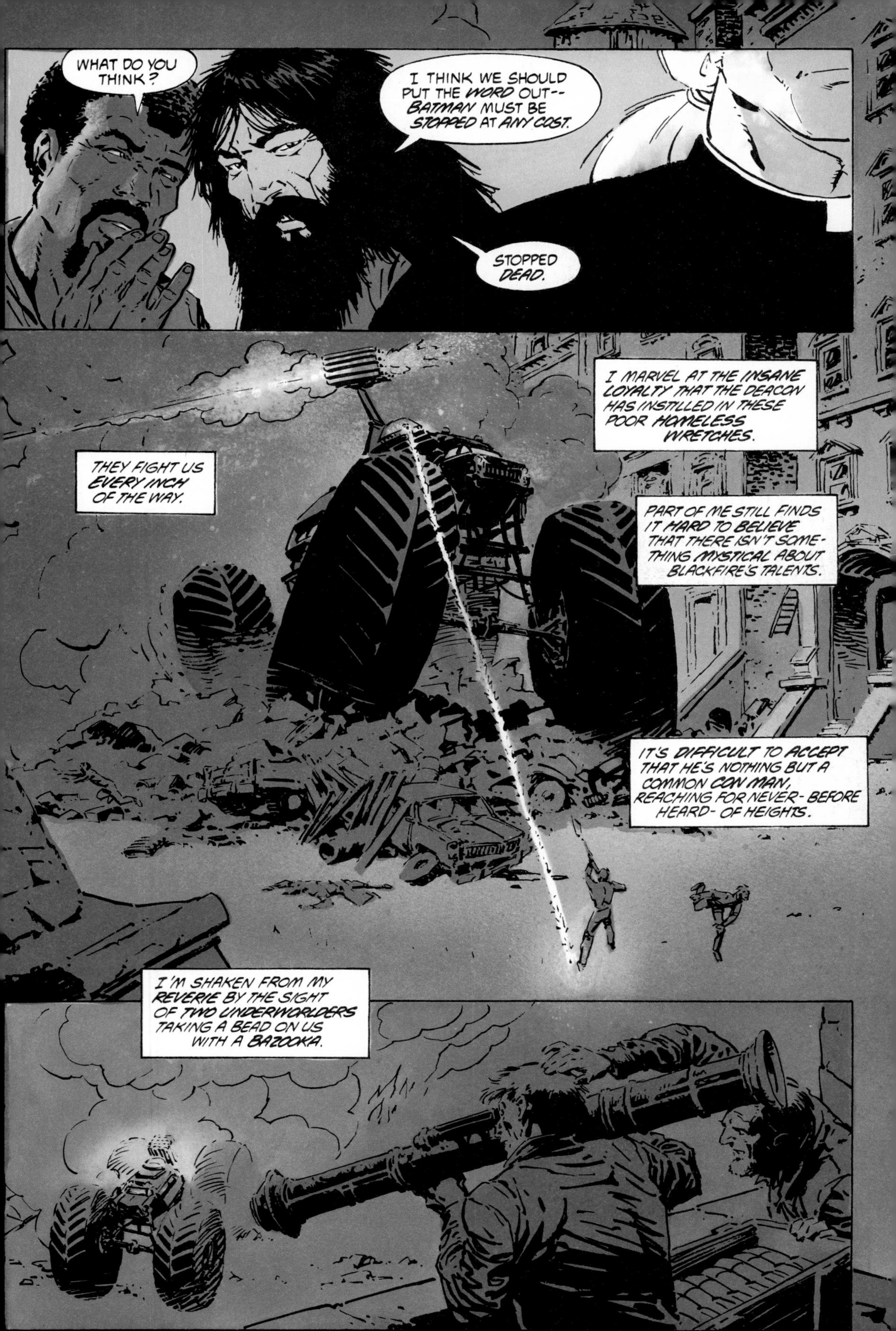

WHAT DO YOU THINK?
I THINK WE SHOULD PUT THE WORD OUT-- BATMAN MUST BE STOPPED AT ANY COST.
STOPPED DEAD.
I MARVEL AT THE INSANE LOYALTY THAT THE DEACON HAS INSTILLED IN THESE POOR HOMELESS WRETCHES.
THEY FIGHT US EVERY INCH OF THE WAY.
PART OF ME STILL FINDS IT HARD TO BELIEVE THAT THERE ISN'T SOME-THING MYSTICAL ABOUT BLACKFIRE'S TALENTS.
IT'S DIFFICULT TO ACCEPT THAT HE'S NOTHING BUT A COMMON CON MAN, REACHING FOR NEVER-BEFORE HEARD-OF HEIGHTS.
I'M SHAKEN FROM MY REVERIE BY THE SIGHT OF TWO UNDERWORLDERS TAKING A BEAD ON US WITH A BAZOOKA.

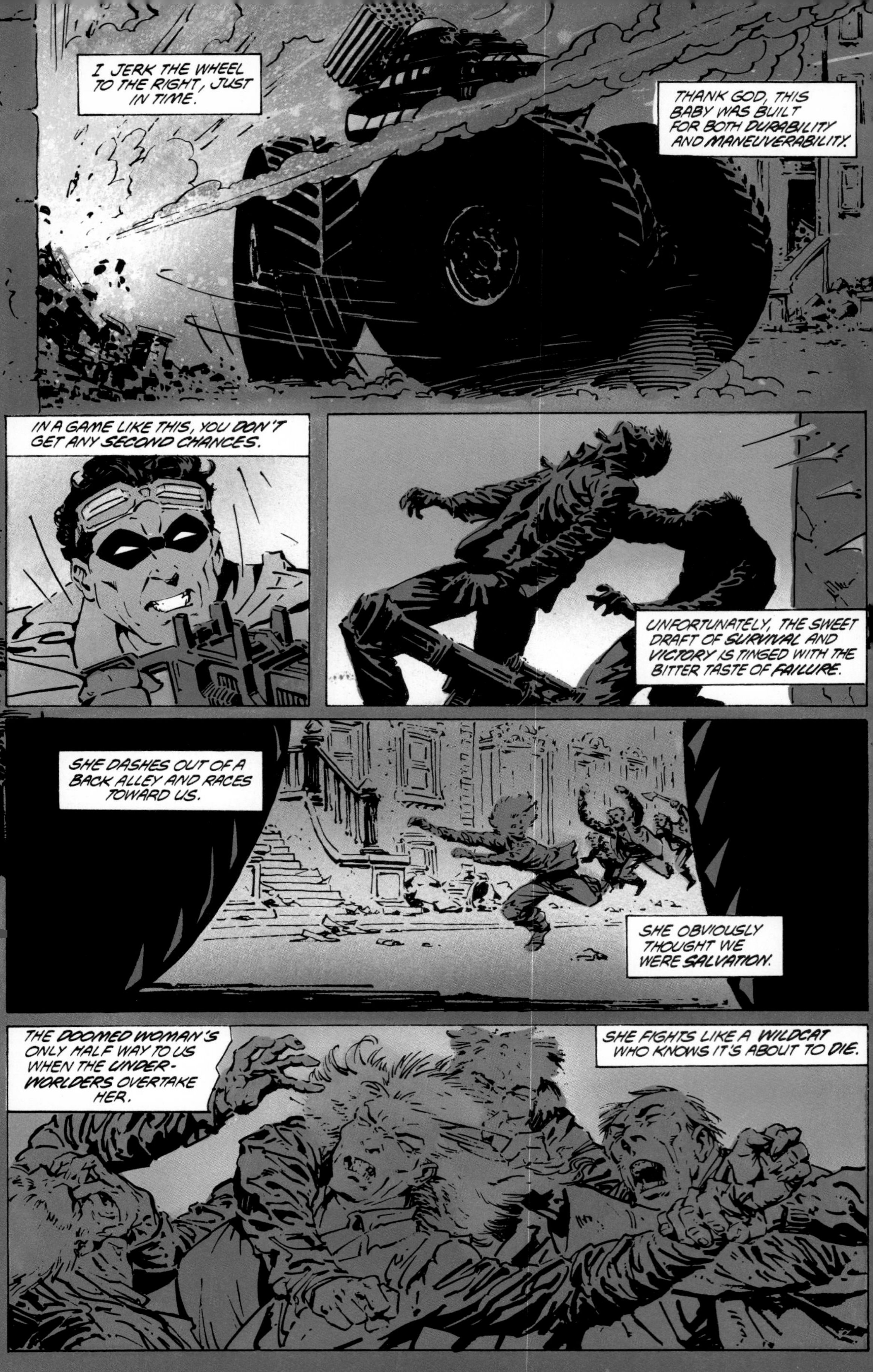

I JERK THE WHEEL TO THE RIGHT, JUST IN TIME.
THANK GOD, THIS BABY WAS BUILT FOR BOTH DURABILITY AND MANEUVERABILITY.
IN A GAME LIKE THIS, YOU DON'T GET ANY SECOND CHANCES.
UNFORTUNATELY, THE SWEET DRAFT OF SURVIVAL AND VICTORY IS TINGED WITH THE BITTER TASTE OF FAILURE.
SHE DASHES OUT OF A BACK ALLEY AND RACES TOWARD US.
SHE OBVIOUSLY THOUGHT WE WERE SALVATION.
THE DOOMED WOMAN'S ONLY HALF WAY TO US WHEN THE UNDER-WORLDERS OVERTAKE HER.
SHE FIGHTS LIKE A WILDCAT WHO KNOWS IT'S ABOUT TO DIE.

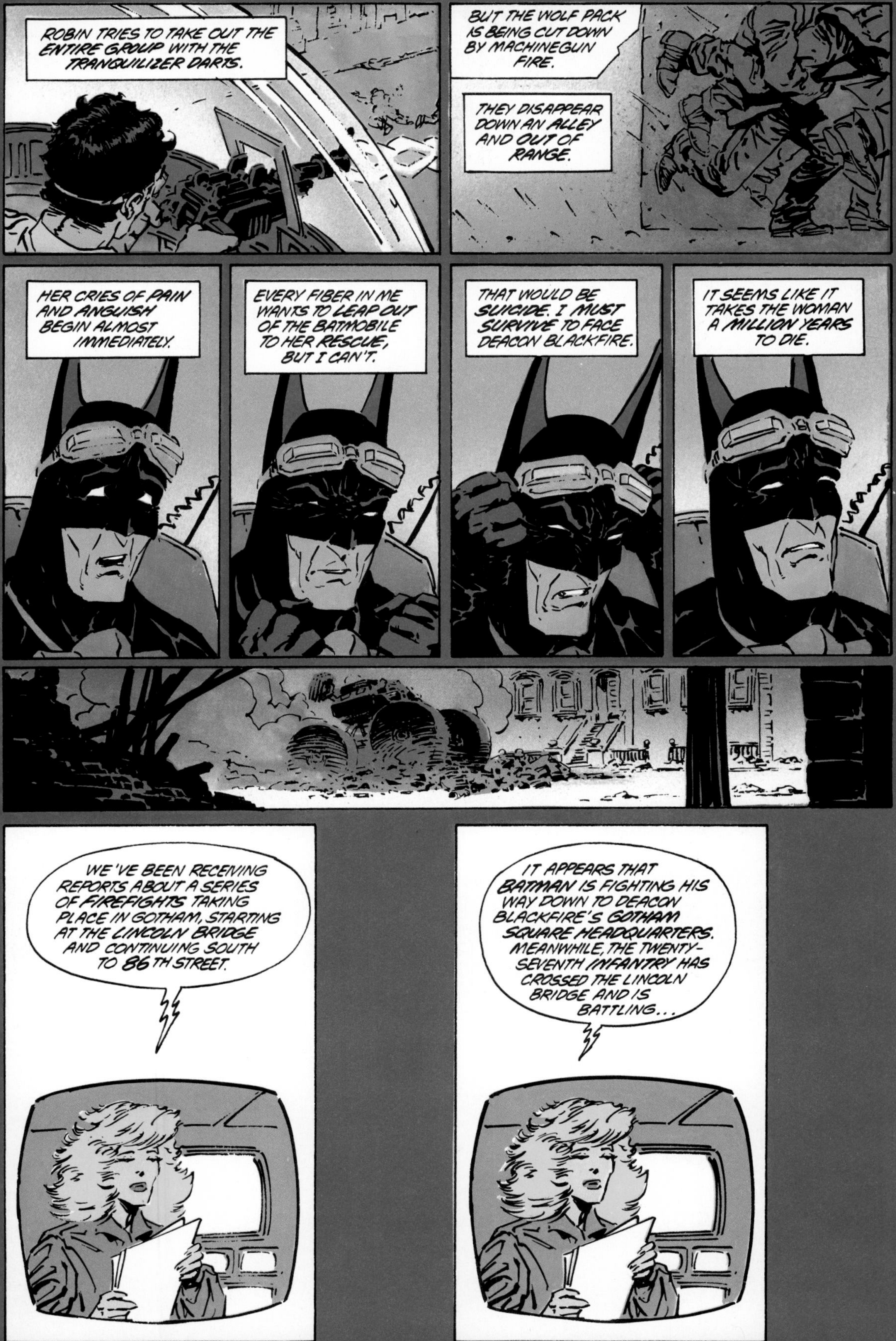

ROBIN TRIES TO TAKE OUT THE ENTIRE GROUP WITH THE TRANQUILIZER DARTS.
BUT THE WOLF PACK IS BEING CUT DOWN BY MACHINEGUN FIRE.
THEY DISAPPEAR DOWN AN ALLEY AND OUT OF RANGE.
HER CRIES OF PAIN AND ANGUISH BEGIN ALMOST IMMEDIATELY.
EVERY FIBER IN ME WANTS TO LEAP OUT OF THE BATMOBILE TO HER RESCUE, BUT I CAN'T.
THAT WOULD BE SUICIDE. I MUST SURVIVE TO FACE DEACON BLACKFIRE.
IT SEEMS LIKE IT TAKES THE WOMAN A MILLION YEARS TO DIE.
WE'VE BEEN RECEIVING REPORTS ABOUT A SERIES OF FIREFIGHTS TAKING PLACE IN GOTHAM, STARTING AT THE LINCOLN BRIDGE AND CONTINUING SOUTH TO 86TH STREET.
IT APPEARS THAT BATMAN IS FIGHTING HIS WAY DOWN TO DEACON BLACKFIRE'S GOTHAM SQUARE HEADQUARTERS. MEANWHILE, THE TWENTY-SEVENTH INFANTRY HAS CROSSED THE LINCOLN BRIDGE AND IS BATTLING...

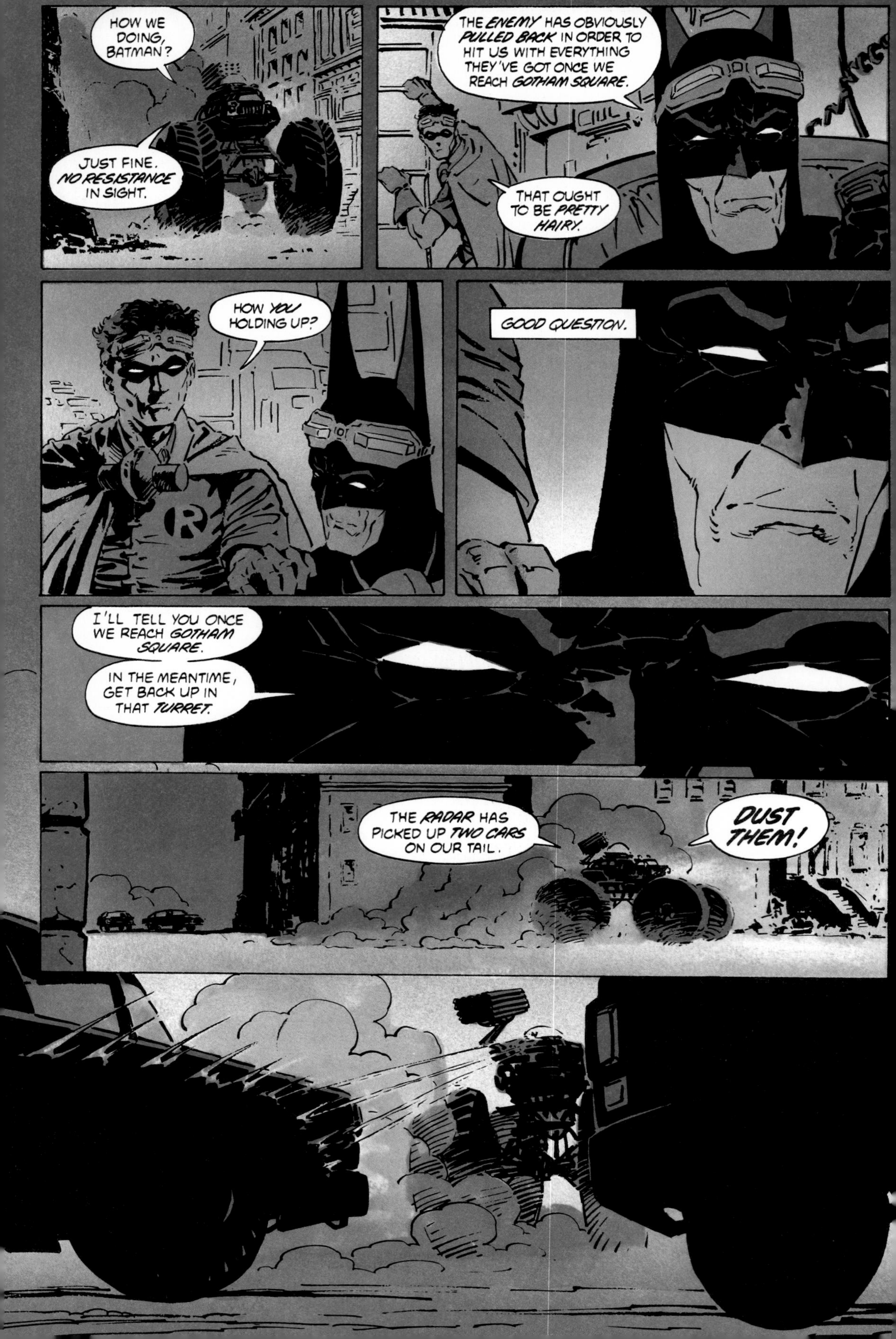
HOW WE DOING, BATMAN?
JUST FINE. NO RESISTANCE IN SIGHT.
THE ENEMY HAS OBVIOUSLY PULLED BACK IN ORDER TO HIT US WITH EVERYTHING THEY'VE GOT ONCE WE REACH GOTHAM SQUARE.
THAT OUGHT TO BE PRETTY HAIRY.
HOW YOU HOLDING UP?
GOOD QUESTION.
I'LL TELL YOU ONCE WE REACH GOTHAM SQUARE.
IN THE MEANTIME, GET BACK UP IN THAT TURRET.
THE RADAR HAS PICKED UP TWO CARS ON OUR TAIL.
DUST THEM!

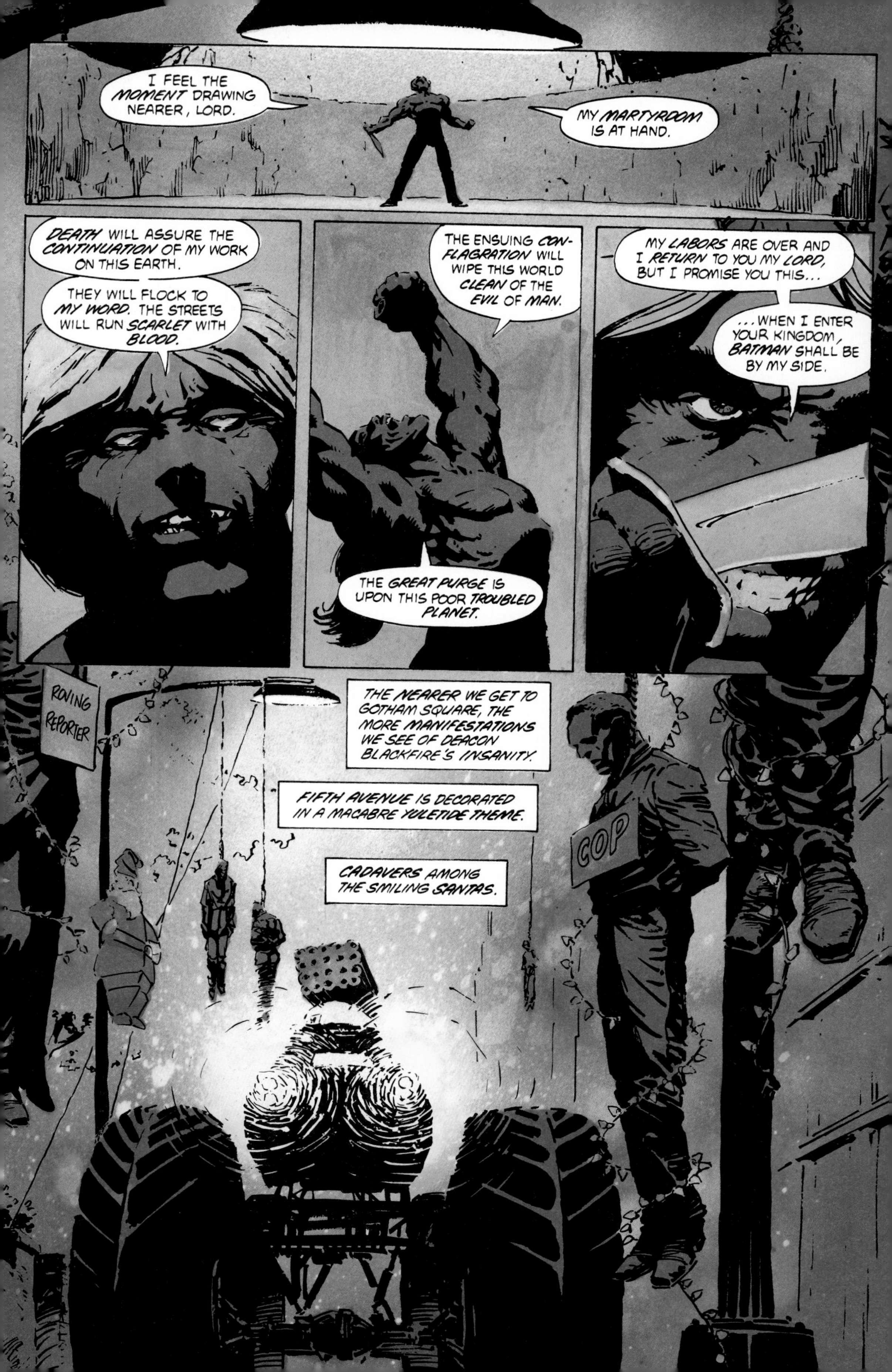

I FEEL THE MOMENT DRAWING NEARER, LORD.
MY MARTYRDOM IS AT HAND.
DEATH WILL ASSURE THE CONTINUATION OF MY WORK ON THIS EARTH.
THEY WILL FLOCK TO MY WORD. THE STREETS WILL RUN SCARLET WITH BLOOD.
THE ENSUING CON-FLAGRATION WILL WIPE THIS WORLD CLEAN OF THE EVIL OF MAN.
THE GREAT PURGE IS UPON THIS POOR TROUBLED PLANET.
MY LABORS ARE OVER AND I RETURN TO YOU MY LORD, BUT I PROMISE YOU THIS...
...WHEN I ENTER YOUR KINGDOM, BATMAN SHALL BE BY MY SIDE.
ROVING REPORTER
THE NEARER WE GET TO GOTHAM SQUARE, THE MORE MANIFESTATIONS WE SEE OF DEACON BLACKFIRE'S INSANITY.
FIFTH AVENUE IS DECORATED IN A MACABRE YULETIDE THEME.
CADAVERS AMONG THE SMILING SANTAS.
COP

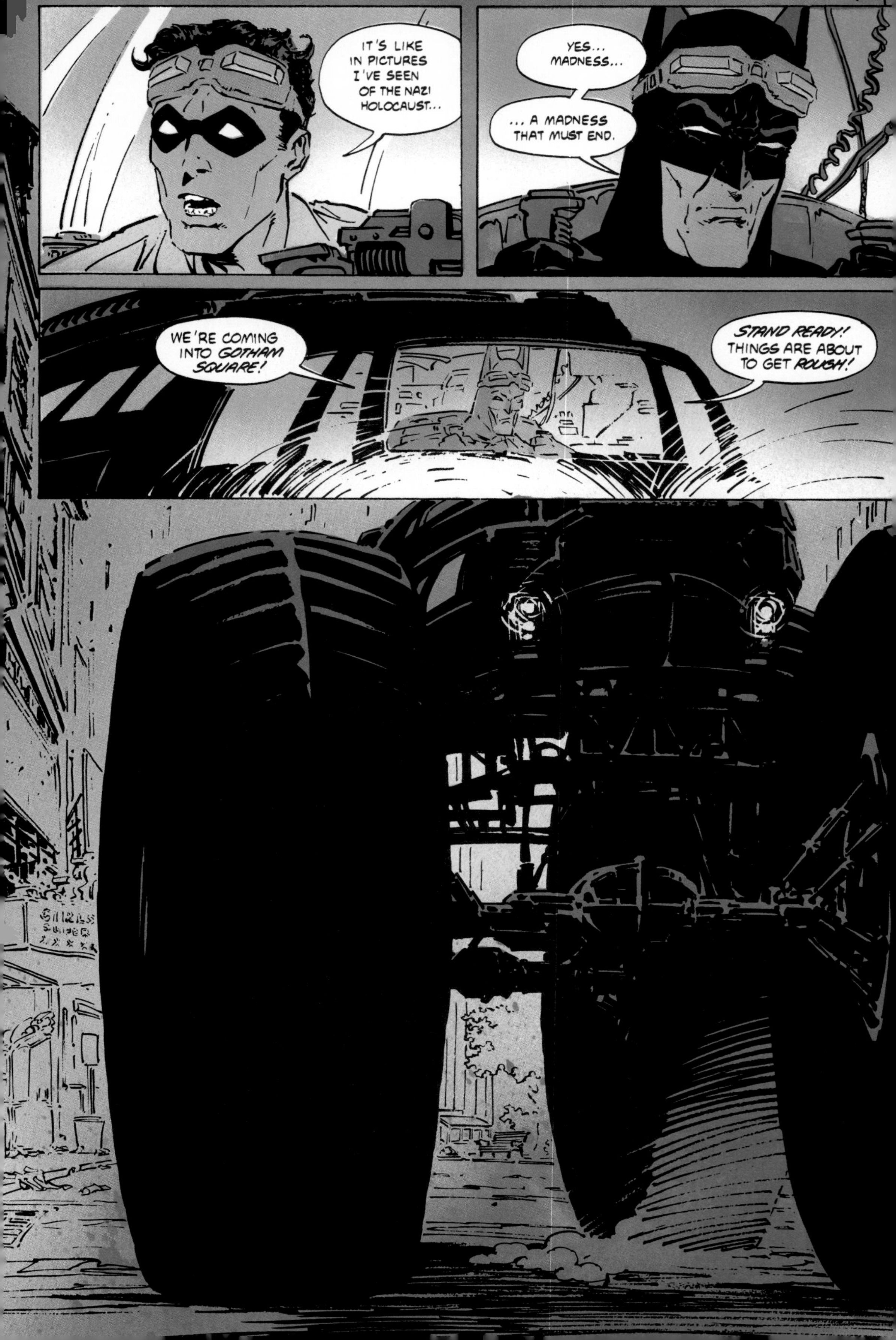
IT'S LIKE IN PICTURES I'VE SEEN OF THE NAZI HOLOCAUST...
YES... MADNESS...
... A MADNESS THAT MUST END.
WE'RE COMING INTO GOTHAM SQUARE!
STAND READY! THINGS ARE ABOUT TO GET ROUGH!

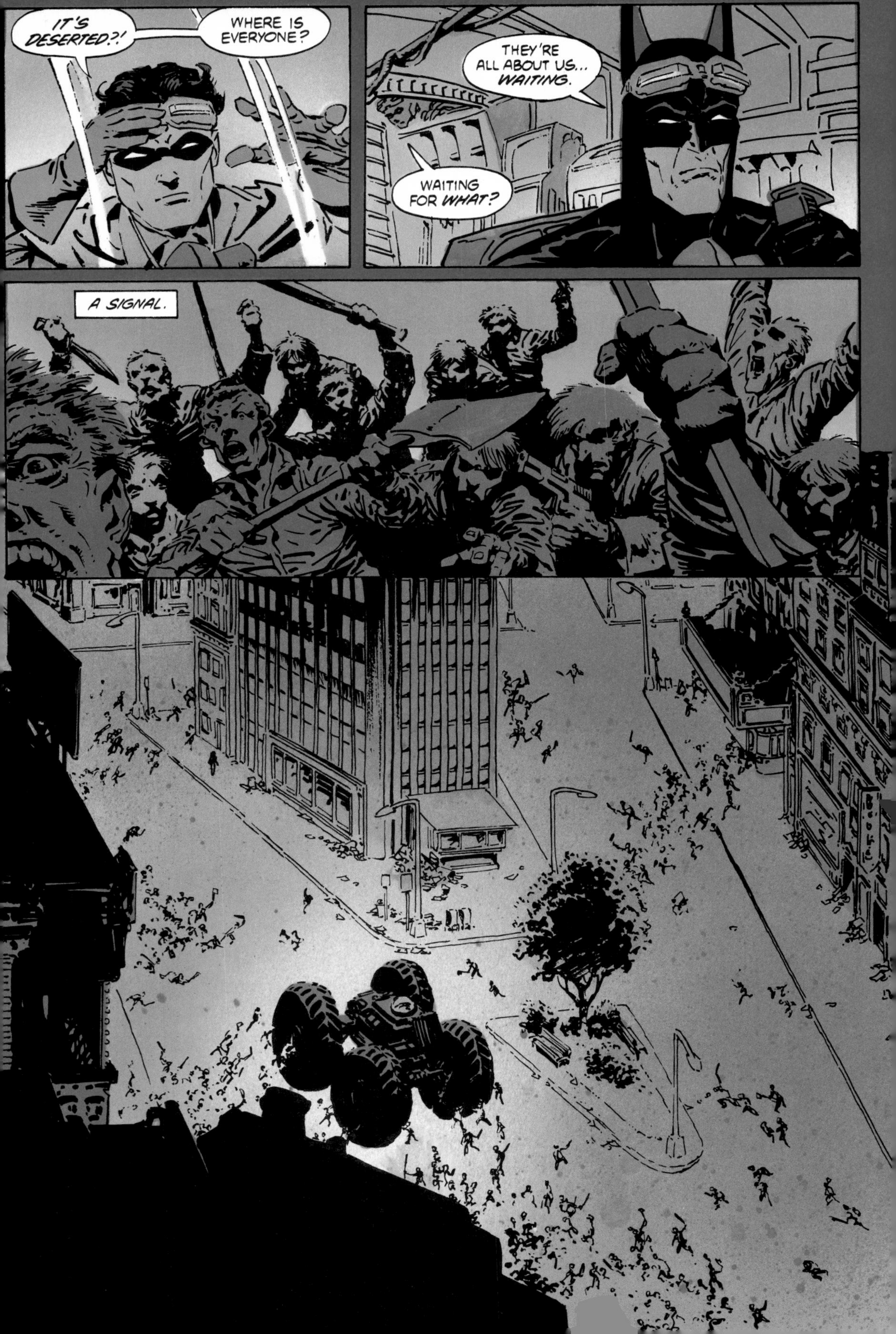
IT'S DESERTED?!
WHERE IS EVERYONE?
THEY'RE ALL ABOUT US... WAITING.
WAITING FOR WHAT?
A SIGNAL.

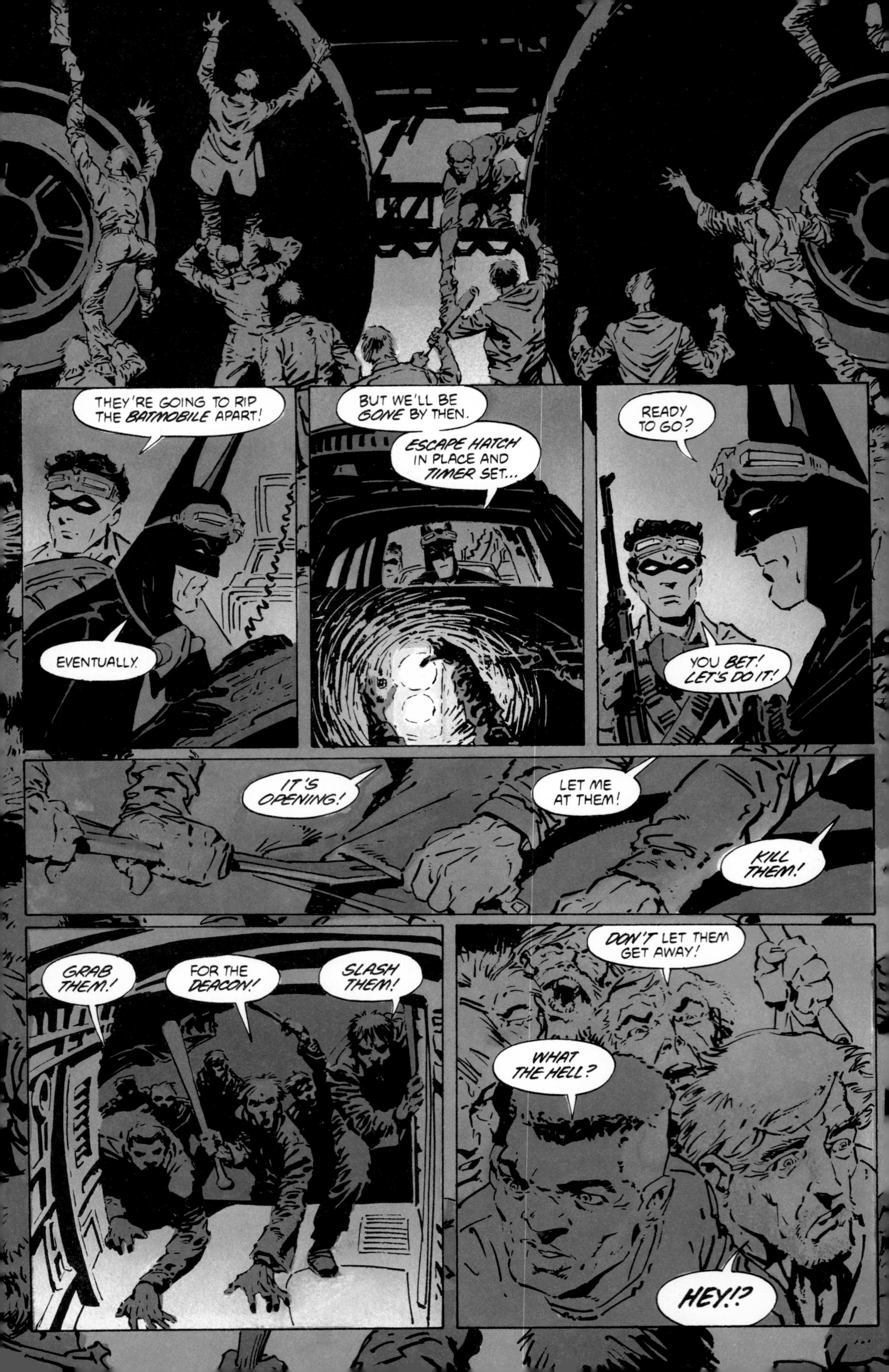
THEY'RE GOING TO RIP THE BATMOBILE APART!
EVENTUALLY.
BUT WE'LL BE GONE BY THEN.
ESCAPE HATCH IN PLACE AND TIMER SET...
READY TO GO?
YOU BET! LET'S DO IT!
IT'S OPENING!
LET ME AT THEM!
KILL THEM!
GRAB THEM!
FOR THE DEACON!
SLASH THEM!
DON'T LET THEM GET AWAY!
WHAT THE HELL?
HEY!?

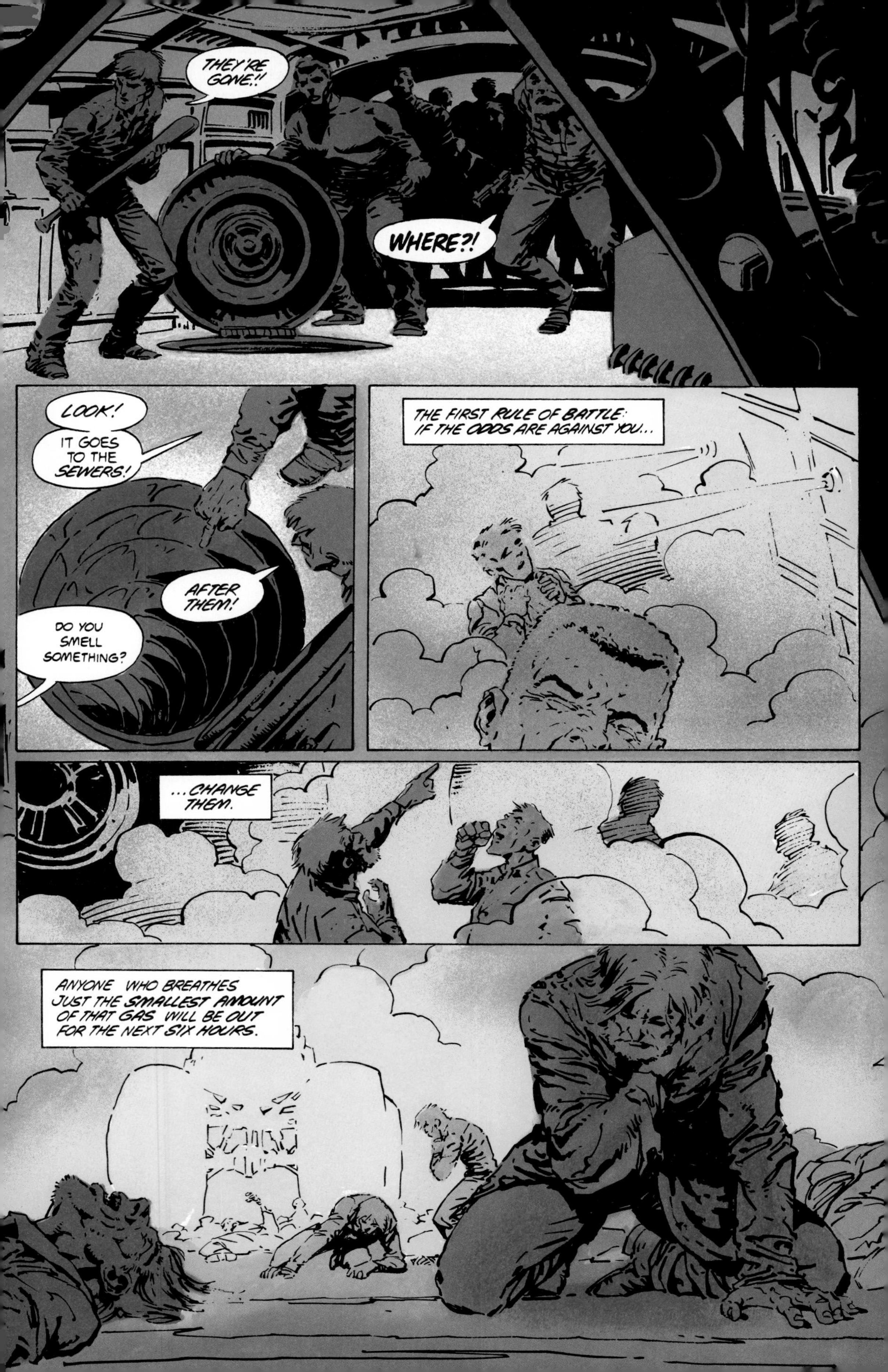

THEY'RE GONE!!
WHERE?!
LOOK!
IT GOES TO THE SEWERS!
AFTER THEM!
DO YOU SMELL SOMETHING?
THE FIRST RULE OF BATTLE: IF THE ODDS ARE AGAINST YOU...
...CHANGE THEM.
ANYONE WHO BREATHES JUST THE SMALLEST AMOUNT OF THAT GAS WILL BE OUT FOR THE NEXT SIX HOURS.

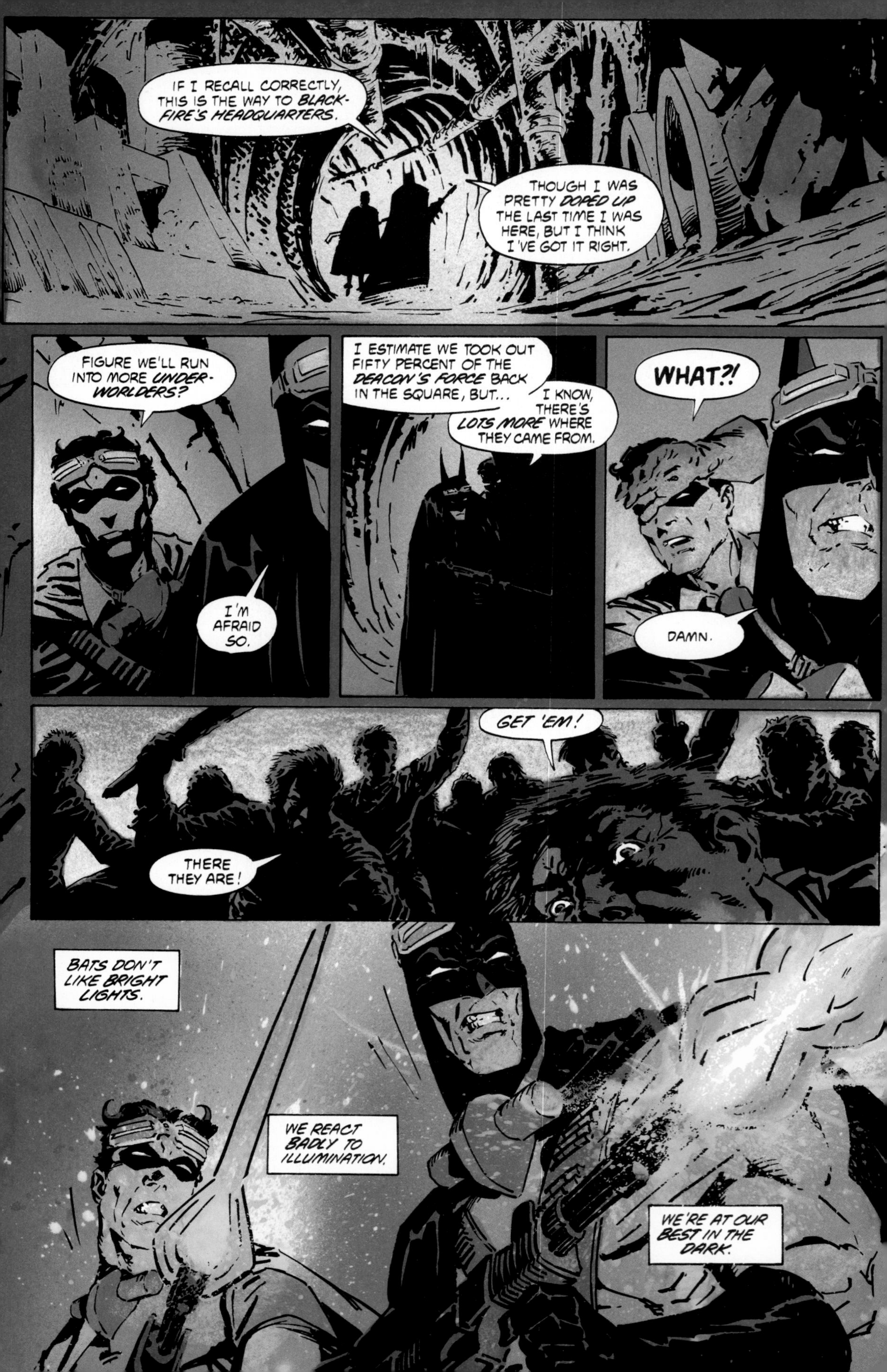

IF I RECALL CORRECTLY, THIS IS THE WAY TO BLACKFIRE'S HEADQUARTERS.
THOUGH I WAS PRETTY DOPED UP THE LAST TIME I WAS HERE, BUT I THINK I'VE GOT IT RIGHT.
FIGURE WE'LL RUN INTO MORE UNDERWORLDERS?
I'M AFRAID SO.
I ESTIMATE WE TOOK OUT FIFTY PERCENT OF THE DEACON'S FORCE BACK IN THE SQUARE, BUT...
I KNOW, THERE'S LOTS MORE WHERE THEY CAME FROM.
WHAT?!
DAMN.
GET 'EM!
THERE THEY ARE!
BATS DON'T LIKE BRIGHT LIGHTS.
WE REACT BADLY TO ILLUMINATION.
WE'RE AT OUR BEST IN THE DARK.

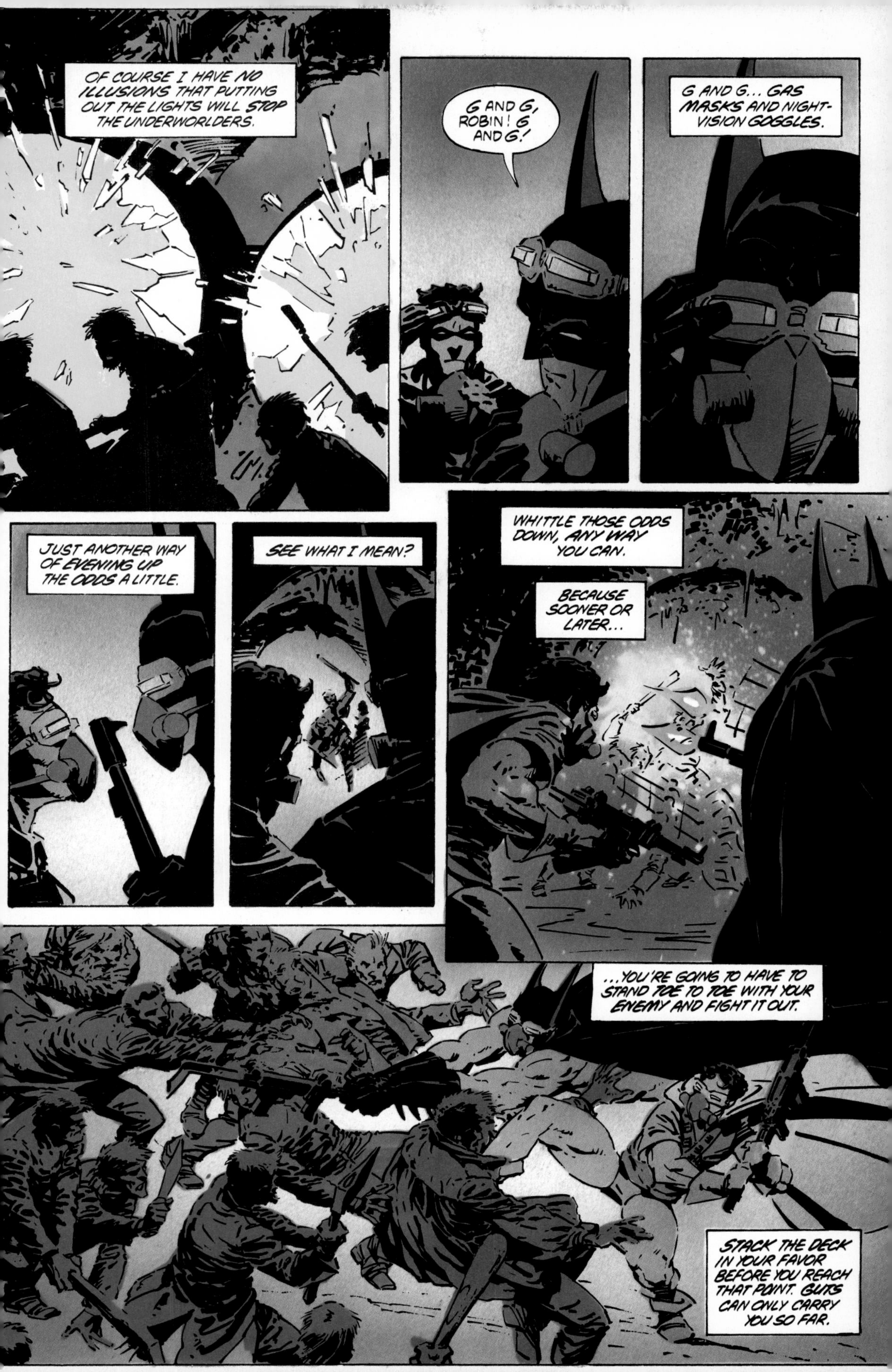

OF COURSE I HAVE NO ILLUSIONS THAT PUTTING OUT THE LIGHTS WILL STOP THE UNDERWORLDERS.
G AND G, ROBIN! G AND G!
G AND G... GAS MASKS AND NIGHT-VISION GOGGLES.
JUST ANOTHER WAY OF EVENING UP THE ODDS A LITTLE.
SEE WHAT I MEAN?
WHITTLE THOSE ODDS DOWN, ANY WAY YOU CAN.
BECAUSE SOONER OR LATER...
...YOU'RE GOING TO HAVE TO STAND TOE TO TOE WITH YOUR ENEMY AND FIGHT IT OUT.
STACK THE DECK IN YOUR FAVOR BEFORE YOU REACH THAT POINT. GUTS CAN ONLY CARRY YOU SO FAR.

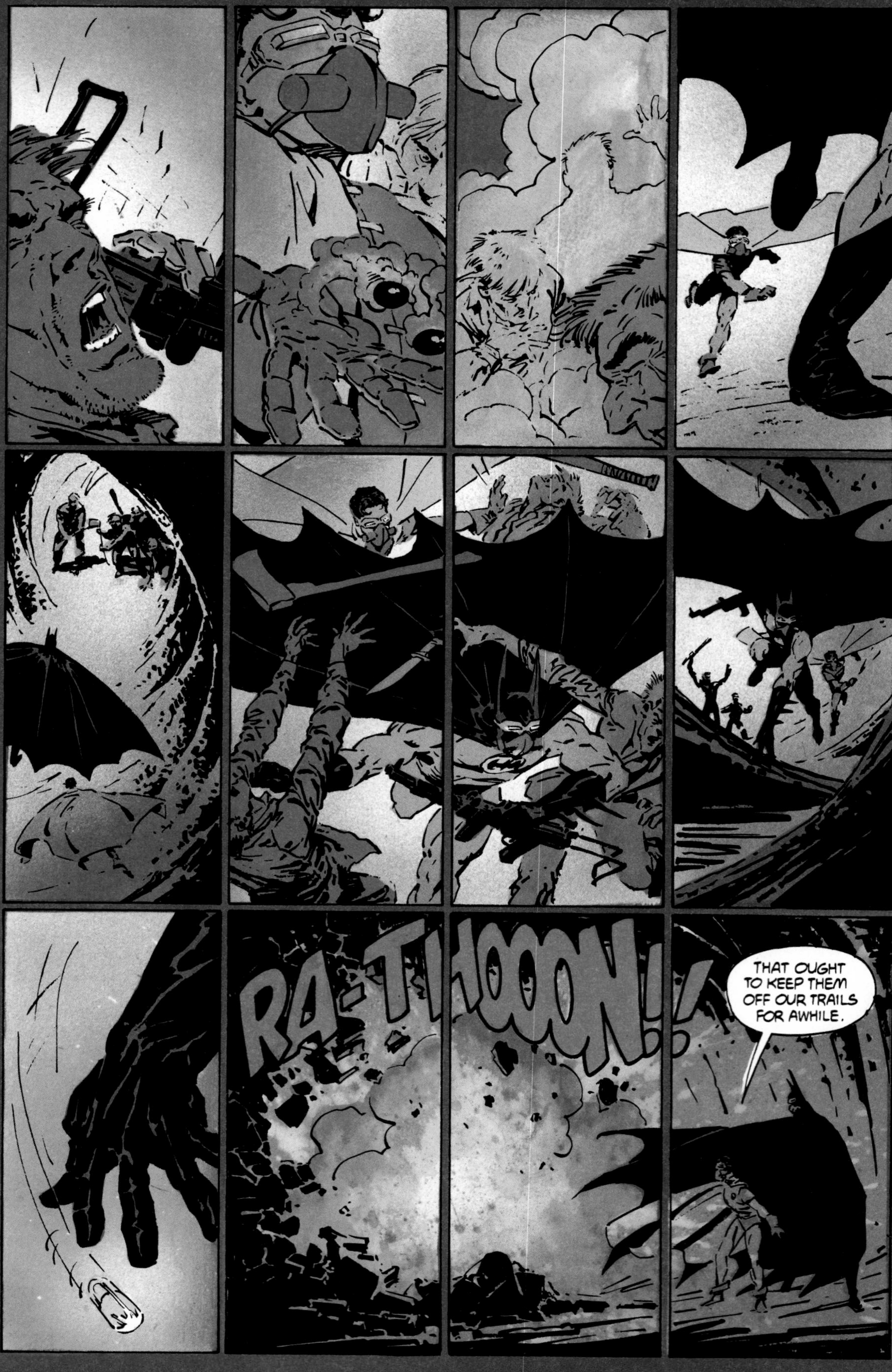
RA-THOOON!!
THAT OUGHT TO KEEP THEM OFF OUR TRAILS FOR AWHILE.

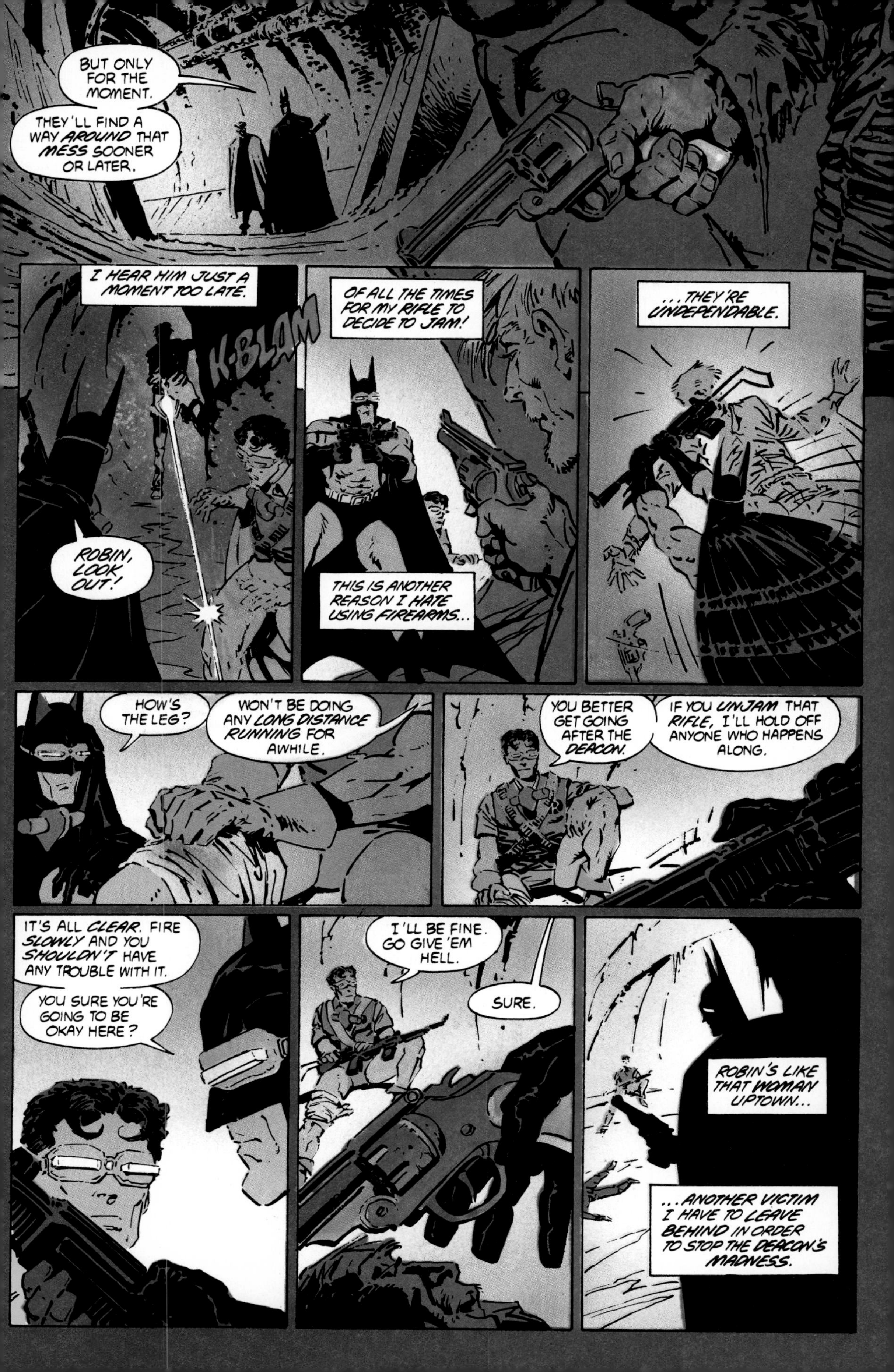
BUT ONLY FOR THE MOMENT.
THEY'LL FIND A WAY AROUND THAT MESS SOONER OR LATER.
I HEAR HIM JUST A MOMENT TOO LATE.
K-BLAM
ROBIN, LOOK OUT!
OF ALL THE TIMES FOR MY RIFLE TO DECIDE TO JAM!
THIS IS ANOTHER REASON I HATE USING FIREARMS...
...THEY'RE UNDEPENDABLE.
HOW'S THE LEG?
WON'T BE DOING ANY LONG DISTANCE RUNNING FOR AWHILE.
YOU BETTER GET GOING AFTER THE DEACON.
IF YOU UNJAM THAT RIFLE, I'LL HOLD OFF ANYONE WHO HAPPENS ALONG.
IT'S ALL CLEAR. FIRE SLOWLY AND YOU SHOULDN'T HAVE ANY TROUBLE WITH IT.
YOU SURE YOU'RE GOING TO BE OKAY HERE?
I'LL BE FINE. GO GIVE 'EM HELL.
SURE.
ROBIN'S LIKE THAT WOMAN UPTOWN...
...ANOTHER VICTIM I HAVE TO LEAVE BEHIND IN ORDER TO STOP THE DEACON'S MADNESS.

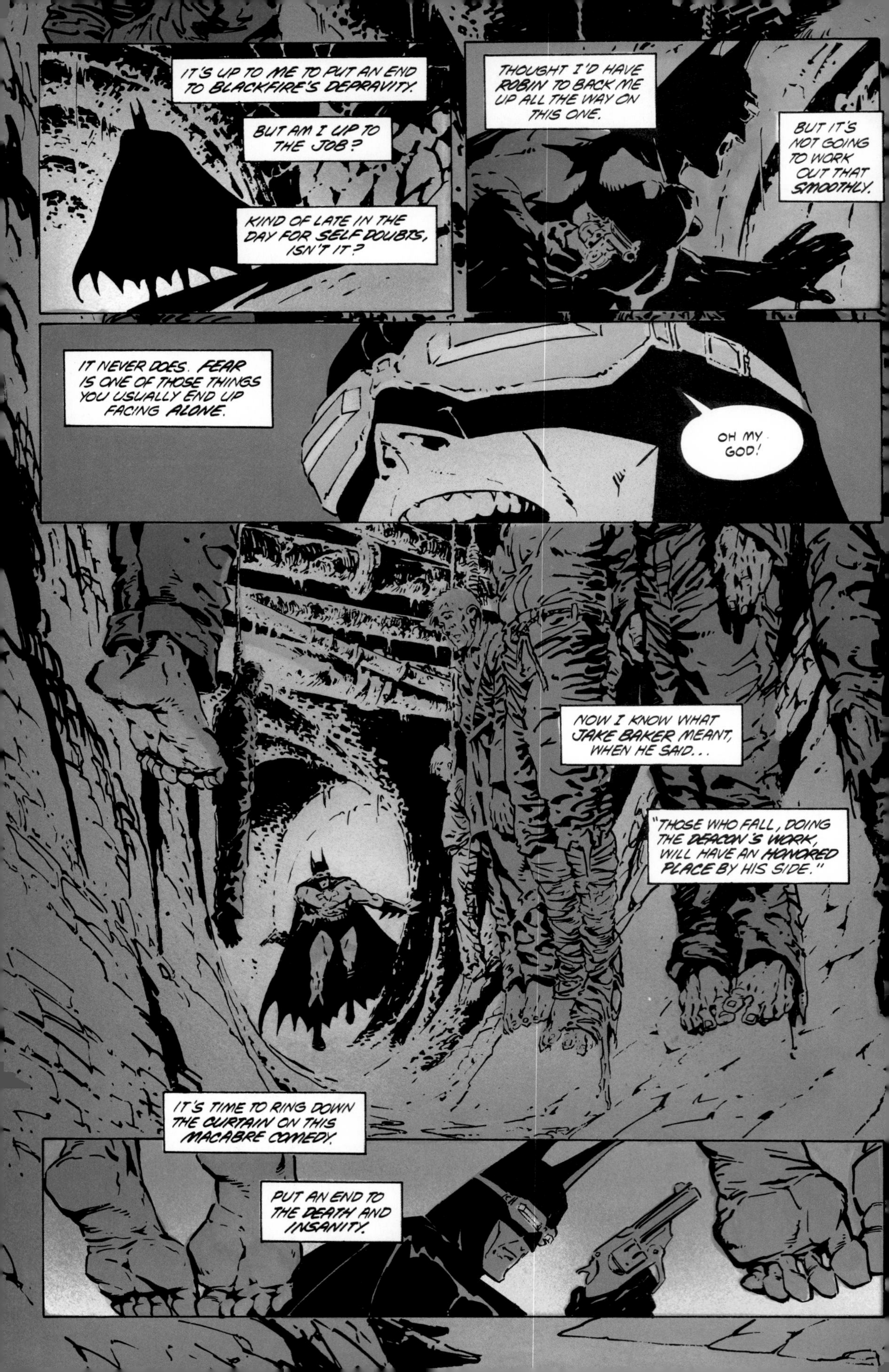
IT'S UP TO ME TO PUT AN END TO BLACKFIRE'S DEPRAVITY.
BUT AM I UP TO THE JOB?
KIND OF LATE IN THE DAY FOR SELF DOUBTS, ISN'T IT?
THOUGHT I'D HAVE ROBIN TO BACK ME UP ALL THE WAY ON THIS ONE.
BUT IT'S NOT GOING TO WORK OUT THAT SMOOTHLY.
IT NEVER DOES. FEAR IS ONE OF THOSE THINGS YOU USUALLY END UP FACING ALONE.
OH MY GOD!
NOW I KNOW WHAT JAKE BAKER MEANT, WHEN HE SAID...
"THOSE WHO FALL, DOING THE DEACON'S WORK, WILL HAVE AN HONORED PLACE BY HIS SIDE."
IT'S TIME TO RING DOWN THE CURTAIN ON THIS MACABRE COMEDY.
PUT AN END TO THE DEATH AND INSANITY.

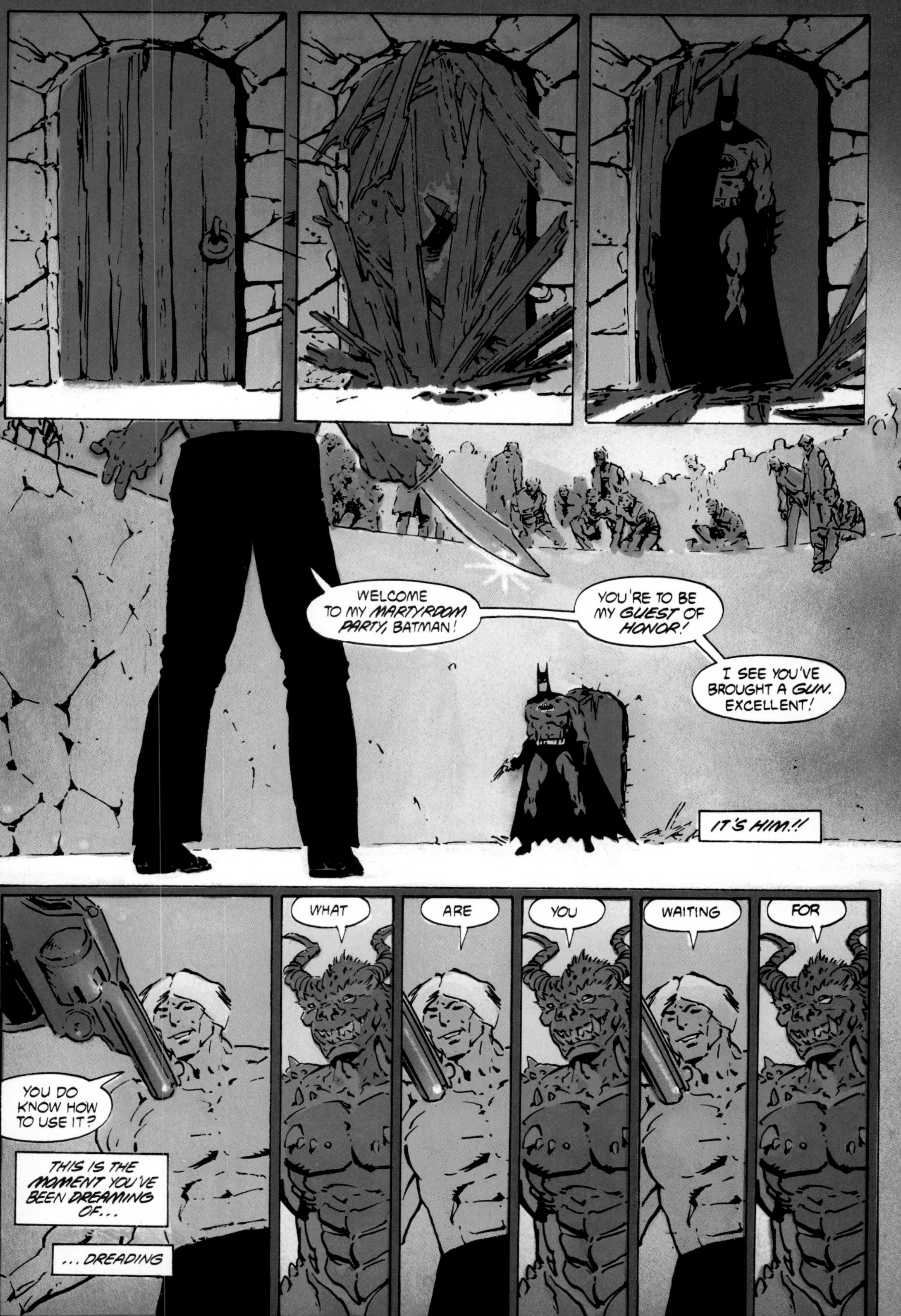
WELCOME TO MY MARTYRDOM PARTY, BATMAN!
YOU'RE TO BE MY GUEST OF HONOR!
I SEE YOU'VE BROUGHT A GUN. EXCELLENT!
IT'S HIM!!
YOU DO KNOW HOW TO USE IT?
THIS IS THE MOMENT YOU'VE BEEN DREAMING OF...
...DREADING
WHAT
ARE
YOU
WAITING
FOR

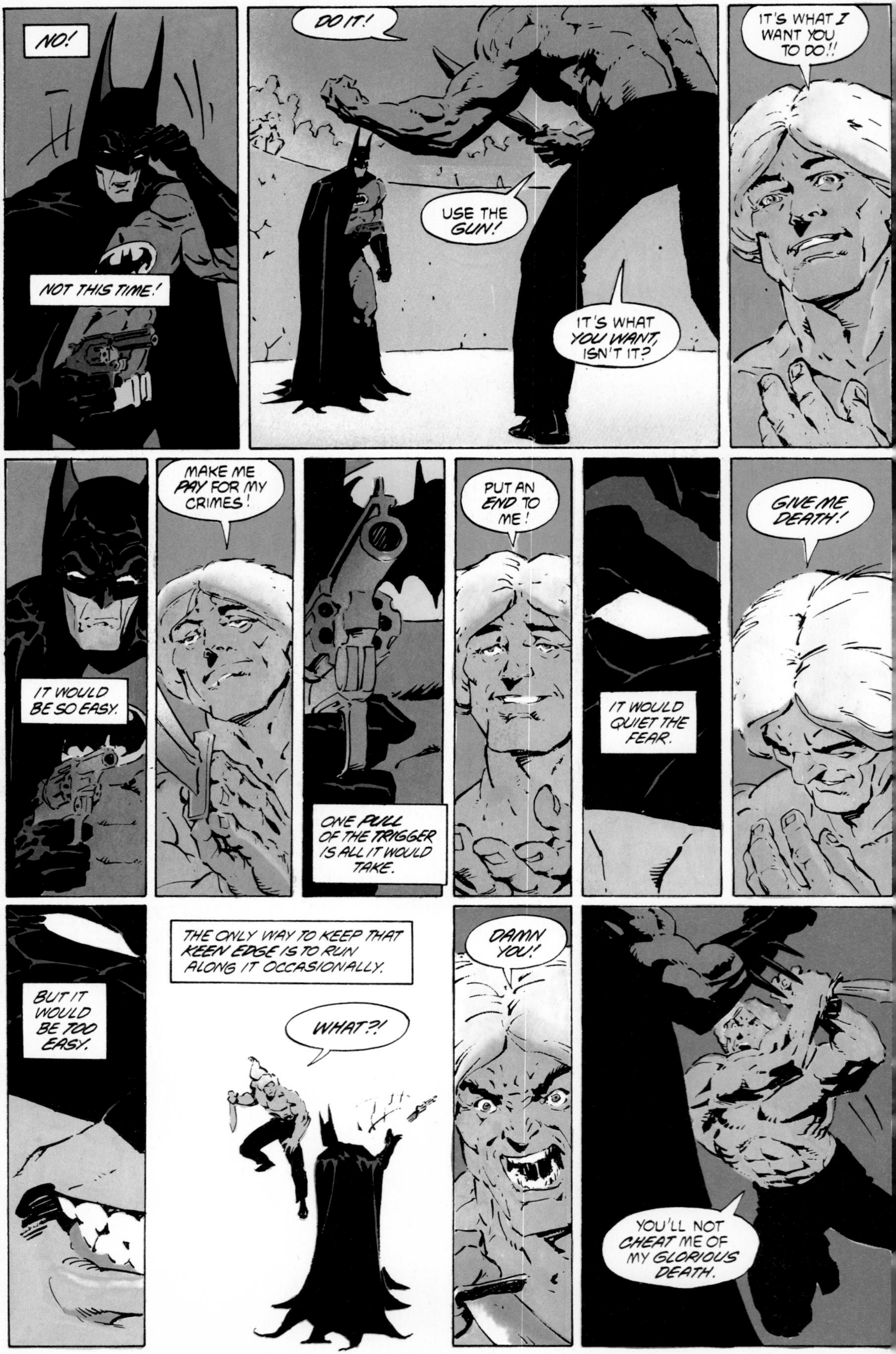
NO!
NOT THIS TIME!
DO IT!
USE THE GUN!
IT'S WHAT YOU WANT, ISN'T IT?
IT'S WHAT I WANT YOU TO DO!!
IT WOULD BE SO EASY.
MAKE ME PAY FOR MY CRIMES!
ONE PULL OF THE TRIGGER IS ALL IT WOULD TAKE.
PUT AN END TO ME!
IT WOULD QUIET THE FEAR.
GIVE ME DEATH!
BUT IT WOULD BE TOO EASY.
THE ONLY WAY TO KEEP THAT KEEN EDGE IS TO RUN ALONG IT OCCASIONALLY.
WHAT?!
DAMN YOU!
YOU'LL NOT CHEAT ME OF MY GLORIOUS DEATH.

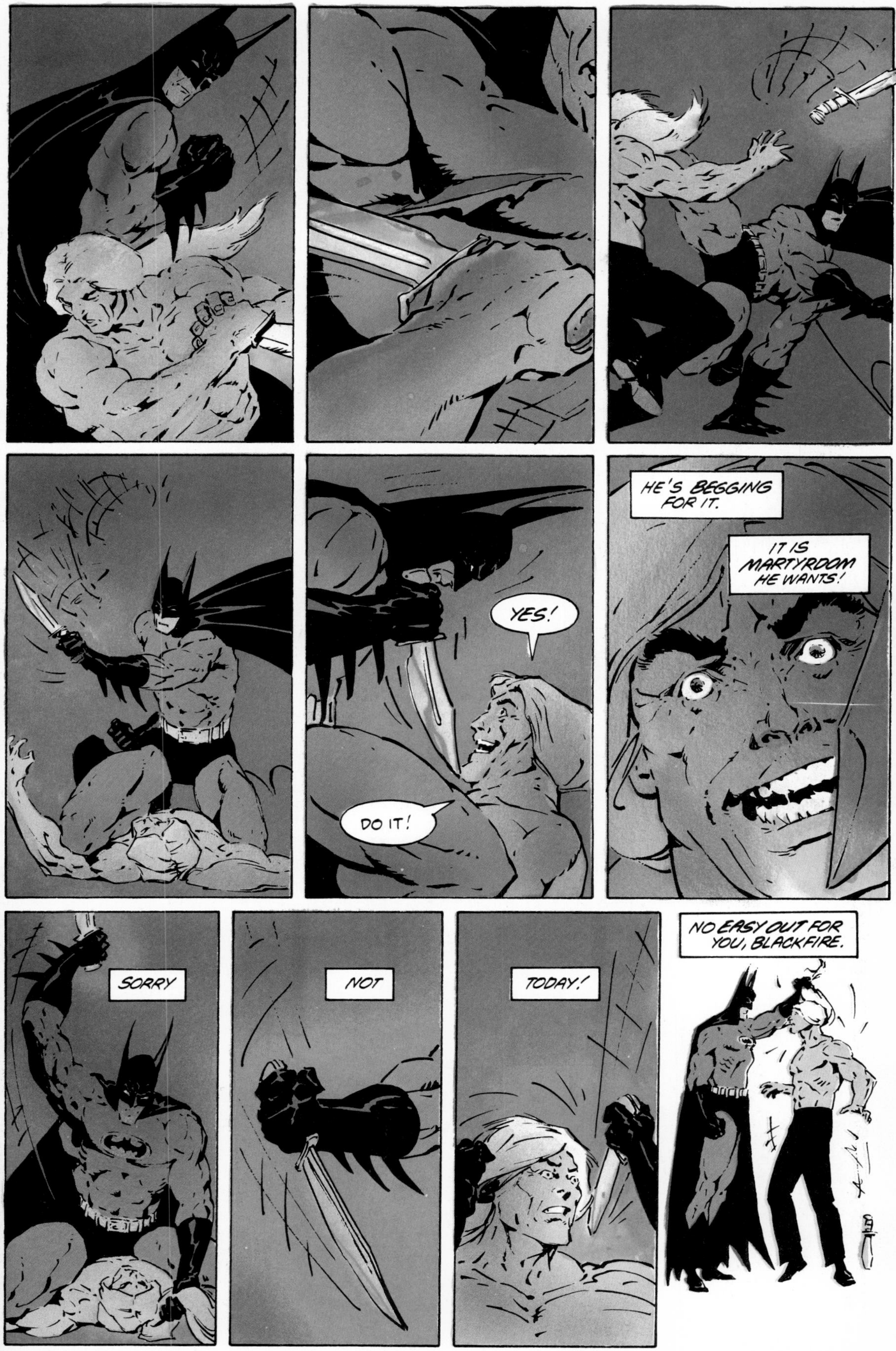
HE'S BEGGING FOR IT.
IT IS MARTYRDOM HE WANTS!
YES!
DO IT!
SORRY
NOT
TODAY!
NO EASY OUT FOR YOU, BLACKFIRE.

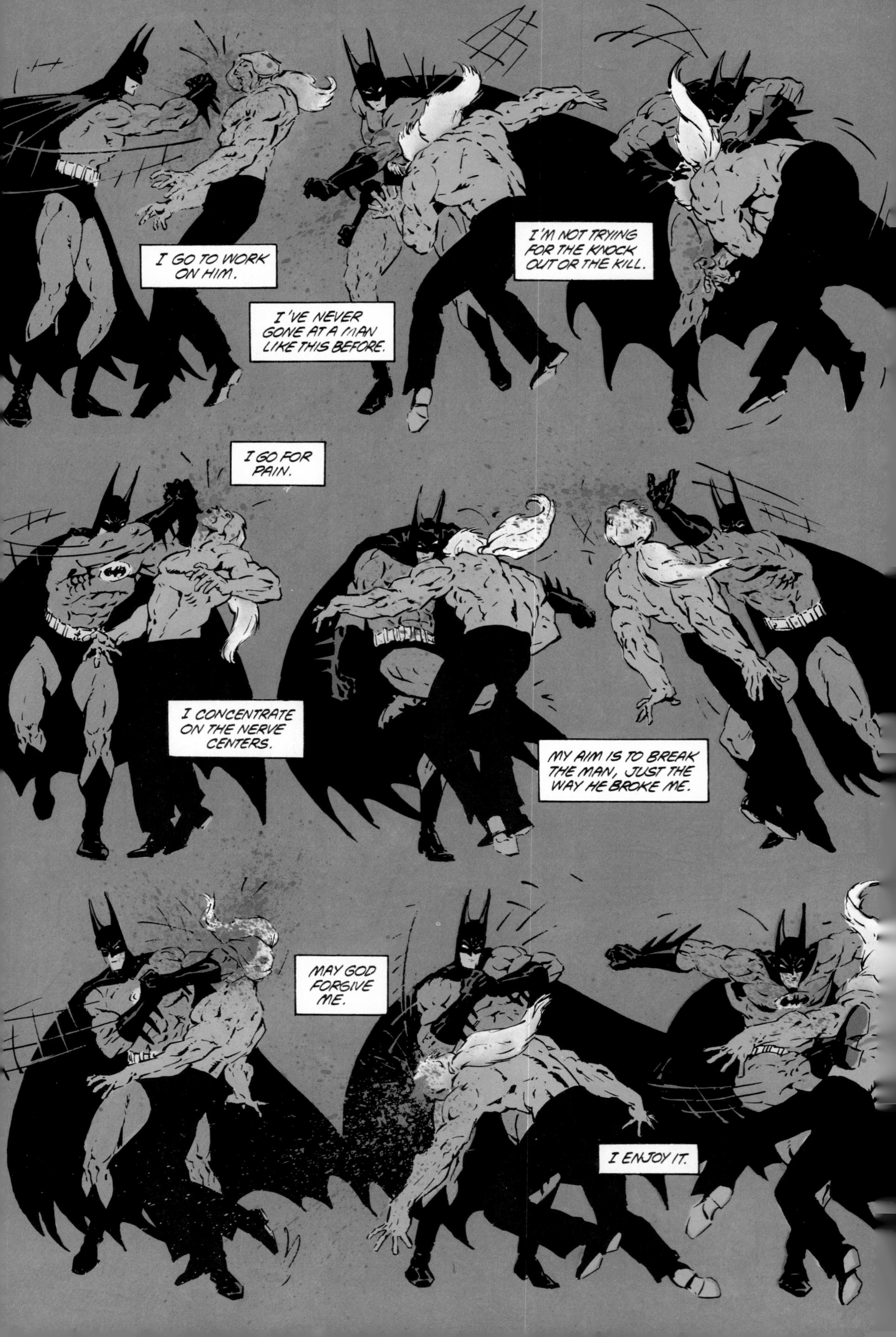
I GO TO WORK ON HIM.
I'VE NEVER GONE AT A MAN LIKE THIS BEFORE.
I'M NOT TRYING FOR THE KNOCK OUT OR THE KILL.
I GO FOR PAIN.
I CONCENTRATE ON THE NERVE CENTERS.
MY AIM IS TO BREAK THE MAN, JUST THE WAY HE BROKE ME.
MAY GOD FORGIVE ME.
I ENJOY IT.

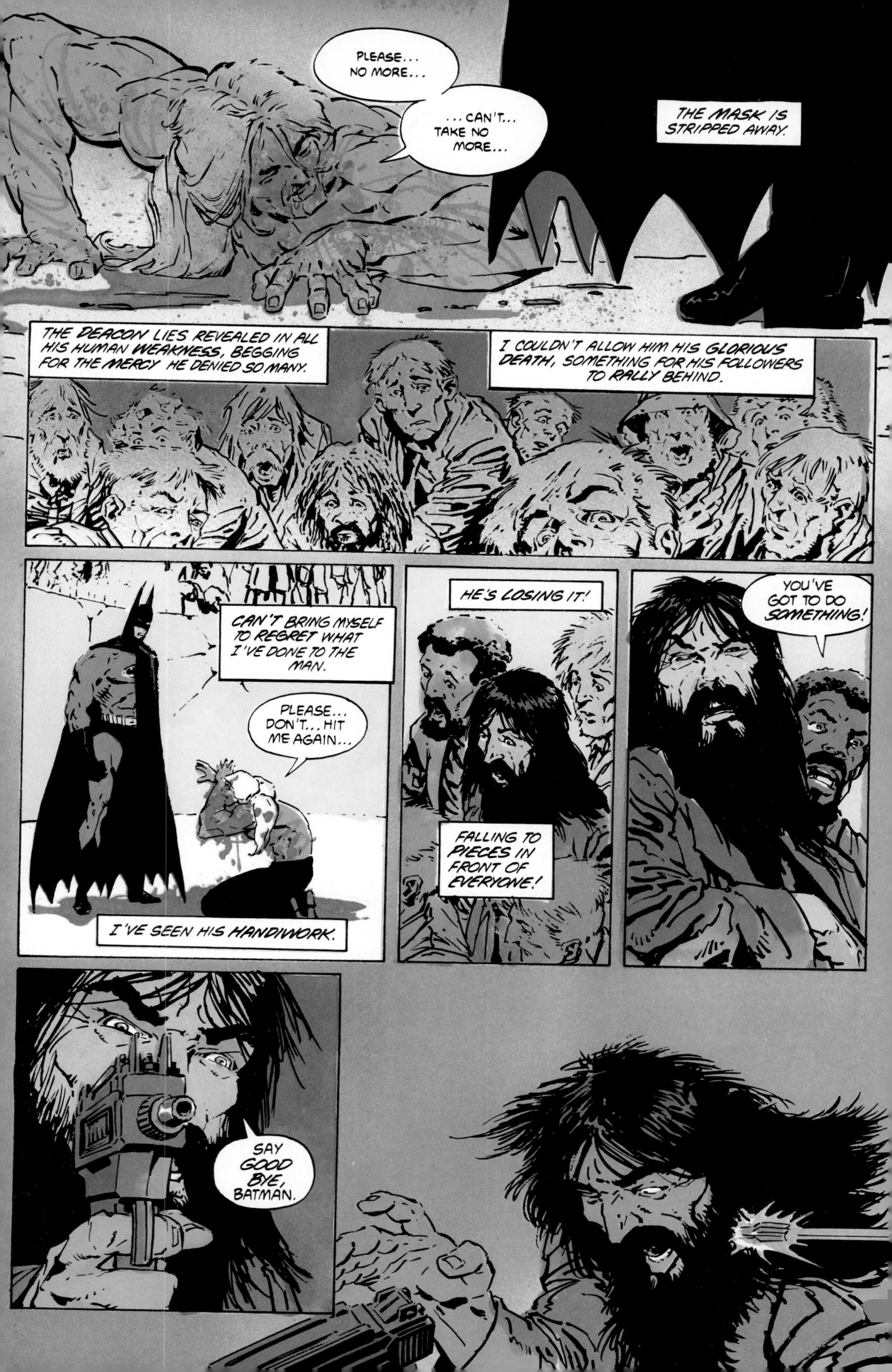
PLEASE... NO MORE...
...CAN'T... TAKE NO MORE...
THE MASK IS STRIPPED AWAY.
THE DEACON LIES REVEALED IN ALL HIS HUMAN WEAKNESS, BEGGING FOR THE MERCY HE DENIED SO MANY.
I COULDN'T ALLOW HIM HIS GLORIOUS DEATH, SOMETHING FOR HIS FOLLOWERS TO RALLY BEHIND.
CAN'T BRING MYSELF TO REGRET WHAT I'VE DONE TO THE MAN.
PLEASE... DON'T... HIT ME AGAIN...
I'VE SEEN HIS HANDIWORK.
HE'S LOSING IT!
FALLING TO PIECES IN FRONT OF EVERYONE!
YOU'VE GOT TO DO SOMETHING!
SAY GOOD BYE, BATMAN.

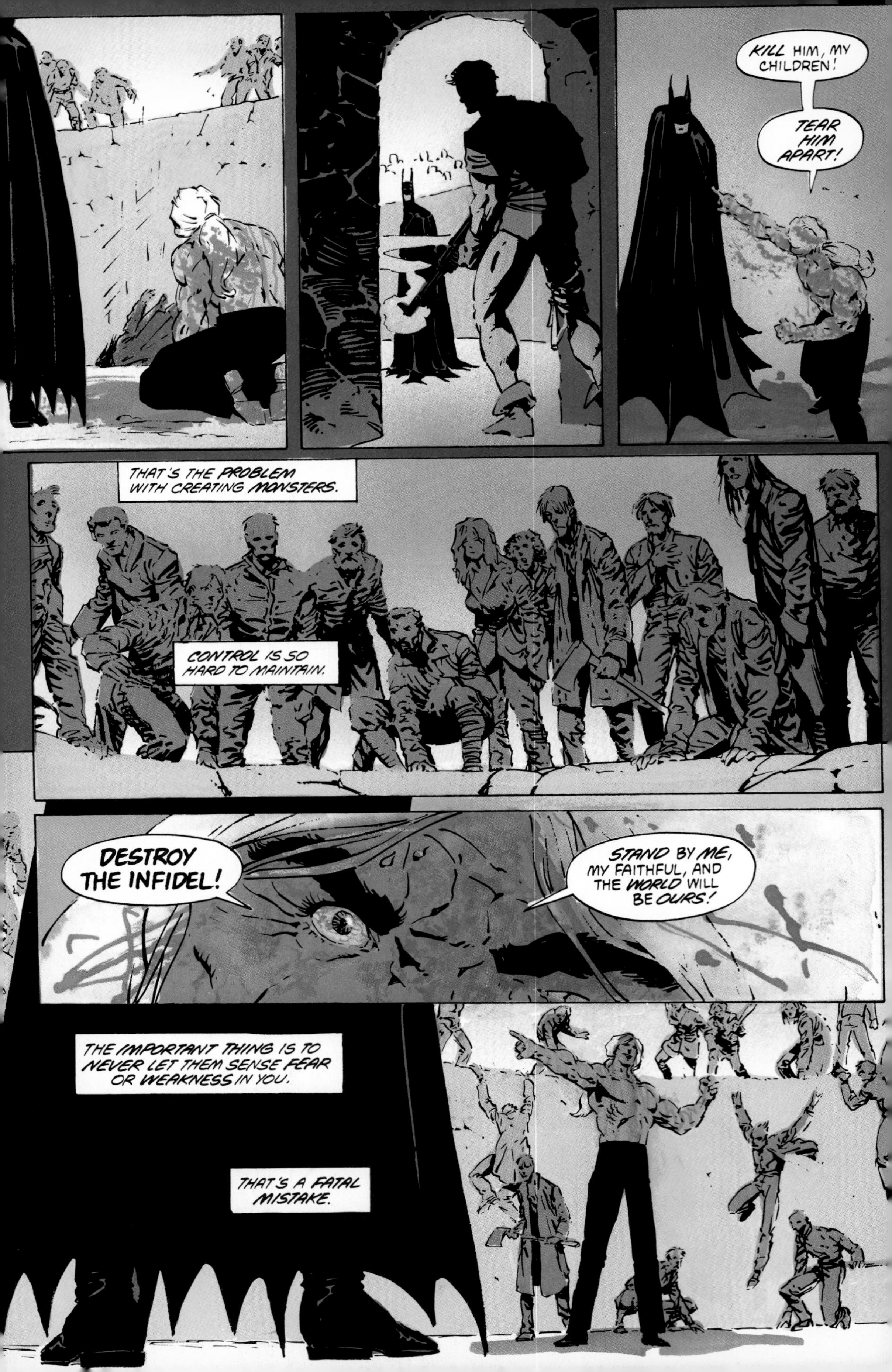

KILL HIM, MY CHILDREN!
TEAR HIM APART!
THAT'S THE PROBLEM WITH CREATING MONSTERS.
CONTROL IS SO HARD TO MAINTAIN.
DESTROY THE INFIDEL!
STAND BY ME, MY FAITHFUL, AND THE WORLD WILL BE OURS!
THE IMPORTANT THING IS TO NEVER LET THEM SENSE FEAR OR WEAKNESS IN YOU.
THAT'S A FATAL MISTAKE.

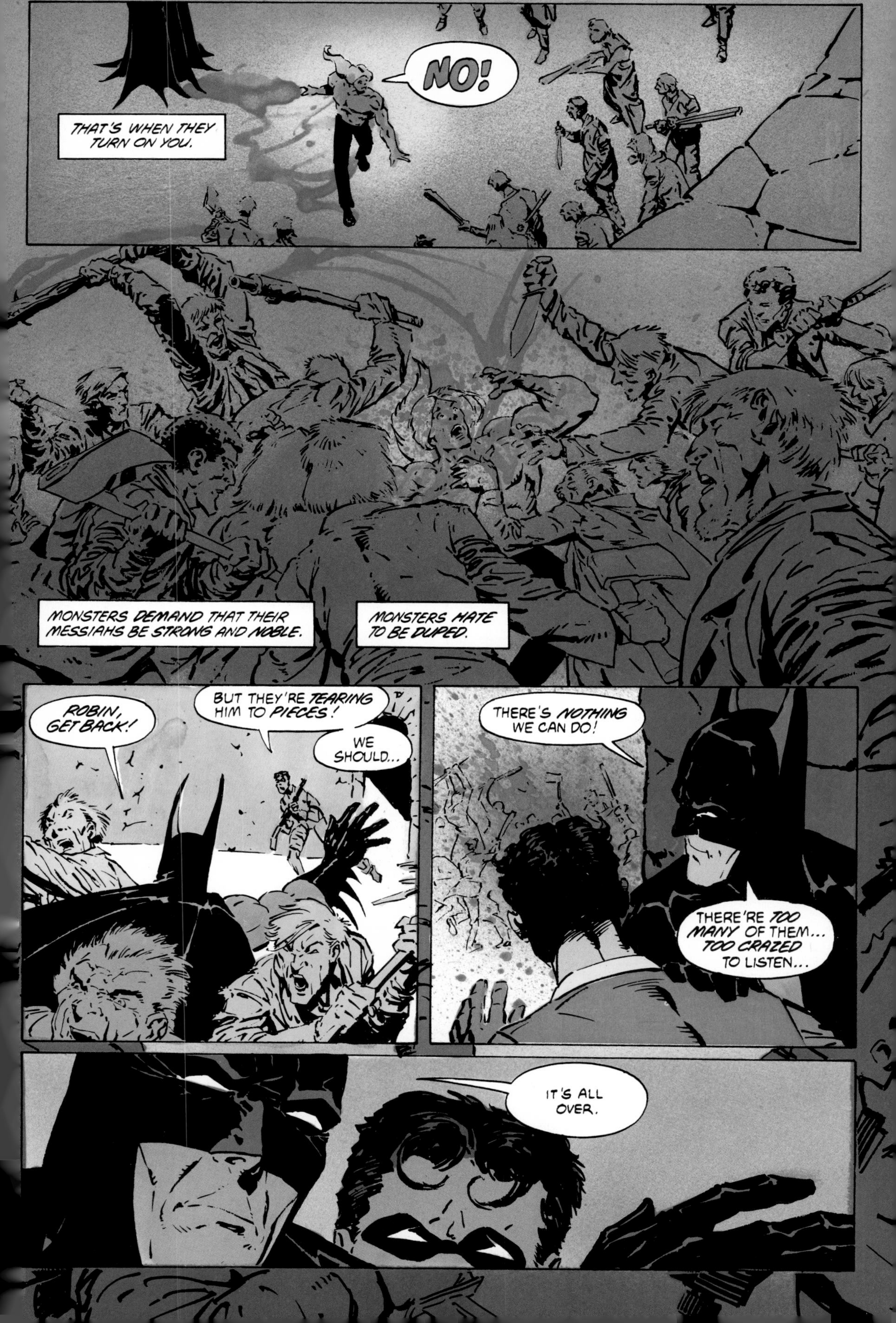
NO!
THAT'S WHEN THEY TURN ON YOU.
MONSTERS DEMAND THAT THEIR MESSIAHS BE STRONG AND NOBLE.
MONSTERS HATE TO BE DUPED.
ROBIN, GET BACK!
BUT THEY'RE TEARING HIM TO PIECES!
WE SHOULD...
THERE'S NOTHING WE CAN DO!
THERE'RE TOO MANY OF THEM... TOO CRAZED TO LISTEN...
IT'S ALL OVER.

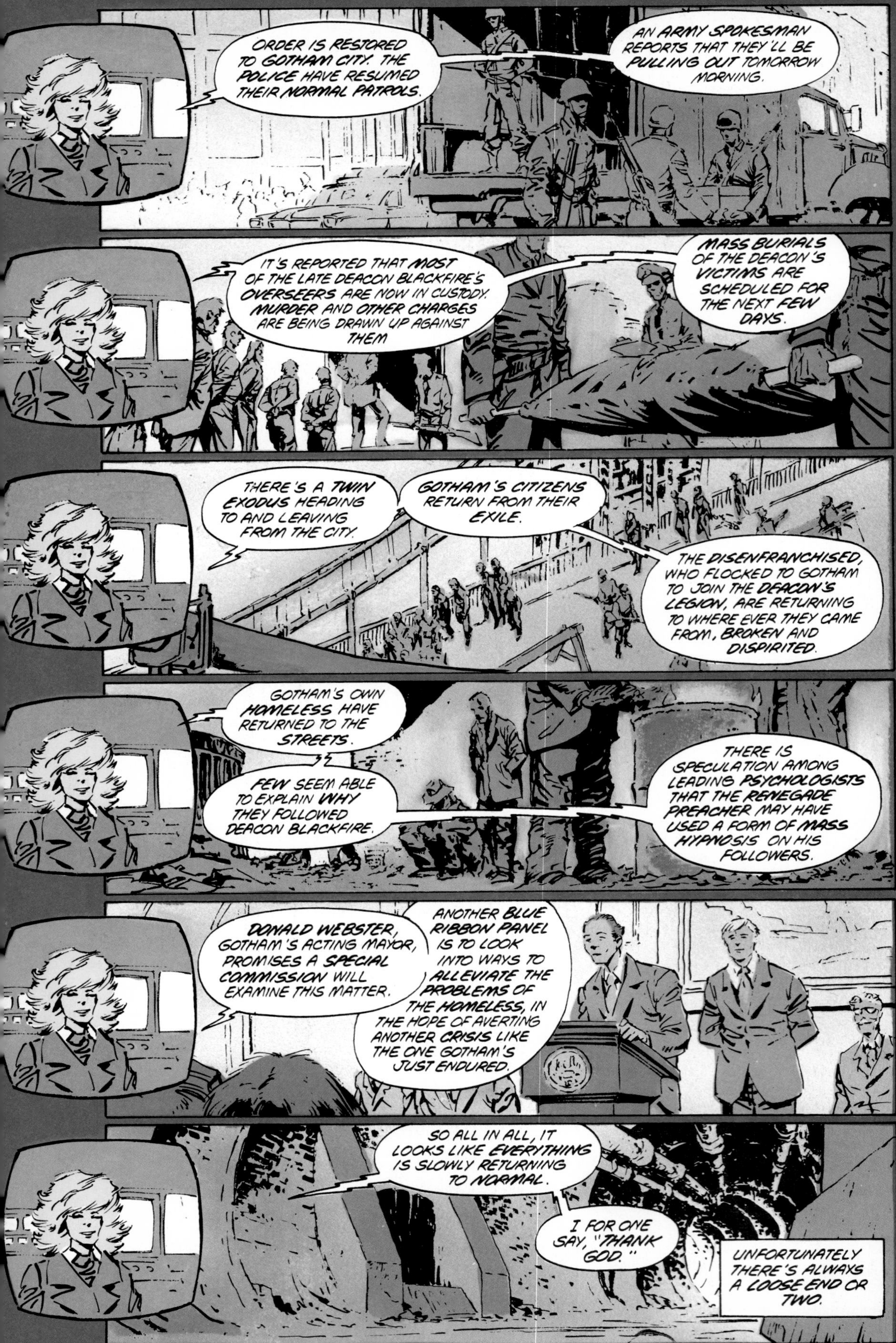
ORDER IS RESTORED TO GOTHAM CITY. THE POLICE HAVE RESUMED THEIR NORMAL PATROLS.
AN ARMY SPOKESMAN REPORTS THAT THEY'LL BE PULLING OUT TOMORROW MORNING.
IT'S REPORTED THAT MOST OF THE LATE DEACON BLACKFIRE'S OVERSEERS ARE NOW IN CUSTODY. MURDER AND OTHER CHARGES ARE BEING DRAWN UP AGAINST THEM
MASS BURIALS OF THE DEACON'S VICTIMS ARE SCHEDULED FOR THE NEXT FEW DAYS.
THERE'S A TWIN EXODUS HEADING TO AND LEAVING FROM THE CITY.
GOTHAM'S CITIZENS RETURN FROM THEIR EXILE.
THE DISENFRANCHISED, WHO FLOCKED TO GOTHAM TO JOIN THE DEACON'S LEGION, ARE RETURNING TO WHERE EVER THEY CAME FROM, BROKEN AND DISPIRITED.
GOTHAM'S OWN HOMELESS HAVE RETURNED TO THE STREETS.
FEW SEEM ABLE TO EXPLAIN WHY THEY FOLLOWED DEACON BLACKFIRE.
THERE IS SPECULATION AMONG LEADING PSYCHOLOGISTS THAT THE RENEGADE PREACHER MAY HAVE USED A FORM OF MASS HYPNOSIS ON HIS FOLLOWERS.
DONALD WEBSTER, GOTHAM'S ACTING MAYOR, PROMISES A SPECIAL COMMISSION WILL EXAMINE THIS MATTER.
ANOTHER BLUE RIBBON PANEL IS TO LOOK INTO WAYS TO ALLEVIATE THE PROBLEMS OF THE HOMELESS, IN THE HOPE OF AVERTING ANOTHER CRISIS LIKE THE ONE GOTHAM'S JUST ENDURED.
SO ALL IN ALL, IT LOOKS LIKE EVERYTHING IS SLOWLY RETURNING TO NORMAL.
I FOR ONE SAY, "THANK GOD."
UNFORTUNATELY THERE'S ALWAYS A LOOSE END OR TWO.

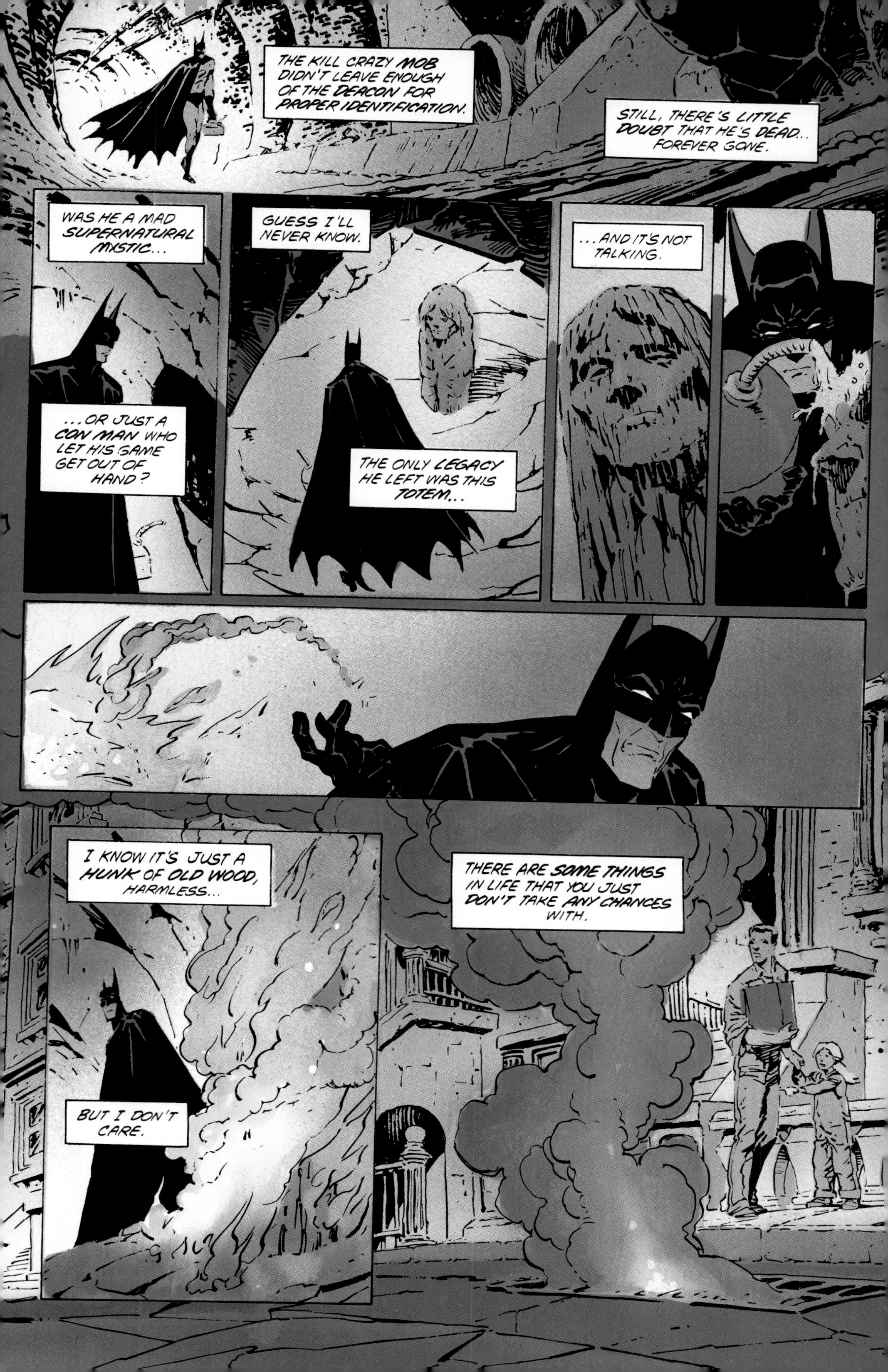
THE KILL CRAZY MOB DIDN'T LEAVE ENOUGH OF THE DEACON FOR PROPER IDENTIFICATION.
STILL, THERE'S LITTLE DOUBT THAT HE'S DEAD... FOREVER GONE.
WAS HE A MAD SUPERNATURAL MYSTIC...
...OR JUST A CON MAN WHO LET HIS GAME GET OUT OF HAND?
GUESS I'LL NEVER KNOW.
THE ONLY LEGACY HE LEFT WAS THIS TOTEM...
...AND IT'S NOT TALKING.
I KNOW IT'S JUST A HUNK OF OLD WOOD, HARMLESS...
BUT I DON'T CARE.
THERE ARE SOME THINGS IN LIFE THAT YOU JUST DON'T TAKE ANY CHANCES WITH.

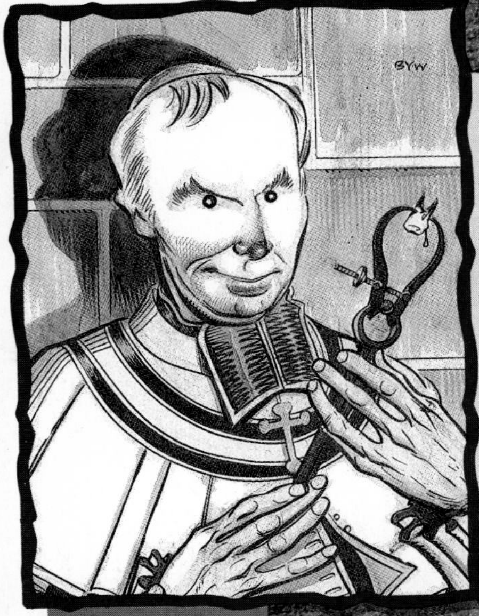
BYW

JIM STARLIN

is one of the most respected writer/artists in the comics industry. His cosmic sagas have given birth to tragic icons such as Warlock, Dreadstar, and Gilgamesh II. His present projects include *THE THANOS QUEST* for Marvel Comics, and the novel *LADY EL* (co-written with Diana Graziunas). He currently resides in New York State.

BERNIE WRIGHTSON

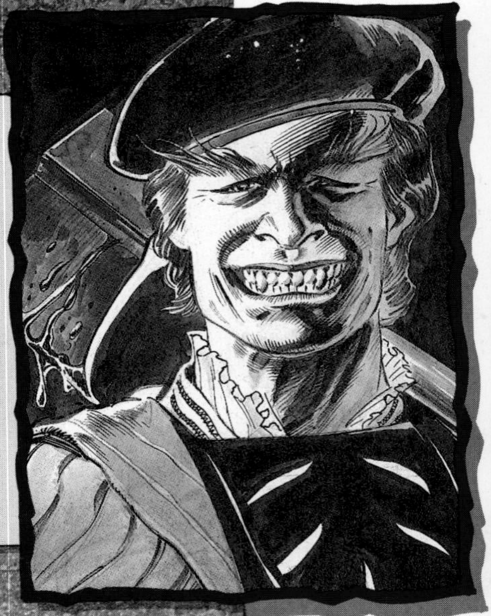

first caught comics readers' attention in the early seventies with his gothic art style on DC's SWAMP THING. He has since become widely renowned as the spookiest artist in any medium. His current projects include *THE PUNISHER* for Marvel Comics. He presently resides in New York State with his wife and two children.

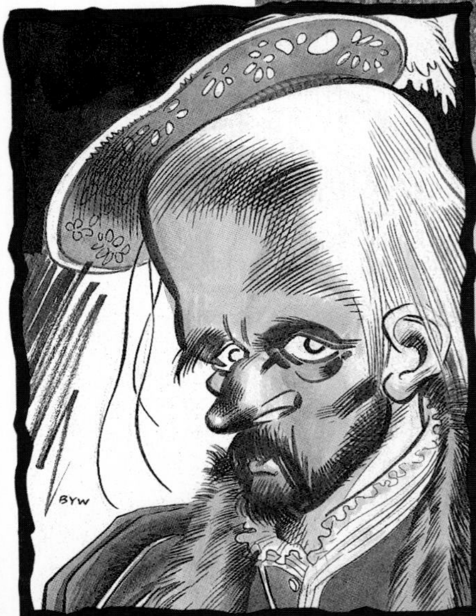
BYW

BILL WRAY

has contributed to a wide variety of comics, from *CRACKED* to DC's avant-garde WASTELAND. Drawing on ten years of experience in animation, his art has covered every genre, from the humorous to the horrific. He is currently inking DC's GREEN ARROW, writing and drawing *WHAT THE...!* and coloring a *PUNISHER* series for Marvel Comics.

Illustrations by Bill Wray